What readers are saying

D0974785

"**Diagonally-Parked** is the socially-anxious person's bible for thoroughly understanding the disorder and getting on the 'yellow brick road' to recovery. It's also an imperative for the support people in their lives. Few writers have brought to light so many of the specific personal life challenges faced by social anxiety sufferers, along with expert and empathetic counsel at overcoming these challenges. The book delivers a message of hope: 'There IS a way out!'"

Colleen Louise Lawrence
Toronto, Canada

"I'm very impressed! I like the detailed stories that let me into the minds and fears of other social phobics, something you don't generally get to experience. Dr. Dayhoff puts into words what it's really like so you can relate to them."

Eric Joffe, editor, **Social Phobia Newsletter**
http://www.spnewsletter.com/

"First chapter, 'Lions and Tigers and Bears, Oh My!' accurately describes my social phobia. It's exactly what I go through everyday at school, even down to the drinking problem to help me get through the day. Anyone who suffers from social anxiety/social phobia must read this book."

Owen G.
Fargo, ND

"Finally a comprehensive guide for anyone who is suffering from any level of social anxiety or social phobia. Only someone who has been there and talked with many others who have been there could have thought to include such a complete list of topics. Anyone with a computer will enjoy the added bonus of finding places to go for support and help from others with this affliction."

Doug (battling social phobia)
Sioux City, IA

"Social phobia is a kind phrase for a highly invisible, disabling disorder. Its intensity is alarming and confusing to those who are caregivers and extremely painful for those who suffer, mostly in silence. IT'S TIME for **Diagonally-Parked in a Parallel Universe**. This book is dynamically informative and compassionately written by someone who has endured SA/SP's grip and ultimately moved past this affliction. Dr. Dayhoff is dedicated to guiding and supporting others in their journey to recovery."

Cynthia Long, Joseph's mom
Sunnyvale, CA

"An excellent and enlightening read which echoes the thoughts I had when I 'didn't know I had' SP."

Orya B.
Cambridge, England

"I found this book enlightening while being very entertaining. Dr. Dayhoff lets us have the facts but laces them liberally with great humor and insight. A great read."

Leslie Day Ebert
Santa Ana, CA

"A comprehensive guide for understanding and overcoming social anxiety and social phobia, covering all the aspects and many important topics not covered by other books."

Roland P.
Berlin, Germany

"I recognize myself in so many situations Dr. Dayhoff describes. The book covers a vast array of important topics, like getting a job, something which is very hard for anyone let alone someone with social phobia. Dr. Dayhoff understands the irrational fear which keeps us alone and afraid of being alone."

A. Mcintyre
Perth, Australia

"It's an immensely exciting discovery for someone who has recently understood that they suffer from social phobia that someone who really understands this condition has written a book on it. This book is a great help for those who suffer from social phobia and those who care for us and support us."

Adrian S.
Adelaide, So. Australia

"Thank you for writing a book specifically and especially for and about those with SA/SP. Now when people don't understand, I can say 'read **Diagonally-Parked in a Parallel Universe** and you'll get a glimpse of what my life is like.' This is also a must read for all who work in the mental health field!"

Barbara
Lafayette, LA

"I think this book will help people. I really related to Dr. Dayhoff's examples, like how social phobics feel more comfortable on the Internet and how one woman's caller ID was more essential to her than her microwave. I started laughing…because she did exactly what I do."

Sherry Mattingly
Louisville, KY

"This book is a must-read to gain a better perspective on understanding both yourself and your relationships with others. It is not just for those with social anxiety disorder. I like how Dr. Dayhoff holds your hand at each step of the process, explains everything in detail, describes, and simplifies. The title really captures the problem we've all experienced to some degree."

Rhonda L. Fallk, Ph.D., Counseling Psychologist
Clarks Summit, PA

"I love the way Dr. Dayhoff writes about social anxiety. It's so casual and conversational. Even though social anxiety is serious, the way she writes about some of her own experiences with it makes me laugh out loud. This addition of humor makes SA/SP all the more understandable and human."

Anne Marie Fetcho
Rio Rancho, NM

"Well-written and in-depth. For anyone who wants to know more about social phobia. The book not only explains it in great detail without being too complex to understand, but also covers areas that other books on the subject fail to explore."

Carolyn
United Kingdom

"I think this book would be useful not only for people suffering from this anxiety but just anyone in general. Everyone suffers from some sort of anxiety at some point in their normal lives. As a worrier, I can relate to some of the situations. I'd absolutely recommend it to a friend whom I thought might find it helpful."

Marilyn J. Westbye
Dresden, ME

"This is a highly readable book that holds your attention and is applicable to everyone (young and old, professional and non-professional). It makes two very important points: You're **not** alone (there are a lot like you) and there's help!"

David I. Fallk, Attorney, Specializing in Anxiety-Disordered Clients
Scranton, PA

Diagonally-Parked in a Parallel Universe

Working Through Social Anxiety

Signe A. Dayhoff, PH.D.

Effectiveness-Plus Publications

Placitas, New Mexico

http://www.effectiveness-plus.com

drsdayhoff@effectiveness-plus.com

Diagonally-Parked in a Parallel Universe
Working Through Social Anxiety

By Signe A. Dayhoff, Ph.D.

Copyright © 2000 by Signe A. Dayhoff, Ph.D.

Published by Effectiveness-Plus Publications
P.O. Box 340
Placitas, New Mexico 87043

Cover design and illustrations by Signe A. Dayhoff

Printed in the United States of America

Publisher's Cataloging-in-Publication
(Provided by Quality Books, Inc.)

Dayhoff, Signe A.
    Diagonally parked in a parallel universe :
working through social anxiety / Signe A. Dayhoff.
-- 1st ed.
    p. cm.
    Includes bibliographical references and index.
    LCCN: 99-90673
    ISBN: 0-9671265-0-9

    1.   Social phobia. 2. Anxiety. 3. Bashfulness.
I. Title

RC552.S62D39 2000   616.85'225
                QBI99-1021

DEDICATION

This book is dedicated to those who inspired me to write it, who clarified my thinking about social anxiety disorder/social phobia, who provided me with different, often unique, perspectives, who suggested topics that weren't covered fully or from the proper perspective elsewhere, and who kept me going with their stories of need, failure, and success: The Social Phobia List.

It is also dedicated to all those others whose voices have been stilled and their lives stalled by this frequently insidious condition.

TABLE OF CONTENTS

ABOUT THE AUTHOR

Signe A. Dayhoff, M.Ed., M.A., Ph.D., is a senior associate with Dayhoff & Kendrick, consultants in interpersonal and presentation skills, social and personal effectiveness, and anxiety management. She received her Ph.D. in Social Psychology at Boston University and continued her graduate studies in Clinical-Counseling Psychology at Framingham State College.

Dr. Dayhoff is also founder of Effectiveness-Plus Publications which provides educational and training materials in interpersonal communication, life effectiveness, and image-management. For ten years she was president of The Mentoring Network which provided seminars and training in career development, networking, and mentoring. She has taught psychology at Boston University, University of Massachusetts, and Framingham State College and consulted on the ethical, legal, and social issues in predispositional genetic testing for the Genetic Screening Research Group.

Author of **Get the Job You Want: Successful Strategies For Selling Yourself in the Job Market**; **Create Your Own Career Opportunities**; **Single and Multiple Mentors: Perceived Effects on Managerial Success**; co-author of **Decision Making For Managers**; and over 100 newspaper and magazine articles, she contributed to Steven J. Bennett's **Executive Chess: Creative Problem Solving By 45 of America's Top Business Leaders and Thinkers,** and for five years hosted/produced the cable television career-development series, the **Inside Track**.

Dr. Dayhoff has done extensive research on social anxiety, social effectiveness, interpersonal perception and communication, decision making, mentoring, networking, and the effects of predispositional genetic testing. As a result, she chaired the Task Force on Mentoring for the American Psychological Association, created a mentoring program for The American Red Cross, and authored New Mexico's 1997 Genetic Information Privacy Act, for example.

In addition, Dr. Dayhoff has done dozens of presentations, seminars, and speeches for diverse organizations, such as Honeywell Bull, Environmental Protection Agency, the Commonwealth of Massachusetts, Merrill Lynch, Suffolk University, Maine Career Educational Consortium, Association of Genetic Technologists, University of New Mexico Health Sciences Center, and Health Professionals for a National Health Program. She has been quoted in publications ranging from **Industry Week** to **Cosmopolitan**.

FOREWORD

I've known Signe Dayhoff for over 15 years yet I was unaware, until recently, she had been suffering from social anxiety disorder for most of her adult life. To me, Signe was a high-achieving consultant, author, lecturer and cable TV talk show host. I never imagined that the woman behind these very public social personas was keeping this "embarrassing little secret" from her family, friends and colleagues. Behind her mask of competence and accomplishment, she continuously experienced overwhelming fears of being evaluated and rejected...of being found out and abandoned.

Dr. Dayhoff's book blows the lid off of SA/SP. Other books on the topic have been research and treatment-oriented. This compelling and insightful volume takes us into the "belly of the beast." Through her own first-person accounts and her interviews with hundred of fellow SA/SP sufferers, she gives us a long-overdue understanding of the often debilitating, misunderstood (this isn't about just being shy) nature of SA/SP.

As a family therapist, I find particularly valuable her focus on relationships. Initiating, developing, and maintaining committed and caring relationships is at the core of our existence. Something on which our physical, social and psychological survival depends. SA/SPers want desperately to make those intimate connections but feel unable to do so effectively. As a result, their primal longings for friends, intimacy, meaningful work and comfortable family relations go unsatisfied.

To realize our life expectations we have to be able to reach out and relate to others. The basic skills so essential to living happy and productive lives have to be learned. But to learn them, those with SA/SP have to put themselves in the social situations they fear and avoid. Feeling they can't take the risk, they often remain on the periphery of life - lonely, afraid and misunderstood.

Signe Dayhoff has triumphed over SA/SP. Her book delivers the empathetic guidance and key strategies vital to recovery. It also gives family and friends the tools necessary to assist in this recovery process. It's the social anxiety self-help manual we all have needed.

Carleton W. Kendrick, Ed.M., L.C.S.W.

(In clinical practice for 20 years, the Harvard-educated Mr. Kendrick is a nationally-known family therapist, the FamilyEducation Network's parenting expert, and an associate with Dayhoff & Kendrick Associates. He has worked with corporate giants, such as CBS and General Motors, on interpersonal communication, work-family conflict, and mind-body issues. He has appeared on nationally-syndicated radio and television shows, such as **Donahue**, and is often featured in **Time** and other national magazines. Several books on children, computers and television have quoted Mr. Kendrick extensively.)

ACKNOWLEDGMENTS

Many individuals generously contributed their time and effort to the making of this book. First, I'd like to thank all those SA/SP sufferers who have shared their experiences, issues, and concerns with me over the last two years.

Second, I want to thank those experts who reviewed early drafts of this manuscript for accuracy and completeness and offered invaluable comments and suggestions:

Richard G. Heimberg, Ph.D., Adult Anxiety Clinic, Social Phobia Program, Department of Psychology, Temple University

Stefan G. Hofmann, Ph.D., Center for Anxiety and Related Disorders, Boston University

Mark R. Leary, Ph.D., Department of Psychology, Wake-Forest University

Neil F. Neimark, M.D., Department of Family Practice, University of California, Irvine, and The Mind/Body Connection

Daniel Perlman, Ph.D., Family Studies and Nutrition Science, University of British Columbia

Thomas A. Richards, Ph.D., The Anxiety Clinic of Arizona

Suzanne M. Sutherland, Ph.D., Department of Psychiatry and Behavioral Sciences, Duke University

Timo Telaranta, M.D., Privatix Clinic.

Third, I want to thank those who answered questions and provided information: Kathryn L. Blackmon. Ph.D., Christer Drott, M.D., James S. Garza, M.D., Amy S. Kloeblen, M.P.H., R.D., Robert C. Meyer, M.D., and Clifford B. Saper, M.D., Ph.D.

And last, but by no means least, I want to thank Robert N. O'Donnell, without whose unflagging support, encouragement, and computer expertise this project would have been impossible.

xviii

ACKNOWLEDGMENTS

INTRODUCTION

Dear Social Anxiety Sufferers (Your Friends and Family),

Everyone has experienced fleeting anxiety in social situations. But what you suffer from is probably more severe and debilitating. It likely insinuates itself into one or more important aspects of your life. Perhaps you suffer from the agonizing pangs of self-consciousness about being on public view or the center of attention and making a mistake, leaving you humiliated. Perhaps you dread meeting people, giving a speech, using a public restroom, eating in public, talking to your boss, or having your social skills or work observed or your competence assessed. Or perhaps you feel threatened in a new social situation where you don't know the rules, avoid such situations altogether, or just want to escape. We all experience social anxiety a little differently yet we're all riding the same skittish horse.

When our social fears are intense and persistent, we have *social anxiety disorder/social phobia* (SA/SP - "sasp" for short). This means every day we're forced to confront the pain of being in the spotlight, evaluated, or being embarrassed by the very social situations we long to embrace. Socially we find ourselves on the periphery of life's dance, trying to follow the choreographed patterns and rhythm, but usually seeming to be one beat out of synch, zigging when we should zag. Often feeling like the butt of a cosmic joke, we see ourselves as the ball in a pinball machine, bouncing from bumper to bumper, missing targets, and always on the verge of "tilt." This is being diagonally-parked in a parallel universe.

Clinically too, having SA/SP puts us in another dimension. Even though SA/SP is the most common anxiety disorder and the third most common psychiatric disorder after depression and alcoholism, it's the least-diagnosed, least-widely understood, and most under-treated. Few mental health professionals are well-versed in the condition or its treatment even as the number of sufferers continues to increase.

Making our situation worse, most of us with SA/SP don't know we have a treatable disorder, that we're not "just shy," and that we can and need to get help. But even when we understand this, we're often reluctant to seek professional help because we're ashamed of the fear and worried that our complaints won't be taken seriously. Then, when we finally do muster the courage to do it, we're often hobbled by the very anxiety for which we seek help: Talking with and being evaluated by others. Together, these factors help keep this major health problem nearly invisible.

This comprehensive book was written to show you how you can

- Significantly and effectively alleviate your SA/SP pain;
- Significantly improve your daily functioning; and
- Effectively work toward your potential.

You benefit from the uniqueness of my perspective. I'm both a social psychologist working in the areas of social and personal effectiveness, interpersonal and presentation skills, and anxiety management and someone who has struggled for 22 years to successfully overcome SA/SP. (I used to worry endlessly about what others might think about me and my not meeting their expectations.) As a result, I understand how it feels to be living- and working through this often-incapacitating disorder and where we SA/SPers need to specifically concentrate our efforts to improve our lives.

You benefit from my knowledge of SA/SPers' concerns, issues, and desires - the result of my two years of talking with and listening to SA/SPers online via lists, news groups, and chats. You benefit from my research, teaching, consulting, training, and coaching experience, as well as my association with professionals in the SA/SP trenches.

To make your SA/SP more understandable and amenable to change, this book provides you with not only the theories and salient research on its origin, triggers, and maintaining mechanisms, but also a broad range of standard and alternative clinical approaches, life strategies, motivational exercises, and empathy. And because I know from extensive experience that your having exercises just thrown at you isn't likely to help you empower yourself and succeed, this book takes you back to square-one. It gives you the psychological preparation you need to jump-start, enable, and maintain your recovery process.

Because we SA/SPers tend to have difficulties with clinicians, this book takes the mystery and risk out of locating and talking to them and guides you through the process: From initiating your search to surviving your first appointment. It tells you what to expect and how to prepare for it. Because we SA/SPers struggle with presenting ourselves socially (whether communicating, socializing, dating, or finding a job), this book addresses each significant life activity, breaks it down into sequential, digestible chunks so you can absorb, assimilate, and achieve it. And, because the Internet has great importance and value for SA/SPers as one of the few means of establishing relationships and comfortable communication we have, the book pinpoints the services and resources available for those with SA/SP.

Since how you think, feel, and behave determines how you interact with your environment (and conversely), this book focuses on your perceptions, emotions, beliefs, and self-presentation. Using real-life stories, typical problems, and their solutions, the user-friendly format takes you logically, incrementally, step-by-baby-step through the multiple-level processes of your recovery. Through concise explanations, thought questions, self-quizzes, and exercises, you systematically develop and apply your cognitive and behavioral strategies to achieve your recovery goals.

In this process you'll assess your social anxiety, determine where you're headed, how to get there, and how you'll know when you've arrived. You'll act as a scientist doing experiments. You'll learn, practice, and apply new skills that will constructively change the way you think about and cope with not only your SA/SP but also the world outside yourself. You'll see yourself make positive changes.

Using this book's clinically-proven methods, you can

reduce your
- *anxiety and fear*
- *depression*
- *negative thinking*
- *anger*
- *loneliness*
- *procrastination*
- *shame and embarrassment, and*

increase your
- *motivation to make change*
- *confidence and self-esteem*
- *ability to handle stress*
- *initiating and maintaining conversations*
- *problem solving*
- *decision making*
- *expressing yourself appropriately*
- *patience*
- *listening to others*
- *social effectiveness*
- *dealing with criticism*
- *dating*
- *networking*
- *creating your own job and career opportunities*
- *understanding of social anxiety, yourself, and others.*

However, just *reading* this book isn't likely to ameliorate your SA/SP any more than just watching others exercise will cause you to lose weight and tone your body (although awareness may provide important identification, hints, and hope). The book's recovery program is action-oriented, requiring your active, committed, persistent participation in order for you to alter all those factors contributing to your SA/SP: Your automatic fear arousal, negative thoughts, mistaken beliefs and assumptions, unrealistic expectations, and counter-productive behaviors.

Note: As much as we all may wish it to be true, there is no finger-snapping, lamp-rubbing, "Shazaam!" magical solution to SA/SP. It took many factors interacting over many years to bring you to your present state. So recovery will not be instantaneous. But if you take the time to make the necessary structured effort toward recovery (whether that includes therapy, medication, or both), you will quickly begin to experience small but significant changes in your thoughts, feelings, and behavior - glimpsing what it'll be like "without SA/SP."

Essential to your SA/SP recovery will be empathy, patience, and your acceptance of yourself as you are. You must believe and feel that you're worthy of becoming better. You must believe that you're not to blame for this problem but that you are responsible for its solution.

The goal of this book is not to make you wildly extroverted or "Spud MacKenzie," the party animal. Unless you're an extrovert lurking under the heavy cloak of SA/SP, that's not likely to happen. What is likely is when that leaden mantle is slipped from your shoulders, your submerged personality, whatever that may be, will be liberated to fly and soar, with the wind beneath its wings.

The goal of this book is not to make you "successful" at everything you try. It can't and you won't be. That's unrealistic. But it will facilitate that happy juncture of the knowledge you've gained through the book, the opportunity to use it, and your careful and focused use of it.

The goal IS your significantly and effectively alleviating your SA/SP pain, your significantly improving your daily functioning, and your effectively and successfully working toward meeting your potential - in a word, *recovery*.

Your actions toward recovery will give you the necessary experience, confidence, and problem-solving strategies you'll need for your new life. Your actions will give you coping, interpersonal, and social effectiveness skills. Your actions will give you a new perspective on yourself, others, and social interaction. Whether you use this book as a guide to work on your SA/SP on your own or as an adjunct to therapy, the following chapters will provide you with everything you need to spark your action, accomplish your goals, and relieve your anxiety.

Always remember, your social anxiety is merely a dysfunctional over-expression of your sensitivity, empathy, and imagination. These are **special gifts** to be valued, cultivated, and nurtured. Yes, you CAN learn how to delight in these gifts and share them with others. I invite you to join me and enjoy finally being "parallel-parked in a parallel universe."

Your recovered friend,

Placitas, New Mexico

August 1999

(The following stanzas are excerpted with permission from)

I Am the Face Behind the Label

By Amy S. Kloeblen © 1998

I am Real. I am your co-worker.
Your best friend. Your neighbor.
Your spouse. Your sibling. Your parent.
Your lover. Your child.

I am a master of deception
Since society deems it necessary
For me to conceal my afflictions.
I don a mask of pleasantness daily,
Yet beneath it I am in turmoil
Lest you discover my terrible secrets.

Overpowering feelings of inadequacy and doubt
Plague me, shadowing my every step, my every breath.
Mocking my persistent attempts to fit in, survive, excel.
Yet I wearily journey on in my quest.

I may falter at times,
Struggling to overcome
The unearned infirmities of my own brain,
Yet I refuse to succumb to ignorance from without!

PUBLISHER'S NOTE

"LIONS AND TIGERS AND BEARS, OH MY!"

"He flung himself from the room, flung himself upon his horse, and rode off in all directions." (Stephen Leacock, *Nonsense Novels*, 1911)

Joanna's tale

Joanna's heart galloped, the surging blood thundering in her ears, painting her face and neck crimson. The butterflies in her knotted stomach were flapping their wings with greater force as the time drew near. Sweat trickled down her sides as her underarms opened their pores and oozed. She was sure everyone could see her soggy, wrinkled shirt, even with her jacket on.

Perched on the edge of her chair in her college English class, 35-year-old Joanna had started the count-down for the instructor's call for the students' five-minute presentations to begin. It was always the same. Whenever she had to speak before a group, her mouth instantaneously became parched. Her tongue stuck to her hard palate. Words caught in her throat. And those incomprehensible phrases that managed to escape, submerged the audience in a tidal wave of croaked stutters and stammers, while she gasped for breath, quaking. You're a mess, girl, she chided herself.

Joanna knew she couldn't present for even five minutes without looking like a laughingstock. Her mindless trepidation was one reason she was still in the process of trying to get through school. Fear of public speaking seemed to malevolently greet her in every other subject, rendering her unable to stick with one major and finish her college degree. Just standing before the group of 19-year-olds reduced her to shimmering guava jelly. Having to speak on top of that totally liquified her resolve. She already knew how the audience would respond: They'd either look disgusted at this pathetic old person or smirk and snicker at the absurdity of her trying to pull it off. Once again she'd be embarrassed, humiliated. Every last one of them, including the instructor, would write her off as being weird, incompetent, or both. Either way, she grimaced, I'm a failure.

Like a coyote-cornered rabbit she felt on the verge of panic...again. Something primitive, ancestrally-wired in her brain, made her want to run, flee, escape. But, no, she couldn't do that. Crazy behavior like that would only draw attention to herself. Joanna mulled it over. A room this packed is a minefield - not something to navigate in a hurry. She chewed her lip and sighed. Maybe I can find another excuse to get me out of the rest of the class period and doing the presentation. But as she sat jiggling her crossed leg, her mind was blank.

Compounding her immediate distress was the knowledge that she needed to do this presentation for her grade. She'd already skipped the others, one way or another, leaving her teacher, who'd tried to talk with her about it, with no other conclusion than Joanna just didn't care. And her grade-point average, which she'd struggled to keep high despite these self-presentation obstacles, depended on her doing well in this class. But to Joanna it was a rattlesnake roundup from the perspective of the snake - a lose-lose situation. At this point she couldn't tell which failure was worse.

As she bounced her leg under her desk, her foot brushed her book bag which fell open, revealing the fifth of Jack Daniels she'd stashed there for emergencies. A fleeting flash of relief played across her face. Her eyes drinking in the label gave her courage. She grabbed the bag and its precious cargo, took a deep breath, then cautiously threaded her way to the door. Once outside the classroom, she bolted for the restroom.

After a couple of healthy swigs, Johanna felt a warming calm wash over her. She was alone, away from scrutinizing eyes. Her hyperventilation was fading in the glow. I've got to find some way to make it work out, she sighed dispiritedly. Her heart palpitations were leveling off too. Sinking to a sitting position on the gray tiled floor, Joanna leaned against the wall and took another drink.

* * *

Barry's tale

With knuckles showing white, Barry finally dragged himself to the Lucky U singles' bar on Saturday night. It had taken him months of pep talks and false starts to steel himself to do it. At twenty-eight, slim with Dylan McDermott intensity, he still had never really dated. Searching his memory, he chuckled and shook his head. After all, you can't count the time my mother arranged for me to take Judy Jones, a 9th-grade classmate and next door neighbor, Christmas caroling with our church group. And, yes, much to his chagrin and embarrassment, he confided, he was still a virgin.

He didn't date because approaching women was like circumnavigating the globe in a kayak, not something a sane person would contemplate. He didn't know the "rules of the game," hadn't read the latest prescription, and he was sure that the women at Lucky U would catch the scent of his inadequacy the moment he crossed the threshold and be lying in wait for their prey. In the movie he played and replayed in his mind he saw them in groups, scrutinizing each male who walked by, sizing him up, ticking off his pluses and minuses, putting him in the "save" or "discard" pile. And if he didn't stack up to their high standards, he was certain they'd make sure he knew it. Barry was convinced they'd take one look at him, and, without so much as a word, label him a geek: An object of derision and laughter in everyone's eyes.

As he stood at the bar in his freshly pressed chinos, oxford cloth shirt, with a Michelob in hand, he fantasized about having a magic lamp. One rub and - poof! - he'd have mentally downloaded the "Winner's Dating Manual." Another rub and he'd be so cool he was hot. He began to survey the crowd. All I really want, he thought, is to meet someone nice. Someone who'd appreciate my thoughtfulness and sensitivity. Hey, he wanted to shout, I don't see women as notches in my belt or slabs of beef in a meat locker. But every time he spotted someone who might fill the bill, his indecisiveness punched him in the gut and his thoughts of failure cemented him to the ground.

I can't talk to her, he'd respond plaintively. *What would I say? I always sound so dull and stupid when I try. Before I can get out what I want to say, she'd get bored and leave. Nobody really wants to listen to me...and I can't blame them.*

Even when a woman returned his gaze and his infrequent, tentative smile, like the vivacious assistant in marketing at his company, he found himself unable to follow through. It was always the same. His face flushed magenta and then he began to stammer. And when he wasn't blushing, he was agonizing over its prospect and the bad first-impression he was sure he had already made on her. It had him coming and going. When he spied her, even when she was forty-five feet away at the end of the hall, he averted his eyes to avoid meeting her gaze. But with or without eye contact, his face continued to glow in her presence. He was at its mercy. Soon he became so obsessed with the possibility of their meeting that he was ever on the look-out for her, armed with evasive strategies. He waited around corners for her to pass. He took the stairs when she took the elevator. He did whatever he could to try to preempt accidental contact.

Suddenly Barry was shaken from his reverie by the three-piece band starting its set. As he turned his attention toward the music, his eyes swept a young woman with long, dark hair, some twenty feet away from him. She was standing and chatting with two other women, but looking directly at him, smiling sweetly. His face became a warning beacon as his heart began to throb. *What should I do?* he asked himself. *Smile back? Go over? And what about the other two women?* He began to breathe more rapidly and shallowly. *Should I talk to them? Ignore them? What if the one with the sweet smile is trying to play a joke on me? I'd be humiliated in front of everyone.* With a laundry list of what-ifs spinning in his head, Barry felt immobilized, glued to the spot at the bar where he stood.

* * *

Joe's tale

Eighteen-year-old Joe sat rigidly behind the wheel of his Camry, concentrating on staring straight ahead as the bumper-to-bumper commuter traffic jockeyed for position around him. As much as he loved the independence of driving, he hated being in this automotive fishbowl with no place to hide and no way to escape. When he was caught in traffic, he was on display, like a street mime, just hanging out there where all could observe him and judge his performance.

Under his Garth Brooks tee-shirt, his shoulders and neck ached with tension as he calculated his options. *If I casually look around and catch the eye of other drivers, they'll start to scrutinize me. They'll think what's that dumb kid think he's doing.* While that was bad enough, what chilled Joe's bones even *more was glancing over and discovering that people in the other cars were already scrutinizing and judging him.*

At critical moments like this Joe always launched into a dialogue with himself. What if that happened? he asked, then replied, I'd look stupid. No matter what he did, he felt his reaction would be awkward at best. What if that happened? Well, I'd do what I usually do and embarrass and humiliate myself. And they'd think I was a real loser.

Whenever other vehicles were moving slowly or running along side the Camry, Joe adopted a look of deep engrossment and began to fiddle with the radio. He'd pretend to be looking for a specific station or tuning it in. His look of rapt attention was intended to convey that he had serious matters on his mind and certainly didn't have the time to rubberneck to see what others were doing. At traffic lights, Joe would try to stop a half-length behind the car beside him, thereby making scrutiny less likely. But when cars covered both his flanks, he resorted to contemplation of the radio dial. If he had been listening prior to stopping, he immediately turned the sound down so no one could hear and evaluate his choice. Driving wasn't the freewheeling expression of teenage freedom he had expected. Instead it was just an exhausting activity. When he wasn't thinking about driving defensively and maintaining the speed limit, he was focusing all his energies on managing his impression on other drivers.

But Joe's fear wasn't confined to his driving. He couldn't bring himself to stand in a line at the bank or the grocery store, sit in the doctor's office, or ride the bus without feeling cold and clammy as dozens of pairs of eyes "bored" into him. He knew it made no sense but that's how he felt. Rather than use a public restroom where someone could see or hear him, he tried never to be too far from home so he could hurry back when urgency called. Being on a plane, a must to avoid, left in him in leg-crossing agony.

He couldn't use the urinals and if someone entered the restroom before he started to urinate, anxiety totally blocked his bladder, leaving him dancing in pain. Once he tried using a Walkman so he couldn't hear himself or others in the bathroom, but turned it up so loud that he inadvertently attracted the attention of other patrons as they crossed the threshold. So as he emerged from the stall, assuming his usual blasé pose, he found all eyes turned in his direction, taking in his 250-pound, six-foot weight-lifter's body with his ginger hair poking out around the tiny blasting Sony earphones. The incident confirmed all his worst fears.

* * *

Sarah's tale

Sarah listened to the shrill ring of her kitchen phone, nagging her to pick up the receiver. The jangling, heart-pumping sound filled her small apartment and fired off her nerve endings. But at 43 years old she just stood by the demanding instrument, indecisive and wringing her hands. She hoped it would soon stop. Panic had gripped her by the throat the moment the phone had started to ring. Instantaneously dread and uncertainty enshrouded her.   In spite of its occasional usefulness, Sarah viewed the phone as her most unwelcomed intruder next to cockroaches.

But maybe the call's important, she counseled herself. A look at the caller identification box she'd had installed was uninformative. It read "unavailable." I can't answer it. I don't know who it is or what they want, she replied, her chest constricting. If it's really important, they can leave a message on the answering machine.

It seemed an eternity to Sarah before the answering machine on her night table next to her bed picked up the call on its fifth ring. She turned up the machine's volume so she could hear the beep. Her heart seemed to stop as she waited, petrified of what was to follow. But on hearing a resounding click and soothing hum of the dial tone, she breathed a big sigh of relief. No message. Thank goodness.

Sarah's caller ID was more essential to her existence than her microwave. When she knew who was calling, she could decide whether or not to pick up. In that few seconds she could begin to prepare herself psychologically for the exchange. Particularly where she had no nonverbal clues to guide her, she needed to be able to exercise some control. Preparation and control were her protective devices. When she wasn't ready, her tongue would seem to fill her mouth and she jabbered. Words tumbled out helter skelter. Once she picked up the receiver, there was no refuge. Her incompetence would humiliate her.

Whenever she saw "anonymous" on the ID readout, she felt palpitations. This meant that someone didn't want her to know their identity. In fact, they had taken measures to block her access to that information. So they had the advantage. One-down, she was a wolf on its back, baring its throat. Anonymous callers who left no message abandoned her to her agony.

But it wasn't just answering phones that was a problem for Sarah. Placing calls too was a masochistic exercise. She could call her mother and Tanya, her best friend, without discomfort but couldn't call anyone else without a script in hand and a half-hour rehearsal. Even with rehearsal behind her, she felt compelled to read from her prepared text, sounding as if she were puzzling over a foreign language. Each time she prayed no one would ask her a question she hadn't anticipated. When they did, it left her flustered, sputtering whatever popped into her head. Sometimes, when things were totally out of control, she had to hang up to keep from destroying all her credibility.

While overall she was glad to have the answering machine to further screen her calls, she hated that others had them too. If she could manage to call people, they could darn well be there. Being pressured to say what she wanted in their prescribed 30 seconds or be cut off in mid-sentence ratcheted up Sarah's anxiety yet another notch. This meant she'd have to say as quickly as possible all the "right" words in the right order.

The "right" words never came easily to Sarah, if they came at all. She could barely walk and chew gum at the same time in social situations. And when they appeared, they never presented themselves either concisely or quickly. Moreover, knowing that her clumsy attempt at speech would be recorded for posterity, for all to hear and evaluate, only tightened her throat *muscles more. I wish everyone communicated by e-mail, she sighed again as she went back to the protection of her computer.*

* * *

Harry's tale

Harry had dealt successfully with people for most of his 56 years. As a pharmacist for 30 of those years, he spent his time checking medication histories and educating customers about drug interactions. He enjoyed the chance for social interchange. In his off-hours he coached the girls' soccer team and acted as secretary for his local chamber of commerce. Short, heavy, and balding, Harry was on everyone's invitation list because of his sense of humor and down-home story-telling ability.

But Harry wasn't this comfortable and composed in all social situations. One, in particular, literally turned him inside-out with skull-screaming anticipation of public scrutiny and judgment: His acting with the town's little theater group.

No matter how many times he performed a role, his repertoire ranging from King Lear to the King of Siam, he always nearly missed his entrance. Night after night, just before his appearance, he found himself doubled over, with his head dangling over the dressing room toilet, retching. It didn't matter that he could practically recite his lines backwards. He didn't care that Sir Lawrence Olivier had suffered the same fate. When it came time to approach the stage, to stand in the wings to await his cue, he went into cryogenic suspension. His fear clapped the eraser and wiped his blackboard clean, leaving only the vision of hundreds of pairs of eye lasering holes into him, searching for a chink in his armor.

As he gasped for breath, his heart started to rattle the bars of its prison. His head swam and his fingers tingled. Before each performance he was sure this was the "big one," the grand finale, the Guinness Book of Records heart attack. If he didn't immediately grab his good luck Walgreens prescription bag and start breathing into it for five minutes, he knew he wouldn't make it onto the stage. Yet, somehow, he never missed a cue. Furthermore, once he was actually out on the boards, involved in doing what he was so thoroughly prepared to do, he relaxed and focused on projecting his character to the audience and giving a good performance.

* * *

Maria's tale

Thirty-seven-year-old travel agent and mother of three, Maria, arrived at her church early on Sunday morning where she was going to meet two friends from her church parents' group so they could sit together for the service. Rosa and Jane wanted to sit up front and asked Maria to stake out their places for them since they thought they might be delayed. But Maria, who always slipped in unnoticed just before the service began and sat in the last row near the door, didn't want to be part of the advance guard in front of the congregation, leading them in the service. Even with her friends physically supplying support, she writhed at the idea of being the focus of attention. But no matter how uncomfortable she was about being observed as she communed with God, she found it impossible to say "no" to her friends.

As the time for the service drew near, and the pews behind her were rapidly filling up, Maria twisted around in the front seat, craning her neck to scan the faces, trying to locate her rescuers. Everyone seemed to notice her frantic behavior. She could hear them clucking to themselves about her unchurch-like antics. The music swelled and service began with no sign of Rosa and Jane. Maria wasn't ten feet from the altar and the gaze of her minister.

Without warning, her heart, like a racehorse, exploded out of the gate, hooves pummeling her chest. The pulsations cannonaded in her ears as sweat bathed her palsied hands, nearly sending the hymnal crashing to the floor. She felt inky coldness taking over, rendering her unable to stand for the first hymn. People on either side of her looked down at her. Simultaneously mortified and terrified she was going to keel over, she just hung her head. She was on the brink of humiliating herself before the entire congregation, her pastor, and God.

As others around her rejoiced in song, one thing became unmistakable. She was either going crazy or about to die. A heavy blanket of suffocating fear had already enveloped her. Wanting to scream or run, she bit her tongue and clutched her seat to keep control, immobilizing herself until the singing subsided. Maria rose just as those around her sat down. Her hymnal which had been teetering on her knee slid to the floor with a echoing slap. She rushed up the main aisle, clutching her purse to her breast, with the assembled watching her with curiosity.

Once she was in the safekeeping of her car, away from the judging eyes and knowing looks, Maria calmed down enough to drive home. Slowly her anxiety was shrink-wrapping her world, squeezing it smaller and smaller. As a result, she didn't go to travel conventions any longer. She rarely went on excursions to check out tourist facilities in the many exotic locations served by her agency. Unless she was with her small group of friends, she rarely socialized. And now she'd guaranteed she couldn't go back to her church, one of the pillars of solace in her life. She'd acted like a maniac and humiliated herself. If she went back, she knew she'd have to deal with others' negative judgments of herself as well.

* * *

What's going on here?

Everyone worries occasionally about what others may think of them. Will they like or dislike me...accept or reject me? So it's only natural for us to be concerned about presenting ourselves in social situations in the best light possible. This means we don't wear aluminum foil or Saran Wrap to work. We don't whistle during a funeral. We don't ride our Harley nude or stop bathing.

While this fleeting concern about being evaluated is common, the fear experienced by Joanna, Barry, Joe, Sarah, Harry, and Maria is neither fleeting nor common. Their concerns about being in the spotlight and the adequacy of their self-presentation are more profound. To them the mere possibility of being observed, evaluated, or having their relationships devalued is a threat like being held at gun point. Every time they enter a social situation they perceive as threatening, they feel as though they're walking on a tightrope above the Grand Canyon. Every shaky step is a potential slide into oblivion. Their lives are hanging by each unraveling thread of the frayed rope. Their fear of stumbling makes their misstep even more probable. The winds of public scrutiny buffet them, making them sway precipitously above another social disaster without a safety net.

"If I could 'shape up' and 'snap out of it,' would I be doing this?"

What does it mean?

What Joanna, Barry, Joe, Sarah, Harry, and Maria endure is an intense and persistent fear which is out of proportion to the realities of the situation. Their lives are not in danger, but their bodies, feelings, thoughts, and behaviors are responding as if they were, urging them to fight or flee. Their arousal system seems stuck in overdrive. They're hypervigilant, alert, and worrying about what "might" happen.

Those of us who have experienced this anxiety in social situations, whether in its milder or more severe forms, can strongly identify with Joanna, Barry, Joe, Sarah, Harry, and Maria in this theatrical production. The cast, the props, and the locations may be different, but the story line, the cast's motivation, and play are basically the same: Social anxiety.

Social anxiety represents a universal concern about what others think. Polls which have been taken over the years on what people fear most have found consistently that speaking in public, formally and informally, is the number-one American fear. This social fear out-ranks even the fear of death. It occurs in all segments of society, regardless of socioeconomic status, race, ethnicity, sexual orientation, religion, or color of skin. Social anxiety is an equal opportunity discomfort. It doesn't discriminate and no one is immune. But our simply being uncomfortable speaking in public, being observed, or evaluated isn't sufficient to fit the definition of SA/SP, as we'll see.

It's important to remember that while we who have social anxiety disorder (hereinafter called "SA/SP") share a lot of similarities, we have a lot of differences too in symptoms, anxiety triggers, and history. We're not wearing a one-size-fits-all label. This is because we're unique individuals who've arrived at our current personal state of anxiety through many different paths.

Like everyone else, those of us with SA/SP often monitor others' reactions to us at an unconscious level, by looking for cues in the social environment to signal how we're being perceived. Of course, it's only human to want to influence or control the impressions we make on others. We want to present ourselves positively and appropriately to make it more likely others won't reject us. Like everyone else we also monitor the effect of our presentation at a conscious level. By monitoring and controlling our self-presentation, we try to maximize the resulting social benefits and minimize the resulting social costs. But unlike everyone else, those of us with social anxiety monitor our impressions to the extent that these self-presentation thoughts predominate, to the exclusion of all others.

Because of this, when we do interact with other people, we tend to behave in ways that reduce the amount of social contact we have with them. We withdraw both physically and psychologically. (For example, I used to stand on the outer perimeter of conversations as long as possible, smiling and nodding, hoping I wouldn't have to try to contribute anything intelligent.) In general, SA/SPers tend not to initiate conversations. But when we're in them, we engage in less eye contact, speak less, allow longer silences, take longer to respond, and don't participate equally. When before large audiences and those perceived to be critical, we also speak less and for shorter periods of time. And some of us, like me, have a tendency to try to say everything in one breath before the other person stops listening or we forget the point we want to make. As a result, we're more frequently seen as reticent, shy, or introverted.

Yet some of us, because of the kind of work we do (such as my consulting, doing seminars, and teaching, are forced to present a more extroverted face). We have to initiate conversations, speak up at meetings, give talks, and interact with authority figures. This apparent level of social competence, however, doesn't necessarily mean that we aren't working very hard to appear comfortable, outgoing, and adequate. It doesn't mean we wouldn't prefer solitariness and solitude, to stay in our little sanctum sanctorums, cuddled up to our computers, never stepping into the spotlight again.

We're concerned about what social psychologist Mark Leary calls the "prospect or presence of interpersonal evaluation in real or imagined social settings." Therefore, we focus our attention inward, on our self-presentation and its implications. All we can think about is how we feel, what we think, what we think others will think about us, and how vulnerable we are. This self-focus creates an ongoing internal dialogue which perpetuates our self-focus. We want to put our best foot (or in this case, "face") forward so we can be seen as competent and socially desirable. Because of this we become totally disengaged from others and the situation.

How motivated we are in trying to manage our impressions depends upon the degree to which we value the outcomes we desire and how important we see the consequences for ourselves. The more valuable the outcome, like getting a date, the more concerned we'll be about obtaining it. The more concerned we are about obtaining it, the more motivated we'll be to create the desired impression.

Most of social life is dedicated to influencing others and being influenced by them in return. One of the primary methods by which we influence one another is impression management. Nearly everything in our Western culture depends upon being seen as competent, responsible, ethical, and friendly. The impressions we make on each other determine many of the central outcomes of our social lives.

Our failure to make the desired impression has important ramifications for us. It means we don't exert the influence we want in situations important to us. As a result, we may not get the job or promotion, be considered for club membership, make the team line-up, or make friends with, date, or marry the people we want. It's important to remember that with or without SA/SP, not conveying the impressions we desire others to see makes us feel excessively tense, threatened, flustered, awkward, and embarrassed.

Social anxiety is generally anticipatory, occurring before anything actually goes wrong (like thinking about the speech I have to give in a month's time). However, on other occasions we may react negatively to situations which have already occurred. We may see people look at us, hear them laugh, and then become anxious, such as in Barry's dating anxiety. We may also recall incidents which made us anxious and re-experience the feeling. Irrespective of when we feel the anxiety, the trigger for the response is the prospect or presence of the social interaction situation. Put another way, our behavior is contingent upon others being able to scrutinize and evaluate us, such as in Joe's anxiety. When this anxiety encompasses many situations, it's *generalized social anxiety*. Generalized social anxiety accounts for about 80% of all those with SA/SP (including me).

Social anxiety may also occur independently in circumscribed instances where we experience anxiety only about a specific performance or task. In this case, our response to the situation wouldn't be contingent upon the presence of others because our response has been predetermined by the specific performance or task characteristic itself. This is *discrete,* or non-generalized, *social anxiety*, also called *performance anxiety*. Discrete social anxiety may occur as a single social anxiety, such as in test anxiety or Harry's stage anxiety, or as part of the multi-component generalized social anxiety like Joe's.

Social anxiety can also occur when we're chronically anxious about others' judging our physical appearance. (I, for example, was a chunky child and was teased mercilessly about it. Today, no matter what I weigh, I tend to see myself as heavier than I am.) We imagine body flaws. As compared with some subjective standard or ideal, we see ourselves as too fat or too thin; too short or too tall; knees too bony or pudgy; nose too crooked, hooked, or bulbous; eyes too close together or too far apart; skin, hair, and eyes the wrong color; too hairy or not hairy enough; our secondary sex characteristics pendulous or puny. Obsessing about these perceived "defects" drives us to constantly monitor others' reactions to see if they're noticing and commenting upon the "flaw."

Physique anxiety creates extreme social anxiety and embarrassment. When this condition is severe enough, it's called *body dysmorphism*.

Drowning in this whirlpool of excessive concern about being perceived unfavorably, we're often left unsatisfied with our interactions. If we're dissatisfied, we expect those with whom we interact to feel the same. As a result, we see ourselves to be less socially skilled. Even if our social skills are intact, our social awkwardness tends to reinforce and perpetuate our social fear. We doubt we can make that desired impression on others. We fear being embarrassed or humiliated in front of others. And because we have an underlying rigidity in our thinking about behavior, we assume there's a "right" way and a "wrong" way to do things and that we're automatically locked into the wrong way.

While the cardinal signs of social anxiety are increased public self-consciousness and exquisite sensitivity to evaluation in social situations, the overarching theme is a fear of being found wanting. Being perceived as inadequate raises all kinds of questions about our general acceptability, self-worth, likability, intimacy and its consequences, and social success. When this high degree of nervousness, self-consciousness, uncertainty, and dread about negative evaluation is severe, lasts at least six months, and significantly interferes with our daily activities, it's called *social anxiety disorder*.

What is anxiety and where does it come from?

In order to understand SA/SP, we have to first understand anxiety. But we all already know what anxiety is. It's that thing that a Gallup Poll says 30-40 million Americans suffer, with 15 million suffering severely enough to warrant treatment. It's butterflies in the stomach on our first date or new job. It's that feeling of apprehension about going to the doctor to bare our souls and our anatomy. It's worry about the future: Whether we'll be able to pay our bills, take a test, or buy the car we need. It's being faced with conflict that's so overwhelming and full of dread that we can't go through our usual problem-solving steps to address it. It's being left without an accurate assessment of the nature of the conflict or an effective plan of action to address it.

So anxiety is an inaccurate, unrealistic speculation about potential dangers. When we're anxious, we inappropriately focus on low-probability events where there's little or no evidence to support the likelihood of those negative outcomes. We believe that what happens around us or what people do can and does directly and adversely affect us. We maintain the belief that we are at the mercy of random events and unpredictable individuals, thus needing to be constantly on guard lest others "push our buttons."

Psychologists usually talk about anxiety in the context of physiological fear or general arousal in response to perceived danger. In some threatening situations our parasympathetic nervous system, which slows everything down, takes over. We respond with an automatic inhibition similar to freezing behavior in animals. Everything shuts down, leaving us unable to move, speak, or think clearly.

In other threatening situations our sympathetic nervous system, which speeds everything up, kicks in, preparing us for action. Our physiological reactions show a state of high arousal. They include rapid heart, shallow breathing, sweating, and tremors. This automatic reaction to anxiety is to fight, avoid, or escape - compelling us to take some action to reduce the threat by avoiding going into the threatening situation or escaping in some manner, either physically or psychologically.

Anxiety is a complex blend of emotions, thoughts (including beliefs, assumptions, and values), behaviors, and physiological reactions which results in that feeling of discomfort about the future. Humanistic psychologist Rollo May refers to anxiety as "...the apprehension cued off by a threat to some value which the individual holds essential to his [sic] existence as a personality." Our values are unique to each one of us and deeply ingrained in our psyches. To some an essential value is being loved by others. To some it's having independence and freedom. To some it's having power and prestige. Irrespective of the particular values we hold, when essential values are threatened, we experience anxiety.

Our emotions in anxiety include not only fear but also excitement, increased anger, and interest. Our thoughts become a welter of perceptions of unpredictability, lack of control over potentially negative future events, and a maladaptive shift in our attention toward ourselves. For SA/Spers, for example, the stronger the perceived uncontrollability in the social situation, the more likely we'll employ avoidance behavior. In general, all these elements combine to prepare us to cope, effectively or ineffectively, with the situation as we perceive it to be.

How does it become a disorder?

The difference between anxiety and an anxiety disorder then is the degree of its severity and its persistence. Just-plain anxiety is like being in a swamped rowboat in a five-foot-deep pond. It's uncomfortable and undesirable but bearable. This feeling lasts just until the situation is over and the survivor makes it to shore. But the anxiety of an anxiety disorder is like being on the Titanic after it hits the iceberg. It's intense, full of extremes of emotion, thoughts, and behaviors. Its effects can be paralyzing for survivors and last for years.

Vulnerability. The core of anxiety disorders is a sense of *vulnerability* which results from the thoughts and feelings which accompany threat. As Aaron T. Beck, the progenitor of cognitive therapy, suggests, vulnerability can be defined as our perception of ourselves as subject to internal or external (or both) dangers over which we either have no control or insufficient control to afford us a sense of safety.

When SA/Spers, for example, enter a socially-threatening situation, we feel as if we're swimming among sharks. There are serious consequences for a single slip or inadequate performance. Our safety requires adherence to a strict set of rules of appropriate behaviors. These can be social expectations, norms, or mores. Our perception of vulnerability is dependent upon a number of factors. One is what we see as the relative power between our evaluator and ourselves. Their "power" is their being able to provide or withhold desired resources, like love or money. The greater we perceive the power of the other to be, the greater will be our impulse to do what is "socially desirable" to get that resource.

Second is the degree of threat, the severity of the consequences, and its probability of occurring. Third is our threat threshold and coping skills. When our threshold to threat is high, we're less vulnerable. When we have good coping skill resources, our perception of threat is low. Fourth is our willingness to confront powerful figures and our skills in presenting ourselves. The more assertive we are the less vulnerable we are. A "confident" persona, or mask, may make us feel more confident and convince our evaluator that we actually are (a method I used successfully for years). As our self-confidence increases, vulnerability decreases.

Fifth is lack of *hardiness*. According to Salvatore Maddi, psychological hardiness is a resilience that some people have which allows them to buffer the effects of stress and anxiety. It's based on our beliefs and our use of certain coping skills, health practices, and support networks. The most important of these beliefs are commitment, control, and challenge. *Commitment* is the belief that persistence in our goals will result in something meaningful. *Control* is the belief that we can influence what's going on around us and are ready to act. *Challenge* is the belief that negative life events can be turned around to result in positive outcomes. Not exactly the SA/SPers' credo.

When we hold these beliefs, we're likely to engage in hardiness coping behaviors. This means confronting disruptive circumstances through changing our beliefs and actions so the circumstances are no longer stressful. We can do this through reframing, or relabeling. For example, rather than see an office Christmas party as upsetting my normal interaction pattern and a personal threat, I'd reframe it as an opportunity to make myself visible with an eye toward future promotions or just becoming acquainted with others to mitigate my loneliness.

Vulnerability is magnified by our distorted thinking and erroneous beliefs. We SA/SPers minimize our positive personal resources, focus on our weaknesses, catastrophize, and expect public humiliation. We have difficulty being objective about ourselves, feel helpless and under attack. We believe we lack important coping skills and doubt our ability to deal with threat. Our resulting lack of self-confidence holds us back from reaching our goals and doesn't protect us from the effects of failure and negative evaluation.

The making of SA/SP

To reiterate, anxiety disorder becomes *social* anxiety disorder when the trigger for our fear response is concern about being scrutinized and/or evaluated by others in a social or performance situation. When there is excessive fear of being embarrassed, humiliated, or judged negatively in these situations. And when our *perceptions* of the social situation, ourselves, and others' motives and behaviors in it are distorted. This anxiety may manifest itself before the event (anticipatory), during, and/or after the event.

Situations which precipitate social anxiety can be classified into four categories, according to Craig Holt and associates:

- *Formal speaking and interaction* (giving a talk before an audience, performing on stage, giving a report to a group, speaking up at a meeting, participating in small groups and acting)
- *Informal speaking and interaction* (giving a party, calling someone we don't know very well, meeting strangers, trying to pick up someone at a bar, dating, having sex)
- *Assertive interaction* (talking to authority figures, expressing disagreement, expressing disapproval of someone, returning goods to a store, resisting high-pressure salespeople)
- *Observation of behavior* (eating while others are watching, modeling clothes, simply being observed while working, taking tests, using a public restroom, or writing).

It's important to note that adults and adolescents may differ on the category of their most feared situations. Recent research suggests that while adults fear formal speaking and interactions most, adolescents and young adults tend to fear informal speaking and interactions most.

Avoidance may or may not be a feature of our experience with SA/SP. Some people avoid some or all feared social situations. Others reluctantly confront the situation and stoically endure the associated distress of doing so. (This is what I did wearing my mask.)

SA/SP is a feedback loop of the four components of physiology, emotion, thoughts, and behavior, each influencing the others, with no one component really starting the process. While physiological arousal is necessary for SA/SP, it is not sufficient to create that sense of vague, unrecognized danger in the future. As with normal anxiety, the arousal needs to be interpreted and labeled for it to have emotional meaning. In general, when we feel heightened arousal, we look to situational cues to determine what label we should attach and how to interpret it. For example, if we experience arousal in the presence of an attractive member of the opposite sex (for heterosexuals) or the same sex (for homosexuals), we'll probably label the feelings as "sexual excitement." If aroused after learning of the death of a loved one, we'll probably label the sensations as "sorrow." If aroused after receiving a severe insult, we'll probably label it "anger."

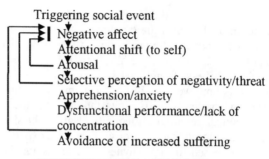

Triggering social event
Negative affect
Attentional shift (to self)
Arousal
Selective perception of negativity/threat
Apprehension/anxiety
Dysfunctional performance/lack of concentration
Avoidance or increased suffering

ANXIETY FEEDBACK LOOP

What we do is called a "cognitive appraisal." We look at various dimensions of the situation and these dimensions determine the situation's emotional content. For example, in a classic experiment conducted by psychologists Stanley Schachter and Jerome Singer in 1962 participants were injected with epinephrine (adrenaline) which produces heart palpitations, hand tremor, rapid breathing, and warm feeling of flushing. All participants were led to believe the injection was an experimental vitamin supplement, but one group (Informed) were told to expect these side effects as a result of the injection. So when the symptoms did occur, the Informed group would, thus, have an appropriate label for their subjective feelings. The second group (Uninformed) were given the injection with no prior warning about the symptoms, and the third group (Misinformed) were told that the injection could produce numbness, itching, and slight headache (all obviously inappropriate to explain the symptoms actually induced).

After the injection, in the 3-5-minute delay before onset of symptoms, each participant was joined by an experimental confederate. The confederate had been trained to act in either an angry or euphoric manner. For participants without an adequate explanation for their symptoms, the actions of the confederate provided an appropriate cognitive label. Results of the experiment showed that participants in the Uninformed and Misinformed groups adopted the label provided by the confederate's behavior, while the Informed participants did not.

Both physiological and cognitive elements are required for the subjective experience of emotional states. As a result, we'll perceive ourselves as experiencing the emotion which external cues tell us we should feel. And when strong external cues are lacking, we look to our behaviors to infer how we feel. I'm laughing so I must feel happy. I'm crying so I must feel sad. I'm eating so I must feel hungry. As we might guess, this inference-from-behavior process can lead to misattribution of emotion. People can laugh because of anxiety, shed tears when joyous, and eat to comfort themselves.

But this is not the whole story. We also unconsciously look at the *pleasantness* of the situation. Pleasantness contributes to a good mood. We look at *agency* to see who has responsibility or control in the situation. If we perceive ourselves to be responsible for a big mistake, we're likely to feel guilt or shame. If we perceive that another is responsible, we're likely to feel anger or contempt instead. But if the circumstances are responsible, like a rainstorm destroying an outdoor wedding reception, we're likely to feel sadness.

Regarding *misattribution*, Philip Zimbardo, the parent of the social psychology of shyness, found that how we attribute causes to our "shyness" behavior affects how we act. In one of many such studies he had shy women (those who had particular difficulties talking with men) and non-shy women interact with a male research confederate. Half of the shy women were exposed to a loud noise and told that the arousal they were experiencing was the result of the noise (as opposed to their shyness). The results showed that shy women who had misattributed the cause of their arousal to a non-social event (noise) acted like the non-shy women. Moreover, the shyness of the misattributors couldn't be detected by the male confederate.

We also look for *uncertainty*. When events are unpredictable and personally uncontrollable, we're likely to feel fear. We look at *attention* and the degree to which we need to stay attuned. If the situation requires little of our attention, we're likely to feel bored. Or if it requires too much, we'll likely feel frustrated.

While most individuals when aroused look to situational or external cues for labeling, SA/SPers don't. Instead, we ignore the full range of external cues. We look internally, focusing on ourselves, for cues. The cues at which we do look are distorted by our erroneous thinking, negative self-talk, and our perceived inability to predict and control future events or obtain desired results in the future. As a result, our attention is narrowed on negative emotional content.

Unconsciously we assess those cues that have personal relevance to our well-being, whether they harm or benefit us. We look for coping options. We look at our expectations about the consequences of our actions. We associate the present situation with past experiences. But when SA/SPers do this cognitive appraisal, we tend to recognize and recall selectively **only** those things which match our negative mood. This becomes our preparatory coping set. These are the auto-pilot action tendencies we put in place so they'll be ready to go whenever the physiological arousal occurs in social situations. It's like having an overnight bag always packed for a sudden business trip.

This internal focus plus our faulty processing of information serves to reinforce all our negative action tendencies, attitudes, beliefs, cognitions, and behaviors because it eliminates the possibility of our finding disconfirming evidence in the external situation. For example, when Barry was debating with himself about the risks involved in speaking to the young woman with the sweet smile, he was so wrapped up in his own concerns about being played for a fool that he never saw her nervously glance away when another young man spoke to her. He didn't see her friends trying to convince her to stay awhile longer. When he saw her shake her head "no" in reply, he interpreted it as referring to him. In fact, she was telling her friends that she really wasn't really interested in the man who had already spoken to her, but in someone else…Barry.

As cartoonist and playwright Jules Feiffer asks, "If you're not able to communicate successfully between yourself and yourself, how are you supposed to make it with the strangers outside?"

So our SA/SP is composed of four primary components:

- *Action tendencies*
- *Perception of lack of control and predictability*
- *Self-focused attention*
- *Physiological arousal.*

The social anxiety feedback loop works like this: We begin with a possible biological predisposition or hypersensitivity to arousal. Then some stressful life events involving performance, such as job loss or relationship failure, create a negative interruption of our functional behavior. We're left feeling uncertain, self-conscious, apprehensive, or helpless. Now we have a psychological vulnerability. The negative emotion we're experiencing becomes associated with perceptions of future uncontrollability and unpredictability. We encounter a social situation we expect not to handle and feel apprehensive. We tell ourselves there's no way we'll be able to take part in the organizational meeting or eat with fellow employees, for example. (It's important to note that how helpless we feel may be moderated by our coping skills, social skills, and social support network. The better our skills and social support, the less helpless we feel.)

Next our action tendencies are geared up and ready to go. Our attention shifts from external monitoring to internal evaluation. We become more aroused as we listen to our negative self-talk, telling us that we're going to muff this meeting too and look foolish. As we become more aroused, we become hypervigilant, looking only at negative emotional content, recognizing and remembering only those things which support our present mood and arousal-interpretation. We're flooded with memories that are painful and unacceptable. These are recollections we're usually able to keep under wraps. Our negative emotion increases further as we keep building layer upon layer of anger and fear. Finally, we're overwhelmed by intense worry which so preoccupies us that we can't perform at the meeting. We stutter, stammer, and blank out. (I was particularly adept at blanking out.) At this point we feel so bad we want to escape.

While SA/SP results from social sources, obviously not all anxiety experienced in social situations reflects "social anxiety." If we're alone at an ATM after dark and several members of a street gang are approaching us, the nervousness we feel isn't social anxiety. If we're waiting to hear from our boss about the future of the company, our tension isn't social anxiety. If the plate of spaghetti the waiter is carrying past us, starts to dip in our direction, our discomfort isn't social anxiety

How many of us are there?

There are a number of anxiety disorders: Agoraphobia, specific phobia, panic disorder, acute stress disorder, generalized anxiety disorder, obsessive-compulsive disorder, and SA/SP. SA/SP is the most common anxiety disorder, least recognized, and most under-treated. In fact, it wasn't until 1980 that SA/SP was listed in the American Psychiatric Association's **Diagnostic and Statistical Manual of Mental Disorders, the Third Edition (DSM-III)**. Then, it wasn't until **DSM-III's Revised Edition (DSM-III-R)** in 1987, and further refined in 1994 with **DSM-IV**, that SA/SP was carefully defined using restrictive criteria to differentiate it from similar conditions, such as agoraphobia. Since then, the National Institute of Mental Health has found that over 13.3% of American adults have this disorder some time over their lifetime, making it the third most common psychiatric disorder, after depression and alcoholism. Of those in whom it's present over 70% experience this social anxiety in three or more socially interactive situations (generalized social anxiety) while 24% experience it in only one or two (discrete social anxiety).

Millions suffer from this life-pervading personal problem in multiple situations. SA/SP interferes with overall satisfaction and enjoyment in life. In its severest form it can lead to functional impairment, such as alcohol and substance abuse, depression, suicidal ideation, dropping out of school, unemployment, and financial dependence.

Specifically SA/ causes fatigue, insomnia, headaches, constipation, diarrhea, gas, and various muscle aches, particularly in the head, neck, and shoulders. It causes us to participate in fewer activities, meet fewer people, have difficulties with work, school, and interpersonal relationships. It causes us to become less outgoing, more solitary and socially isolated, often relying on our pets and the Internet for companionship. We work at whatever is available that requires less self-presentation from us (like my early years working as a secretary, and doing it miserably, rather than teaching which is what I was qualified to do). This means we're likely to go from flipping hamburgers to working in a stockroom, from seeing patients to hunkering behind a microscope, from working with adults to playing with children. As a result, we frequently feel stuck in a no-win situation. We see our dreams of having a college education and well-paying job, owning a home, or having a permanent relationship, one by one, slip away out of reach.

As a result, SA/SP has national health consequences. Perhaps the most significant of these is that those of us with the condition frequently turn to alcohol and illegal drugs for temporary relief from this tension, dread, and uncertainty. Because of this, the disorder is now seen as a cause of alcoholism and drug abuse and a candidate for public health prevention strategies.

The number of SA/SPers is increasing. It's now estimated that up to 50% of the population of the U.S. have experienced social anxiety at some point in their lives. This results from an interaction among four factors:

- *Individuals' predisposition to anxiety*

- *Society's predisposition to intrusive stress processes*

- *Individuals' precipitating psychological reactions to stress*

- *Society's precipitating social stress events.*

Test yourself for SA/SP

Do you think you have SA/SP? Answer the following questionnaire "yes" or "no" to find out. (This assessment is for information purposes only and is not to be used for diagnosis.)

___*Do you experience intense and persistent anxiety when you're exposed to feared social or performance situations?*

___*Do you feel nervous anticipating future feared social or performance situations?*

___*Do you feel nervous about meeting strangers?*

___*Do you feel nervous being observed or scrutinized by others?*

___*Do you feel nervous about being evaluated by others?*

___*Do you feel your nervousness is excessive or unreasonable for the real danger present?*

___*Do you avoid these feared social or performance situations or endure them while experiencing considerable distress?*

___*Does anxious anticipation of the feared social or performance situations significantly interfere with your activities, relationships, or normal routines?*

___*Does avoidance of the feared social or performance situations significantly interfere with your activities, relationships, or normal routines?*

___*Have you ruled out a medical condition or the effects of drugs or medications to account for your anxiety?*

The greater the number of "yeses" the greater the likelihood you have SA/SP as defined by the DSM-IV (inventory adapted from DSM-IV definition).

Are worry and anxiety the same?

"Anxiety" and "worry" are often used interchangeably, but are they the same? Or is worry qualitatively or quantitatively different? Worry, like anxiety, has been defined as a narrow, intense emotional focus on the future with accompanying symptoms of arousal. But worry is like a rehearsal for dealing with danger. Specifically, we focus our minds on the problem, ostensibly so we can search more efficiently for a solution. But we never follow through.

"What if the Prize Patrol rings my doorbell or I have to pee in public?"

According to clinical psychologist Thomas D. Borkovec, who founded the Worry Clinic at Pennsylvania State University, everyone worries. Some degree of worry is expected and normal. Most people fit into the categories of "non-" and "moderate worrier." "Non-worriers" make up about 30% of the population and report worrying less than one and a half hours a day and don't consider it a problem for them. "Moderate worriers," who constitute about 50%, spend between one and a half and seven and a half hours a day worrying and probably consider it a problem. "Chronic worriers," which is about 15-20%, spend nearly all their time in apprehensive turmoil, unable to deal with it or extricate themselves from it. (I even worried whether I was worrying the *right* amount.)

Results of a survey I conducted on worry behaviors showed distinct differences between self-described "worriers" and "non-worriers." "Worriers" and "non-worriers" had similar spheres of concern: Family, home, interpersonal relations; finances; work, school; and illness, health, injury. About two-thirds worried about family matters and one-half worried about finances, with work close behind. Illness was just over 10%.

However, when "non-worriers" encountered a problem, they first assessed its magnitude. If it was trivial or beyond their control, they forgot it. But, if it had significance for them and they believed they could affect it, they imagined the things that could happen next. Then they brainstormed some solutions, picked one, and acted on it in their own best interest. It was worry that motivated them to address the problem directly and deliberately. Their worry behavior resulted in "getting organized," "performing better," and "solving problems." They exerted only the energy necessary to put the things they wanted in motion.

"Worriers," on the other hand, thought about their problems and became anxious. Some got headaches, others nausea, a knot in their stomachs, or tight shoulders. Some responded by eating, drinking alcohol, tossing and turning all night, doing nothing, or becoming depressed. They became distracted, had difficulty concentrating on things, and couldn't completely shut off their worry. Their worry took on a life of its own, became self-perpetuating, and part of the problem. Their philosophy (and mine) seemed to be "Why should I waste my time reliving the past when I can spend it worrying about the future." This is despite their acknowledgment that the things that never seem to happen worry them the most. Those "worriers" who became immobilized in the present as a result of things that were going to or not going to happen in the future would fit Borkovec's category of "chronic worrier."

So worry experienced by the "non-worrier" and "moderate worrier" would be considered to be within normal limits and would be called "anxiety." But that experienced by the "chronic worrier," exceeds those bounds. This anxiety tends to block thinking. It becomes an end in itself where we're caught up in a downward spiral of increasing anxiety, resignation, and failure. This maladaptive and dysfunctional type of worry is called *generalized anxiety disorder*.

What about stress disorder?

Stress is everywhere, pushing us on and holding us back at the same time. Stress and anxiety seem synonymous. But is an anxiety disorder the same as a stress disorder? In an anxiety disorder the focus of attention is internal, on ourselves, what we think and feel. In stress disorder, on the other hand, the focus of attention is external, on the situation or event itself, such as a disintegrating marriage. While anxiety has emotional, cognitive, behavioral, and physiological symptoms of fear, stress has only physiological symptoms, such as rapid heart, shallow breathing, and sweating. So only anxiety is associated with increased worry, negative affect, and a feeling of helplessness.

Effect of culture on social anxiety

It's important to remember that how SA/SP manifests itself is a function of the culture in which it occurs. The culture gives it form and dictates how and when members of the culture perceive themselves to be the object of threatening social evaluation. Each culture has its own set of social expectations for its members to follow. This means that to understand social anxiety in any given culture we have to understand the norms for behavior and social skills, and how deviations are verbally and nonverbally expressed.

In several East Asian countries, such as Japan and Korea, the culture defines the individual not as individual but as a member of a group: Family, social group, or community. As a result, the individual's behavior, whether good or bad, is seen as a direct reflection of the group. Deviation from the norm and "individualism" are not tolerated. One is responsible to the group for the welfare of the group and is dependent upon their evaluation. SA/SP in this culture, called *taijin kyofu-sho* (fear syndrome) in Japan, focuses on fear of offending or embarrassing others in public because it brings shame to the social group to which one belongs. This offense and embarrassment may also result from blushing, displaying unsightly body parts, or emitting body odors.

One study of Japanese children showed that these social fears are prevalent at an early age. For example, fear of eye contact was found in 40-50% of children aged 10-17, while fear of blushing was 20-40% in that group. These fears appear to occur mostly among young East Asian men and may reflect the cultural concern about and emphasis on politeness. Thus, as a child and adult in these cultures, one deals with social anxiety through social avoidance, demonstrated by deferential behaviors, such as showing respect and excessive modesty.

In Western cultures individuals are defined by their individualism and independence. Being unique, self-aggrandizing, and standing out from the crowd are not only accepted but also expected. One's primary responsibility is for oneself. In these cultures the focus of social fear is embarrassing and bringing shame to oneself.

Being overwhelmed by social stressors

Defining the present cultural climate in which we in Western societies experience SA/SP is important for our overall understanding of the predisposition and prevalence of the condition. Over the last several decades, the number of social stressors has increased dramatically, prompting many to dub this last quarter-century the "Age of Anxiety" and the 1990s the "Decade of Social Anxiety." Paraphrasing media analyst Marshall McLuhan, one might suggest that this age of anxiety is, in great part, the result of trying to do today's job with tomorrow's concepts and yesterday's tools. With each successive year things have only gotten worse. This has led to system overload for many, perhaps helping trigger clinical symptoms of SA/SP. Under this accumulating burden, we seem unable to process all the inputs from our environment. This may be because there are either too many inputs for us to cope with or they come too fast for us to process them in the proper order.

This is the situation to which we all are forced to adapt. Even though this overload distorts daily life on every level - from the physical to the psychological, from the social to societal - most of the time it leaves the majority of us still able to set priorities and make choices. But social stressors interfere with the roles we play, as parent, child, worker, friend, and lover. They interfere with how we follow social norms, such as becoming independent and productive members of society or helping those who depend on us. They significantly and negatively impact SA/SPers by creating and maintaining a negative atmosphere. Let's take a look at some of the many factors contributing to this overload.

Value shift. Everything around us seems to be in a state of flux, producing feelings of insecurity and worry. There are no stable, consistent socially-accepted and socially-enforced standards or values by which to live. A two-year study by the Josephson Institute for Ethics reports that large numbers of young Americans admit to stealing, lying, and cheating at school, work, and home. Another study which indicated an unprecedented rise in cohabitation before marriage also showed that couples who do live together are more likely to divorce than those who don't. One in every three marriages will end in divorce.

In addition, over the last 35 years the pendulum of ethics has swung from the position of favoring group/community rights and individual duties to individual rights and group/community duties. For the individual the transition has been from dependence and interdependence to independence. Our continuing emphasis on "me" and "self" creates a climate of narcissism and perpetuates our sense of isolation, alienation, and loss of community.

Mobility. Sense of community has been rapidly disappearing since the 1950s when increased individual mobility made it easier to travel and travel in ever-widening circles. Always on the move, we've grown accustomed to brief encounters and accept them as the norm. We see time as a precious commodity, in short supply. So much to do and so little time in which to do it. As a result, we don't want to have to wait to build relationships in order to communicate our message of who we are. It's no longer a small, closed world where we have known everybody with whom we'll interact since our childhood.

Density. Everywhere we look space is at a premium. New houses are being built closer together with postage-stamp lots. Developments are springing up like crabgrass. Every piece of green open space along our byways is being sacrificed to strip malls and parking lots. In all but the most rural areas the roads and highways are filled to capacity from morning til night. People are becoming denser and seem to be carrying this density around with them as they move at a fast clip. This crowding and pace create an unremitting level of arousal for those even remotely touched by it.

Efficiency. In this big, wide, hurry-up world we need to be both effective and efficient. Efficiency suggests creating and relying upon first impressions to do the job, despite their superficiality and seeming artificiality. We sell cars, food, politicians, movies, and wars through impression management. In fact, spin doctoring has become a proficiency in demand.

Social support. With mobility also comes disconnection, the breaking up of the nuclear family, and loosening of the extended family ties. Families today come in lots of shapes and sizes. The traditional definition no longer applies. Rarely do three generations live in the same house, in the same neighborhood, or even in the same town. Social support networks, which are interdependent groups consisting of friends and family found to be so important to our mental and physical health, especially in times of stress, likewise are becoming more difficult to establish and maintain. Often we hardly know our neighbors much less have the time, energy, or interest to socialize with them and become involved.

Business trends. Competition, mergers, and business- and industry downsizing often have debilitating social and economic effects. The downsizing ax affects everyone, leaving victims of all ages and economic status behind. Competition, mergers, and downsizing are also changing workers' perception of loyalty. Jobs have become simultaneously more demanding and less secure. No longer is it a given that if we work well and hard for a company that we'll be rewarded by being guaranteed a place with them until we retire - if we can afford to retire. Our perceived entitlement in this area is becoming a thing of the past.

Jobs. We can no longer define our self-image by our job. Competence, experience, and knowledge are no longer the linchpins of our getting the rewards of our labor. It's become harder to hold onto the belief that upward mobility is a "birthright." Instead, it's concern for stockholders and profits that often supersedes a business's concern for its employees, the community in which it resides, its social responsibility, and product or service quality.

Despite this environment, we tend to expect more from our job, not less. We expect our jobs to use our talents, be a challenge, be an avenue of self-expression and meaning, and provide us a means of contributing to society. But the reality is work has become more routine and specialized, offering less satisfaction and remuneration.

Youth. Particularly hard hit is the so-called Generation X, or Twentysomethings. This generation of young adults, born between 1965 and 1980, faces an economic situation for which it has been inadequately prepared. Imbued with the unrealistic expectation of continuing economic prosperity, of having things better than their parents did, they are unsuccessfully grappling with underdeveloped self-sufficiency, unemployment, and underemployment in all but a few circumscribed areas. Psychologically, they have been used to having more than their parents did at that age and, consequently, expecting the situation to only improve with time. But this sense of entitlement and specialness creates a resentment of the kinds of compromise necessary to effectively survive. They find themselves without an expectation of economic fluctuations, an understanding of the implications of change, and the survival skills necessary to deal effectively and efficiently with them. As a result, this group is left feeling disillusioned and alienated.

Privacy. Loss of privacy looms large in our psyches. Computer data collection, storage, and retrieval by large corporations, such as TRW, Equifax, and the Medical Information Bureau, make personal details of our lives easily accessible to employers, insurance companies, law enforcement, and a whole host of others. Our "confidential" medical records are anything but confidential. It has been estimated that at least 75 people have access to our individual medical files at any given time and not all of these individuals are health care professionals with a need to know. Employers listen to our telephone calls, read our e-mail, search our lockers, and require testing of our personality, honesty, and urine. Closed-circuit television cameras monitor our actions everywhere we go, whether in stores, businesses, bathrooms, or on the street. While there's always been and will continue to be some unwanted intrusion into our lives, restricting the access of others to what's intimate in our lives is even less under our control today.

Crime. Fear of crime is escalating. Even as crime rates are dropping, sales of handguns are increasing because we feel alone, anonymous, unprotected, unable to predict and control an alien environment. This anonymity is a double-edged sword, however. It has the advantage of greater tolerance for or acceptance of individuality, eccentricity, and stigmatized others. This means, for example, that SA/SPers are less likely to be singled out as deviant (though we'll still perceive them to be doing it). But it also has the disadvantage of a lessened willingness to trust and assist strangers. A heightened sense of physical and emotional vulnerability makes us think twice about reaching out a hand to another.

The resulting social isolation means less familiarity with those outside ourselves, which, in turn, tends to breed "them" versus "us" thinking. In this environment those who already lack adequate social and job skills and have fewer opportunities to develop them will tend to feel even more alienated, detached, and be indifferent to others. They will be less likely to experience those emotional exchanges found in social ties which lead to social sharing, understanding, and cooperation, thus potentially leaving us all in harm's way.

Technology. Technological changes are occurring rapidly too, barely allowing us time to adjust before the next wave hits, such as the appearance of for-profit managed care or genetic discoveries and their ethical, legal, and social implications. Many of these changes produce a sort of "techno-anxiety" because we are not sure how they'll affect our lives, if they'll impact our values, families, or economic status. Many of these changes also reinforce our isolation by further reducing face-to-face interaction. We no longer need a teller to get our money; we can use a card at the ATM. We no longer need a station attendant or a cashier in order to get gas or pay for it; we can use a card at the pump. We no longer need a telephone operator to make a call; we can dial the pre-recorded information we need and use a card at the phone. This automation offers efficiency, convenience, but no human contact.

Computers. Similarly computers are providing access to an overwhelming array of information so that we can spend hours every day surfing the web, doing research, collecting and sending e-mail, playing video games, listening to music, and watching CD-ROM movies. In general, we chat anonymously and superficially with disembodied others. Because we are unable to observe the verbal and nonverbal aspects of these social interactions, we may feel less of a personal connection. Personal connection mediates our behavior toward others. As a result, some of us may even be at-risk for becoming disinhibited on lists or in chat rooms. Unfettered by face-to-face social norms, disinhibited individuals may insult others, make threats, or be aggressively argumentative. For these people civility, consideration, and respect for others and their opinions may take second-place to their achieving whatever it is they want. Fortunately, this incivility seems to occur less frequently among social anxiety cyber-surfers.

Some of us may prefer online relationships. Real-time relationships, which are guided by social norms, are messy, awkward, and sometimes stifling. They require attention, emotion, problem-solving, decision making, and work. But in cyberspace the "rules" governing interpersonal relations and interaction are more ambiguous. We can be whoever we want. We don't have to pay careful attention to what the other is saying or meaning. We don't have to contribute our emotion or work through problems. It's there only if we choose to log on.

And, if we wish, we can simply and easily walk away from it all with just click the mouse, reinforcing our avoidance of social situations.

Financial & health security.   There are justified fears that Social Security, Medicare, and Medicaid will not be available when people are of the age or financial situation to need them.   A recent SunAmerica Financial Services survey found that four out of five Americans in their prime working years (25-55) believe they will not have enough money to live on when they retire.   Of these 71% of African-American, 59% Hispanics, and women in general were "very concerned." With over 41 million without health insurance many cannot be sure they'll have access to health care. For-profit managed care has taken over health care.   Its lean-and-mean approach achieves its cost-cutting goals by cutting back on referrals, tests, psychological treatment, and de-skilling (replacing trained professionals with untrained technicians) of health care staff. As a result, we cannot be sure if we'll receive health and mental health care or of the quality of the care that we do get.

Media image.   All the while the media reinforce and perpetuate unrealistic expectations about what "should be" through TV, movies, and advertising. Perfection is the goal: Speaking flawlessly like a Peter Jennings or Tom Brokaw; looking thin and beautiful like a Cindy Crawford; being rich, famous, and seemingly without problems like an Oprah Winfrey, Leonardo DiCaprio, or CNN's Ted Turner. Life becomes a fantasy of endless possibilities where we're taught to desire more, imagine more, and expect more. By feeding on our inadequacies, embarrassment, alienation, and withdrawal, the media promote consumerism, materialism, and instant gratification as the solution to the void in our lives. But in holding out false hope that the right deodorant, Docker's trousers, whitened teeth, or a 36D cup will make us feel better about ourselves, they make us feel cheated and doom us to disappointment and even greater feelings of self-doubt, cynicism, confusion, and dread.

What this summary suggests is that all these social forces serve to increase everyone's fears and insecurities. They focus our attention on ourselves. They decrease the amount of face-to-face social interaction we experience. They decrease our learning both social skills and communication skills or practicing the skills we have.   At the same time they increase our lack of human connectedness, our isolation, and our loneliness. Our inability to fully cope with this overload increases our predisposition to anxiety and helps set the stage for SA/SP. As Henry David Thoreau writes, "The mass of men [sic] lead lives of quiet desperation." Is it any wonder that the number of individuals with social anxiety is increasing?

Species: *Stressus resultus*
Numbers increasing

CHAPTER 2

DISSECTING SA/SP - WHAT IT IS & ISN'T

"Why worry about the future? The present is more than most of us can handle."

What are its social characteristics?

When SA/SP actually begins is unclear, but 47% of us with it report a lifelong disorder or its onset prior to the age of 10 (although mine didn't really reveal itself until I was in my 20s). However, what is clear is that since SA/SP involves public self-consciousness and concerns about negative evaluation by others, it can't begin until we have a developmental awareness of others and ourselves as objects to be evaluated. This occurs around 8 years old. A majority of us are capable of showing embarrassment by the age of 3, but this is more likely to represent a fearful shyness rather than a public self-consciousness. We need to remember that findings in this area may conflict since earlier works used the **DSM-III** for definition of SA/SP and later studies have used **DSM-III-R** or **DSM-IV**'s most restrictive definition. Also much early research was on shyness, not SA/SP.

Diagnosis of SA/SP in children has slightly different characteristics than it does in adults. Because the condition is dependent upon our understanding the impact of social relationships, the child must be at a stage where it's able to have age-appropriate social relationships with familiar others. This anxiety must occur in peer settings and not just with adults. Moreover, children, unlike adults, don't necessarily recognize that their social fear is excessive or unreasonable.

While onset is most common in adolescence and young adulthood, SA/SPers who present for treatment tend to do so 15-25 years after the onset of the disorder. Our mean age at presentation is 30 years. Our concern over social threat, however, is relatively stable over our life span. This suggests that if untreated, our social fears will likely have a fairly chronic course.

In most anxiety disorders there's a marked predominance of females; however, in SA/SP there seems to be an equal distribution across the sexes presenting at clinics. While females are more likely to report social anxiety, males are more likely to seek treatment for it. This discrepancy may be attributable to the effect of social influences relating to sex roles.

Sex roles. Western society generally expects males to be socialized to be aggressive. Specifically, their sex-role holds expectations that they be more assertive than females, have higher career aspirations and achievement, and initiate both romantic and non-romantic contact. But males who exhibit social anxiety or shyness won't meet that expectation. As a result, they may receive negative feedback from parents and peers that their behavior is inappropriate.

While sex-role stereotypes allow females to be withdrawn and non-assertive, they punish males for it. Parents are more likely to admonish their sons than their daughters for shy and inhibited behavior. Because of a fear of appearing passive and "feminine," boys may restrict their interests and their ability to engage in a wider range of human activities. Social anxiety/shyness then may be a major social impediment for males' social development. It may lead to less effective interaction and relationship satisfaction and more interference with life than for females, thus motivating them to seek help.

The female's sex-role, on the other hand, expects and rewards reticence, withdrawal, and non-assertiveness. The "up-side" of this (if you can call it that) is that females can hide their disorder behind these perceptions and expectations. The down-side, however, is that these same perceptions and expectations make it difficult for females who seek help to be seen as needing help. Depending upon the health care professional's sex-role stereotypes, she may be seen as perfectly "normal."

Relationships & career. By its very nature SA/SP interferes with all interpersonal relationships, but particularly romantic relationships. In general, SA/SPers are less likely to marry. A 30-year study looking at life-course patterns of shy children found that shy males were likely to marry and have their first child three years later than non-shy males. They tended to enter steady careers three years later as well. This not only increased their chances of career change but also decreased their chances to achieve. Overall, they achieved less. This, however, was not found to be the case for females. Shy females were less likely to work outside the home. This means that if they entered the work force in the first place, they were less likely to re-enter after childbirth. Overall, according to a study on **DSM-III-R** psychiatric disorders, 69% of male and female SA/SPers believed their anxiety interfered significantly with their social relationships, 92% felt it significantly interfered with their occupational functioning, and 85% with their academic functioning as well.

For both males and females shyness is negatively correlated with a number of behaviors considered to be important career-wise. Shy people will be less likely to seek out information, network, look for mentors, work in teams, and make the decisions so instrumental to career advancement. Many SA/SPers find it difficult to pick and stay with a career path. In school we're guided by the amount of interpersonal interaction required of us. As a result, we may change majors multiple times, not because our interests have changed, but because our fear of evaluation is greater than our desire to pursue a particular field.

The same holds true for work. We tend to have poor work records, with 12%-reduced work productivity, because we're frequently overwhelmed by the self-presentation requirements of our jobs. When the pressure is too much to handle, we move on. Some 11% of us are unemployed, as compared with 3% of non-SA/SPers, and 23% of us report substantially impaired working performance which is due to our SA/SP. So as shyness, or SA/SP, increases, these career behaviors decrease.

As pointed out in Chapter 1, those of us who react to a single, discrete fear situation, like test-taking, performing, or public speaking (some 6% of SA/SPers), respond differently from those of us who react to many fear situations. In one study individuals who were fearful about public speaking showed greater cardiac response to that stimulus than did those who were fearful about social interaction in general. It appears that we discrete-situation SA/SPers may be showing a specific fear response (as in a specific phobia, like fear of heights) whereas we who respond to many social situations may be showing a more general, variable, and inconsistent anxiety response.

One study by Stefan Hofmann demonstrated that while both SA/SP subtypes tend to pause frequently during public speaking, those with generalized SA/SP spend more time doing it, up to 25% of their time. Generalized SA/SPers also report higher levels of anxiety. Interestingly, there appears to be no difference between SA/SP subtypes in gazing behavior in a public-speaking situation.

However, it may be that there are really three subtypes of SA/SP: Two clinical and one sub-clinical. Hofmann has found that in the area of public speaking anxiety there are not only generalized and discrete SA/SPers but also generalized non-diagnostic "SA/SPers." This subtype shows an elevated level of symptoms but doesn't meet the DSM-III-R diagnostic criteria These individuals experience social anxiety as severe as that of generalized SA/SPers but don't consider ourselves to be socially phobic because we don't avoid fearful situations and don't let it interfere with our activities. We gird our loins and push on through. (While I exposed myself to fearful situations, I definitely knew I wanted to avoid them. I did it because the long-range gains seemed to outweigh the immediate costs.)

How are shyness, high sensitivity & introversion related?

There seems to be a lot of confusion about shyness, high sensitivity, introversion, and SA/SP. Are they the same? They appear to be. Prior to the **DSM-III-R,** studies tended to use the terms "shyness" and social anxiety" interchangeably because they seem to spring from a fear of negative evaluation when engaged in social interaction. But they really are different.

Shyness. Shyness is a normal personality trait, not a mental disorder, which shares with SA/SP a fear of humiliation, embarrassment, and negative evaluation by others. Other shyness behaviors include inhibited behavior, wariness of unfamiliar people, timidity in situations that contain risk or harm, and cautiousness in situations which contain risk of failure. But this isn't considered to be dysfunctional for the individual whereas SA/SP is.

One important difference between shyness and SA/SP seems to be how information is processed in social situations. While both shy and socially anxious people experience anticipatory anxiety, shy people tend to check out others in the situation for cues on how to interpret the situation and respond. If others' behaviors don't support having negative thoughts and feelings, shy people may simply stop those thoughts and feelings. SA/SPers, on the other hand, look specifically for cues to support their negative thoughts and feelings. Because of this we're unlikely to end the process even if confronted with contradictory information. However, in general, both shy and socially anxious people appear to have knowledge of appropriate social behavior but don't believe we have the ability to use it or we are less willing to do so.

Another important difference, as pointed out by clinical and behavioral psychologist Samuel Turner, is that SA/SPers more extreme deficits in daily functioning than do shy individuals. The course of our disorder is more severe. Avoidant behaviors are more extreme. And, furthermore, our physiological reactions to social situations are stronger. Where a shy child might hang back from participating in class, a SA/SPer might look for the nearest exit, use it, or desperately want to.

Still it's hard to discern where shyness ends and SA/SP begins because there are no clearly defined clinical criteria for "shyness." In most cases the trait is self-defined. As Philip Zimbardo says, "if we think we're shy, we are shy." Far-reaching in its prevalence, shyness affects some 84 million people, generally some 15-20% of the population at any given time. This is almost twice as many as are affected by SA/SP.

Developmental psychologist Jerome Kagan's work on the "shy personality" suggests that shyness is the result of fear arousal and *behavioral inhibition*. Children are said to exhibit behavioral inhibition when they respond to novel stimuli or events with excessive sympathetic nervous system arousal and behavioral withdrawal. Kagan's work suggests this sympathetic arousal may be inherited. Specifically, he found that children who are generally fearful or inhibited will tend to have higher heart rates, higher levels of urinary epinephrine and salivary cortisol, and more spontaneous fluctuations in their resting galvanic skin response (GSR) (all indicators of stress). This syndrome may begin as early as four months and persist until age 7 ½ years. It's estimated that 10-15% of Caucasian 2-3-year-olds show behavioral inhibition (data are lacking on other racial groups). While shyness may be a general temperamental factor, there's been nothing to suggest that social anxiety is as well.

There are two sub-categories of shyness. One is *fearfulness*. This first appears after 3 years of age as a response to novel stimuli, such as strangers, new toys, new locations, and the intrusion of others. When we're very fearful and inhibited in unfamiliar situations at the age of 2, we'll tend to be quiet and socially avoidant at the age of 7. Our inhibition may be demonstrated by avoidance, cessation of ongoing activity, retreat, isolation, clinging to our caregiver, and vocalization.

While children with behavioral inhibition have seemed to have higher rates of phobic disorders, overanxious disorder (now called "generalized anxiety disorder"), multiple anxiety disorders, as well as disorders of a social-evaluative nature, 1998 follow-up studies found no support for the hypothesis. History of behavioral inhibition doesn't appear to be associated with anxiety symptoms in general or social anxiety symptoms in particular. This means that while behavioral inhibition exists as part of shyness, how it relates to anxiety, if at all, is still unknown.

The other sub-category of shyness is *self-consciousness* which appears later in development, 4-17 years of age, and is a response to a situation in which we are the focus of scrutiny.   Self-consciousness, either public or private, is characterized by the thoughts we have.   *Publicly shy* people report being uncomfortable when our behaviors are observed. We feel dis-ease when we're being awkward, failing to respond appropriately, or being too quiet for the situation. *Privately shy* people, on the other hand, are bothered by our own experience of anxiety *per se* and focus on our body's cues.

Family environment is important in shyness.   Where there's high family cohesion, high emotional expressiveness, lower conflict, and emphasis on intellectual, recreational orientation, and social and cultural development, there's a decrease in shyness in children aged 1-2 years.   Maternal responsiveness also is correlated with decreased shyness in girls, but maternal characteristics of nervousness, dysphoria (feeling of unpleasantness, discomfort), irritability, and shyness-related inhibition are correlated with increased shyness in girls (there are no data on boys).

Children who are temperamentally fearful and inhibited AND have parents who are unsupportive, perceived to be unavailable, and unresponsive will tend to feel insecure and become shy.   Our level of shyness has been found to increase with decreased maternal acceptance and increased maternal control. Mothers of shy children are more likely to believe that social skills should be taught by direction or coercion, rather than by personal experience.   They tend to feel angry, disappointed, guilty, or embarrassed by their child's unskilled behaviors. Witness how some parents of Little Leaguers act when their child isn't Mark McGwire at the plate or Roger Clemens on the mound. In addition, both parents tend to be more rejecting, overprotective, less emotionally warm, and more concerned about others' opinions regarding appropriate behavior. Similarly, we SA/Spers rate our parents as more rejecting, overprotective, and less emotionally warm.

Peers likewise frequently react to shy children's withdrawal and reticence as a form of deviance from age-appropriate social behavior. They too, males and females alike, tend to respond with rejection. They may tease, pick on, ridicule, victimize, or neglect. Even teachers perceive shy children negatively, becoming frustrated and annoyed at our reluctant behavior. As a result, they tend to rate shy children as less friendly and sociable.

Selective mutism.   One result of experiencing social distress in childhood is selective mutism (formerly called "elective mutism") wherein there's a persistent refusal to speak in selected social situations despite being able to communicate fluently in spoken language. According to the **DSM-IV**, these children may show excessive shyness, fear of social embarrassment, social withdrawal and isolation, and negativism. Because of these symptoms some believe selective mutism is a variant of SA/SP, rather than a separate diagnosis.

But until controlled trials demonstrate this, making a differential diagnosis will be difficult.

High sensitivity. High sensitivity or hyperarousability is also seen as a normal personality characteristic. This is where we're easily stimulated, overly aroused or stressed by stimuli. It's estimated that 20% of the population share this trait. To the highly sensitive person (HSP) lights seem brighter, sounds louder, fabrics coarser, smells stronger, and pain greater. Temperature-, humidity-, and barometric changes may be very noticeable. We startle easily. We tend to pick up on nonverbal and verbal nuances others miss. We may feel the highs, lows, and subtleties of life more deeply. Music, art, and poignancy touch us. For this reason we may avoid violent content in movies, television programs, books, and newspaper accounts as well as other highly-arousing situations. Where there is too much stimulation, overload occurs, which may make us (especially me) appear irritable, touchy, and picky. This overload increases our arousal and interferes with thinking, recognition, and recall, and may create conflict with others.

Elaine Aron, developer of the concept of the *highly sensitive person*, believes everyone has a range of stimulation with which they feel comfortable. Too little and we feel bored; too much and we feel on edge. However, the degree to which we're aroused in a particular situation by a particular stimulus differs from individual to individual. Highly sensitive children may appear frightened, apprehensive, irritable, with digestive problems, or as loners. But we may also appear as aware, imaginative, and creative. As adults we may tend to overwhelm ourselves by working too hard, too long, with too much interpersonal interaction, or under adverse conditions, unaware of our sensitivity thresholds.

When highly sensitive persons encounter too much arousal, regardless of the situation or stimulation, we tend to become confused and distressed. We feel less in control. (I've found noise particularly bothersome and capable of nearly driving me to distraction.) Increased awareness and reflection only serve to magnify the experience. Without boundaries or safety- or comfort zones, HSPs may become overwhelmed, avoidant, and enervated.

As a result, HSPs tend to avoid situations which are over-stimulating. We may also respond negatively to and seek to avoid situations where we may be observed, judged, or criticized because of the outward appearance or effect of our hyperarousability. The mere existence of hyperarousal in HSPs makes us look to observers as if we're fearing or avoiding specific situations, whether we are or not.

Introversion. Developed in 1923 by Swiss psychiatrist Carl Gustav Jung, a disciple of Freud, introversion is a psychological temperament used to describe our personality. It represents one pole of the Introversion-Extroversion continuum. Sometimes referred to as "subjectivity," introversion today may be thought of as a social-attitude dimension. In general, personality is conceived of as a hypothetical structure or organization of behavior, which can be identified by patterns and preferences on a test.

Those of us who tend to live in a highly personal, contemplative, subjective world of experience may be thought of as closer to the introversion end of the continuum.   Psychotherapist Carl Rogers felt that this world has a more significant influence on our behavior than does more objective experience because observable behavior is unintelligible without reference to it.

Those labeled as "introverted" orient ourselves toward our inner, more introspective world.   We're more wrapped up in the intrinsic aspect of things, ideas, thoughts, impressions, reflections, emotions, and our imagination.   This inner world is the generator from which we draw our power, energy, and motivation.   Because we prefer and value this inner-orientation, we rely less on socializing for stimulation, meeting our needs, and satisfaction.   (While I spend my days doing "extroverted" things, my activities' preference is inner-directed.) This doesn't mean, however, that we don't enjoy meeting and being with others. On the contrary, we do, but we enjoy them in smaller doses, and in deeper, longer-lived relationships.   Crowds and short-lived, superficial connections not only don't interest us but also tend to drain our batteries.

It's important to remember that we're talking about places along a continuum.   This means degrees of introversion.   At either pole we'll find extremes.   We must bear in mind also that the environment in which we find ourselves at any given moment has a large effect upon our social attitudes and behavior.   When those with introversion are with intimates, for example, we're more likely to come across as very social, although, in general, getting to know us isn't easy.

Some suggest that "reserved" is a more appropriate and descriptive term than "introverted," which is burdened with negative connotations.   We reserved people don't reveal ourselves quickly or easily to others. We tend to keep to ourselves.   We're more quiet, more a listener than talker. This, however, is a positive quality since conversations and social relationships wouldn't exist long without us.

Because of our reserve we tend to bottle-up unexpressed feelings.   As a result, outwardly we seem focused, serious, and cautious, guarding the inner space we hold so dear.   If given the option of relaxing with our computer or partying with a group, we'd likely choose isolation and our solitude.   According to Aron, approximately 70% of HSPs tend to be "reserved."

Where the similarity ends. One study found a more frequent history of childhood shyness in those of us with generalized social anxiety (although this wasn't the case with me).   Along with this were significantly higher introversion scores and higher frequency of traumatic conditioning episodes than for discrete social anxiety.   (However, I did experience many traumatic episodes since I moved frequently and was always the "new kid" outsider.)   This introversion tendency may make it more likely for us to be shy and vulnerable to negative experience.   Those with discrete social anxiety, on the other hand, showed greater anxiety.   What does it all mean?

Shyness, high sensitivity, and introversion seem very similar yet there are no data at present to link these factors.   They all have a lot in common with

SA/SP, but not all individuals who have these personality characteristics develop SA/SP. Conversely, not all SA/SPers have these characteristics. This has led some, such as Samuel Turner and his associates, to hypothesize that shyness is a predispositional factor for SA/SP but that other factors, such as traumatic conditioning experiences in childhood, trigger development of the disorder. Hypersensitivity and an introverted temperament may likewise act as independent predisposing factors to SA/SP. This means that if we add the right environmental elements over time to this susceptibility, we may be able to produce SA/SP. However, this is still conjecture and has yet to be demonstrated empirically.

Assessing the place of embarrassment & shame

Embarrassment is the emotion closely associated with blushing which, in turn, often occurs in SA/SP. It's an uncomfortable aroused state of awkwardness, mortification, and chagrin. It results from knowledge that others could notice, whether or not they actually do, our doing something we'd prefer them not to (like trembling, stumbling, stammering, sweating, blushing, misspeaking, or forgetting). Our doing something in public that we perceive as awkward or stupid upsets our expectations of what's appropriate. We fear communicating unwanted impressions of ourselves to others. Because of this, our embarrassment motivates us to repair, if possible, or escape, if necessary, the awkward situation.

One of my most embarrassing moments occurred when I was 28, living in San Diego, attending bi-weekly singles' dances. Over the course of 7 months I developed a pure-and-chaste-from-afar crush on a popular man whose look and lithe dance movements seduced every woman on the dance floor. I loved the feeling of dancing with him.

Suddenly one evening he asked me for coffee at, as it turned out, his apartment, a place I'd resigned myself to never seeing. After etiquette-required preliminaries, we started to make out on his day bed. I was so thrilled that he finally liked me as much as I liked him. Then the phone rang. Grinning slyly, he began to tell the caller what he was doing. While looking at me in my disheveled state, he graphically detailed all his moves and my physical and emotional responses to them. He laughed and handed the phone to me. His male friend on the line was laughing too. I was the object by which they were mutually mentally masturbating. My expressions of anger were barely a squeak above my humiliation. I never went to the dances again.

Grounded in the existence of our public self-consciousness, embarrassment is the ability to think and be concerned about what others are thinking about us. This ability to look at ourselves through the eyes of others is thought to begin around the age of 3 years, when we gain the capacity to understand the abstract idea of "self." This means that embarrassment does not exist at birth, but develops along with our cognitive abilities and socialization. Once we develop the concept of self, we can begin to suffer the consequences of trying to see ourselves as others might.

Of course, our social image may be accurate or inaccurate. But what we operate on is our belief about it, not reality. Some suggest that embarrassment may be considered a signpost of what it is to be human because it motivates us to try to correct awkward social situations. Interestingly, individuals who don't show this emotion where others expect them to are perceived to be less human or less "normal." Specifically, they're thought to be insensitive, thoughtless, and uncaring.

Frequently when we experience embarrassment, we blush. As Mark Twain is oft quoted as saying, "Man [sic] is the only animal that blushes or needs to." Blushing is one of the most characteristic features of embarrassment and the principal physical symptom of SA/SP. It distinguishes it from other anxiety disorders. It differs physiologically from our body's reaction to fear. Typically fear signals the sympathetic nervous system to constrict blood vessels. Typically dilation of blood vessels, as seen in embarrassment, is thought of as a parasympathetic nervous system response. However, strangely, facial blushing appears to be an atypical sympathetic response instead.

Not everyone blushes (though I did: Loudly, long, and often). When we're embarrassed, we may engage in a number of discomfiture behaviors, such as agitation and increased body movement, averted gaze, sheepish grin, face touching, as well as blushing. Exhibiting embarrassed behaviors has an important social function. It shows others that we're aware that we've breached some social rule. Our embarrassed behaviors influence how others respond to us in those predicaments. People tend to be drawn to embarrassed persons. But depending upon the situation, embarrassment can elicit compassionate support or hostile rejection.

While embarrassment and social anxiety share a common awareness of and concern for what others will think of us, they're also different. Social anxiety is composed of fear, dread, and apprehension. It's anticipatory and depends on concern about what we think about the situation. It begins with public self-awareness and ends with distress.

Embarrassment has no anxiety component. It's composed of startled surprise and abashment. It's reactive, occurring only after the event has taken place. It has nothing to do with what we think about the situation. It begins with our public self-awareness which leads to our distress which ends in our feeling dumb.

Occasionally the terms "embarrassment" and "shame" are used interchangeably. Both embarrassment and shame result from events which communicate unwanted images of ourselves to others. Both are found in SA/SP. However, they are two distinctly different emotions.   As we just said, embarrassment results from minor breaches of convention, manners, or poise. It's associated with the unforeseeable, mistakes, goofs, and accidents. These events aren't serious and have no moral implications. When we're embarrassed, we feel foolish. Others attribute our embarrassment-behavior to the situation and see it as only a limited and temporary *faux pas* on our part, as when we drop food in our lap in a restaurant.

Shame, on the other hand, is a breach of important and fundamental standards of conduct or rules. It's associated with the foreseeable, serious, awful, or unforgivable actions and dereliction of duty. As such, shame has strong moral implications. When we're ashamed, we feel regretful, guilty, and depressed. We're afraid of exposure because public revelation of these behaviors leads to extremely unfavorable assessment of us, as when we're caught going through a friend's private financial records. Others attribute shame-behavior to a defect in our personality, morals, or character. Further, they expect it to be ongoing and likely to recur in all types of situations. Unlike embarrassment which can occur in the absence of others, shame occurs only when others actually become aware of our behavior.

Differentiating overlapping disorders

There are a number of disorders which are similar to SA/SP and may even occur with it (co-morbid). In fact, 70-80% of cases of SA/SP are complicated by co-morbid conditions. Co-morbidity increases symptom severity, disability, and suicidality. These disorders include panic disorder, agoraphobia, specific phobias, school refusal, generalized anxiety disorder, depression, avoidant personality disorder, schizophrenic spectrum disorders, and alcoholism. It's important for us to be able to differentiate them from SA/SP both for understanding and appropriate treatment. Unfortunately, there's a low recognition rate for SA/SP in primary care due to the presence of co-morbid conditions. In these cases, the co-morbid condition is the one likely to be recognized and treated. Still, only 50% of us with a co-morbid condition go to outpatient services, with only 38% to psychiatric services. Overall, only 20% of all SA/SPers have used mental health services of any kind.

Panic disorder has as its core element **panic attacks**. Panic attacks are sudden episodes of acute apprehension or intense fear which occur without any apparent cause. Intense panic usually lasts only a few minutes. During the attack, we're likely to experience any of the following symptoms:

- *Heart pounding or palpitations*
- *Shortness of breath*
- *Faintness or dizziness*
- *Sweating*
- *Shaking or trembling*
- *Sensation of choking*
- *Feelings of unreality*
- *Nausea*
- *Tingling in hands and feet*
- *Chest pain or discomfort*
- *Fear of losing control or going crazy or dying*

• Hot and cold flashes.

Individuals with panic attacks don't have these attacks because they fear places or social situations. Their attacks are spontaneous and unexpected, with no phobic component. Panic attacks become **panic disorder** when we have at least three such attacks in a month's time and at least one of these attacks has been followed by a month's worth of concern or worry about having another attack and its implications. We SA/SPers may have panic attacks as part of our disorder. Our attack results from apprehension about a feared social situation or performance. (I regularly experienced them before and during social gatherings, meetings, and presentations.) Paraphrasing psychologist Isaac Marks, while those with panic disorder fear the crowd, SA/SPers fear the people who make up the crowd. It's important to note that panic disorder is different from **agoraphobia** in which individuals fear having a panic attack in public, being embarrassed by it, and not being able to escape or find help.

Agoraphobia, which affects one in 20 in the general population, appears to stem from panic disorder and may have a balance-impairment component. It's common for agoraphobics to avoid various types of situations. These include public transport (subways, planes, buses, trains), confined or enclosed areas (highways, bridges, tunnels), crowded public places (stores, restaurants, theaters, churches), and being alone (anywhere one can't reach a "safe person").

The central issue which differentiates SA/SP from agoraphobia is the reason for fearing the social situation or performance. In SA/SP it's the social situation where we may be evaluated which directly elicits our fear of embarrassment. In agoraphobia social situations do not elicit fear of having an attack. Instead it's being in an unfamiliar, strange, or challenging place or just being away from one's security.

Specific phobias, as noted earlier, are intense, out-of-proportion fear and avoidance of a specific object or situation, which results in marked distress or impairment. Like SA/SP they may involve panic attacks which are either situationally bound or situationally predisposed. Even though 33% of those with speech phobia attribute their phobia to panic attacks, it's not known whether panic attacks are the cause or the consequence of phobias.

While this fear may occur in social situations, it's not a fear of scrutiny, embarrassment, or humiliation (which involves arousal, thoughts, feelings, and behaviors). The primary emotional component of phobias is fear alone (which involves arousal and behavior). Phobias are oriented in the present. Generally, individuals see the object/situation or make an association with it, feel afraid, and try to avoid it. "Specific phobia" is the label applied to avoidance of some situation not covered by another diagnostic label.

This differs from SA/SP, which occurs only in socially-related situations and is a fear of scrutiny, embarrassment, and humiliation. While the primary emotional component in SA/SP is fear also, there are other significant emotions present, such as anger and excitement. SA/SP is primarily anticipatory, and, therefore, oriented in the future. We worry about what might happen.

Therapy for phobias is primarily behavioral which tries to break the connection between the stimulus, feared object, and the fear response through imaginal or in vivo (real) exposure over time and desensitization.   SA/SP therapy uses behavioral techniques, but also relies on cognitive reshaping of our thoughts and beliefs, improving coping and social skills, enhancing self-confidence and assertiveness, nutrition and exercise, and use of psychopharmaceuticals.

School refusal (previously referred to as "school phobia") is a behavioral symptom of anxiety and other disorders. It may be related to avoidance of a negative situation, attention-getting, separation anxiety, or some reward reinforcement. It may also be related to the flight from feared social situations or evaluation found in SA/SP. In one study of children referred to an anxiety clinic, 15% demonstrated school refusal with overtones of SA/SP, while 9% showed social anxiety symptoms unrelated to school (in the general population, 5-10% of children have mild social anxiety while 1% have severe). Symptoms for school refusal include the following:

• *Refusal*

• *Tantrums*

• *Complaint of stomachache, headache, or nausea*

• *Chronic school absence*

• *Panic attacks*

• *Crying*

• *Shyness*

• *Petulance*

• *Opposition*

• *Cringing*

• *Unhappiness.*

Generalized anxiety disorder (GAD) is a driven, unending process, characterized by a chronic state of anxiety or worry which lasts for at least six months. It has no accompanying panic attacks or phobias. Focusing on two or more life stresses, such as health, job performance, or finances, GAD results in our entertaining a stream of thoughts and images about possible or traumatic events in the future and how we might deal with them. Individuals spend all their time considering feared what-if possibilities so that no solutions are reached in terms of actually dealing with the future. For a GAD diagnosis there needs to at least three of the following six symptoms:

• *Feeling keyed up*

• *Difficulty concentrating*

• *Difficulty sleeping*

• *Muscle tension*

• *Irritability*

• *Feeling easily fatigued.*

GAD can be aggravated by any stressful situation. This includes ones which elicit fears, such as fear of not being in control and fear of rejection. Both of these fears are seen in SA/SP. There are few differences found between GAD and SA/SP so it's easy to misdiagnose SA/SP as GAD. Insomnia, headaches, and fear of dying appear to be more common with GAD than SA/SP, whereas frequent sweating, flushing, and shortness of breath are more frequent with SA/SP. However, the primary difference appears to be that GAD has none of the significant fear of embarrassment or humiliation that SA/SP does.

Depression is the leading psychiatric disorder in the U.S., followed by alcoholism, and SA/SP. A large proportion of SA/SPers meet the criteria for depression or dysthymic (mood) disorder, with 40-50% of us presenting at primary care with major depression. In 75% of patients development of SA/SP precedes this major depression by over a year. It's characterized by a persistent

• *Sadness*

• *Loss of interest in all or almost all activities and pastimes*

• *Decrease in energy*

• *Feelings of worthlessness or guilt*

• *Self-denigrating ideas*

• *Difficulty in concentrating or thinking*

• *Indecisiveness*

• *Social withdrawal and avoidance*

• *Helplessness*

• *Hopelessness*

• *Suicidal ideation.*

Common to depression and SA/SP is a sense of helplessness, focus on self-denigrating ideas, fatigue, and insomnia. In addition, both depression and SA/SP exhibit social withdrawal and avoidance; but the motivation for that behavior is different in each disorder. In depression those behaviors result from lack of interest and energy. In SA/SP they result from fear of being scrutinized or judged by others. (However, there is an atypical subtype of depression which is characterized by hypersensitivity to rejection or criticism, which bears a similarity to SA/SP.) Individuals with both disorders tend to attribute causes for negative events which occur to them to internal factors, like lack of social ability (or my not believing I was lovable). They see these factors as stable, characterological, and present across situations.

There are two elements that best discriminate depression from SA/SP. One is the presence of a sense of hopelessness. Depressed individuals operate in a continuous state of pessimism. For SA/SPers our hopelessness and negativity depend upon the specific situation. The other is the degree of activation present. Individuals with depression don't engage the world. They don't act upon their circumstances in order to try to change or improve things. They can't; they have no energy. We SA/SPers, however, do engage the world, despite our fears and desire to avoid situations. We do act upon our circumstances to try to change or improve things. Our anxiety is nothing but energy.

Avoidant personality disorder (APD) is a deeply ingrained, enduring, inflexible, and maladaptive pattern of fearful perceptions, thinking, and behavior about social interaction. As such, it's a severe form of social fear, characterized by an exquisite sensitivity to rejection or humiliation. Its primary characteristics include

• *Avoidance of occupational and other interpersonal activities*

• *Fear of criticism, disapproval, or rejection*

• *Preoccupation with being criticized or rejection in social situations*

• *Restraint in intimate relationships, no close friends*

• *Inhibition in participating in new interpersonal situations or taking risks*

• *Feeling of social inadequacy and inferiority*

• *Fear of embarrassment, shame, and ridicule.*

Avoidant personality disorder and SA/SP have considerable overlap. In fact, several studies demonstrate high rates, in the range of 50-89%, of APD among individuals with generalized SA/SP, those who experience symptoms in all or nearly all situations, but lower rates, 21-23 %, among those who experience SA/SP in only one or two specific situations. Individuals with both disorders have a fear of criticism and tend to be disturbed by the lack of relationships. However, there seem to be two significant differences.

It appears that those with APD tend to have little desire to confront their phobic event. As a result, they adopt avoidance as their coping mechanism and lifestyle, withdrawing from opportunities to develop close relationships where they fear they'll be criticized, humiliated, or rejected. SA/Spers, on the other hand, frequently desire to confront the avoided situation. We sometimes do so, but at great sacrifice. Individuals with APD often feel justified in avoiding social activities because of their perception of the criticality and unreliability of others. We SA/SPers are distressed that our fears and anxieties keep us away from people and potentially rewarding activities. We want to change and feel better.

APD and SA/SP may not be qualitatively but quantitatively different, perhaps representing different places along a social avoidance continuum. Specifically, APD appears to have a greater degree of severity, negative affect, impairment, and co-morbidity with other mental health conditions. Interestingly, while most personality disorders respond only to intensive psychotherapy, APD, like generalized SA/SP, responds to MAOI antidepressants and cognitive-behavioral therapy, suggesting more similarity than dissimilarity.

Schizophrenia spectrum disorders (SSD) represent a loss of a sense of reality and an inability to think and act normally. There may be mood changes, social withdrawal, and delusional or paranoid social fears. However, this fear and avoidance of social situations are thought to be the result of a lack of social interest or perhaps delusional fears of harm. There are no data to suggest they result from fear of embarrassment, humiliation, and negative evaluation.

Alcoholism overlaps SA/SP because alcohol abuse and dependence commonly accompany SA/SP and increase with the severity of the anxiety disorder. Consumption of alcohol as self-medication is particularly effective short-term in reducing our fear to social threat. It generates a sense of personal power which those of us with social anxiety frequently lack. This accounts for its widespread use and abuse. Under its influence we feel less inhibited and more willing to participate in activities we normally fear but desire, like meeting people, talking, dancing, and performing.

However, when the relaxation effect disappears, the anxiety reappears, prompting us to reach for another drink to regain that feeling of adequacy and control. Studies indicate that severely fearful and anxious people develop alcohol dependency more quickly than less fearful and anxious people.

While alcoholism in the general population has a lifetime prevalence of 8-10% in men and 3-5% in women, in the SA/SP population it's 16-36%. Patients often report that their social anxiety symptoms preceded their alcohol abuse or dependence, yet SA/SP symptoms frequently occur as a consequence of alcoholism, where cessation of drinking leads to remission of the anxiety. Individuals suffering from both alcohol dependency and severe anxiety have difficulty differentiating the symptoms of anxiety from those of alcohol withdrawal. This may be because withdrawal from alcohol increases the excitability of neurons in the brain which then stimulates severe anxiety.

Even with all the work that's been done on various theoretical aspects of SA/SP since 1980, there's still a common perception among clinicians that SA/SP is a minimal and relatively unimportant problem in the lives of its sufferers. This perception is mirrored in the relative paucity of research on the clinical aspects of SA/SP. It's mirrored in the lack of knowledge of it by primary health care providers. It's even mirrored in the scarcity of psychotherapists, clinical psychologists, licensed social workers, psychiatric clinical nurses, and psychiatrists who recognize the disorder and appropriately treat the individual who has it.

Henry David Thoreau suggested that "If a man [sic] does not keep pace with his companions, perhaps that is because he hears a different drummer." What we need is for mental health professionals and our support people to hear our drummer too.

"What do you mean you can't talk to your uncle on the phone?"

CHAPTER 3

SEARCHING FOR ORIGINS AND TRIGGERS

"Speak roughly to your little boy, and beat him when he sneezes:
He only does it to annoy, Because he knows it teases"
(Lewis Carroll, *Alice's Adventures in Wonderland,* 1865)

How does social anxiety originate?

So how do we acquire SA/SP? Is it evolution? Genetics? Physiology? Family? Upbringing? Conditioning? Stress? Trauma? Cognitions? Behaviors? Yes...and no. The one thing that seems crystal clear is that no one factor creates the disorder. The condition is generally thought to be an interplay of factors which predispose us, factors which trigger the clinical signs, and factors which maintain the symptoms long enough to make them a psychiatric disorder. What makes understanding SA/SP difficult is that each clinical manifestation appears to be an individualized permutation of the possible contributing factors. Because we're all individuals with individual difference, our SA/SP will be individual and different too.

We're going to look at some of the more significant predisposing and triggering factors. (Categorization adapted from Edmund Bourne.) Maintaining factors will be found in the next chapter.

What are its predisposing factors?

Predisposing factors are those which create our vulnerability or susceptibility to the condition. They may include biochemistry, genetics (as demonstrated by genetic tests, twin and family studies, evolution, development, childhood upbringing and experiences, and cumulative stress.

Biochemistry. From the **biochemical** perspective this condition can be seen as a physiological imbalance in our neurotransmitters. Research in neurobiology suggests that SA/SP may be related to one or more neurotransmitter-receptor systems which cause either a deficiency or excess of particular neurotransmitters in the brain. Neurotransmitters which have been implicated in SA/SP include serotonin, dopamine, norepinephrine, and gamma-aminobutyric acid. This biochemical imbalance may be acquired or inherited.

Here's a crash course in neurobiology. The central nervous system controls and coordinates our entire body, including our behaviors such as memory, thoughts, emotions, pleasure, sleep, and anxiety. The system uses electrical impulses to carry input from our senses to our brain and then relay directions from the brain back to our body. These electrical impulses are generated and transmitted by chains of nerve cells which run throughout the body for the purpose of sending or stopping particular messages. The actual mechanism which sends or ends the impulse is a group of chemicals called "neurotransmitters."

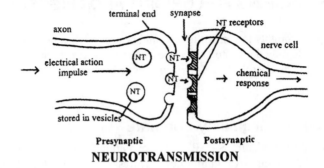

NEUROTRANSMISSION

Neurotransmitters (NT) are selectively released from the end of the nerve cell ("nerve terminal") when stimulated by an electrical impulse ("action potential"). Neurotransmitters cross the space ("synaptic cleft") between the first cell and the next in line and look for receptors on the adjacent structure to match their chemical composition. A match produces a specific physiological response. The response is a signal to release more chemical, stop releasing the chemical, or stop inhibiting the release of the chemical so the chemical can continue.

All neurotransmitters derive from amino acids and are referred to as "amines." They're considered to be either "excitatory," geared to continue sending the message forward, or "inhibitory," geared to stopping the message right there. Any deficit in neurotransmitter storage, release, synthesis, degradation, and change in receptor sensitivity could lead to incorrect transmissions, resulting in clinical disorders. Neurotransmission is a very sensitive process, being increased or decreased to meet the requirements of any situation.

While SA/SP has been hypothesized to be the result of a physiological imbalance of neurotransmitters, most studies on the effects of neurotransmitters on mood disorders have been done on depression and panic disorder. Very little has been done on SA/SP specifically. It's important to note that what may hold for anxiety disorders in general or depression may not hold for SA/SP in particular.

What do we know about neurotransmitters and how they affect our moods? How are they related to the drugs prescribed for SA/SP? Let's take a brief look.

Receptors for benzodiazepines (like Valium, Xanax, Klonopin) appear to match those of the inhibitory NT gamma-aminobutyric acid (GABA). The hypothesis is that the benzodiazepines enhance GABA in its blocking signals to the emotional center of our brain, the limbic system, to prevent triggering anxiety. Therefore, by increasing the stopping signal, we produce a calming effect. Not having enough GABA available or having too many receptors for the amount of the chemical present would then also trigger anxiety. GABA is found the basal ganglia and cerebellum.

Monoamine oxidase (MAO) is a complex enzyme system throughout our body. "Monoamine" refers to the type of amine and "oxidase" (or enzyme) breaks down, burns, or deactivates that particular amine. An increase in monoamines leads to a corresponding increase in serotonin, dopamine, and norepinephrine and a decrease in depression, for example. This suggests that to decrease depression and some forms of anxiety, we need to stop the oxidase from deactivating the monoamine. We can do this by employing a chemical which inhibits the oxidase, called a *monoamine oxidase inhibitor* (MAOI), like Nardil and Parnate. By inhibiting MAO, the cell prolongs the effective life of these amines in our brain.

Serotonin is derived from the amino acid tryptophan, is found in the raphe nucleus, and is metabolized by MAO. *Selective serotonin reuptake inhibitors* (SSRIs) are drugs like Prozac, Paxil, and Zoloft which have been found to help some SA/SPers. They work by preventing the cell's receptors from reabsorbing the serotonin, thus continuing its effect.

Dopamine derives from the amino acid tyrosine, is found in the substantia nigra, midbrain, and hypothalamus, and is metabolized by MAO. Even though MAOIs, which have an effect on dopamine, serotonin, and norepinephrine, are useful in SA/SP, the specific role, if any, of dopamine in this disorder is unclear, as of this writing.

Norepinephrine is made directly from dopamine, is found in the hypothalamus and locus ceruleus, and is metabolized by MAO. We SA/SPers tend to have higher levels of norepinephrine in our blood than do those with panic disorder or normal non-SA/SPers.

Because several classes of drugs (for example, MAOIs, SSRIs, and benzodiazepines) are known to be effective on different aspects of social anxiety, some have suggested that perhaps none of these drugs targets a common pathway in the creation of SA/SP. Perhaps there is no common pathway. There may be parallel neural pathways or the disorder may be a group of seemingly similar but neurobiologically different conditions.

Genetics. Genetic research by Klaus-Peter Lesch and colleagues in 1996 found an association between a test-quantified personality trait for "neuroticism" (including worry, pessimism, and fear of uncertainty) and a serotonin-transporter gene (5-HTT). They used this test because the "neuroticism scale" can predict anxiety and depression. Those who had the presence of a particular form of the 5-HTT gene scored higher on the neuroticism test than those who didn't. The authors of the study theorize that this gene may account for 3-4% of total variation and 7-9% of inherited variance in anxiety-related personality traits.

Unfortunately, relating a functional gene variant to the observable properties of humans isn't easy. One problem is that it's difficult, in most cases, to assess the meaning of an association. However, it is particularly so when the association is between what one chooses to check off on a paper-and-pencil test and the results of genetic analysis of white blood cells. There are 200 potential neurotransmitter metabolic, receptor, and transduction genes which may play some small part in predisposition to anxiety. In addition, what's relevant for anxiety in general, should any gene variant be a factor, may or may not be relevant for SA/SP in particular. For example, the presence of lactate, a by-product of muscle exercise, creates anxiety and panic in individuals with panic disorder. But lactate doesn't create anxiety for SA/SPers.

While there may turn out to be a genetic predisposition to SA/SP, the susceptibility will more likely result from a number of genes working together. To-date no one gene has been found to be the cause of any mental disorder though some genes appear to be implicated through linkage and association studies.

Twin studies. Twin studies have been done to attempt to provide clues to the relative contribution of genes versus environment to SA/SP. These studies compare identical twins, who share 100% of their genetic information, with fraternal twins, who share 50% of their genetic information. Generally, these twins have been reared separately. Twin studies in anxiety, in general, have suggested that members of the identical twin pairs were more likely to suffer from anxiety to a similar degree. However, adoptive studies have shown that shy children were found to have both biological and adoptive mothers who were more socially anxious and less sociable than those of non-shy children, suggesting environmental influence. And, the similarity of twin environments both before and after separation confounds some of these findings of identical-twin concordance. To-date there have been no twin studies reported using the strict **DSM-IV** definition of SA/SP..

Family studies. Family studies (which assess first-degree biological relatives - biological parents, full siblings, and children) likewise have looked to see whether SA/SP tends to aggregate within families. Some studies suggest a familial transmission of the generalized, more severe form of the disorder, but can't pinpoint genetics, social learning, or a combination of both as the cause of it. The **American Journal of Psychiatry** in 1998 reported an interview of 106 first-degree relatives of 23 SA/SP patients and 71 first-degree relatives of 24 individuals without the disorder. The study, conducted by Murray Stein at University of California, San Diego, showed that the SA/SPers had a strong history of the disorder, 26.4% as compared with those without. While the findings suggested SA/SP was a heritable trait, the researchers allowed that the patients could also have learned the behavior from their socially anxious parents. At this point there is no way to determine that each family member with SA/SP shares a particular gene variation that is specifically associated with SA/SP.

Both twin and family studies suggest the presence of a genetic component. But it's important to remember that at one level everything human can be said to have some genetic component. Genes are what write the software for everything we do and then carry those programs to every cell in our bodies to make everything work properly. Genes can be altered both internally, by DNA replication errors, and externally, by assault by environmental toxins or stress.

Not all genetic variations will be passed on from generation to generation. It will depend upon whether the genes in question are in the sex (germ) cells or body (somatic) cells. Only sex cell variations are inherited.

The "genetic" - "inherited" distinction is important. Let's use cancers as an example. Cancers result from variations occurring in the genes. Generally the cell that will become cancerous has to take a "hit" about three times. Maybe the first hit is a vulnerability or predisposition resulting from the particular form of the gene present. Maybe the second is a DNA mismatch on replication. And maybe the third is exposure to radiation, hormones, or stress. While all cancers are genetic, only about 10-15% are hereditary, where the genetic variation is actually passed on to the children.

Single-gene diseases, like cystic fibrosis or Huntington Disease, are relatively uncommon. Most conditions will result from a combination of a number of genes and environmental factors. This is particularly true with something as complex as human behavior which is also so closely tied to culture, environmental context, and what we define as "abnormal." Of the many components in the mix some will be discernible, some will not. The National Institute of Mental Health's (NIMH) 1998 report, **Genetics and Mental Disorders**, concludes, "Despite strong evidence [from twin studies] for genetic susceptibility, no specific gene has been unambiguously identified for common forms of mental disorders. ...[R]esearchers now believe that several susceptibility genes interact with each other and with environmental factors to influence the risk of developing a particular disorder."

Evolution.   Evolutionary theory suggests that early human beings developed the capacity for social anxiety to prepare for and aid their survival. As psychologist Roy Baumeister says, social anxiety is a natural consequence of our concern about our individual and collective social bonds. Specifically, individuals alone in the wild were vulnerable in defending against predators, the elements, and other environmental factors. But individuals in groups could work together against predators, elements, and environment and, thus, be more likely, both individually and collectively, to survive and reproduce.

This can be seen in Abraham Maslow's conception of the hierarchy of human needs. Maslow proposed that we humans possess an individual tendency to seek goal states that make our life rewarding and meaningful. These desires are innately arranged in an ascending order of priority or potency. Lower-order needs, such as the physiological need for food, water, air, and sleep must be satisfied before another, higher-order need can take its place. Once we have satisfied our physiological and safety needs, we strive to address our need to belong.

Belonging is nearly as necessary as the air we breathe. It shows social approval of us by others, recognizes us and confers visibility upon us. It legitimizes our existence, implies acceptance, and provides us with a sense of not being in jeopardy of rejection. It establishes social bonds. Furthermore, it specifies how we can generate power and control over the consequences of our behavior and our environment .

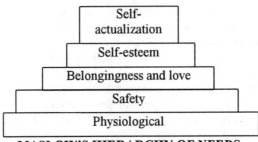

MASLOW'S HIERARCHY OF NEEDS

Perhaps this is why we humans are very social creatures. We're drawn to one another to form all kinds of relationships and bonds, from casual to intimate, in order to accomplish our individual and mutual goals. But to stay a part of a group and derive group benefits, early humans had to find ways to prevent their exclusion, rejection, and ostracism from the group.

This could have been done by appeasement, or submissive, behaviors, such as blushing and grinning sheepishly. In monkeys behaviors similar to those observed in humans have been associated with attempts to communicate their lack of threat or their subservience to dominant others. Primate reassurance behaviors, such as greeting, holding, hugging, kissing, grooming, and grinning, likewise appear to be geared to maintaining the connectedness among interdependent members. An extension of these stabilizing mechanisms may be seen in humans in the systematic use of civility: Etiquette, politeness, apologizing, paying compliments, and performing reciprocal behaviors, such as taking turns in conversations. Humans may, then, be predisposed to worry when we fail to make the desired impression since self-presentation failures are associated with possible social exclusion.

Those dominance-submission behaviors observed in animals may be an analogue to our status behaviors.. For humans the status of interactants plays a large part in how we respond to one another and how we're accepted. High status is synonymous with power, having access to and discretionary use of resources valued by others. These resources today include money, fame, physical attractiveness, knowledge, and competence. For early humans access to food, mates, and protection may have been the primary high-status resources.

When we're in the presence of or interacting with someone we consider to be powerful, specifically one who has access to the resources we want, we tend to defer to that person. We tend to take on low-status, "submissive" behaviors. However, it's important to remember that status is in the eye of the beholder. A person has power or influence only if certain conditions are met: (1) Others believe that person has it; (2) That person encourages that belief; and (3) That person resolves to make use of it and others know and believe it. In other words, high status really depends on the presence of one's supporters or true believers.

Today our perception of power, who's down and who's up, may play more of a role in our pressure to perform and make the desired impression in order to be accepted. The degree to which we perceive our relative power in the interaction determines our level of self-confidence and impacts our performance. If we perceive ourselves to be one-down or in an inferior position, we're likely to feel less confident, less competent, and more vulnerable. We're less secure about our place in the group's membership.

Our behaviors will then reflect this position. We may opt for submission over confrontation for a number of reasons. Once there's a confrontation, the results will likely tell the tale. A confrontation may well confirm our "inferior" status which will cause us pain. But until then, we may "feel" inferior, but it's not an established fact for all to see. As a result, we may see avoiding or withdrawing from the situation as preferable. By doing so, we neither experience the pain nor confirm our suspected inferiority.

While early people were, no doubt, concerned about status and competition within the group, it may be likely that they were even more concerned about cooperation and belonging. Social anxiety is a common response by humans in a social context. It's present in situations where dominance and competition occur, as in vying for mates. But it's also present in situations where dominance and competition don't occur, such as mutual caring for the young or exchanging desired resources where status differential between givers isn't an issue.

If avoidance of social rejection is a human goal, it follows that a fear of social rejection would create social anxiety. This being the case, early people would be motivated not to make undesired impressions on others. They would be motivated to stop any such presentations when they discovered them occurring. And, when necessary, they would be motivated to be submissive or repair any damaged image they'd created. Restoring, fostering, and maintaining supportive relations with others would increase their acceptance and reduce their social anxiety.

Social psychologists Mark Leary and Robin Kowalski assert that this capacity for social anxiety may be directly related to fostering inclusion and indirectly to reproductive fitness. Specifically, if we fear social anxiety, we're likely to behave so as to reinforce our social desirability, which, in turn, increases the probability of inclusion in the group. The more desirable we are, the greater our breeding opportunity is. Evolution favored early humans who acted in ways that promoted group inclusion and attracted mates. Social anxiety then may increase our capacity for social concern and promote socially adaptive behavior. This would imply that modern humans would have hardwired tendencies to reinforce and perpetuate social connections, to be aware of others' responses to our self-presentations to them, and feel anxious when we aren't successful at conveying the desired impressions. SA/SP then may be thought of as an over-expression of an evolutionary protective, primitive fear.

These biological factors suggest is that social anxiety may occur when there's a biochemical or genetic predisposition which affects how our body responds to its environment. How and to what degree the biological, genetic, and environmental elements of SA/SP are involved and interact is as yet unknown - and, indeed, may be unknowable. Like many other complex problems we encounter and have to deal with, SA/SP is very probably the consequence of an interaction with no one factor the initiating component.

It's very much a chicken-and-egg situation. For example, a psychological factor, such as trauma, can affect a biological factor, such as neurotransmission of serotonin. A stress factor, such as death in the family, can also affect serotonin levels. Serotonin levels can lead to feelings of anxiety. The stress of divorce or job loss can also lead to anxiety, which can further affect serotonin levels. Each factor can trigger or maintain the others. As a result, it's important to note that addressing or eliminating only one of these factors will not eliminate our problem.   Since SA/SP is a problem with many components, it likely requires solutions with many components.

How developmental factors affect us

How we cope with anxiety may, in part, relate to what we learned and mastered as we passed through our stages of development. Developmental psychologist Erik Erikson created a psychosocial model of development which consists of eight stages through which we all pass.

The stages are biologically-based and constitute a fixed, universal sequence. Each stage represents a conflict of old attitudes and abilities versus new that we must address and resolve before moving successfully forward to the next. This is because behaviors that served us well at previous stages no longer fit or suffice. Resolution of each conflict results in our developing a sense of competence. Without this sense of competence, we lack self-confidence, suffer from low self-esteem, and feel anxious and vulnerable.

Throughout our life cycle we acquire a series of competencies primarily through interaction with our physical and social environment. However, we never totally resolve these conflicts during each developmental phase. As a result, some of the aspects of the competencies to be mastered continue through succeeding stages, like extra baggage. Of all the conflicts to be resolved establishing a strong sense of identity is most critical, especially to SA/SPers.

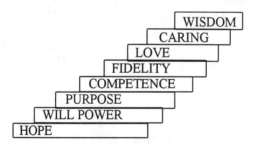

ERIKSON'S PSYCHOSOCIAL DEVELOPMENT STAGES

The degree to which our intimacy, middle-age productivity, and old-age acceptance are successfully achieved depends upon our development of a strong sense of identity in adolescence and early adulthood. With a strong sense of self we are more likely to accept adult freedom and responsibilities and our roles in family and community.

Trust vs. Mistrust. Erikson contends that one of the most basic elements of a healthy personality is a sense of trust that we develop toward ourselves and others.   Trusting is often very difficult for SA/SPers. This develops during the first year of life as we react to our environment. If our needs are met with warmth, certainty, and regularity, we feel comfort, security, and confidence that significant others (maternal person) will be forthcoming in getting what we need from the world. If not, we'll have lingering doubts about significant others' willingness to provide necessities for us. This mistrust can lead to a sense of loneliness and feeling of isolation. If Mother responds to our cries of hunger, wetness, or fear with infrequent attention and when she does respond her actions are abrupt and distancing, we're likely to mistrust her, and later, others, being there for us. Successful resolution is the capacity for *hope*.

Autonomy vs. Shame & Doubt. Between 1 and 3 years of age, we begin to act upon the world, to test our capabilities in relation to significant others (parental persons) in order to see ourselves as able individuals. Once again, our view of ourselves depends largely upon the responses of others to our actions. Our perception of independent action will tend to last throughout our lives. If, however, our attempts to spread our wings and explore are met with disfavor and criticism, as in, "You shouldn't do that," we may be left feeling unsure as to what is appropriate to try or certain that any attempts to be independent will be seen as punishable. This leaves us in a quandary: Do we persist in reaching out or do we acquiesce. SA/SPers tend to acquiesce because we're afraid not to. Successful resolution means attainment of *will power*.

Initiative vs. Guilt. Between the ages of 4 and 5 we expand our testing of our abilities to our trying to influence the outside world (the family). We do this through competition, manipulation, power-seeking, and aggressive behavior.   Now that we've discovered that we're a "somebody" we have to determine *who* that somebody is. Now that we know we're autonomous, we want to show ourselves to be responsible for actually initiating behavior. Since not all our manipulations of the world will have the desired effect, we'll feel thwarted, angry, and antagonistic. This can produce guilt because we want to act but know that such impulses have had negative repercussions in the past. SA/SPers often have strong guilt feelings because we were chastised for acting. Successful resolution leads to a sense of *purpose*.

Industry vs. Inferiority. Between ages 5 and 12, we concentrate on mastery of cultural, intellectual, and technical tools in the outside world (school). It's at this stage that we reinforce our sense of selves, our identities, and that we can *do* things. We want to learn things that we perceive meet the expectations of our social environment. For example, a very rural culture may be more likely to transmit the values of manual skills, whereas a very urban culture may be more likely to transmit the values of intellectual skills. By meeting these expectations, we hope to build on our "somebody-ness." Critical to our identity development is our awareness of our competencies. This means that we're especially aware of negative evaluations, where being seen as a "bad" student may create a feeling of inferiority. Teachers and students often label SA/SPers as "bad" or "different." This may result in our feeling bad and doing badly in school. To compensate for this some may feel compelled to be a trouble maker or the class clown. Successful resolution facilitates feeling of *competence*.

Identity vs. Identity Confusion. Between ages 13 and 19, we develop a sense of identity with respect to peer- and reference groups and leadership models. We try to discern how we're similar to and different from our parents and what our rights and responsibilities are. It's a confusing and ambiguous time, heavy with mixed messages. If we're 18, we can go to war, vote, but not write contracts. We're expected to demonstrate responsible behavior but not to be totally responsible. Adults in some ways, but not in others. Our primary questions are "Who can I be?" "What do I want to do with my life?" and "Who's my social group?" This last question is particularly important since at this time we no longer view parents as the end-all and be-all of information and approval. Instead, we look to our peer- and reference groups as the prime source of our answers and guidance. But SA/SPers are at a disadvantage because belonging to a group is difficult for us. This reduces our identity-production options.

Identity-determination possibilities abound, leaving us with a conflict. We can accept a clearly defined self (a parental ideal, for example) or we can expend a great amount of energy experimenting with a variety of roles, even negative identities, to see what really fits us. A negative identity will result from negative, unresolved issues of earlier crises, such as guilt and mistrust. But whatever the final identity that we choose, whether positive or negative, it'll incorporate our earlier acquaintance with unresolved guilt and incompetencies.

It's at this time that parents sometimes relate to us in a way that's not conducive to our developing a healthy personal identity. Parents may resent our being on the brink of new life, with a world of possibilities open to us and years in which to explore them. While parents have already been there and done that, they don't necessarily want, or will accept, it to be over. SA/SPers' acting independently is difficult because we risk negative evaluation. As a result, parents may find fault with everything we do, having nothing good to say about us and our choices. Or they may see this as a new life for themselves, not for us, and try to relive their youth through us. This doesn't mean appreciating and enjoying what we do with our lives. This means their directing our lives so they can achieve what they want, effectively not letting us be ourselves. When we don't feel separate from our parents, we tend to not act independently. As a result, we may identify ourselves through what our reference- or peer group wants or doesn't want. Successful resolution produces the ability to sustain *loyalties and fidelity*.

Intimacy vs. Isolation. Between ages 20 and 30, we take on the adult role along with its responsibilities. By now we've established a philosophy of life, explored occupations, established ourselves within a peer group, and become secure in our own identity. As a result, we're ready to begin to relate to others in a way that can develop meaningfully, whether it's friendship, sex, task cooperation, or competition. Close, stable relationships require us to share all aspects of ourselves (feelings, ideas, goals) unconditionally without fearing the loss of our identity. They also require us to be receptive to those same things from our partner.

But moving toward intimate partnerships creates risk for all of us, but particularly for SA/SPers. If we have a weak sense of self, we'll need a great deal of reassurance and praise. The strengths of our partner, when we can form relationships, may be perceived as threatening so we may be more willing to accede to the other rather than share decisions and reach compromises. Further, our partner may quickly tire of our dependence, of giving us constant support, and getting no useful input or feedback. In this situation, we find ourselves exposed and vulnerable. If we're unable to share and be shared with by others in this way, we'll feel alone, lonely, isolated, and alienated, which most SA/SPers do. Successful resolution supports *love* as a *commitment* of ourselves to others and abiding by that commitment.

Generativity vs. Stagnation. Between ages 30 and 60, we begin to contribute to the maintenance and perpetuation of society through productivity. We can do this by creating goods and services or by producing, rearing, and socializing children. We begin to make our assessment of the fulfillment of our dreams. We look at what's still available and accomplishable. We acknowledge that some things that we'd dreamt of now will never be. We make peace with the reality of these fantasies of youth. We also begin to invest our creativity and energy in projects outside the family. Specifically, we look to promote social good that will make things better for the next generation. Our goal is to "give something back."

But if we're unable to let go of those old dreams, as most SA/SPers "can't," and if we're unable to make the transition, we'll be held prisoner to them. Not allowing ourselves to close the door condemns us to spinning our wheels, wasting the present in service to the past - a past which we see as lacking satisfaction and fulfillment. This leads to a sense of stagnation where we're aware of our weaknesses and defects. We may also feel frustrated and depressed because we perceive ourselves caught between the demands of two generations (adolescent children and aged parents). Further, because of relationship obligations we see our opportunities to pursue our own interests rapidly declining. Successful resolution engenders *care* and the conviction that someone or something outside ourselves matters.

Integrity vs. Despair. Between the age of 60 and death, we look for a meaning to our lives and how our life fits globally into some larger whole. We seek to accept that the life we've lived has been worthwhile. It's a time when we want to bring everything into harmony with the end of our life. We have to find worth and purpose in our lives as we have lived them. We have to forgive ourselves and others for imperfections and mistakes. If we've successfully progressed through the previous stages, we'll face old age with acceptance, equanimity, if not enthusiasm. But if we can't accept all that has gone on before

and feel our life has been wasted, we'll "not go gently unto that good night,…" but "Rage, rage against the dying of the light" to quote Dylan Thomas. We'll spend our last years, our precious remaining time, bemoaning the lack of time to do all the things we missed because of our SA/SP. We'll mourn our inability to make up for past mistakes and fear a too-rapidly-approaching end while emotionally bobbing in a cesspool of anger, frustration, and despair. Successful resolution effects life experience *integration, maturity,* and *wisdom.*

Thus, unless SA/SPers find effective ways to build those competencies, our future could be bleak.

Looking at childhood upbringing and experiences

Overly cautious parents. Parents of children with fears are more anxious or fearful than the average parent, often being overly concerned about potential dangers. They impart this concern to us by how they respond to their environment and their frequent admonitions to us to "be careful," "watch out," "don't talk to strangers," "wear your galoshes or you'll get pneumonia." When this happens, we come to think of the world as dangerous, threatening, untrustworthy, and something to avoid. Instead of taking risks and exploring the world and the people in it, we tend to become excessively concerned with our vulnerability and personal safety. We may feel less able to rely upon others and feel anxious about their responses. Because we worry about what we can and should do, we don't want to put ourselves in harm's way and, therefore, restrict our activities accordingly.

Joe. *Whenever one of 9-year-old Joe's classmates was ill, his mother kept him home from school. His father wouldn't let him ride on the school bus because it lacked seat belts. When he started wearing glasses in the 7th grade, which he was sure resulted from his not heeding his father about lying on the floor to watch TV, both his parents cautioned him about dropping, sitting on, breaking, or losing his glasses. Joe began to worry so much about the safety of his glasses and what his friends would say about his efforts to protect them that he finally gave up the neighborhood baseball games that he loved.*

Overly critical parents. Parents who set very high standards for their children tend to be perfectionistic. For them "good enough" is not acceptable. This leaves us doing whatever we can to please and maintain the approval of our demanding parents. No matter how hard we strive to look good and "do the right thing in the right way," we never can achieve our goal because the yardstick is constantly being readjusted upward. For example, *when my father made suggestions on how to write a civics essay, I followed his directions religiously, wanting his hard-to-obtain approval. But after several hours of writing and several draft critiques, I received only further criticism for what he considered an unsatisfactory final result.*

Nevertheless, we act like puppies, overly eager, trying to please our master. This leaves us unsure of and insecure about our own acceptability and true feelings. It also stifles our capacity for assertiveness, or standing up for our own rights. Because of our being socialized in this environment, we'll learn to expect this behavior, learn to respond to it, internalize our parents' values, and incorporate this criticality into our own thinking. As a result, we too will likely have very high standards for ourselves and others and be perfectionistic and overly critical of everyone. As Johnny Carson says, "A perfectionist is one who takes great pains and gives them to other people."

Joanna. *While Joanna's father was very dominant and her mother very submissive, both were very critical of everything she did. Her father concentrated on her school work. He was never quite satisfied with her performance. Rather than praise her for what she did right, he always pushed her to do better. Her mother instead focused on how Joanna looked: What kind of statement she made to the world about herself and her family. From the barrettes in Joanna's hair to which ankle socks to wear with her patent leather shoes, her mother dictated her wardrobe. The dress-yes/blue jeans-no approach allowed for no expression of Joanna's individuality. Her acceptability was always in question.*

Both overly protective and controlling parents (research studies are generally done on mothers) tend to have lower expectations for their anxious children. They expect us to be more upset and less competent to cope in stressful situations. So they tend to attribute our undesirable behavior to our disposition and desirable behavior to factors outside us, generally and specifically. For example, if we strike out in softball, we're incompetent or uncoordinated. But if we hit a homer, we're lucky or the pitcher threw an easy one. In other words, they perceive us to have neither ability nor control in the situation. Unfortunately, we tend to fulfill their and others' expectations of us.

Assertiveness-suppressing parents. Parents who operate under the dictum that "children should be seen and not heard" tend to be overly controlling. They want us to obey and act like miniature adults (as was expected in my parents' home). As a result, they continually suppress our expression by reprimanding and punishing us for any instance of speaking out, getting angry, or acting impulsively. This suppression suggests that we don't have the right to state what we feel. To do so puts us in jeopardy. This behavior leads to our internalizing this restrictive attitude as well as bottling up our feelings. Bottled-up feelings can lead to anxiety, depression, anger, and passivity.

Barry. *When he was a child, Barry often thought he was in the Army. He was told when to get up, what to wear, what to eat, how he could use his time, and with whom he could spend his time until he left for college. When he was a teenager, he broke the cardinal rule and he spoke back to his father. "Why," he asked, "Can't I go for a Coke after school with my friend?" His father became so enraged at his insubordination that he grounded him for a week, cutting Barry off from his one connection to the outside world.*

Parental beliefs affect parental behavior which affects children's behavior. Parental beliefs also affect how children see themselves and the world.

Emotional insecurity. We can develop a sense of insecurity from the experience of neglect, rejection, physical, psychological, or sexual abuse, or abandonment. This abandonment isn't just the intentional physical cutting of ties with us as a child, as in leaving us in a basket on someone's doorstep. It's also the perceived emotional and physical cutting of ties that results from divorce or death.

I learned early that I couldn't rely upon my father to protect me. That was made abundantly clear every time we visited my paternal grandfather who ruled his world literally and figuratively with an iron fist. Part of every audience with him was a ritual greeting that all the grandchildren had to endure. With my father and his two brothers looking away in parental conflict, my grandfather lined the children up then demanded that we each shake his hand. I was first. Knowing what was about to happen, I started to cry and begged my father not to have to. He half-heartedly commanded me to comply. Wrapping his meaty paw around my 6-year-old's hand, my grandfather began to squeeze and squeeze... and squeeze. As I screamed and writhed, struggling to get away, he riveted his icy gaze at me, smiled, and squeezed just a little more for good measure.

Dependence. Children of alcoholic parents and alcoholics themselves tend to be overly concerned with control. As such, we think about things as black-and-white, all-or-nothing. We try to avoid our feelings and have difficulty trusting others, yet we bend over backwards to please others, even at our own expense. We passively allow others to assume responsibility for areas of our lives. As a result, we may subordinate our needs to those on whom we depend to avoid the possibility of having to rely upon ourselves. Feeling unable to function independently, we lack self-confidence. As children who respond to insecurity with dependency, we will tend to rely on safe harbors: Safe places and safe people.

How cumulative stress impacts us

Stressors are conditions of threat or loss which produce varying degrees of physiological arousal. They can also be anything that places a demand for change, adaptation, or readjustment on us, such as death, divorce, marriage, job loss or promotion, financial loss, sexual problems, childbirth, relocation, severe or chronic illness, pregnancy, retirement, physical aging, or menopause. Throughout our life cycle we're bombarded with numerous stress-arousing general life events and required life changes. As indicated in the Holmes and Rahe Social Adjustment Rating Scale, which ranks forty-three life events by degree of stress, the most stressful event is death of a spouse. That's followed in descending order by divorce, marital separation or end of a relationship, jail term, death of a family member, personal injury, illness, and miscarriage.

In addition, we often have to bear the burden of unresolved psychological conflicts (such as love-hate issues with our parents) which we carry with us. Each of these events, changes, or conflicts has stress associated with it. It doesn't take long before these events and their resulting stress begin to accumulate, effect a chronic state of arousal, and make their presence physically and psychologically felt. What this means is that when we recover from our arousal for a specific event, our stress level doesn't return to baseline but stops at a higher level. Each time we're stressed, the baseline changes, becoming higher. When we can no longer marshall our body's resources adaptively or there are too many stressors to which to respond, we will start to succumb to the stress overload.

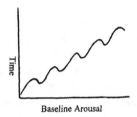

CUMULATIVE STRESS

What triggering mechanisms do

Triggering mechanisms are short-term events which set the anxiety-producing process in motion. One such mechanism is a single, acute stress condition resulting from a significant personal loss, life change, or trauma. Another is the use of stimulant drugs.

Behavioral (Conditioning). In this frame of reference, SA/SP may be thought to be the consequence of one or more traumatic experiences which result in our fearing some object or situation. This conditioning occurs when we associate something neutral, such as a microphone, with the strong anxiety we experience when giving a speech. So while initially only giving the speech elicited anxiety, now the mere presence of a microphone elicits anxiety too.

This conditioning can also occur by avoidance. When we avoid the object or situation which creates our anxiety, we reduce the anxiety. Reduction is rewarding, making avoidance is rewarding. So we learn to avoid the situation.

This may be what happens with direct trauma conditioning. It can be a single acute experience, such as being humiliated by a teacher in front of the class or chronic experiences, such as moving constantly from town to town as a child where there's continual newcomer rejection and little opportunity to practice social skills. At least two studies demonstrate the relationship between direct traumatic conditioning and the origins of SA/SP. In one study 44% of SA/SPers recalled traumatic experiences. When that number was broken down by subtype, 56% had discrete SA/SP and 40% had generalized SA/SP.

Sarah. *When Sarah was 7, her father told her he had wanted a boy instead of a girl. Since she knew that boys weren't supposed to cry, Sarah swallowed her grief and started dressing in a tee-shirt and pants like her father. When she walked, she swaggered and spoke to her dog, Ralph, in a deep-pitched voice. Since she rarely saw her father who traveled a lot, when he was around* *she tried to participate in whatever he wanted to do, which, unfortunately, included shooting at crows. This was very conflictful for Sarah who loved animals and wanted to be a veterinarian someday. Would a son object? It didn't matter because she saw this activity as the only viable connection to her father left to her and she feared severing it.*

Observing someone else's fearful behavior in the presence of some previously neutral object or situation also may cause this fear conditioning. While research on observational, or vicarious, learning has not been extended to social fears in humans, it's easy to imagine children learning how to respond to situations by watching a parent. For example, if we see our parent respond to high-status individuals by grinning, nodding, and deferring or respond to crowds by cringing, looking agitated, and withdrawing, we're likely to follow suit. Ruth Stemberger and others looked for possible developmental factors in SA/SP. They found two things: One is a relationship between social anxiety and a childhood traumatic conditioning event. The other is that conditioning **plus** shyness tended to predict the likelihood of SA/SP.

Since not all who undergo traumatic or vicarious conditioning actually acquire clinically significant levels of fear, we may need to have some prior experience with the conditioning stimulus for the conditioning to have a powerful effect. Individuals will differ widely in the degree to which our fear is maintained over time and whether it generalizes to other objects or situations over time. Such as whether fear of the public speaking microphone expands to include lecterns, auditoriums, etc. Some of this difference may come from environmental factors (other negative and stressful life events) which may prepare us to experience fear. The more prepared we are to experience the fear, the more rapidly we'll acquire it, and the more resistant it'll be to being removed, or extinguished. Moreover, the larger the number of aversive social experiences we have, the greater the likelihood is that we'll expect these social situations to continue to be negative and feel anxiety when approaching them. Conversely, the larger the number of rewarding social experiences we have, the greater the likelihood of our not experiencing anxiety approaching them. If every time we approached the feared microphone we received acclaim, the microphone would lose its negative association.

Some of the individual response difference may come from temperamental variables, such as behavioral inhibition. Behavioral inhibition is related to negative emotion, introversion, lack of impulsivity, and fear of novelty and strangers. It makes animals more socially anxious and submissive. As previously mentioned, behavioral inhibition may be a risk factor for SA/SP.

Learning theorist Albert Bandura postulates that whether people undertake particular actions, attempt to perform tasks, or strive to meet specific goals depends on whether or not they believe they will be effective, or efficacious, in performing those actions. *Self-efficacy* is a control-related belief that we have the ability to manage particular kinds of activities, mobilize motivation, control our own cognitive and emotional reactions to it, and achieve desired outcomes. It's sometimes synonymous with self-confidence. While it tends to be task- and context-specific, it may generalize to other areas of activity. As a result, it's related to goal-setting.

It's a dynamic process which changes over time as new information and task experiences are incorporated. The more efficacious we perceive ourselves to be, the greater and more persistent will be our effort toward a task. So if we believe we know what to expect at a group meeting and are prepared to interact with others on particular topics, we are more likely to attempt to do it.

It's important to note that threat is not a fixed property of social situations. Threat exists if we believe it does. It's a function of the relationship of our appraisal of possible danger and our perceived ability to deal with it. Appraisal of the likelihood of a negative event relies on our interpretation of the information we encounter.

Believing we can't cope with perceived potential threats is what makes us anxious and avoidant. Bandura has found that low levels of perceived self-efficacy are associated with increased levels of stress, anxiety, and depression. Children who are high in perceived self-efficacy, for example, may cope more effectively with negative events like death of a parent, divorce, school transitions, and academic failure. Mastery helps buffer us from the aversive psychological effects of failure in general.

People who believe they can exercise control over potential threats don't engage in anxious thinking and are not disturbed by such threats. As seen in the concept of hardiness, hardy beliefs not only buffer this stress but also prevent it. But because we SA/SPers don't perceive ourselves to be in control over future events, we experience high levels of anxiety. To control our arousal we must believe in our coping, ability to forestall or mitigate the negative events. We must believe in our controlling our dysfunctional anticipation so we can envision success scenarios that foster problem solving.

Degree of perceived controllability of stressful situations may also be a contributing factor to SA/SP. In animal studies when an intruder rat was introduced to an existing rat colony and had no way to escape from the aggression against it, the intruder developed submissive behaviors. Even when that rat was then given an escape route, it didn't learn to escape. A dominant rat when placed in the same inescapable situation in a new colony likewise became fearful and submissive. The rats appeared to learn that they had no control over their situation and no escape, irrespective of the true situation. Their perception of uncontrollability and inescapability intensified and maintained their fear.

Some have equated the rats' experience of uncontrollability with the concept of *social defeat*. Repeated defeat seems to have led to their increased reluctance to retaliate when attacked. The greater the number of social defeats, the greater their resulting submissiveness to all dominant animals and the lower their position in the rat hierarchy. Some have suggested that this learned submissiveness may be parallel to the decreased assertiveness found in SA/SPers, particularly with respect to persons in authority. It's in this situation that merely the inescapable visual presence of a dominant animal is enough to create considerable physiological stress.

Since SA/SP is predicated, in part, on fear of being observed, some have suggested that inescapable visual presence has a role in our human disorder. However, SA/SP also deals with self-consciousness, a fear of evaluation, embarrassment, and humiliation resulting from that observation. Because of this one would be hard pressed to conclude that fear of observation in defeated rats and in humans with SA/SP is the same thing or represents the same thing.

Monkey studies have demonstrated that early extensive experience controlling one's environment prepared the animals to successfully cope with novel and threatening situations. This experience acted as an immunization against the effects of the stressors. It indicated the importance of the perception of controllability and an early history of actual control over our environment. What this emphasizes is the usefulness of knowing what specifically to expect in social situations and preparing for it so we can increase our self-efficacy and reduce our anxiety.

Of course, we need to be careful generalizing from other animals' behavior to that of humans. While they may appear to be similar, we can't know whether the behaviors are demonstrating a similar biological function or even similar evolutionary origins.

"She just said her first word .....Prozac?!"

CHAPTER 4

KEEPING SOCIAL ANXIETY GOING

"Deep into that darkness peering, long I stood there wondering, fearing,
Doubting, dreaming dreams no mortal ever dared dream before."
(Edgar Allan Poe, *The Raven*, 1845)

What are maintaining mechanisms?

As we've seen, once we're primed for anxiety by vulnerability, negative life experience, and cumulative stress, we have to experience a trigger to actually start the process. But simply setting this process in motion isn't enough. Anxiety is temporary unless there are other factors available to maintain it to keep the process going. What sorts of things do SA/SPers feel helps keep the process going?

• Them: "I see you've set aside this special time to humiliate yourself in public."

• Us: "You're validating my inherent mistrust of strangers."

• Them: "Someday, you'll look back on this, laugh nervously, and change the subject."

The primary maintaining mechanisms for SA/SP include our core beliefs, self-presentation, and negative self-talk.

Core beliefs. We all develop beliefs in childhood about ourselves, others, and the way the world is, what it does, and how it *should* operate. According to psychologist Jeffrey Young, they represent categories of

• *Value (self-worth)*

• *Security (self-safety)*

• *Performance (self-competence)*

• *Control (self-power)*

• *Love (self-desirability)*

• *Autonomy (self-independence)*

• *Justice (life fairness)*

• *Belonging (being a part)*

• *Others*

• *Standards (self norms)*.

Cognitive therapist Judith Beck suggests that when these beliefs are negative, they can be classified as representing either "helplessness" or "unlovability" or both. Beliefs are personally-formed thoughts that are often culturally-determined and -shared. They're composed of *unconditional beliefs* about ourselves, *conditional beliefs* about social evaluation, and *excessively high presentations standards*.

Unconditional beliefs about ourselves are:

- *I'm stupid.*

- *I'm helpless.*

- *I'm undesirable.*

- *I'm a failure.*

Conditional beliefs about social evaluation are demonstrated by, "I'll be seen as stupid, helpless, undesirable, or a failure *if* I speak up in class." Excessively high presentation standards are embodied in thoughts such as, "I must be perfect or everything will be ruined."

These are our *core beliefs*. These beliefs are so central and fundamental to our existence, and sense of self that we regard them as absolute truths. They act as a frame of reference for all we encounter. They determine what we see as "fact" and how we interpret its meaning. When these core beliefs are activated, they become the filters through which we perceive and interpret everything. The truth or falsity of our belief is inconsequential because the belief focuses selectively on information which supports it. As long as our belief is "supported," it'll continue. Irrespective of what predisposes us to SA/SP and triggers our disorder, we develop this system of negative beliefs which leads us to view ourselves as at-risk.

Core beliefs result from a variety of sources: Parental and cultural values, group stereotypes, and conclusions drawn from specific incidents about what happens and why. We frequently don't know whether our beliefs are correct or not because, as a general rule, we don't test them. So if we see social situations as being inherently dangerous and feel we have to be perfect or we won't be acceptable to others, we're less likely to feel comfortable in social situations and less willing to take risks regarding them.

Similarly, we may believe that we are "personally responsible for everything that happens to us." This belief implies that "illness," such as SA/SP, is a personal failure. If we're responsible, we caused it, and, therefore, we can cure it. Even though a belief such as this could be harmful, we tend to take it at face value, accept it as gospel, and operate on it. As a result, these mistaken beliefs may become self-fulfilling prophecies because we look for information to support them.

As we work from our inner mind to our outer limits, we can see the expression of these core beliefs in our *attitudes*, *expectations* or *rules*, and *assumptions*. Breaking the core belief "I'm a loser," for example, into its components, we're likely to see the following:

- *Attitude - "It's perfectly awful that I'm a loser."*

- *Expectation - "I have to do everything I can to prove that I'm not a loser."*
- *Assumption - "If I do everything I can, I might be able to just get by."*

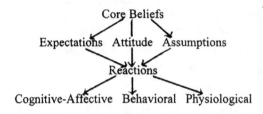

BELIEF HIERARCHY

Negative self-talk. These representations of our core beliefs make up our negative self-talk. These are the automatic, pre-conscious or just barely noticeable repeated statements we make to ourselves about:

- Perceived *inadequacies*
- What *should* be
- *What-ifs* ("What if I say something stupid?" "What if they think I'm a jerk?" "What if I can't handle it?")
- *If-then* premises ("*If* I approach a woman, *then* I'll be vulnerable to attack").

They cause us to anticipate worst-case scenarios, embroil us in self-criticism, compel us to work toward perfection and assume a feeling of helplessness. Just thinking about potential consequences of being in a threatening social situation sets our automatic anxiety in motion.

Consequently, when we're actually in the social situations, we tend to think of ourselves negatively. We overestimate the degree of threat associated with the situation and simultaneously underestimate our ability to cope with it.

But, it's important to note that this occurs *only* in social situations we fear. When we're alone or in non-threatening situations, we tend to think of ourselves more positively and feel more adequate. Thus, when Joe's car is the only vehicle on the road, he doesn't feel stupid or inadequate. When Harry can spin his tales any way he wants, he shines at parties. When Sarah is with her mother or Tanya, she's funny and outgoing.

Since social anxiety is anticipatory, dealing with possibilities and what-ifs, much of what we agonize over is imaginary. This fact makes our automatic anxiety program ineffective and inefficient. We become caught up in a spider's web of negative social thoughts and self-focused attention. This excessive attention to anxiety cues from our body, emotions, behavior, and thoughts wraps then immobilizes us in a silken cocoon of apprehension.

So when SA/SPers enter a feared situation, we approach it with a distorted view and go on negative cognitive auto-pilot. We choose negative evaluations for ambiguous situations, catastrophic interpretations for mildly negative situations, and underestimate our presentation. No longer do we focus on others or on the social environment. We think and feel we're the center of attention. To us thinking we've done something dumb is the same as our having done something dumb. Feeling out of control is the same as being out of control. External information to the contrary doesn't make it through our filter. We either discount or dismiss it so it doesn't get checked out.

What sorts of things do we say to ourselves about ourselves?

- *"I'm not so much a has-been as a definite won't be."*
- *"When I open my mouth, it's only to change feet."*
- *"I have delusions of adequacy."*
- *"I have a knack for making strangers immediately."*
- *"If you see two people talking and one looks bored, I'm the other one."*
- *"The wheel is turning but the hamster is dead."*

What sorts of things do we believe others are thinking about us?

- *"She's a prime candidate for natural selection."*
- *"He's depriving a village somewhere of an idiot."*
- *"She brings a lot of joy whenever she leaves the room."*
- *"Some drink from the fountain of knowledge, but he only gargled."*
- *"He donated his brain to science before he was finished using it."*

Then we look to physiological symptoms to support our threat perception: "My heart is racing and I'm breathing fast, I must be anxious about the situation." We monitor our thoughts: "Everyone's looking at me. What if I make a mistake?" The greater our social anxiety, the more likely we'll overestimate the degree to which our anxiety is observable or observed by others. We monitor our emotions: "I'm frightened by what others might do. I feel angry that they're evaluating me."

Meeting standards. Part of our evaluation process is our checking to see how our perceived self-presentation matches some ideal or standard. But trying to make this match creates a discrepancy, or cognitive dissonance, within us. This discomfort motivates us to do something to reduce it. To do this we can change our behavior to bring ourselves closer to the ideal. We can change the situation. We can change our attitudes. Or we can direct our attention elsewhere.

Suppose we want to go to a new movie featuring Harrison Ford but are afraid of being scrutinized by other movie patrons. We're confronted with the unpleasant arousal of dissonance and, as a result, are on the horns of a dilemma about what to do. We may decide to go but disguise ourselves and sit in the back by the exit. We may wait for the film to come out on video, go to another theater which is virtually empty, or wait for it to show up at the local drive-in. Or we may tell ourselves we really don't want to see the movie, because the reviews weren't five-star, or we don't want to spend the money, or we really have to clean the bathroom right now. In SA/SP we frequently reduce this conflict by making our thoughts and behaviors consistent with the fear-based thought and find an excuse for not going or doing what we'd like to.

Typically, following any such conflictful social event, we'll review in all its gory details what we perceived to have happened. We'll microscopically dissect and analyze it, not once but over and over again, through our negative filter. We'll compare it with past failures. This is especially easy to do since we have a better memory for negative information about ourselves than we do for positive information. When we're done, our sense of social defeat will be amplified and our embarrassment and shame deepened. Moreover, the negative effect of the event will be chiseled in granite so we can torture ourselves some more the next time we take a trip down our memory lane of "failure."

The process becomes a vicious circle of self-perception and erroneous feedback. As a result, our self-focused attention leads to self-dissatisfaction and bad feelings. In turn, this increases our social anxiety which further inhibits our self-presentation.

Safety behaviors. When in social situations, SA/SPers also attempt to reduce the risk of negative evaluation through safety behaviors. For example, when Sarah answered the phone, she adopted a monosyllabic vocabulary and one-word answers to avoid misspeaking and self-disclosure. When Joanna gave a class presentation, she spoke rapidly without pause so classmates wouldn't think the pauses meant she wasn't prepared. When Barry feared he would tremble in the presence of an attractive woman, he braced himself against the nearest stationary object. And when Joe wanted to keep from making eye contact, he'd avert his gaze and fiddle with the radio knobs.

While these behaviors feel comfortable, serve a useful purpose, and seem to be only a minor distraction strategy for preventing feared outcomes, they are, in fact, forms of avoidance. They actually reinforce our overestimation of others' negative evaluation of us and its social consequences. They reinforce our negative thinking and feared behaviors. Their use makes some anxiety-reducing techniques, like exposure, less effective. But while eliminating these safety behaviors can reduce our anxiety significantly, keeping some of these available for emergencies may not be unreasonable as we get our recovery program up on its feet and underway.

When Joanna races through her speech, she doesn't allow for audience feedback which might disconfirm her fears. She doesn't get to see how her classmates would actually respond if she paused at expected intervals. When this behavior reduces her fear, she feels rewarded for doing it and is likely to continue doing so. It's the same with Barry and Joe.

However, safety behaviors may be perceived as negatives or deficits by others. For example, those listening to Joanna will likely feel disconcerted that she doesn't pause where they expect she should according to generally-accepted standards of presentation. If so, her safety behavior may create a negative pattern of interaction and have a negative effect on the way she appears to others. If Joanna sees her audience's frowns and looks of puzzlement, it will likely confirm her worst fears about public speaking. This then will further reinforce her SA/SP and, in effect, become a self-fulfilling prophecy for her.

Self-Presentation. As Mark Leary and Robin Kowalski argue, social anxiety is essentially a reaction to real or imagined self-presentation difficulties where we believe the impressions we make may cause others to devalue, avoid, or reject relationships with us. The possibility of our relationships being regarded as not as important, close, or valuable as we desire makes us anxious. Relationship devaluation tends to occur in four situations, where we're perceived to be (1) inept or incompetent, (2) physically unattractive, (3) violating some group rules or standards, and (4) a socially unappealing interactant.

While it would be nice to be certain that we'll make the impression on others that we desire, unfortunately there's no way to do that. This is because we're dealing not only with our performance but also with someone else's perception of it. While we may have some control over the former, we have very little over the latter.

In order to influence others to perceive and evaluate us in certain ways, we try to determine what factors will produce the reaction we want. Then we have to pay careful attention and devote time, effort, and thought to creating the desired impression. We seek information in the social situation to provide us with clues. When we know what to expect and are prepared for it, our expectations of conveying the desired impression increase and our anxiety decreases. When we're uncertain or the situation is unstructured, ambiguous, or lacking clues altogether, we can expect awkward, stilted interactions and an increase in our anxiety.

Joanna. *When Joanna began as a volunteer at the local homeless shelter, she found her boss, Irene, worked from a wheelchair as a consequence of an automobile accident. From the moment of their introduction, Joanna never knew where to look when talking with Irene. If she looked at her face, she'd be staring at the scar tissue that covered Irene's right cheek. If she looked lower down, she had her eyes on Irene's right arm which was amputated at the elbow. What are the rules? Joanna asked herself. Where are the clues?*

Joanna didn't know how to handle the situation. Because of the uncertainty and ambiguity she was wracked with questions and guilt. Should I stoop or squat when I talk to Irene so she won't strain her neck looking up? Do I pick up things for her or wait for her to ask me first? Joanna wanted to escape interactions with Irene and would talk with her only when it was absolutely necessary. She kept her conversations short, touching only the essentials. Whenever possible, she would try to avoid Irene altogether when she thought she could do so without seeming to reject her.

Joanna's anxiety shot sky-high everyday she went to work. She so wanted to make a good impression but hadn't the slightest notion how to do it. There was no question in her mind that she was doing everything wrong and looking like an insensitive jerk as a result.

Novel situations or roles likewise provide us with no road maps on how to conduct ourselves. In addition to her concerns about Irene, Joanna didn't know when she began at the shelter what was expected of her. How was her role defined? Was she a person in the background? Was she supposed to get involved with the shelter's clients? If she was expected to interact, how was she to do it?

This is similar to Barry's role-questions in the singles' bar. How should I act? What's expected of me? Should I mimic others' behavior here? Without the necessary preparation both Joanna and Barry will worry about breaching norms and rules of etiquette and, consequently, will likely experience anxiety. Those of us who value manners and adherence to social norms will be particularly distressed when we don't follow, or don't think we follow, the rules.

As poet T.S. Eliot says, "Prepare a face to meet the faces you meet." According to the self-presentation model of social anxiety, we experience social anxiety when we are motivated to make a particular impression on others but doubt we'll be able to make the desired impression successfully. If either that motivation to make the desired impression OR the doubt that we will isn't present, our social anxiety won't occur. In other words, if we don't care if we make the desired impression, we won't experience social anxiety. If we're sure we'll make the desired impression, we won't experience it either. What this suggests is that any internal factor, such as our disposition, or external factor, such as the particular situation, which increases that motivation to succeed or decreases the probability of succeeding will precipitate or heighten social anxiety.

Status. The identity of the person who'll evaluate our impression is important to our motivation to manage the impression. As a result, we look for significant, defining interpersonal characteristics, such as status, for identification. We assign the label "high-status" to those whom we see as powerful, competent, attractive, knowledgeable, gifted, or socially skilled. We tend to see those individuals as having not only more value but also more value to impart to others. We see high-status peoples' evaluations as being more valid than those from others. Since individuals with these characteristics can mediate valuable social rewards for us (from jobs to friendships), we perceive more to be at stake in our interactions with them. Consequently, we tend to be more anxious in dealing with those with high status.

Gender. Gender also is a motivating factor for us. Cross-gender encounters tend to create anxiety for heterosexuals because of personal and cultural rewards. Being perceived as desirable not only raises our self-esteem and self-confidence but also makes it more likely that we'll participate in culturally-desired relationships (from dating to marriage). This participation allows us to be seen as meeting society's expectations and to be rewarded for it.

Social comparison. SA/SPers evaluate ourselves by comparing ourselves to others. We see that they're socializing, dating, holding good jobs, going to school, making presentations, and enjoying life and we're not. This social comparison process appears to be an intrinsic need for people in general.

That is, we need to evaluate our own opinions, beliefs, and behaviors for correctness. People actively seek out social evaluation whenever uncertainty exists. We look for information in others against which to judge ourselves. Finding another who disagrees with us shakes our confidence and creates uncertainty. This uncertainty creates an even stronger need for our evaluation of the correctness of our views or behavior. We need certainty in order to take adaptive action. We're seeking social agreement between what they do and what we do.

If we know what is acceptable in a given set of circumstances, we can predict the likely outcome and perhaps take appropriate action. This also applies to our comparison of standards. We may compare what we see as others' evaluations of us with our own internal standards for performance. SA/SPers tend to see others' standards as being high. The higher their standards, the greater our social anxiety.

Number of people. The number of people present in social situations is important. As the number of people present increases so does our motivation to make the desired impression. Greater numbers tend to lead to a perception that our impression will have greater impact because there are that many more to observe and evaluate it. Greater numbers lead to a decrease in our confidence that a desired impression can be made. Furthermore, they likewise lead to greater social anxiety, although the increase in anxiety is less as the number continues to increase. Ten people may be twice as anxiety-provoking as five, but forty won't be twice twenty. There is some threshold beyond which the increase is smaller per each additional person.

The number of people performing with us also affects our level of social anxiety. The greater the number of performers, the less our anxiety. This may result from a diffusion of responsibility wherein no one member is responsible for an unfavorable impression. Instead, responsibility is spread across the group. The reduction in anxiety may also be related to the audiences' attention being divided among group members.

Confidence. The degree to which we feel we can make the desired impression is a measure of our self-confidence, or self-presentation efficacy. When we evaluate ourselves negatively or engage in negative self-talk, we lower our self-confidence and raise our social anxiety. Likewise, when we raise our self-confidence, we lower our social anxiety.

The more confident we are in our appearance, the more likely we'll feel we'll make the desired impression. Conversely, the less physically attractive we think we are, the less likely we'll feel we can. Attractive people are given gold stars in our Western culture. We see them as smarter, friendlier, and more likely to succeed. Interactions with attractive people are seen as more satisfying than those with unattractive people.

SA/SP avoidance behaviors tend to be seen as unattractive. When we avert our gaze, have infrequent eye contact, and demonstrate a general lack of participation in the interaction, we may be seen as aloof and unfriendly. As a result, we'll be evaluated more negatively. Others mirror this response to us and we then feel less attractive.

People who respond appropriately in social situations, that is, with clear, effective, and well-timed reactions, are thought to possess good interpersonal skills. Because of our reticence and withdrawal in social situations, which is often interpreted as avoidance behaviors, those observing our performance will see us as lacking social skills. Yes, we do speak less, look less, interrupt less, and nod, smile, and uh-huh more. Yes, we do remain quiet or leave the situation. Yes, we do allow ourselves to be only minimally engaged in the in situation for social image protection. And yes, we do ask more questions and make fewer statements of fact or self-disclosure. But these behaviors are also skillful ways to handle difficult social situations. If we have any doubt about how to present ourselves, these behaviors allow us to deal with the interaction safely.

There are no data to support the notion that these overt displays of social anxiety have any connection with poor interpersonal skills. Those of us with SA/SP may believe we're less socially skilled, but that doesn't mean we actually are. Since our perceptions of our abilities tend to be so negatively distorted, it's hard for us to tell objectively. All we do know is that encounters will be more effective when both participants contribute and tailor their responses to the interaction.

Avoidance. Avoidance can be summed up in the following advice, "On the keyboard of life always keep your finger on the escape key." Once we've started avoiding feared situations, we tend to continue to do so. However, as long as we continue to avoid the fear, the fear remains a viable and disabling enemy. We'll continue to worry about social situations. In extreme cases we may simply avoid social encounters. Studies show that socially anxious students will tend to choose living accommodations which allow less interaction, in general, and with members of the opposite sex in their residences. Where they are required to interact, they'll tend to do so at greater distances. It's important here not to confuse having a quiet nature or a desire for solitary activities with avoidance.

There are other ways we avoid what we fear that aren't so obvious. For example, when required to defend our behavior, we can offer empty explanations, such as "Because I wanted to do it." We can claim we really have a good reason but can't tell it because "You wouldn't understand it" or "It's a national security matter." We can simply refuse to account for the behavior, saying "I don't have to explain my actions." And we can leave the situation without a response.

Denying feelings. In SA/SP we experience an array of strong emotions, but are afraid to express them because of how we think others will judge us as a result. Denial is an unconscious refusal to admit into our awareness those aspects of reality that we find consciously unacceptable. When this happens, we refuse to accept some particular event (the sadness from the death of a loved one) or to face what seems to be an intolerable situation (not being able to trust and depend upon one's parent any longer). Put another way, denial is also a distortion of reality to make it conform to our individual wishes. *I used to deny my fear of confronting others. I always had an altruistic excuse for acceding to others' wishes and letting them walk all over me. It was geared to make me look good but I always felt bad just the same.* While we deny our anger, frustration, sadness, and excitement, we often feel stuck, depressed, and vaguely anxious without knowing why. Furthermore, what we deny frequently shows itself in some other way.

Lack of assertiveness. In order to feel good about ourselves, to keep our self-esteem and self-confidence high, we need to assert ourselves. Specifically, we need to express our thoughts, beliefs, and feelings in a direct, firm, and socially acceptable manner.   Assertiveness is a behavioral style which involves our awareness of our right to stand up for ourselves, ask for what we want, and act in our own best interests without harming or infringing on the rights of others. It's expressing ourselves in an honest, appropriate, reasonable, firm, and respectful manner.

An assertive person would say, "This is what I think about that." Assertiveness is expressing how we see the situation, how we feel about it, and what we'd like to see happen. It's expressed in "I-messages" ("When you didn't show up for our date or call to explain, I felt angry and disappointed. I want you to call when you're going to be late or not show") not critical or accusing "you-messages" ("You didn't show up for our date. You didn't even call. You're a thoughtless creep").

Assertiveness is significantly different from aggressiveness, though sometimes we confuse them. Assertiveness is also the middle ground between aggression and passivity, or non-assertiveness. Aggression is a form of self-enhancement but, unlike assertiveness, it's at the expense of the other person. It's a dominating, controlling, and attacking behavioral style. Only indirectly standing up for our rights, it violates the rights of others, denying and devaluing them. The aim is humiliation and winning.

While assertiveness exerts a positive influence, aggressiveness exerts a negative one. It manifests itself in blame, negative evaluation, and labeling of others' behavior and attitudes. It says, "This is what I think and what you think is stupid or doesn't count."

In order to produce and host a program on cable television I had to be trained in all aspects of production and be available to crew on other shows, all of which I did. The evening of my first produced show I arrived about 15 minutes before my guests, checked with the director about the script I'd supplied earlier, checked graphics, slides, videos, props, then greeted my guests. The interview went okay and everything seemed fine, except for my throat-clutching SA/SP, of course. For my second show I arrived as I had for the first and was immediately attacked by the director/program manager for the station. Shouting at me in front of the crew, she challenged me, "Who do you think you are arriving so late for this shoot! Everyone else has been here 45 minutes already and you waltz in just before we start!" I was shocked, mortified, and abysmally confused. "No one told me I was expected to crew my own show as well, " I sputtered impotently, "or I would have been here." She continued belittling me for my "arrogance," stating that I "should" have known. When she finished, I greeted my guests and stumbled through the show.

Why do some people act aggressively? There are a number of reasons. We may feel threatened and powerless. Perhaps we fear losing our control over others. We may be expressing frustration from prior non-assertive behavior. We may be overreacting because a present association brings out memories of past negative emotional experiences. We may believe that the only way to get what we want is to attack. We may feel deficient in appropriate skills. We may find that aggression evokes an immediate "positive" response for us. While others of us may find our culture reinforces aggressiveness as a sign of status and power.

The overall consequences of aggressiveness are negative. The behavior leads to tension, hostility, losing relationships, alienation, and retaliation. Only in the short term does the behavior seem rewarding by creating a feeling of power.

Non-assertiveness, on the other hand, is not standing up for our rights. It's an expression of self-denial and fear (as in my playing doormat). When we're non-assertive, we violate our own rights by not expressing our honest thoughts, feelings, and beliefs directly and appropriately. Instead, we're self-effacing, apologetic, and overly agreeable. It demonstrates a belief that we're not as deserving as others, and thus must sacrifice by subordinating our needs and wants to those of others. Our message is, "I don't count so you can do whatever you want, even take advantage of me." Non-assertive behavior allows others to easily disregard us.

A non-assertive person will seldom initiate actions or deal directly with others to address problems. We exert no influence by acting in a diffident, self-effacing manner. When we don't assert ourselves because we're afraid, we feel resentment. Specifically, we feel angry with those against whom we can't assert ourselves and angry with ourselves as well. We feel trapped and helpless. When we lack assertiveness, we're always going to be at the mercy of others. Non-assertiveness is:

- *Suffering silently because you're afraid to assert yourself in public or private, with strangers, family and friends;*

- *Kicking yourself afterwards for not having said the things you really wanted to say;*

- *Being afraid people will disapprove of you if you express how you feel;*

- *Holding your tongue until you can't stand it any longer and then exploding.*

Why do people act non-assertively? We may mistake assertiveness for undesirable aggressiveness and, thus, avoid it. We may equate non-assertiveness with politeness and believe this is how we should act. We may not be able to accept that we have personal rights which allow us to get what we want. We may fear the consequences of acting assertively. Others of us may mistake non-assertiveness for behavior that's supportive and helpful to others.

The overall consequences of being non-assertive may also be negative, leading to feelings of frustration and submerged anger. The cost of appeasing others and avoiding conflict can be loss of integrity and, sometimes, dignity.

As novelist James Baldwin writes, "Not everything that is faced can be changed, but nothing can be changed until it is faced."

Being assertive rather than aggressive will help us gain control of ourselves. Being assertive rather than non-assertive will help increase self-respect. When we're confident and in control, we are more likely to be able to influence the way individuals behave toward us.

Perfectionism. Perfectionism is setting unrealistically high standards for both our performance and that of others. It's not to be confused with motivation to do a good job or a heartfelt wish to achieve something as perfectly as possible. Instead, perfectionism is rigid adherence to these strict standards and a compulsive striving to achieve unachievable goals. By being "perfect" we try to guarantee for ourselves the approval and acceptance of others. *When I was a child I composed a list of goals which I hoped would place me above reproach: To dance like Martha Graham, to sing like Birgit Nilsson and Ella Fitzgerald, to play piano like Vladimir Horowitz, to write like John Steinbeck, to act like Katherine Hepburn, to look like Grace Kelly, to be loved like Walt Disney, to be a leader like Winston Churchill... .*

If we're perfect, the thinking goes, others can't negatively evaluate us in social situations and we won't be publicly humiliated. But demanding approval from every significant, or insignificant, person in our lives only sets us up for failure. From a history of feeling emotionally and physically deprived we might fear rejection and abandonment and despair that our needs will never be met. This may lead us to expect the worst so as not to feel hurt and then feel disappointment in not having our needs met.

In this process we equate our self-worth with our performance, productivity, and accomplishments. We nag ourselves about our failures. We think that if we don't achieve our goal, it will be "terrible," a catastrophe. This makes our "failure" even more devastating. And being the hard taskmasters we are, we allow ourselves no relief from self-condemnation. As we heap on the self-recrimination, our anger, frustration, resentment, depression, demoralization, and stress swell to gargantuan proportions. If, on the other hand, our unrealistic expectations are too low about ourselves, we'll experience depression, resignation, low self-esteem, and underachievement.

Unrealistic expectations lead to poor coping with frustration, difficulty with problem solving and decision making, and a generalized sense of disappointment. Interestingly, according to psychoanalyst Karen Horney, when we have these high standards, we tend to perceive ourselves as morally, if not intellectually, superior to others. We are, after all, giving our all to achieve perfection. Anyone who does less either has lower values than we do or is too lazy to do what's "right." Because of our perception of others' inferiority, we may unconsciously and consciously hold them in contempt.

We express these unrealistic expectations in terms of *should, shouldn't, must,* and *ought,* or what Albert Ellis, the parent of rational-emotive behavioral therapy (REBT), calls *"must*erbation." Believing that there are some rules etched in marble that we are expected to follow makes us try to adhere to them out of guilt. ("I must be able to talk with strangers without having medication or therapy" or "You must wash those dishes right after dinner"). These rules we subscribe to all require that we work methodically, meticulously, and endlessly.

These *musts* and *shoulds* create a mental trap for us. While we are beating ourselves about the head and shoulders in order to coerce ourselves into motivation, we are inadvertently undermining our efforts to succeed at achieving our original task. We're so stifled by what we *should* do and how we *should* do it that there's little wiggle room for being spontaneous and original. Our work becomes slow and unproductive, leaving us overworked and exhausted.

To fulfill our *shoulds* we are likely to make strenuous efforts to measure up, to meet our duties and obligations, to be polite, mannerly, and punctual - make the totality of our conduct exemplary. But failure to be perfect, according to our own individual criteria, relegates us to incompetence, inadequacy, and poor character. In this sense, perfectionism is perceiving and believing that we and our work are never "good enough." As a result, we *should* be punished for this discrepancy between performance reality and fantasy.

Shoulds aren't the only illusions engendered by unrealistic expectations. We may expect will power to overcome all. We may expect that there's only one true course in life and we have to find "it" or we have nothing. We may also expect to define ourselves as acceptable only through our actions. So if our actions don't meet our standard, we're unacceptable. However, we need to remember that expectations themselves aren't the problem. The problem is our relationship to them, how tied we are to the wish and to the anticipation of the expectation being fulfilled or unfulfilled.

Expectations may be positive or negative. Positive expectations are based in an assessment of the situation and a wish for a particular course of events. When positive expectations (being surprised by flowers) are unmet, they result in disappointment. Negative expectations (our birthday will be forgotten), on the other hand, are defensive, mirroring fears that our wishes won't be gratified.

Expectations we have for others that are too high likewise produce negative feelings. We tend to expect them to intuitively know what we want and need and then to act on that knowledge. When they are unable to meet that expectation, we resent their failure to do so. We scorn and condemn them. After all, if **we're** fair and just, we're entitled to fair treatment. Receiving anything less than what we expect is perceived as unfair because it unbalances our mental accounting ledger. This leaves us feeling angry and disappointed. We need to remember the words of humanistic psychologist Fritz Perls, "I am not in this world to live up to your expectations. And you are not in this world to live up to mine."

Perfectionism often leads to an inability to feel satisfaction because we perceive that we have to give more than 100% all the time. Just as we approach the high-jump bar, someone raises it higher so it's once again out of reach. But we can't let go. We can't stop worrying about our errors, obsessing over our failures. Tied up in an emotional straitjacket, we lose our grip on the possibility of self-acceptance and inner peace.

Perfectionistic thinking is often characterized by fear of failure, procrastination, an all-or-nothing mindset, task paralysis, workaholism, anxiety, depression, and lowered self-esteem. This means immobilization. If we can't be perfect or do something perfectly, there's no reason to try. This means not taking risks or exploring new territory. But without failure we learn nothing and experience no growth.

Irrespective of the particular expectations we hold, when we increase our perfectionism, we increase our anxiety, our fear of public exposure, our withdrawal, and our loneliness. If we're going to eliminate and prevent perfectionistic thinking, and its attendant anxiety, we have to either change our expectations to more closely approximate reality or accept feeling continually disappointed by most human behavior, especially our own.

Anger and hostility.   Anger can be a natural, spontaneous, and unavoidable self-generated arousal response to many stimuli. It originates from a sense of helplessness which is inherent in our anxious state. It may be the result of our feeling trespassed against and robbed of what is rightfully ours. Or it may be the result of our immature demands, false ideas of grandiosity, devaluation of others, perceived necessity to mete out blame and harsh punishment, and lack of assertiveness.

It's created and maintained by our belief that something "shouldn't be." In general, it's short-lived, although it can become chronic. Those of us who withdraw from social situations and who cling or try to please tend not to demonstrate our anger directly. We fear exposing ourselves and alienating those on whom we depend for a sense of security. As a result, our anger is buried and accumulates over time, putting those others at risk of an inadvertent explosion.

But dwelling on anger or giving in to ranting or explosions is neither healthy nor useful. When we don't control the expression of our anger, its power increases and we often hurt others as well as ourselves. As Aristotle says in **Nicomachean Ethics**, "Anyone can become angry - that is easy. To be angry with the right person, to the right degree, at the right time, for the right purpose, and in the right way - this is not easy."

Hostility, on the other hand, seems to stem from a blend of conflicting feelings: Anxiety, anger, and unresolved rage. As our anxiety increases, so may our hostility. We feel ourselves to be in constant danger of a real or imagined threat of external attack so we adopt hostility to protect us. We have to defend continuously against these attacks because we see ourselves as powerless, alone, and the object of great and irreparable injustices. When not thinking about defense, we're contemplating avenging the injustices and hurts we believe we've suffered.

Hostility may result from our having felt deprived of love, recognition, fair treatment, or opportunities. It may result from our having been made to feel inferior, inadequate, or worthless. It may result from our having been hindered in some way, from rigid discipline, excessive criticism, or lack of respect.

In general, that which initially ignited this persistent feeling of bitter resentment is long gone, but the resulting antagonism and anxiety live on in our thoughts and feelings, gnawing at us, constantly refreshed by cognitive distortions and mistakes. In our self-centeredness we assume that if we feel ill will toward them, they feel the same toward us. This further justifies in our minds our thoughts, feelings, and behavior. We see ourselves as right and, in extreme cases, are unable to admit our errors. So if we're right, then that means others must be wrong and are automatically to blame. With all of this we don't see or don't want to admit that our attitudes or behaviors are even in part responsible for this ill will we perceive.

How hostility is expressed depends upon our personality and behavior. While we may present ourselves as cool, aloof, and disengaged or charming and engaging, hostility may slip from behind our mask as cutting remarks, sniping at others, putting people down, or sarcasm. If we are shy, non-assertive, or highly anxious, we may express our hostility as greater fear rather than as anger. The greater the level of hostility we experience, the greater our inability to express it. We may stutter, choke up, or become incoherent altogether, further incensing us yet making us even more fearful of letting it show.

Our only release seems to be indirect or oblique. We become masters of passive-aggressive behavior. We "innocently" do things to thwart those we feel have hurt us. We're late for appointments. We make mistakes that inconvenience others. We send mixed messages (with words saying one thing and behaviors saying the opposite) about our concern or support.

Like termites slowly eating away the structure of a house, hostility cuts us off not only from others but also from ourselves. We're so preoccupied with anger and defending that we alienate ourselves from our warm and vulnerable feelings. This leaves us further isolated. Without concerted efforts to identify and understand this state of emotional poverty, we can find ourselves on the brink of chronic withdrawal and depression.

This hostility may be deadly to more than just relationships and social interaction. Back in the early 1970s physicians Meyer Friedman and Ray Rosenman discovered that individuals with a particular behavior pattern were at greater risk for coronary artery and heart disease. The pattern, which consisted of free-floating hostility, time urgency, and excessive competitiveness, was named "Type A behavior." Since then, some studies have indicated that it's only the hostility component of the Type A pattern that is the determining factor in heart disease, while other, more recent findings, have suggested that individuals who harbor constant feelings of negativity, distress, inhibition, and inadequacy (known as "Type D personality") are three times more likely to suffer recurrent heart attacks than their "non-D" counterparts.

Cognitive errors. These result from systematic distortions in the way we process information. They bias how we think and show up in our negative self-talk. The following are some of the more common ones (they are addressed in detail in "Self Talk" in Chapter 7):

- *Arbitrary inference*
- *Over-generalization*
- *Magnification and minimization*
- *Personalization*
- *All-or-nothing thinking*
- *Mental filter*
- *Disqualifying the positive*
- *Jumping to conclusions*
- *Mind reading*
- *Fortune telling error*
- *Emotional reasoning*
- *Should statements*
- *Labeling*
- *Rationalization.*

Low-self esteem is a sense of worthlessness and insecurity, a lack of uniqueness and belonging. It's based on how we compare ourselves with others and to what degree we meet the dictates of our internal standards. We ask ourselves, "Who am I to know?" "Who am I to judge?" "Who am I to decide?" It's determined not only by our feelings about ourselves, particularly as children, but also by things that happen to us.

These feelings promote behaviors that tend to reinforce them. If we feel bad about not being able to solve a problem, we're unlikely to want to try to solve another and risk feeling bad again. These feelings may stem from parental criticism, neglect, abandonment, abuse, or overprotection as well as our not having positive models for self-nurturing behavior. They are the result of what others tell us about ourselves and what our observations of our own behavior and its consequences tell us about ourselves. These feelings form gradually over time and are cumulative. Deprivation then underscores the hurt of our inner child.

Having internalized the standards and beliefs of those who judge us, we come to describe ourselves in terms of how we deviate from the norm. As a result, we accept our culture's pay-off system: Performance at or above the norm is rewarded. Performance below the norm is punished. Buying into this system puts us in further danger of experiencing the anxiety associated with others' evaluation of our performance.

If we have low self-esteem, we're likely to avoid situations that provoke anxiety. We're likely to demean our own talents and feel others don't value us as well. We'll tend to believe we'll be unable to cope with different social situations. Furthermore, we'll likely doubt that we'll make the impressions we desire to make on others.

All of this promotes our feeling frustrated, defensive, and powerless. It leaves us without the capacity to care for our needs and nurture ourselves. In the face of life demands for action and responsibility, we feel inadequate. This feeling of inadequacy leads to feelings of insecurity, self-doubt, being unfit for reality, and increased anxiety. However, having high self-esteem is not a panacea for psychological problems in general or SA/SP in particular.

Guilt is a vague but potentially corrosive feeling which results from self-punishment for our not having met some conscious or unconscious standard of behavior. Expressed in terms of "should" and "ought," guilt is the product of our internalization of others' expectations of "right" and "wrong." Guilt is the gold standard for our personal behavior so we can recognize our violations of some societal or other rule. When the life we live doesn't match up with the life we want to live or feel we should live, our conscience regales us with recriminations and bad feelings. Even though there's no relationship between what we do and whether we feel guilt, we make our meeting these standards the measure of our self-worth. While feeling guilt may not stop us from doing something "unacceptable" or make us do something "acceptable," it will make us feel terrible for having done it.

Barry. *Barry's elderly grandmother is in the nursing home and he has trouble visiting her. One reason is that she taps into his well of guilt and social confusion every time she makes an indirect request of him. "I wish you'd visit more but I know how busy you are. I don't ask because I don't want to be a bother." Her mixed message tells Barry she's disappointed he's not visiting more, implicitly but not explicitly asks him to visit, but then excuses his not doing so.*

Procrastination is a decision to delay or do nothing. It can occur when we have something that is useful, necessary, or unpleasant to do. It occurs when we wish or agree to do something, but postpone doing anything, berate ourselves for it, delay some more, and berate ourselves some more. Based on self-defeating compulsiveness, procrastination persists through anxiety and self-recriminations. According to Albert Ellis and William Knaus, it can be categorized by the behavior involved, such as maintenance, self-development, or irresponsibility to others.

Maintenance is where we put off essential duties, like paying bills or our income tax until the last possible moment, thus making our lives more inconvenient, out of control, and less enjoyable. This makes us feel inconvenienced and out of control. *Development* is where we routinely avoid anything having to do with self-improvement activities, constructively working toward meeting realistic goals we desire. This makes us feel depressed, immobilized, and frustrated. *Irresponsibility* to others involves sabotaging others by dawdling. Procrastination can be the result of many factors, such as self-doubt, organizational problems, powerlessness, hostility, self-indulgence, low frustration tolerance, perfectionism, need for love, depression, guilt, shame, and fear of disapproval. Irrespective of the source, the behavior creates a vicious circle.

Muscle tension refers to tightness and rigidity in any of the large muscle groups of our body. This extreme, continued contraction restricts our blood flow and reduces our breathing to shallow breaths. It's one of the many physiological changes that occur when we experience anxiety's arousal. Like the release of adrenaline and liver-stored sugar into the blood stream, it's designed to help us survive by preparing us for fight or flight. Our muscles tense, ready to spring into action. The muscles that are particularly affected are the thighs, back, shoulders, arms, jaw, and face. When stress is prolonged, this tension can become a chronic response. Our muscle tension may also be indicative of suppressed feelings such as anger, frustration, or resentment and leads to anxiety.

In order to feel less anxious, we need to decrease physiological arousal. One way to do this is by learning how to control our breathing. A second, which often goes hand in hand with the first, is by eliminating muscle tension through progressive relaxation. (See Chapter 6.)

Nutrition and stimulants can contribute significantly to our experience of anxiety. Use of stimulants, such as caffeine and nicotine, trigger the physiological arousal associated with anxiety through increasing the neurotransmitter norepinephrine. They interfere with sleep and deplete B-vitamins (B1, B2, B6, B12). B-vitamins, which are also depleted by stress and anxiety, are necessary for a healthy nervous system.

Those of us who use mental health services, or need to, tend to ingest a lot of caffeine - from 5-10 times as much coffee as non-patients, averaging 10-15 cups per day. This exacerbates our anxiety and irritability and increases our problem with insomnia, thus making our condition worse than it already is. It can also interfere with some antipsychotics, sedatives, and lithium.

Low intake of calcium, vitamin C, and amino acids, the precursors to neurotransmitters, also leaves us vulnerable to stress. Moreover, our use of alcohol, a depressant, depletes both B-vitamins and C, and, in excess, can destroy brain cells.

Refined sugar acts as a stimulant to our body's hormone insulin, which breaks down sugars and starches. Excessive sugar sends our insulin level soaring, often overshooting, and leaving us with rapid heat rate, feeling jumpy, irritability, weakness, and sweating. This is very similar to the body's response to stress and mimics the symptoms we associate with anxiety.

Yet, paradoxically, we find eating the sugar somehow comforting. This appears to be related to a selective effect insulin has on amino acids. Which amino acid is transported to the brain depends upon which has the highest concentration in the blood stream at the time. Insulin in the blood stream causes all amino acids but tryptophan, the precursor of serotonin, to be taken up by muscles and other tissues. Tryptophan, as the amino acid with the highest concentration, is then transported to the brain. When the tryptophan is converted to serotonin, we feel rewarded for eating the sugar. As a result, diet can have a profound effect on our daily functioning in general and on anxiety in particular.

Allergic reactions can cause psychological as well as physiological symptoms: Anxiety, panic, depression, mood swings, irritability, insomnia, dizziness, fatigue, confusion, disorientation, and headaches. Frequent culprits are wheat, milk, chocolate, peanuts, soy, and citrus. Oddly enough, foods to which we're allergic are the ones we tend to crave. Let me share a related experience.

Anxiety and physiological dependence. *It took me most of my adult life to come to the realization that I'm an addict - out of control, unable to resist a seductive, toxic substance. I used it daily and relied on it to make everything right. No matter how bad I felt after the buzz wore off, I didn't stop. I had to have it.*

Was I hooked on cocaine, heroine, crack, or amphetamines? Nothing so obvious. In a way, my substance was more insidious because it's widely used, labeled by the Food and Drug Administration as "generally recognized as safe," and often invisible. I'm talking about processed sugar.

Unless you're consciously avoiding sugar, you eat it all day, every day of your life. According to the American Dietetic Association, the average American consumes in excess of 130 pounds of sugar a year; in other words, 6 ounces a day or 2.6 pounds a week. Over 70% of all processed foods contain some form of sugar because it's used as a preservative, flavor enhancer, fruit plumper, acid reducer, curing agent, fermentation medium, crust colorant, moisture holder, shelf-life extender, and provider of bulk, texture and body.

I've always loved sugar in any form, from fudgicles to birthday cake to spoonfuls of brown sugar right from the box. My early love affair with it never seemed a problem, until my 20s when I developed constant headaches. They were present upon rising and going to bed, often erupting during the day into migraines. As a result, I ate Excedrin (which contains 65 mg. of caffeine per tablet) by the handful, upwards of twelve a day, every day. In addition, my periods were getting worse with simulated labor pains and water-weight gain up to 10 pounds.

Anxiety insinuated itself into my every thought. I worried about the occurrence of the improbable and impossible. Depression slowly settled a dark, suffocating blanket over me. By the time I was in my 30s, I'd run the gamut of neurological tests, but nothing revealed itself or helped.

I was tired all the time, weak, and cried at a moment's notice. To comfort myself I ate some Brach's Bridge Mix, 'Nilla Wafers, or Breyer's Fudge Swirl Ice Milk, only now in larger portions, more frequently to round off the sharp corners.

As I turned 40, I developed night sweats, a 120-beats-per-minute heart rate, and insomnia. A prescription for the beta-blocker propranolol slowed my racing heart in between binges. By this time I was eating all the sugar-laden food I could lay my hands on. If I didn't have candy around, I'd go to the store at any time in any weather to get it, bake a coffee cake, or eat raw sugar. Heartburn and gas were a constant problem.

Then one day I chanced to see physician on television, talking about the controversy over sugar's hypothesized effect on mood and behavior. I began my research and found a description of my own health picture. With a glimmer of hope, I copied all the names in which processed sugar (simple sugar) appears: Sucrose, dextrose, lactose, fructose, crystalline fructose, corn syrup, high-fructose corn syrup, turbinado, raw sugar, brown sugar, molasses, malt syrup, maltol, and maltodextrin. Immediately I eliminated from my diet all processed foods that contained any of the list. The only "sugar" I consumed was moderate amounts of fresh fruits (complex sugars) and carbohydrate vegetables, but only in combination with protein, to mitigate any minor sugar reaction, and lots of water.

The first several days without my precious sugar I was screaming inside my skull. Something down deep inside like a caged rat gnawed at my soul, eating me alive from within. I'd find myself physically doubled over, hugging myself, rocking back and forth in psychic agony. Then, on the fourth day as I awoke and habitually reached for my Excedrin, I realized I didn't have a headache. The first time in 20 years.

By the end of the first week I actually began to feel "up." The knot in my stomach had untied itself in non-social situations. My life looked brighter and held promise. I've been off sugar for over five years now and have experienced no recurrence of my previous condition except when I tested this cause-and-effect relationship. There's no question that, at least for me, sugar is "addictive" and significantly increases general anxiety symptoms, making my SA/SP worse.

Lifestyle is how we live. "Many people unknowingly subject themselves to unnecessary stress by adopting and maintaining patterns of behavior, habits, relationships, activities, and obligations that add to their stress scores day by day," says Karl Albrecht, corporate stress-reduction consultant. When we have a stressful lifestyle, we tend to experience chronic, unrelieved stress, struggle with stressful interpersonal relationships, and feel trapped in continuing stress situations. Often, we're involved in work we find unpleasant and unrewarding. In addition, we worry about potentially aversive events in the future.

The Type A behavior pattern we already mentioned briefly is an example of a negative or stressful lifestyle. Those with the Type A pattern are embroiled in a chronic, incessant struggle to do more and more in less and less time. There's a time urgency, a fear that there's not enough time for all that needs to be done. Because of this when Type A people (like me) are faced with environmental challenges, we'll try to achieve work goals to the exclusion of other activities. We tend to accept high-pressure and stressful situations with few complaints, even conforming to punishing social roles whenever they're demanded. All this is done without a whimper. Our pre-occupation with productivity leaves other activities, whether it's social, sexual, leisure, or exercise, someplace on the periphery. Likewise, our health may suffer from poor habits such as eating fatty foods, smoking, alcohol, lack of exercise, and poorly-balanced life. For those of us with this behavior pattern work may be a defense against our anxiety.

There are several lifestyle and health behaviors that contribute to how we experience stress. Personal factors include our beliefs about control, our resilience and hardiness, and our coping skills. Environmental factors include those physical aspects over which we have little or no control, such as noise, air pollution, high-density crowding, heat, and public and organizational policies. Cultural factors include those goals of culture toward which we work or the values we want to preserve, such as quality education for all.

From the cultural perspective, Western societies generally admire and reward aggressive, competitive, productivity-oriented behavior despite its potentially negative effect on workers' health. This is because our health is not a highly-valued commodity, or certainly not as valued as workaholism in an employee. Health is something to be purchased when needed and not thought about much or attended to in the ordinary course of events. Responsibility for its maintenance then falls to delegated specialists. When we have a toothache, we go the dentist; when we have an anxiety disorder which significantly interferes with our lives, we go to a mental health worker. Unless there's actually a pressing problem, we tend not to think about our health.

Healthy lifestyles and behaviors, like preventive medicine, are not systematically taught at any societal level. Too frequently they seem to be given mere lip-service, and may be abandoned altogether when their prescription conflicts with cultural expectations. If the culture had to choose between "stress-free workers" and "achievement-obsessed workers," there's little doubt that Western societies would choose that which creates a profit over that which fosters health.

Lack of meaning in life leaves us without a sense of purpose or a direction to follow. Our psychological health depends upon our having a "why" to live. It depends upon our finding meaning in our suffering in order to survive. All humans have a need for meaning.

According to existential psychologist Viktor Frankl in **Man's Search For Meaning**, it doesn't matter to what external conditions we're exposed or that affect our lives because ultimately we're free to choose our reaction to those conditions. In other words, we can, if we want to, ultimately rise above our circumstances. Our continuing need to search for meaning supplies us with the purpose for our existence. The more we're able to transcend ourselves, get past our immediate needs and self-gratification in order to give to others, the more fully human we become (and the more we can get beyond our anxiety).

For those who value having a religious faith, our personal belief appears to aid in transcending psychiatric disorders and health problems in general. Numerous studies have demonstrated that religious faith helps people cope with their illnesses and makes them less likely to be depressed when ill or hospitalized. Patients report that their faith provides them with a sense of control and meaning and purpose to their suffering.

Search for meaning involves our personal responsibility for finding our own way and keeping at it once we find it. It means our giving to the world and taking experience from it. This is not something that parents, friends, significant others, or therapists can do for us. We constantly have to meet life's challenges and stretch toward our potential or we'll find ourselves in a vacuum of aimlessness, apathy, emptiness, boredom, and anxiety.

When "anxiety" isn't anxiety

Before we begin any journey toward recovery from our anxiety, whether it's with a psychotherapist or by ourselves, we need to be sure the anxiety we feel has a psychological root. There are many medical conditions which mimic the symptoms of anxiety disorders. Therefore, before we apply the strategies in this book or any other, we need to appropriately rule out medical conditions as the cause or complicating problem. This requires having a complete physical examination plus blood chemistries. The following conditions are more fully detailed in Mark S. Gold's **The Good News About Panic, Anxiety, and Phobias** and James Morrison's **When Psychological Problems Mask Medical Disorders**. This listing is a heads-up and guide for further investigation and is not for medical diagnosis purposes. An asterisk (*) marks the most common of the following anxiety-related medical conditions.

Asthma - unpredictable periods of breathlessness and wheezing caused by stress, environmental conditions, or foreign substances. Symptoms: Difficulty breathing, tight chest, anxiety.

Brain tumor - tissue growth in brain displaces normal structures. Symptoms: Headaches, weakness, confusion, seizures, nausea, vomiting, memory loss, cognitive decline, depression.

Cerebral Arteriosclerosis - thickening, hardening, or loss of elasticity of arterial walls. Symptoms: Headache, dizziness, memory defects, anxiety.

*Chronic obstructive pulmonary disease - loss of elasticity and absorptive surface area in lungs. Symptoms: Shortness of breath, dusty skin hue, headaches, insomnia, panic, depression, anxiety.

Congestive heart failure - loss of heart's pumping efficiency due to heart disease or arrhythmias. Symptoms: Shortness of breath, weakness, edema, bluish skin, cold extremities, panic, anxiety.

*Diabetes mellitus (hyperglycemia) - reduced effectiveness or availability of insulin to metabolize food. Symptoms: High levels of blood glucose, increased hunger, increased thirst, increased urine output, weight loss, panic, depression, anxiety.

Emphysema - air sacs in lungs which exchange gases become distorted or destroyed. Symptoms: Decreased oxygen and increased carbon dioxide in blood, increased burden on heart, increased blood pressure, difficulty breathing, fatigue, anxiety.

Epilepsy - recurrent paroxysmal disorder of cerebral structure of brain. Symptoms: Sudden, brief attacks of altered consciousness, motor activity, depression.

Essential Hypertension - most common type of high blood pressure. Symptoms: No symptoms, headaches, ringing in ears, lightheadedness, and fatigue.

Fibromyalgia - ill-defined cluster of symptoms. Symptoms: Muscle pain and tenderness, stiffness, chronic fatigue, depression, anxiety.

Hyperparathyroidism - over-reactive parathyroid gland. Symptoms: Increased serum calcium, weakness, tremors, nausea, abdominal pain, personality change, depression, anxiety.

*Hyperthyroidism - increased production of thyroxin. Symptoms: Heart palpitations, sweating, weight loss, increased temperature, insomnia, depression, panic, generalized anxiety.

*Hyperventilation syndrome - rapid, shallow breathing. Symptoms: Decreased carbon dioxide in blood, dizziness, shortness of breath, trembling, feelings of unreality, tingling in lips, hands, and feet, anxiety.

Hypocalicemia - decrease in blood calcium from hypoparathyroidism, kidney failure, lack of vitamin D leading to irregular heartbeat and muscle spasms.

*Hypoglycemia - decreased blood sugar level from stress, improper diet, severe alcoholism, pancreatic tumor. Symptoms: Shakiness, weakness, dizziness, disorientation, anxiety.

Hypokalemia - decrease in blood potassium caused by malnutrition, dehydration, treatment for diabetes, hypertension, and use of diuretics. Symptoms: Muscle weakness, reduced respiration, low blood pressure.

*Inner ear disturbances (Meniere's syndrome, infection, allergy) - pressure from swelling in the inner ear. Symptoms: Dizziness, lightheadedness, ringing in the ears, unsteadiness, nausea, vomiting, panic, anxiety.

Lyme disease - tick-transmitted infectious inflammatory disease. Symptoms: Arthritis, headache, fever, chills, pain, fatigue, depression, anxiety.

*Mitral valve prolapse (MVP) - slight defect in valve separating upper and lower chambers of left side of the heart which keeps the valve from completely closing, thus allowing back-flow of blood. Symptoms: Non-dangerous arrhythmic heartbeat, panic, anxiety.

Myocardial infarction (MI) - blood clot interrupting the flow of blood in the heart results in damage. Symptoms: Sharp, intense pain radiating to neck or left arm, indigestion, irregular heartbeat, discomfort, anxiety.

Niacin deficiency - where maise forms major part of diet and has not been alkali-treated. Symptoms: Weakness, headaches, rough and red skin, diarrhea, depression, anxiety.

Pheochromocytoma - adrenal cell tumor which secretes catecholamines (neurohormones). Symptoms: Increased blood pressure, headache attacks, sweating, palpitations, nausea, panic, anxiety.

Porphyria - genetic metabolism deficiency. Symptoms: Abdominal pain, dark urine, constipation, nausea, vomiting, increased heartbeat, sweating, depression, anxiety.

Post-concussion syndrome (head trauma) - non-penetrating injury to brain with temporary or permanent symptoms. Symptoms: Headache, dizziness, fatigue, mood swings, anxiety.

*Premenstrual syndrome - fluctuations in estrogen and progesterone occurring 7-10 days before period. Symptoms: Weight gain, breast pain and tenderness, edema, fatigue, irritability, depression, anxiety.

Seasonal affective disorder (SAD) - insufficient exposure to sunlight. Symptoms: Depression, irritability, insomnia, agitation, anxiety.

Vitamin B1 (thiamine) deficiency - inadequate intake of polished rice or where increased requirement due to hyperthyroidism, pregnancy, lactation, fever, severe diarrhea, alcoholism. Symptoms: Fatigue, irritation, poor memory, chest and abdominal pain.

Vitamin B12 (cobalamin) deficiency (with or without anemia) - inadequate or vegetarian diet, chronic alcoholism, small intestine disorders, hyperthyroidism, liver or kidney disease. Symptoms: Shortness of breath, increase heartbeat, weakness, edema, sensory changes in extremities, amnesia, anxiety.

Drugs, medications, and environmental toxins

Other substances and situations too have the capability of mimicking anxiety symptoms:

- Alcohol
- Amphetamine withdrawal
- Aspertame
- Caffeine
- Carbon dioxide
- Cocaine
- Codeine withdrawal

- Diet pills with stimulants
- Heroin withdrawal
- Indomethacin (non-steroidal anti-inflammatory)
- Insecticides
- Laxatives with mercurous chloride
- Lidocaine (local anesthetic)
- MAOIs
- Marijuana
- Mercury
- Nicotine withdrawal
- Volatile hydrocarbons.

"I'm not socially-avoidant. I'm fear-approach-challenged."

CHAPTER 5

APPROACHING RECOVERY

"Climb high, Climb far, Your goal the sky, Your aim the star" (Inscription on Hopkins Memorial Steps at Williams College, Williamstown, MA

How others respond to us

As those of us who suffer from it know, SA/SP is the source of great distress. It generates discomfort, pain, and incapacity. It damages beliefs and values, commitment, and social relationships. It forces us to live with fear, uncertainty, insecurity, dread, and apprehension. And it results in embarrassment, humiliation, shame, guilt, and loss of dignity. This is something that the majority of family, friends, and health and mental health professionals don't seem to understand.

Family and friends. Those close to us often seem unable to understand not only the depth of the distress created by the disorder but also how they can appropriately and helpfully relate to our suffering. While some are apparently clueless about what we're going through, others seem to have at least an abstract idea. However, both these groups tend to be guilty of trying to get us to "put on a happy face." They downplay our fears, feelings, and thoughts, as if we were exaggerating or just being negative. They want us to "cheer up," "look on the bright side," and "accentuate the positive." Aside from the fact that this approach is highly unlikely to work, it trivializes how and how deeply we feel, undermining the legitimacy of our claim of suffering.

This mind-set suggests that we're giving in to silly and easily controllable fears and that we should "shape up" and "pull ourselves up by our bootstraps." If only we'd "just do it!", as the Nike ad goes, we could transcend the problem. It's okay for us to feel our discomfort, but after a reasonable period of time, we should get on with it. This attitude makes it doubly difficult for us because we fear and feel threatened by others' evaluation of us. This means we're saddled with the disorder itself as well as others' judgments about how "appropriately" we're dealing with it.

So why does just about everybody throw these positive prescriptions at us? Our Western culture rewards cheerfulness in the face of adversity. This means we're expected to conceal symptoms or, at least, minimize them. Even when someone asks, "How are you," they really don't want to know, don't expect us to tell them the nitty-gritty truth, and, indeed, become uncomfortable when we do. Frequently, unexpected, non-affirmative responses don't even get acknowledged. People urge us to be positive when we're in pain because our pain is a burden for them. They can't handle our feelings and the situation without some emotional cost to themselves.

People also urge us to be positive in order to reinforce the notion that all human beings have control over such things in our lives. For if we don't have control, they don't either. This means that things may happen randomly to them (as they do to us). If this randomness were true, the world would not be the "just place" they'd like to believe it is. They want to believe the world is a place where we're responsible for what happens to us and we get what we deserve. Because the thought of its being an "unjust world" is threatening, we all tend to blame the victim of the misfortune. Not only for getting themselves into the position in the first place but also for not getting themselves out of it in the second place.

Some people are frustrated with our behavior - our indecision, hiding, and running away. They shake their heads, roll their eyes, and sigh. They feel we're not holding up our end but have no idea what to do about it. Our symptoms and self-presentation don't add up to "illness" in their eyes. Instead, our behavior seems merely non-normative, maybe even a little deviant, immature, and, perhaps, irresponsible. Sometimes their response is to tell us, "You shouldn't feel that way." If we're not perceived to be ill, we're not entitled to these feelings. Our reaction to this often is to apologize, become defensive, feel guilty, or shut down any attempt at communication. Once again we're being told that if only we'd simply control our emotions, we'd fare better with the world around us.

After all, they have to deal with problems face-to-face so we should too. They have to meet cultural expectations so we should too. They have to encounter lots of situations they don't like, but they have to do what's required, so we should too. Furthermore, we appear to spend our time whining "Poor me. Understand me. Support me," something they'd like to be able to do on occasion but don't feel they can.

Some people have well-meaning intentions to help when they urge us to "let a smile be our umbrella on a rainy day." They believe what they're saying will be inspirational, promote a positive outlook, and help lift us out of the doldrums. While this may be useful in some specific instances with SA/SP, to get our attention or encourage us, it's not a good overall approach. It implies that if we had the right motivation, we could just "snap out of it." Unfortunately, even with all the motivation, skills, and help available, we're not going to do that. It's not a hop, skip, and a jump to move from chaos to self-acceptance and empowerment, even for the mildest case of SA/SP.

When these individuals are unable to respond appropriately to our distress, they also give what are called "Mrs. Lincoln responses." The response style is based on a sick joke which asks, "Other than that, Mrs. Lincoln, how did you like the play?" As counselor Brooke Collinson points out, this style shows insensitivity, denial of others' pain, and a refusal to acknowledge our human condition. Something as innocuous as, "Are you okay?" is often such a response. This question is generally asked of someone who's in distress and obviously not okay. People tend to feel obligated to ask and offer their help.

This then relieves them of their responsibility with a clear conscience. We who are distressed feel guilty if we don't let them off the hook so we generally let them continue on their way unconcerned and uninvolved.

Sometimes people will try to identify with our distress by letting us know that they know of someone who has experienced what they think we have: That the other either suffered Biblical plague and pestilence, so we should feel lucky, or is doing fantastically well, so we shouldn't worry. Either way once again our feelings aren't being accepted or accepted as legitimate. But, perhaps more importantly, when this "other" person is brought into the conversation, that person then becomes the focus. This further distances the responder from us and the intensity of "our" problem. Even if the responder wants to be close to us but just doesn't have the appropriate mechanism to do it, we're still left without comfort and support.

"I feel really terrible" is a response we hear to our situation, suggesting we're making others feel bad. (A similar phrase is, "I don't know what to say.") The thinking goes that if only we were sensitive to and protective of others, we wouldn't share our problems with them and cause them pain. Of course, by not reaching out or sharing, we cut ourselves off from the possibility of support.

Trying to be empathetic with our situation, people will often tell us, "I know exactly how you feel." Unless we know this person to be experiencing SA/SP or shyness or to be working with those who do and, therefore, to have an inkling of what we're going through, we're likely to respond internally with anger, "Oh, yeah?!" with some colorfully-graphic profanities. In trying to communicate their perceived understanding of our situation, they're depriving us of our unique experience of our private event.

Even when others try to be authentic and honest by telling us, "I'm glad it's not happening to me," they're really saying they're glad it's happening to **us** instead. Or when they say to us, "I don't know how you stand it," they mean they can see we're standing it, obviously doing okay, and don't need their help. Or "You're lucky cognitive-behavioral therapy worked," implying that our knowledge, skill, effort, and just plain hard work had nothing to do with our progress or successful recovery. Even with their best intentions, when family and friends don't know what to say, we're likely to suffer.

Professionals. Health care professionals likewise tend to underestimate our distress. They're concerned with the quantitative, objective, and technical so they tend to miss or ignore the qualitative, subjective, and personal. There's a lack of information about the disorder, that it's serious but treatable. As a result, when we present at primary care for help, all that professionals can see is our depression or alcoholism. Sufferers and professionals alike tend to think of SA/SP as shyness, part of our personality, or something everybody experiences. Despite the spate of medical journals focusing on SA/SP and medical schools emphasizing physician's sensitivity and clues to anxiety, our condition tends to be invisible or insignificant to health professionals.

The quality of the physician-patient relationship has a great influence on our therapeutic outcome. Granted, it's often difficult to fully understand the multiple, and often disguised, emotional meanings of what we say. It's hard to figure out what's significant even in the best of circumstances. But since we may have to interact with physicians in some manner regarding our SA/SP, it's important they don't dismiss our distress.

If physicians don't know about SA/SP and don't appear eager to learn, they may reject our conjecture and chalk our symptoms up to temporary anxiety or a consequence of underlying depression. They may prescribe an antidepressant which may or may not be helpful. This leaves us feeling angry, helpless, and questioning whether there's any help available if the professionals don't seem to know or care. If, on the other hand, physicians ask questions to screen us for SA/SP and understand more of what we're experiencing, listen to the answers, and make the interaction a sharing process, we're likely to feel that there's hope for recovery.

What physicians need to do is get beyond the ignorance, insensitivity, and haste. In spite of their fatigue or overload, they need to look for the real message that we're sending. This means recognizing our fear and the brittleness of our defenses against it. It means attending to our strengths as well as our sense of helplessness. It means responding to our need for both reassurance and information. It means acknowledging that different people perceive and cope with things differently, that one size does not fit all, that pat answers, quick and easy solutions, and gimmicks will have a negative impact. Without some change on the part of physicians, it will be difficult for them to overcome their message distortion or failure to hear us at all.

Aiming at recovery versus cure

Murphy's Law: Nothing is as easy as it looks.
        Everything takes longer than you think.
        If anything can go wrong, it will.

SA/SP is not like a having a cut finger. Sewing up the wound, putting a bandage on it, and giving us some antibiotics will not cure the problem or restore us to our "former (?)" state of health. The problem of SA/SP, especially the generalized form of it, is too deep and far too complex for such a simple solution. Many of us have literally built our lives around the limitations of SA/SP. It's also not something that has a definite end. The finger heals and the tissue goes back to normal. But despite all the psychopharmaceuticals and psychological therapies available to us, we won't go back to "normal" (however we arbitrarily choose to define it). Besides, what is "normal" for us as individuals anyway? There is always likely to be, at the very least, an imprint (both positive and negative) of the disorder on our thoughts, feelings, beliefs, and behaviors.

This is because we've lived *with* our SA/SP and *through* it for a long time. What we are today is, in part, a result of it. Specifically, it's part of how we perceive and act upon the world. It's what we've learned to do to protect and comfort ourselves. It's the strategies we use to cope, adapt, and accommodate to change so we can manage to achieve some degree of success in our lives.

Anything which impacts the psyche so completely and insinuates itself into so many aspects of our lives can't be shed like a snake's skin or wiped out by anxiety-targeted penicillin.

It may be useful to think of SA/SP as part of our "personality," even though, strictly speaking, social anxiety is not a personality trait. This implies that hating our disorder is counter-productive and tantamount to hating ourselves. Trying to separate the disorder from who we are creates conflict. Our acceptance of it as an aspect of ourselves that we want to positively change makes that change easier and more likely. This shift in attitude paves the way for improvement.

But while we may make things better for ourselves and be able to function satisfactorily and enjoy life more, we shouldn't expect to be totally exorcised of this bedevilment. For this reason we really need to think of treatment in terms of "recovery," not "cure."

Recovery is not an event like the Fourth of July or Christmas or Passover. It's a series of steps and tasks. It's a journey which leads us out of chaos and despair into the Promised Land. Like any other journey it requires our deciding on a destination, anticipating problems, and making careful preparations.

In this context it's also important to remember that for almost any change process, setbacks occur but they are **not** our fault. No one (except ourselves!) expects us to do it perfectly on our first try. It's both expected and normal to relapse many times before achieving a stable change. Each go-around shows improvement, teaches us what we need to do differently the next time, and gets us closer to recovery. And because of what we've already learned, we don't have to go back to the beginning, to start all over again. Relapse can occur at any stage and, indeed, appears to be a normal and necessary part of the overall process. For this reason we should not let this reality dishearten, depress, or discourage us.

A guiding principle of any type of recovery program is what Reinhold Neibuhr penned in the first stanza of his "Serenity Prayer":

> "God, grant me the Serenity to accept the things I cannot change;
> Courage to change the things I can; and the
> Wisdom to know the difference." (or, as one wag put it, "…The Wisdom to hide the bodies of the people I had to kill because they pissed me off.")

As self-efficacy psychologist Michael Aleksiuk suggests, acknowledging one's sense of powerlessness is the first step in understanding that we're not powerless at all, that we only *feel* that way. His 12-step approach "Powerlessness Anonymous" can be adapted for SA/SP.

You need to:

1. *Admit you feel powerless.*

2. *Believe feeling powerful could enhance your self-esteem.*

3. *Commit yourself to becoming more personally powerful.*

4. *Assess yourself, your good points, and what you want to change.*

5. *Accept that you need to change and share this need and desire with others.*

6. *Prepare yourself to use personal power to work on your negative thoughts, feelings, and behaviors.*

7. *Give yourself to the empowering process and change - don't fight it.*

8. *List those you've hurt or alienated with your SA/SP behavior.*

9. *Makes amends to those people. Forgive yourself and forget it.*

10. *Monitor SA/SP behavior and continue to make amends where necessary.*

11. *Reconnect with your intuition and common sense and use them.*

12. *Keep personal empowerment an ongoing process toward health, happiness, and recovery.*

The goal of recovery in SA/SP is personal empowerment or enablement. Through the recovery process presented in this book we'll examine our beliefs and determine our strengths and weaknesses. We'll learn how to let go of negative thoughts, such as irrational self-talk and cognitive distortion. We'll learn how to deep-six stress, guilt, shame, and fear. We'll learn how to terminate our dependence on others for security and self-worth. We'll learn how to increase our self-esteem, control, self-confidence, and social effectiveness. We'll learn how to be more accepting of our ups and downs as well as our human flaws. Recovery means our finally taking charge of our lives.

Stephen Schlesinger and Lawrence Horberg demonstrate that there are three stages, or "**E**"s, to the recovery process: Exasperation, Effort, and Empowerment. *Exasperation* is when we're in emotional pain, feeling isolated, and afraid of change. For SA/SPers it's a time when we're locked in a closet of shame, helplessness, hopelessness, and vulnerability. *Effort* is when we're going through the motions in order to survive, without a clear goal in mind. We're experimenting and exploring but unsure there's hope of achieving anything worthwhile. *Empowerment* is when we begin to live with meaning and purpose to our lives, with a sense of vitality. This is the time when we take risks and responsibility, make commitments, and become involved with others.

To better understand this let's look at each stage more closely. In the *exasperation stage,* our conflict interferes with our needs and pleasures. Most of what we do is safe, socially acceptable but bland. Addressing, much less fulfilling, our deepest needs seems, at this point, totally impossible. We're not even sure we know what would satisfy us. We may dream about having a romantic partner or satisfying job but not do much else. We find little about ourselves to be admired and believe that others feel the same about us. What strengths we have are not evident. In fact, when we can recognize a strength, we tend to dismiss it and label ourselves as an impostor. We do the same with our feelings. We either discount or deny them.

In the *effort stage,* we still see others doing things we perceive ourselves as yet unable to do, but we recognize our having succeeded at some things. We enjoy our success and even venture to share it with others, believing they'll admire our actions. We have made plans for improvement and have tentative confidence in them. Still not knowing how to appropriately evaluate our strengths, we depend, to some degree, upon the opinions of others. Our feelings now are less negative but fear, emptiness, and sadness cast a pall. Because we're skeptical about positive actions and events, we tend to blunt our positive feelings when we get good results.

In *empowerment stage*, we have achieved confidence in ourselves. We perceive others as less threatening and believe that whatever threats still lurk can be handled. We accept our faults, foibles, and idiosyncrasies, and cut others the slack they didn't seem to give us before we recovered. We still get confused but accept confusion not only as a human inevitability but also as a precursor to growth and change. No longer unable to stand up for our rights, we put aside aggression and passivity and begin to assert ourselves. In fact, we feel secure enough to share our personal feelings with others. At our fingertips now is a full-range of both positive and negative feelings.

Further, we have evolved a sense of purpose and self which allows us to follow our own values, take responsibility for our behavior, and withstand the pressure of disappointments. As our plans and dreams come together, we particularly enjoy the accomplishment because our dreams represent a true understanding of our needs. Commitment to challenges becomes important to us and we follow through on them.

Recovery can be thought of as a growth process. This is where we develop and mature emotionally, cognitively, and behaviorally over time. Graduation to the next step is predicated on mastering the step before. With this in mind we need to look at six basic questions which we should keep in mind as we work through recovery:

- *What kinds of experiences do I want right now?*
- *What actions would I admire in myself in this situation?*
- *What strengths that I have would be valuable in this situation?*
- *How do I feel right now?*
- *What am I doing right now?*
- *What do I expect?*

Edmund Bourne adds that in order to reach empowerment, or recovery, we must :

- *Take responsibility;*
- *Be motivated;*
- *Make a commitment to ourselves;*
- *Be willing to take risks;*
- *Define and visualize our goals.*

Responsibility. We must *take responsibility* for making our SA/SP situation better. This means discarding the bumper sticker that reads, "I assume full responsibility for my actions except the ones that are someone else's fault." Responsibility is the ability to fulfill our needs and to do it in a way that doesn't deprive others of the ability to fulfill their needs. It's learned and acquiring it is a complicated, lifelong problem. If it were easy to fulfill our needs, social anxiety would probably not exist as we know it today.

Taking responsibility for making our SA/SP better does **not** mean we caused or are responsible for its initiation. We need to tattoo across our forehead," My condition is **not** my fault." Placing blame on ourselves is an unproductive, no-win tactic in recovery. All it does is bog us down and immobilize us. On the contrary, we need to forgive ourselves for real, not imagined, errors and award ourselves the credit we deserve. We've done the best we could under the circumstances. Limited knowledge of the disorder and available resources set the boundaries on what we could achieve. But in spite of this, we're the ones who'll determine if we're going to continue to suffer with it or if we're going to make our life more productive and enjoyable without it.

When we're responsible, we do things which give us a feeling of self-worth and being worthwhile to others. But the push and pull of pride and self-condemnation make it difficult for us to see the connection between our behavior, thoughts, and feelings and the disorder, as well as between our behavior, thoughts, and feelings and our recovery. Not seeing the connection or shirking the responsibility for change makes it harder for us to face and overcome the problem.

It may be useful to think of "responsibility" as Jack Schwarz does: "Response-ability" is the ability to respond. Once we have it, we then have the power to change our behavior in the situation, to act constructively to benefit ourselves.

Responsibility also means that if we are to get what we want from life, we must master our destiny by making choices and decisions and standing by them. President Harry S Truman's succinct pronouncement applies: "The buck stops here." So if we make a mistake, we make a mistake. It's a fact of life. We're fallible human beings and fallible human beings make mistakes…lots of them.

I've made some doozies, like the time I was part of an informal awards ceremony at the college where I was doing my post-doctoral clinical studies. When the clinician who sponsored me introduced me to the college president, he extended his hand and asked what award I was to receive. I stood there, "Twilight Zone" theme music booby booby booby boobying in my ears, with my mouth agape. Rendered mentally comatose by my anxiety, I couldn't even think to feign deafness or an asthma attack. But the compulsion to respond was over-powering. Some place in the darker recesses of my brain a small voice commanded me to speak, to say something - anything. What unconsciously rolled off my tongue stopped the interaction cold: "Beats the hell out of me!" I said. The president did a double-take and my mortified sponsor whisked me away to find a sock to stuff in my mouth, an exorcist, or both.

We mustn't make excuses for our mistakes. We mustn't try to shift the blame to something outside ourselves ("The Devil made me do it!"). It's far easier and less painful in the long run to accept responsibility for an error, learn something from it, live with it, and move on. Even executives who make only 50% of their decisions correctly can be successful.

Since part of accepting responsibility is learning from our mistakes, we need to treat mistakes as occasions for learning. Even though we do learn through insight, most of our learning is through trial and error. The reality we should etch inside our skulls is that "we are not perfect and will never be." Believe it or not, other people, in general, really don't expect us to be perfect. Why? Because most other people tend to be more objective and realistic about our human limitations.

Ironically, however, while those others are allowing **us** this latitude, they too are expecting **themselves** to be more nearly perfect, much to their own disappointment. This is the *self-other expectancy paradox*. Expectations of **others** tend to be realistic, objective, and flexible, with reasonable standards. Expectations of **self** tend to be unrealistic, subjective, and rigid, with unreasonably high standards. Perfectionistic thinking isn't the exclusive domain of SA/SP.

According to philosopher and architect R. Buckminster Fuller, "Mistakes are sins only when not admitted." Accepting responsibility for our actions means allowing ourselves to be human and make errors. "If-onlys" apply only if we have the power to go back in time to alter events. But we don't. So we need to change what we can, stop dwelling on what we can't, put the issue aside, and get on with our recovery and life.

Motivation. *Motivation* is "the possibility of contemplating, determining, acting upon, and maintaining a specific strategy for change." This means, the greater our motivation, the greater our likelihood of actual adherence to the action plan. Motivation, however, does not appear to be a general trait. It isn't just sitting there waiting for us to apply it any time anywhere. Instead, it depends upon the specific situation, our relationships, and the environment. Growth psychologist Carl Rogers thinks of "motivation" as "...springing from a self-actualizing tendency of life itself, a tendency of the organism to flow into all the differential channels of potential development, insofar as these are experienced as enhancing." But even if we are "programmed" to develop ourselves in positive way, creating the motivation necessary to take recovery action steps is still not an easy task.

Before we can initiate any change, we must be motivated to put aside whatever rewards we're getting from our present behavior. For example, avoiding a negative social situation makes us feel better so we're likely to continue to do it. Likewise, being perceived by others as snobbish or a loner may keep us from having to deal with social interactions we don't want to participate in. But ours aren't the only rewards. Others may be rewarded by our SA/SP. For example, a partner who is authoritarian and controlling may like our being dependent on them for security and decision making. These payoffs, which are called "secondary gains," erect highly resistant barriers to recovery. By discovering our positive, non-avoidant intention, we can more easily accept our negative behaviors for what they are and be better able to identify positive substitute behaviors to meet those intentions.

We tend to do things when there are enough incentives to do them. When either there are no incentives, the incentives aren't strong enough, or there's punishment involved, we'll tend not to do them. Psychological pain will increase our motivation because change ultimately will decrease the pain. However, it can motivate us only if the pain of being helped is less than the pain of having the problem. If the reverse is true, we're likely to resist change.

Issues of intrinsic importance to us, like saving an intimate relationship, protecting our children, or not losing our home, will tend to motivate us, unless we're also severely depressed. Similarly, how much psychological and physical effort is demanded affects our motivation. If we need transportation, have to travel long distances, locate child-care, or don't have the money and time readily available to go through therapy, we'll feel less motivated. The easier the process is for us, the more likely we are to work at it.

Expectations of the likely results of a particular course of action also act as incentives. If we expect the positive results to outweigh the negative, we'll tend to be more motivated to work toward recovery. If, on the other hand, we expect the negative to take precedence, we'll resist efforts toward change. Negative expectation can also quickly become a self-fulfilling prophecy. If we anticipate and believe we won't do well, we won't do well. Unconsciously we'll set ourselves up to fail.

How much we require of ourselves makes a difference. If we demand too much, we may become demoralized and quit. But if we demand too little, we may see no progress and quit.

Other factors which interfere with our motivation are our beliefs. We may believe we're undeserving of a life without SA/SP. As if to punish ourselves, we hang onto guilt-inducing behaviors, such as failing to make a scheduled meeting and, therefore, disappointing our team. Or we may hurt ourselves in order to punish someone else, such as losing job after job so our parents, who were never there for us as children, have to be there now. We may also believe that there's too much to do to make any appreciable change. By dwelling on what's entailed and the time it will take, we discourage ourselves and keep the process from ever starting. Furthermore, we are less likely to change if those in our lives make it easier for us to continue with the problem, make it seem normal, ignore it, or protect us from the consequences of it.

Commitment. We must *make a commitment to ourselves to do it and follow through* with the effort once we begin. Commitment is our strong motivation to bind ourselves to our decision to adopt or resist some idea or action. When we commit, we create beliefs which sustain future related ideas, activities, or involvement. Commitment means change. Once we make a behavioral commitment, our attitude change is likely to follow. For example, if we start setting up recovery goals, we're likely to come to believe we're doing it because we think it's important and useful. We're also likely to start using ingenuity to interpret and implement this change in a way that ensures success.

Commitment means our publicly acknowledging that our recovery requires constant attention. The more public we make it, the more committed we'll feel.

Writing down our intention to recover and giving it to those important to us creates a strong social incentive to continue.

Our recovery requires frequent and consistent practice of all the effective techniques, skills, and strategies available to us. It's like our preparing for the Boston Marathon. We'd have to work out every day, doing our running, then doing our weight training. First working on this group of muscles, then working on that, but always working on breathing, relaxation, nutrition, coordination, and timing. Commitment is essential because the motivation required to lift ourselves back into the sunlight is difficult to sustain over the long haul.

Taking risks. We must be *willing to take risks*. To experiment with and to explore our feelings, behavior, and life is to take a big risk. Not taking risks means doing things the same way. It's knowing what's going to happen all the time, rigidly adhering to a life plan we can count on. The result is a life which offers no surprises, no challenges, no growth, just sameness. This predictability provides some semblance of security to those of us wallowing in insecurity, like an insurance policy.

But as we know, in reality no such plan can exist because it requires the outside world to conform to our wishes. It mandates that no one ever require us to give a presentation, participate in a group, stand in a line at the bank, go to school, eat in a restaurant, use a public bathroom, or sign a check in front of others. Like it or not, we have little control over those things that happen outside ourselves. We can't always predict and control the behavior of others or find a job or relationship that's totally satisfying. Trying to make the world conform to our expectations is an exercise in frustration and futility.

External security is a myth. As Helen Keller said, "Security does not exist in nature. ...Avoiding danger is no safer in the long run than outright exposure. Life is either a daring adventure or nothing." The only real security we have is internal security. Our confidence in ourselves to adapt and survive-to-succeed.

Our inability or reluctance to try something new results from our fear. It can be fear of failure, disapproval, humiliation, rejection, abandonment, loss of self-esteem, and loss of love. It results from our concern with loss of control and predictability of the situation. We respond with avoidance and look for old, familiar ways to accomplish our goals rather than attempt new ones. In fact, when we feel uncertain or confused in social situations, we're more likely to identify and use prototypic, or routine, actions, rather than those that would be most successful in the situation.

The problem with doing the same old thing is that our standard operating procedure in SA/SP simply will not work in all social situations. Trying to fit this procedure into each new situation often leads to further feelings of dissatisfaction. While we may be comfortable with the process, we're uncomfortable with the product. We're still left with uncertainty, dread, and stress. If we're unwilling to meet our fears head-on, we won't be able to conquer them.

It's important to remember that even when the amount of risk taking seems small, the benefits derived can be significant. Robert Frost crystallizes this awareness in his poem "The Road Less Taken,"

> "Two roads diverged in a wood, and I—
> I took the one less traveled by,
> And that has made all the difference."

Goal visualization. We must *define and visualize our goals* for recovery. We need to ask ourselves

- *What are your goals, that is, the most important positive changes you want to make?*

- *What do you need to achieve those goals?*

- *What are your expectations of how you'll feel, think, and act when you've achieved them?*

It's important to make our goals and expectations as concrete and specific as possible. We need to be able to identify with and relate to them, to hold and examine them as if they were a diamond we're about to polish. We need to be able to experience the final faceted gem with all our senses. The road to recovery isn't always smooth. There will be frost heaves, pot holes, and boulders to recognize and get beyond. One such obstacle is ambivalence.

Ambivalence. *Ambivalence* is a state of mind wherein we have coexisting but conflicting feelings or thoughts about something. "I want to, but I don't want to." We feel it when we seek help for our SA/SP. One part of us says, "I need to get help. I want to behave differently," but the other part counters out of fear, "But it's not that serious." Or "I'd better wait until I'm feeling better." In a therapeutic encounter, for example, we can see the effect of our ambivalence where we can go from feeling vulnerable to defiant back to vulnerable in only a matter of minutes. We can see it too in our everyday interactions where we feel unhappy and lonely. We want to be with people in a closer relationship yet fear rejection because we feel we won't be perceived as attractive or worthwhile.

We are both attached and attracted to our problematic behavior. We're not exactly sure what we should do about the situation because the problem offers us positive rewards. The degree of conflict we experience, from severe to minor, will vary with the individual. It can either increase or decrease over time. The more attached we are to the behavior the more difficult it is to move away from it. A good way to think of this conflict is an *approach-avoidance* situation. This is where we are simultaneously both attracted to and repelled by aspects of our SA/SP. If it weren't so serious, if we didn't feel so stressed and stuck, it would be almost funny. Yes...no. Yes...no. All our cognitions, emotions, and behaviors are locked up in this ambivalence. Even though this is a normal part of the process, we end up feeling like a yo-yo.

Occasionally we find ourselves in an *approach-approach* situation. This is where we're torn between two equally attractive alternatives, such as having many comfortable social acquaintances or several intimate relationships. And sometimes we find ourselves in an *avoidance-avoidance* situation. This is where we have to choose between two equally unpleasant alternatives, such as feeling suicidal at home or going to school. The last two types of these conflicts, however, are less likely to be at the core of our ambivalence than *approach-avoidance*.

Sometimes our ambivalence is misinterpreted by others. Some may actually think it represents a mental-, personality-, or judgment problem. Often others consider our uncertainty, irrespective of it cause, as merely unacceptable. When this interpretation occurs, whether it's by family, friends, coworkers, bosses, teachers, physicians, or therapists, those individuals will believe we need to be confronted, educated, persuaded, and overtly directed. But when we're approached this way in our state of ambivalence, we tend to dig in our heels. We become resistant and even more entrenched in defense of our problem.

It's important to remember that the competing sides of our conflict each have both perceived costs and benefits. For example, recovery from SA/SP means we have to go through a lot of fear and pain (-) in order to have more friends, work at a job, but we can enjoy life more (+). Not recovering from our disorder means we stay lonely, have difficulty working and maintaining financial independence (-), but we don't have to expose ourselves to fear and pain or give up our protective devices (+).

This is similar to the story about a Southern Congress member who was asked about his attitude toward whiskey. He replied,

"If you mean the demon drink that poisons the mind, pollutes the body, desecrates family life, and inflames sinners, I'm against it. ...But if you mean the elixir of Christmas cheer, the shield against the winter chill, the taxable potion that puts funds in the public coffers to comfort little crippled children, then I'm for it. This is my position and I will not compromise!"

The value of each item in the conflict may shift over time from positive to more or less positive, negative to more or less negative, positive to negative, or negative to positive. As a result, sometimes we'll be willing to try, and other times we just won't care. We seem to seesaw, going back and forth, making ourselves crazy. When we're in this mode, it doesn't take long before we begin to think there's something wrong with our decision-making capabilities. We ask, "What's the matter with me? Why can't I understand?" We're left confused and frustrated by this normal state of affairs.

Finding the key to motivation

People often think that self-esteem is the key to motivation and recovery from SA/SP. While bolstering self-esteem may be useful and occasionally a necessary prerequisite to creating motivation, self-esteem is not the real key to motivation.

Why is self-efficacy important?   The real key is self-efficacy. *Self-efficacy* is our expectation of success in the tasks we undertake. It's grounded in

self-confidence which is the positive appraisal we make of our personal assets and resources to master, or solve, problems and deal with threats. It's our belief in our ability to carry out plans, reach goals, and succeed with our specific task or meet a challenge. It's also our belief in our ability to protect ourselves from harm and its consequences.

If we believe we can't accomplish something, we'll have no hope of achieving that goal. When there's no hope, we'll expend no effort. No effort means no change. But if we believe we have the ability to do it and that it's possible to do, we'll feel the hope, make the effort, and effect the change. Changes in self-efficacy cause changes in behavior and self-esteem. Studies have strongly demonstrated that increased self-efficacy leads to increased coping ability and decreased anxiety. This is particularly important where our activities depend upon our perceived competency level.

Self-efficacy has many benefits. It

• *Creates positive emotions;*

• *Increases effort;*

• *Improves concentration;*

• *Reinforces setting and pursuit of goals;*

• *Affects strategy;*

• *Increases psychological momentum.*

Even those of us who have low self-esteem will do it. This is demonstrated by approaches such as that employed by Alcoholics Anonymous which emphasize personal powerlessness over a problem but stress self-efficacy to change.

Social and cultural factors also affect all aspects of the recovery process. They affect how we feel and think about SA/SP. They suggest if we're to see it as a real dysfunction. As a mental or behavioral problem. As immaturity. Or as escapism. Those factors determine what labels are applied as well as the implications of using them. For example, labels carry a certain stigma in the public mind. Having a "mental illness" is seen more pejoratively than "being shy," "having stage fright" or the desire to avoid a social situation. Everyone can relate to and identify with some instance of shyness as a child and the stage fright of public speaking as an adult. Unlike "mental illness," they are seen as behaviors within the "normal" and "acceptable" range.

Social and cultural factors affect how we evaluate the costs and benefits of change, when it should occur and how. They affect our assignment of the responsibility for change, specifically whether the individual has the free will and competence to make decisions and bear the consequences of them. They also affect our willingness to commit to projects, others, and ourselves. Our family, friends, and community, likewise, all have an impact on the decisions we make, how we make them, and the values we adhere to in the process. Since these factors interact and influence us, we can't fully understand our motivation outside the social context.

Conflicts. As we begin to consider making a change, we move along a continuum from being vaguely unaware to being more fully aware of our conflicts. But the more aware we become the greater the ambivalence we experience. Then as we come to understand and work through our ambivalence, we come closer to determining what we want and making a decision. When we resolve our conflicts, our motivation emerges, and promotes our readiness for change.

So how do we resolve our conflicts? How do we decrease our ambivalence? How do we ignite our motivation? The first thing we need to do is express *accurate (or therapeuti)c empathy* for ourselves. By *empathy* here we don't mean putting ourselves in another person's shoes or fully understanding another's feelings, thoughts, or motives. This accurate empathy is the same as acceptance. Acceptance is telling ourselves and believing that we're okay. Conversely, non-acceptance is when we tell ourselves that if our behavior is bad, we're bad, and we *must* change (as opposed to "want to"). For real, stable change to occur it must come from within (intrinsic). It can't be from without (extrinsic). And, it can't be the result of coercion. When we feel genuinely accepted, we'll feel free to change.

To be accurately empathic we need to do three things:

• S*eparate ourselves from our behavior;*

• A*ssess our behavior non-judgmentally; then*

• A*ccept and respect ourselves irrespective of our behavior.*

In other words, we may hate the behavior, but we love the person. When we do this, we act to support our own self-esteem. We reinforce and perpetuate our notion of our worthiness. In essence what we're doing in this process is what we hope a therapist would do: Give us *unconditional positive regard.* That is, we're acknowledging that we have value and worth as a human being no matter what we do.

Unconditional positive regard is analogous to respect and love. It's a valuation of others for who they are. We all have a compelling and pervasive need to seek positive regard in order to make ourselves feel accepted, approved of, and loved. Unfortunately, we don't always receive it. In our infancy, for example, we may have received only conditional positive regard. Specifically, the love we received may have been conditioned upon our actions, like our "proper" behavior. So if we dropped our bottle out of the crib, we would have received disapproval. If we cried too much, we would have received disapproval. As a result, we would see love and positive attention predicated upon our doing the "right" thing. Then after a while, we would internalize this attitude and begin to even disapprove of ourselves when we acted in an "unacceptable" way. The message that would continue to ring loud and clear would be, "I'm okay *only* when I don't make mistakes."

The upshot of this is developing *conditions of worth.* These are the particular - the only - times when we feel worthy. For the child of demanding, perfectionistic parents one condition of worth is when she brings home an "A" on her test. Her worth as a child and human being is based upon her test grade. Anything less and she has no demonstrable value to those who matter to her.

When we perform unacceptable behaviors or perform acceptable behaviors badly, we feel guilty and unworthy, feelings we must defend against. When we feel defensive, we feel anxious. Carl Rogers says this defensiveness limits our freedom to interact fully and openly with our environment. It cuts us off from many experiences.

All this suggests that the primary requisite of a healthy personality is receipt of unconditional positive regard. Does this mean if we didn't secure it in infancy or early childhood, we're lost? No. We can still achieve it. One way to do this is to look at our behavior, thoughts and feelings the way an objective, nonjudgmental person would. Before we react to the substance of the behavior, thoughts, or feelings, we need to assess these elements and ask:

- *"Is it helpful to getting what I want?"*
- *"Is it true?"*
- *"What is its overall impact?"*
- *"Would I be acting this way if I didn't have SA/SP?"*

Joanna's Positive Regard Assessment

Joanna often found herself thinking, "I can't do anything right. I'm a failure." Assessing her thoughts, she answered each question as objectively as possible.

"Is it true?" *"No, not exactly. I do do some things right. For example, I tutored a high school student in math. I get good marks in college when I don't have to make presentations. I help save unwanted animals. I'm a loving daughter. I'm not really a failure because I have succeeded at achieving goals, like going back to college and making a living for myself."*

"Is it helpful to get what I want?" *"No, it just makes me feel bad and not want to try."*

"What is its overall impact?" *"It makes me less confident and worthy."*

"Would I be acting this way if I didn't have SA/SP?" *"Probably not. I'd feel pretty good about myself, working, making friends, and having fun. I wouldn't be beating up on myself or putting myself down."*

After doing this assessment, Joanna had to decide if she wanted to keep and repeat such thoughts. Her answer was, "No."

We can show ourselves this respect by seeing ourselves as unique human beings. We can care about our welfare and demonstrate a willingness to work toward it. We can become free of our present inhibition and the unreasonable expectations imposed by our parents and society. We can support our desire for self-determination and assume the best of our intentions. We can suspend critical judgment and take the time and effort to listen to what we're really saying to ourselves and about ourselves. We can become flexible and open to all new experiences, including formerly-threatening social situations. Once we become accepting of ourselves, we can address the discrepancies that make up our conflicts.

Making the recovery decision

According to turn-of-the-century psychologist William James, "There is no more miserable human being than one in whom nothing is habitual but indecision." Before we can make a change we have to have a solid foundation for it. We need to become acquainted with our expectations as well as the process and content of that change. Being able to identify what's happening to us at any given stage of recovery enables us to take steps toward positive and lasting improvement. The change process requires us to go through four basic steps:

• *Awareness*

• *Understanding*

• *Acceptance*

• *Change.*

No change can occur until there is *awareness* of the problem. Fritz Perls describes this as the "ah-ha" experience. The light bulb flashes on and we say, "yes, a problem exists and I want to do something about it."

Understanding comes from discovering something about not only the problem's present manifestation but also the problem's origin. This doesn't mean we have to have total insight into our intrapsychic processes or early experiences. It means we should have at least a clue: That we had specific traumatic experiences, that our parents suppressed our assertiveness, that we were shy or hypersensitive as a child. Understanding, then, is an integration of new and old knowledge. It's our seeing how they interact. It's our realizing that the whole of our problem is greater than the sum of its parts.

Acceptance is taking responsibility for the change, being both willing and able to respond. *Change* is a decision-making process which starts with inspiration and ends with implementation and success.

Starting the decision-making process

Henry David Thoreau encapsulated the idea of recovery when he said, "If you build castles in the air, you need not be lost; that is where they should be. Now put foundations under them." Decision making puts that foundation under our dreams, wishes, hopes, and plans for the future. To initiate the decision-making process we first need to assess the information that is available:

• *What are the viable alternatives from which to choose?*

• *What is the predicted outcome of each alternative?*

When the problem is simple and the outcome of each alternative is known because information is available, the decision we have to make is generally *routine*. For example, our physician asks if we want to increase our medication. We've been on 20 mg/day and find it working well, so we decide not to change dosage.

When the problem is more complex but the outcome of each alternative can be computed because information is available, the decision is straightforward and *analytical*. For example, if we wanted to estimate the statistical probability of maintaining our B+ in our history class while skipping an oral presentation, we could employ a probability formula and plug in information about our grade so far, what percentage of the grade the presentation represents, the number of tests remaining and their percentage of the grade.

These types of decision making are well-informed, certain, structured, and objective. As such, they involve little risk. However, when we address SA/SP recovery, we have to make decisions in the absence of complete information. In this situation it's not clear what the outcomes of each of our possible actions will be. It's likely that each alternative has several possible outcomes, not just one. Our recovery decisions are subjective or *judgmental*. Nothing is certain. There is no pre-determined structure to follow. Moreover, it's not obvious exactly what each of us has to do to achieve our goal.

Choices. For each problem we have a set of choices for actions. These are possible ways we can achieve our goals. What we do and what we are is the result of these choices. Since the key to our success is recovery, we need to choose a recovery that's right for us, not necessarily what works for others. To repeat, one size doesn't fit all. Each of us is a unique individual with a unique combination of needs, desires, thoughts, beliefs, attitudes, values, feelings, behaviors, physiological responses, experiences, and life circumstances. These all have to be factored into the mix.

We have only some information about the outcomes of these choices. To assess and evaluate the relative merits of the choices available, we must recognize their limitations. For example, do we want to try medication, therapy, both, or neither as part of our recovery. Medication doesn't work on cognitive distortions but it does have fairly rapid effects. Cognitive-behavioral therapy doesn't provide immediate relief but is provides enduring relief. Together they're twice as expensive but potentially more effective. Self-help doesn't work for everyone but it offers us more control over the process.

We must then establish our preferences and our means of dealing with them and their uncertainty. All decisions on our choices have varying degrees of risk. The degree of risk depends primarily on our goals and the environment in which the decision is being made. As we go through this rational assessment process, we determine the value (perceived contribution to our goal attainment) of the various alternatives.

It's important to remember that since we can't be sure of the consequences of any given action, we can't make a perfectly rational decision. What we want to strive for is "good enough." This, of course, is not easy when many of us SA/SPers suffer from the demands of perfectionism.

Level of risk. Decision making requires that we first distinguish between alternatives which have acceptable and unacceptable levels of risk. For example, we may be anxious to tell a new significant other about our SA/SP. What should we do? Three alternatives are (a) telling the person now and possibly losing the embryonic relationship - *unacceptable*, (b) waiting until the relationship is more secure before telling - *acceptable*, and (c) deciding that our significant other would never accept our problem anyway, therefore, we should act immediately to break off the relationship so as to avoid rejection later on - *unacceptable*.

Next we need to distinguish between real unacceptable risk and the irrational fear of taking any risk at all. Our fear of risk-taking is like the rest of the fears experienced in SA/SP, inappropriate, self-defeating, and arising from the inaccurate negative statements we make to ourselves. In other words, our risk-taking fear is likewise the result of distorted thinking.

When we're experiencing a negative mood like fear, we tend to employ more rigid strategies in dealing with social situations than if we're in a positive mood. The more positive we are, the more flexible we are, and the more aware we are of multiple ways of dealing with the situation.

If, however, the fear of risk is not a big consideration for the given decision, then we can choose the alternative with which we feel comfortable. We need to choose an alternative, such as (b), that intuitively appears either to be "good enough" or to maximize our expected outcomes. Comfortable decisions strive to maximize the benefits and minimize the costs.

Risk taking is the ability to make decisions in the face of uncertainty of the outcomes. Reluctance to take risks drastically reduces our decision-making effectiveness. Taking moderate, calculated risks and trying new things is a prerequisite for recovery from SA/SP. Fear of risk-taking inhibits our ability to grow, develop, and achieve in all aspects of our lives. Consequently we need to reverse this thinking and become aware of how our emotions impact our thoughts and the exercise of self-control. A lot of things that seem like threats can be turned into opportunities. There's no such thing as a riskless recovery.

Risk-taking assessment

*To make decisions you need to ask yourself, "How willing am I to confront the unknown?" Test yourself by replying **Yes** or **No**.*

1. *Are you afraid to try a new activity because you can't do it well? You say, "I don't know what to do so I'll watch." Or you dismiss it by saying, "It's not a very intelligent thing to do anyway."*

2. *Do you stay with the same old job even though you dislike it because you feel apprehensive about exploring the unknown of a new job?*

3. *Do you find yourself unable to change your plan when an interesting alternative comes up, for fear that the new situation will not conform to the way you do things?*

4. *Do you hang around with the same group of friends or associates and never branch out to become acquainted with new and different people?*

5. *Do you hang back because of fear of what might happen if you started talking with a stranger on new topics?*

*If you answered **Yes** to any of the above questions, you need to look specifically at your risk-taking behavior. You need to determine the particular types of situations in which you are unwilling or reluctant to take risks.*

In order for us to make the decisions necessary for recovery we must:

• *Surrender the notion that it's better to tolerate the familiar than confront the unknown;*

• *Allow ourselves to be spontaneous and not cling to accustomed and standardized behavior;*

• *Allow ourselves to act independently rather than adhere to what we think is expected of us (by others, society, and ourselves).*

Formulating risk-taking decisions

Taking risks isn't easy but it's essential. It involves knowing what to do and when to do it. Of course, knowing these things is rarely clear-cut. Thus, in order to do it we need to make our risks more calculated and better grounded. We can do this by perceptively assessing the problem, sizing up the situation, and recognizing the real risks involved and what's at stake. We need to become scientists, to look at ourselves under a microscope. "There's an erroneous belief. Sweep it away. There's a distorted thought. Push it aside. Oops, there's a cluster of negativity. Hasta la vista, baby."

We have to conceptualize the dimensions of the problem. We have to feel the urgency to solve it. We have to assess the probable consequences of not solving the problem. So to make moderate and calculated risk-taking decisions we must follow a logical process. This process requires that we:

• *Ask the right questions;*

• *Make rational assessment of the answers before acting.*

Once we've recognized that a problem exists and have identified it, we need to assess whether or not it's a situation for which we have a ready and appropriate solution or one that requires a subjective or judgmental approach.

Next we need to establish our goals. Generally speaking, a *goal* is a statement describing a long-range outcome we desire. *Objectives*, on the other hand, are the short-range steps that work toward our reaching our goal. Goals must be based in an understanding of ourselves and a determination of what resources and assets we have. Goals come from our heart and mind. So achieving our goal is the end-product of the problem-solving/decision-making process.

In setting goals we need to look at both the present and the future and ask ourselves:

- *What do I want to do or achieve now?*
- *What do I want to do or achieve in the future?*

Next we need to spell out *whats* and *whens* of those goals in clear, concrete, specific terms:

- *What exactly do I want?*
- *By what date do I want it?*

Goal-setting and -achieving are part of a solution-focused approach. To be solution-focused goals have to be

- *Positive (it's what we want, not what we "don't" want)*
- *Specific and concrete (we know the boundaries and substance)*
- *Attainable (it's within our control)*
- *Observable (we know what it is when we see it)*
- *Measurable (we can precisely determine that we've achieved it)*
- *Stated in terms of the present (it's what we want to do here and now)*
- *Action-oriented (it's stated in terms of what we'll be doing to achieve it).*

It's important to remember that once we're satisfied we know exactly what we want to achieve and when we want it, we need to determine what resources are necessary to actually achieve the goal. Do we already have all the resources we need? If not, who has them? How do we gain access to them?

For us to accomplish our goals it's essential that we not confuse wishes and complaints with goals. "I wish I could go to parties" or "I never meet anyone" won't get us any closer to being social. We have to translate wishes and complaints into what it is we want and are willing to go after. For example, "I wish I could go to parties" translates into "I want to go to parties." But what does that mean specifically and concretely? "I want to be able to feel comfortable talking with others." What does "feel comfortable" mean? "I want to feel less anxious and concerned about what others think." This then breaks down actually into two goals: (1) I want to reduce my physiological arousal in social settings and (2) I want to think positive thoughts about my self-presentation.

With our broad goals of our overall recovery established, we need to look next at our specific objectives. These are the immediate, intermediate, specific results we want. Saying we want to feel less anxious at work is a vague goal. Less anxious than what? On any given day we're less anxious than on some other day. By when will we know we've achieved it? Tomorrow, a month from now or next year? We have to put our objectives into well-defined behavioral terms with deadlines such as " "I want to give a 5-minute speech before my colleagues at work by the end of next month." This is a concrete, specific, realistic, and meaningful objective. Clearly we can determine if we've achieved it. These are the standards by which we'll judge the effectiveness of our decisions.

It's useful to think of our objectives in terms of the SA/SP problem components we'll be addressing, specifically the physiological, cognitive, emotional, and behavioral. For example, a physiological objective would be to "daily work on muscle relaxation, breathing exercises, and cutting out caffeine and sugar." A cognitive objective would be to "use positive self-talk whenever I think others are thinking I'm a failure." An emotional objective would be to "recognize my hostility, sarcasm, and anger in dealing with others." A behavioral objective would be to "construct a hierarchy of anxiety-provoking situations and gradually expose myself to them."

Then we need to compile a creative and complete list of all possible ways to handle each problem. They can be applications of new ideas to the situation to provide the desired response, existing ideas, **or** new combinations of existing ideas. For example, to handle the problem of relaxation we can do progressive muscle relaxation, yoga, transcendental meditation, biofeedback, self-hypnosis, visualization, and/or autogenic training. The permutations of all the different ways we can address relaxation are nearly endless.

When we look at each of our alternatives, we need to ask ourselves five important questions:

- *Does this alternative have some lasting value to me or my situation? Is it worth it?*

- *Does this alternative help me meet my objectives and goals either directly or indirectly? Will it further my recovery?*

- *Is this alternative an efficient and effective approach?*

- *Is this alternative necessary and sufficient to achieving my success in general or in this particular situation?*

- *How much control can I still exert to achieve what I want if I use this alternative? Or does this take the control out of my hands? How do I feel about it?*

It's important to remember that as we move through the five questions, we look for negative responses. These signal doubt about the appropriateness of the alternative. What we want are alternatives which generate positive responses for us. As we apply each of these questions, we begin our evaluation of each alternative.

Evaluation consists of looking for:

- *Effects*
- *Probability of desired/undesired effects*
- *Seriousness of these effects if they occurred.*

Finally we make our risk-taking decisions by selecting the intuitively-acceptable alternatives which offer us the:

- *Highest probability of working*
- *Highest desirability*
- *Highest number of positive outcomes*
- *Lowest number of negative outcomes.*

Decision making is a form of thinking-plus-intuition that results in making a choice among alternative courses of action for a desired result. At every turn in our recovery we have to make decisions. Decisions to work toward recovery. Decisions about how to do it. Big decisions and little decisions alike.

Decisions are action-oriented. They're the key to our flexibility to change. Our implementation of the chosen alternative will tell us if this solution will accomplish the goal and objectives we want. It'll tell us if our desire to achieve recovery is stronger than our risk-taking fear.

As the Koran says, "If you don't know where you're going, any road will get you there."

Developing a general timeline for achievement of objectives gives us something to which to refer and helps keep us on track. We need to specify how long it reasonably will take us to accomplish those objectives. To do this properly we need to be detailed. Therefore, we must write out as much as is necessary to communicate what we want to achieve. But all this verbiage is cumbersome, so we need to go back over and over, distilling our objectives to a sentence, then a sentence fragment, finally to a phrase. The more concise and precise they are the easier it'll be to remember and achieve them. It's also helpful to list our goals and objectives both in order of priority and chronologically. Priority shows us what must be done when and chronology guides our everyday efforts toward it.

Recovery Timeline

Today's Date_____

Goal	Time Needed	Deadline
1. Read book on SA/SP	*1 week*	*May 15*
2. Make appointment with therapist	*3 weeks*	*June 5*
3. Start relaxation exercises	*4 weeks*	*June 15*

Problem solving model

Phase I - Problem recognition

　　　1. *Identifying, defining, and assessing problem*

　　　2. *Committing self to solving problem*

　　　3. *Generating list of alternative solutions to problem*

4. *Evaluating alternatives*

    a. Concrete and specific

    b. Observable and measurable

    c. Achievable

    d. Risk-level

    e. Likelihood of success

    f. Gut-level reaction.

Phase II - Decision making

1. *Deciding on solution*

2. *Prioritizing elements of solution*

3. *Putting elements in workable, meaningful order*

4. *Creating program to implement solution.*

Phase III - Acting

1. *Creating a timeline*

2. *Implementing solution actions*

3. *Observing, recording, measuring, and analyzing action outcomes*

4. *Evaluating progress.*

How can we become risk takers? We become risk takers by learning and practicing risk-taking behaviors. This learning process begins with our awareness that

- *Our fear exists.*

- *Trying new things can be beneficial.*

Over time we can learn to treat stumbling blocks as stepping stones. Peak performers, for example, treat real failure and rejection as only temporary setbacks. We too can choose to replace fear of risk taking with new, exciting activities to bring growth, development, and pleasure to our lives through recovery.

Change guidelines

1. *Know yourself and your personal resources: Your time, skill, and courage.* Over-extension of ourselves leads to stress, burnout, hostility, increased anxiety and depression, negativity about change, and resistance.

2. *Think through the desired change and make certain you're willing to go through with it.* Stopping in the middle is generally perceived negatively,

as a failure, and may only make matters worse. "If it isn't worth doing, it isn't worth doing well."

3. *When you decide to change, do it well; that is, pull out all the stops and leave no stone unturned.* "If it's worth doing, it's worth doing well."

4. *Plan and arrange your recovery.* We can't sit back and wait for things to happen. Opportunities don't just knock and recovery doesn't just happen to us. We create opportunities and we create recovery by participating and effecting change.

5. *Don't try to do too much too fast.* A slower, steadier pace of exercises, practice, new experiences, and rewards will chip away at SA/SP. Think baby steps.

6. *Know and accept the tradeoffs necessary for your change to materialize, such as money, time, effort, discomfort.*

7. *Visualize what your recovery ideally would be like.* We need to see how specifically our life may change for the better. Looking at different aspects of our lives, we ask ourselves how we'll think, feel, and act. We focus on those areas which are important to us (such as, family, relationships, job, school, activities) and picture the details of that problem-free existence. We do this in a relaxed state and practice it daily to increase our confidence in a successful recovery.

It's important for us to document the entire recovery process. We've listed and scheduled our goals and objectives through our Recovery Timeline. But this is not enough. We also need to keep track of what specific tasks we're doing to meet those goals. We need to monitor our intermediate progress. We can do this by keeping a journal of our daily progress notes. A loose-leaf notebook is often best because it uses 8 ½" x 11" paper, which is useful for diagrams, lists, charts, and calendars, and allows us to add items easily and shift materials around. The notes will detail what we've done, when we did it, and any changes that have occurred. It will also detail "successes" (when things worked out well because of our recovery program) and "stalls" (when things didn't work out because we backslid). The successes and stalls highlight change that's occurring, where we need to continue what we're doing, or change, and where we need to put in more effort.

Daily Progress Notes

*Today's Date*_____

Week's Goals: *1.*

       2.

       3.

                       M   T   W   Th   F   Sat   Sun

Physical -   Do muscle relaxation

Do abdominal breathing
Cut out caffeine
Cognitive - Practice self-talk
Emotional - Listen for anger
Behavioral - Work on hierarchy
Positive changes:
Backslides:
Proposal to correct backslides:

Need for balance

Our recovery generally isn't the result of our focusing on a single area of our lives. For most of us our SA/SP shows up in and impacts our overall personal satisfaction, all our interpersonal relationships, our participation in community, our education and careers, and how we conduct our lives. All these areas contribute to our sense of well-being and level of functioning. As a result, we need to make sure we include all these areas in our recovery plan.

Recovery

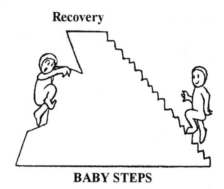

BABY STEPS

Recovery has three criteria which must be met for it to be said to have taken place. The first criterion is *objective*: Our SA/SP symptoms and avoidance must have reduced significantly or disappeared. The second is *adaptive*: We must have achieved a level of functioning which permits us to express our potential. And the third is *subjective*: We must perceive our having achieved a state of well-being. Personal change requires time, effort, perseverance, and courage. To lose sight of this fact is to doom ourselves to disappointment. But, as Abraham Lincoln said, "The best thing about the future is that it comes one day at a time."

CHAPTER 6

TARGETING AROUSAL

"What does the baby chick know which we overlook? The shell around us won't crack of it own accord." (Anonymous)

What does psychological treatment entail?

Is there a single treatment, psychological or pharmaceutical, that's best for SA/SP? Even though researchers and clinicians tend to have their own pet theories which they strongly defend, nothing has demonstrated that one, and only one, exists.

SA/SPers aren't an homogeneous group. We aren't anxious for the same reasons. We have different personalities and backgrounds which may require different approaches. For example, degree of introversion or extroversion will affect our comfort with specific approaches.

Another important reason that no one treatment is best is that irrespective of treatment modality, when we're motivated to recover and expect to improve, we're likely to do better than when we aren't. This suggests that most credible psychological interventions will provide *some* benefit. It would then follow that when we're motivated and have many credible interventions available to us with which to deal with the physiological, cognitive, emotional, and behavioral factors of SA/SP, we're likely to do better. This is, in part, because we're able to individualize our treatment.

Psychological interventions that are the most commonly used for SA/SP fit into four general approaches, according to the factor they address:

- *Physical (arousal)*
- *Cognitive-Affective (thoughts and feelings)*
- *Behavioral*
- *Social skills (assertiveness, interpersonal relations).*

This chapter deals with the physical approach and arousal.

Relaxing with physical techniques

Relaxation techniques are based on the premise that our physiology forms not only a major component but also the very foundation of our anxiety. According to William James, "The greatest thing then in all education is to make the nervous system our ally instead of our enemy." When we anticipate a "fight or flight" situation, we automatically and involuntarily tense our muscles in preparation for action. Simultaneously, our rate of breathing increases to meet the additional demand for oxygen by the brain. Blood moves into larger muscles, making it easier for us to run. These two bodily functions are also under our conscious control and, thus, can be used to modify our arousal.

Therefore, in order to reduce our arousal, to calm and relax ourselves, and to reduce our anxiety, we have to reduce our physiological manifestations of it. Specifically, we have to lower our increased

- *Heart rate*
- *Respiration rate*
- *Blood pressure*
- *Muscle tension*
- *Oxygen consumption*
- *Alpha brain wave activity.*

The various physical techniques are designed to provide us with a method of coping with them. The goal is to monitor and recognize early signs of our anxiety, cope with them before they snowball, then counteract the arousal symptoms. The specific techniques are:

- *Muscle relaxation*
- *Autogenic training*
- *Abdominal (diaphragmatic) breathing*
- *Visualization*
- *Meditation*
- *Biofeedback*
- *Physical exercise.*

Common to many of these techniques is what Harvard Medical School-affiliated mind-body expert Herbert Benson calls the "relaxation response." This relaxation response came about because the innate human response of "fight or flight" generally can't be acted upon in our everyday lives. As a result, we have had to psychologically adjust to the demands of those situations, leaving ourselves in a state of tension-filled readiness. What Benson found is that irrespective of the relaxation strategy, whether meditation or progressive muscle relaxation, there are four shared ingredients which make them beneficial and effective. Those elements are having a:

1. *Situation or environment which is quiet and without interference.*
2. *Word, phrase, or sound which can be repeated over and over.*
3. *Passive attitude in order to disregard intrusive, distracting thoughts.*
4. *Position which is comfortable.*

Relaxation techniques are most effective when we have the opportunity to practice the skills in the social situations in which we experience the anxiety. This means that we need to learn the technique, recognize early signs of our physiological arousal, then apply the training before, only sometimes during, and after anxiety-provoking social situations.

Progressive muscle relaxation. Relaxation involves learning to alternately tense and relax various muscle groups until we are capable of voluntarily arriving at a state of deep muscular relaxation. This is a state which is diametrically opposed to that characterized by our anxiety. Devised by Edmund Jacobson in 1938, the method has been used successfully to slow heart, pulse, respiration, and lower blood pressure rates.

The calming effects of the relaxation strategy are concomitants and consequences of our *voluntary* efforts to decrease our muscle tension. Experiments have shown that when muscle relaxation was induced non-voluntarily or passively by injection of a curare-like drug, there was no calming effect on the individual's anxiety. In addition, as behaviorist Joseph Wolpe states, there's a definite relationship between the extent of muscle relaxation and the production of emotional changes opposite those of anxiety.

Progressive muscle relaxation technique requires no necessary sequence of steps, but whatever sequence we adopt should be orderly.

You should begin by finding a comfortable place and position in which to relax. The surface on which you'll perform the exercise should be neither too hard as to be uncomfortable nor too soft as to induce sleep. Clothing should be loose and non-distracting. Undoing belts and other constricting apparel is useful. You should remove your shoes. Lying on your back is an ideal position if it's comfortable and convenient for you. A small pillow under your neck and one under your knees (this is particularly important if you have a history of low-back strain) may be more comfortable. In the absence of a knee cushion, you can flex your knees slightly and achieve the same effect. You should avoid falling asleep since the goal of the exercise is to consciously experience relaxation. Keep distraction and disturbances to a minimum. This includes animals, children, television, radio, sunlight, clocks, telephone, and pagers.

*You're going to tighten certain muscle groups and study the sensations that come from these muscles when they're tense. Then you're going to relax them and notice what changes occur and how they are different. (Note: **Individuals with physical problems, infirmities, or limitations should consult their physician before doing these exercises.**)*

It's important to note that as you begin to practice this exercise, intrusive thoughts will occasionally interfere with your focus. Sometimes a lot. Sometimes a little. This is a normal part of the process and is to be expected. You must look upon the interruptions with dispassion so as not to further distract yourself. You shouldn't take this intrusion personally. Their presence isn't due to your weakness. At this point, you simply have no control over them. They are a normal occurrence.

What you need to do about these thoughts is calmly, gently push them aside, telling yourself you'll deal with them later, set a specific time, then resume the exercise where you left off. And if the intrusion recurs, and it will, you should simply repeat the process. Whatever you do don't allow yourself to become angry or frustrated. That will erase all you've accomplished up to that point and you'll have to start over completely.

Over the coming weeks, you'll find the intrusions gradually fading away as the relaxation deepens. Remember, relaxation comes at its own speed and it can't be forced. Your being patient and passive will allow it to deepen more rapidly.

Start by clenching your right fist while keeping all other muscles of the body relaxed. Study the feelings of tension, where they start, and how they flow. Note the location of the muscles when tensed. Hold the constriction for about 10 seconds. Relax the arm totally, letting the tension drain away, leaving the arm feeling heavy with relaxation. Now do the same procedure with your left fist.

You're going to work from your hands and forearms to your upper arms, shoulders, upper back and chest, lower back and abdomen, pelvis and buttocks, thighs, lower legs, and feet. Then you'll travel to your neck and throat, head and face, eyes and jaw. (Note: Beware of muscle cramps particularly in the legs and feet when tensing muscles.)

In each muscle group concentrate on locating separate muscles. See how many you can find. Tense and relax each. These muscle actions should even include raising eyebrows, wiggling ears, frowning, wrinkling the nose, retracting the upper lip, puckering the mouth, and clenching the teeth. Muscles that need special attention are the head, neck, shoulders, and jaw. (Note: If you've chosen to do this exercise sitting in a chair, relaxing the neck muscles may make your head fall forward. The head's weight pulling on the muscle fibers that are still contracted may result in discomfort or pain.) Continual practice should lead to relaxation of these neck muscles as well, allowing the chin to rest on the breastbone comfortably. If, however, this forward thrust of the head is too uncomfortable, you can practice relaxing with the back of your head resting against a high-back chair.

When you finish this sequence, consciously relax your whole body, starting at your toes and working your way to the top of your head. Tell yourself that your muscles are becoming heavy with relaxation. Visualize each of your muscle groups as white, knotted, and cool-feeling. As you further relax them, visualize the muscles as unknotting, becoming smoother, longer. As the blood can flow more freely through them as you relax, you see them as becoming redder, warmer, and heavier. See the relaxed muscles as large rubber bands, hanging loosely between bone attachments. See your whole body as limp.

Practice this relaxation technique for 30 minutes per day every day for at least a month to develop the skill. You need to expect only limited success when you're first attempting to relax. Good relaxation takes time.

You can tape record a step-by-step description of what you're doing to play back. Or you can memorize the sequence of exercises for daily recall. (SA/SPers frequently are more comfortable, at least initially, having the tape direct us so we don't disrupt our concentration by worrying about remembering the next step.)

It's important to note that progressive muscle relaxation *by itself* is considered to be of little value in the treatment of SA/SP. Its primary usefulness is with anticipatory anxiety. In general, it should be thought of as setting the stage and removing the barriers of stress, so that other techniques can be acted upon. This means muscle relaxation is necessary to SA/SP recovery but not sufficient.

Autogenic training. Developed by psychiatrist Johannes Schultz in 1910, autogenic training, also called autosuggestion, is a systematic program to teach our minds and bodies to respond to verbal commands to reduce our arousal. It does this by inducing specific physical sensations that are associated with relaxation. This is not the same as autohypnosis, or self-hypnosis, because we do not actually hypnotize ourselves in this process. In hypnosis we go into a trance-like state which is characterized by a narrowing of consciousness. While both the hypnotic and autogenic states are "waking" phenomena, hypnosis relies on active concentration while the autogenic process relies on passive concentration.

Autogenic training allows us to take the characteristics of a relaxed body (with increased blood flow where the blood flows freely) and superimpose them on our tense body (with decreased blood flow where the flow is constricted). By using phrases to suggest the sensations, we come to feel the warmth that we associate with blood flowing throughout the body. We come to feel the heaviness we note when our muscles are relaxing.

The key to this process is making suggestions and allowing our body to respond. If we try to consciously control our body, to make it feel what we want it to, we'll fail. Trying too hard creates excess tension which only adds to the stress we're trying to relieve. To be successful we have to let go, to give in to the relaxation. This is often very difficult for us SA/SPers because we need to feel in control.

What autogenic training produces is a state of relaxation which is physiologically identical to that induced by meditation and other Eastern techniques. Where autogenic training differs from Eastern techniques is in its focus on physical sensation and not on abstract mental states. What makes this easy to perform is that it involves concrete tasks and experiences and provides immediate feedback. We can feel if it's working.

Because the technique is easy to learn and easy to do, success occurs rapidly with practice. We can employ it any time we start to feel tense or anxious. We can do it in the car at a stop light, on the bus, at our desk at work, in a restaurant, in line at the grocery store, before a social gathering, or in bed before going to sleep. Autogenic training has been used in conjunction with biofeedback as a means of directing attention and obtaining relaxation when a biofeedback instrument isn't available.

You can perform autogenic training when you're either sitting or lying down. If you choose to sit, you should sit comfortably but straight in a straight-back chair with your knees bent at slightly more than a 90-degree angle, with feet planted firmly on the floor, slightly ahead of the knees. In this position as you relax, you'll tend to crumple straight down with your neck bent forward. You should place your arms on top of your legs, with your hands just behind the knees, with fingers spread apart. This position is thought to create the least muscular tension.

*If you choose to lie down, lie flat on a bed or the floor, with a pillow supporting your neck and knees. Let your legs spread slightly and place your arms away from your body, palms on floor with fingers apart. If you're chilly, cover yourself with a light blanket. If you find that lying down makes you more likely to fall asleep, assume the sitting position. Wolfgang Luthe in **Autogenic Training** suggests that this technique be done before meals or in the afternoon, whenever there is less likelihood of your falling asleep as a result. To prevent interruption or distraction, choose a time when you're likely to have quiet. It may be easier to use a tape recording of the exercise while you're learning the progression, although many continue to use it as a matter of course. This allows you not to have to think about it at all.*

As with progressive muscle relaxation, you want to let extraneous thoughts flow away. You want to become totally involved in the physical sensations and nothing more. Check to see that you're breathing slowly, deeply, and evenly. Make sure you're comfortable before you begin. The basic procedure requires that you say each phrase three times slowly, pausing between each repetition, then go on to the next.

Start by telling yourself, "I feel relaxed and calm. I'm feeling more and more relaxed." Note how your body feels as you say it.

Focus on your limbs and feel their heaviness. Start with the right side of your body if you're right-handed, or the left if you're left-handed. Concentrate on you right arm and tell yourself, "My right arm is heavy. It's getting heavier and heavier."

Concentrate on your left arm, telling yourself, "My left arm is heavy. It's getting heavier and heavier."

Tell yourself, "Both my arms are heavy." Note how they feel.

Concentrate on your neck and shoulders, telling yourself, "My neck and shoulders are heavy. They're getting heavier and heavier." Note how they feel.

Concentrate on your right leg and tell yourself, "My right leg is heavy. It's getting heavier and heavier."

Concentrate on your left leg, telling yourself, "My left leg is heavy. It's getting heavier and heavier."

Tell yourself, "Both my legs are heavy. My arms and legs are heavy. I feel calm and relaxed." Note how you feel.

Focus on your limbs and feel their warmth. Concentrate on you right arm and tell yourself, "My right arm is warm. It's getting warmer and warmer."

Concentrate on your left arm, telling yourself, "My left arm is warm. It's getting warmer and warmer."

Tell yourself, "Both my arms are warm." Note how they feel.

*Concentrate on your shoulders, telling yourself, "My shoulders are warm. They're getting warmer and warmer." **(Note that the neck area is being omitted from warming for those who are susceptible to headache related to dilated blood vessels.)***

Concentrate on your right leg and tell yourself, "My right leg is warm. It's getting warmer and warmer."

Concentrate on your left leg, telling yourself, "My left leg is warm. It's getting warmer and warmer."

Tell yourself, "Both my legs are warm."

Tell yourself, "My arms and legs are warm. I feel calm and relaxed." Note how it feels.

Concentrate on your abdomen, telling yourself, "My abdomen is warm and relaxed."

Concentrate on your heart beat, telling yourself, "My heart rate is regular and calm."

Concentrate on your breathing, telling yourself, "My breathing is regular and calm."

*Concentrate on your head, telling yourself, "My head feels relaxed. My forehead is cool." **(Note that the head is treated in a similar fashion to the neck with respect to warmth. Excessive blood flow in the head may trigger a migraine headache in some people.)***

Concentrate on your entire body again, telling yourself, " I feel relaxed and calm. I am relaxed and calm. My whole body feels quiet, comfortable, and relaxed. I feel quiet. My mind is quiet. My thoughts are quiet. I am relaxed."

Finish the exercise by bringing yourself back to full wakefulness. Tell yourself, "I'm feeling refreshed. I'm feeling alert. I'm awake and ready to resume my day." Say this slowly three times, then take several deep breaths, stretch your arms and legs, slowly open your eyes. When you feel ready, get up and move around. You should practice autogenic training at least once a day. It may take a month before you achieve a state of deep relaxation.

Abdominal (diaphragmatic) breathing. As noted previously, our breathing responds to our arousal. The tenser we become, the more rapid and shallow our breathing becomes. We begin to breathe only in the upper portion of our lungs. This type of breathing reduces the oxygen supply to the brain and muscles. It stimulates the sympathetic nervous system which is associated with anticipation of threat. The mind races and we're unable to focus our attention. Shallow, rapid breathing produces poorly oxygenated blood which contributes to anxiety, depression, fatigue, and irritability. This results in exhalation of large amounts of carbon dioxide which can lead to hyperventilation and panic-like symptoms. These symptoms include palpitations, dizziness, a sense of unreality, shortness of breath, tingling in the lips and fingers, and increased heart rate. In its more severe form, hyperventilation can lead to unconsciousness.

Breathing is controlled only partly by our autonomic nervous system and partly by our voluntary nervous system. This is why we're able to consciously control our breathing to some degree. By breathing slowly, deeply, and rhythmically, we can relax. Since the autonomic nervous system also controls our emotions, we can influence our emotions by controlling our breathing.

*(**Note: If you have asthma, emphysema, or other lung problems, consult with your physician before initiating this exercise.**) Sit in a reclining position*

where you can rest your head, back, and shoulders or lie down, whichever is more comfortable. Rest your hands on your upper abdomen. Your hands will act as monitors of correct movement of your diaphragm as you breathe. Close your eyes.

Inhale slowly through your nose to the count of six (if you can't reach six, aim at four). As you draw air into your lungs, you should be pushing it down toward your lower abdomen. This should make your lower abdomen it rise. Inhalation should be slow, unhurried, and unforced. When inhalation is complete, pause for 2-3 seconds, then slowly exhale. As you exhale through your nose to the count of six, you should push from your abdomen as if you were shoving out the air. This should make your abdomen fall. Carefully monitor your abdominal movement to determine if you're using your diaphragm properly.

Repeat the pattern 15-20 times. The exercise may take a total of five minutes. With this breathing sequence comes the total-body heaviness and warmth which accompanies relaxation. After completion of the exercise, become aware of your body and its sensations. Once you master the exercise, you can use it in any tense situation to reduce arousal. It will result in your increased ability to cope.

Biofeedback. Biofeedback training is like autogenic training in that it aims at general receptivity of ourselves to ourselves. But this training also teaches us to monitor our physiological responses, such as heart rate, blood pressure, muscle tension, skin temperature, and electrical activity of the brain. This is accomplished by means of a specialized instrument, a biofeedback machine, which converts our physiological activity (which is internal) into a bioelectric signal (which is external) and amplifies it so we can detect it.

This signal provides us with continuous external feedback regarding our autonomic responses. It's like when we check our pulse, we're monitoring our heart, thereby giving ourselves biofeedback. Biofeedback information helps us learn to bring our automatic responses under our voluntary control.

When we alter our visceral state or make it correctly match some predetermined criterion, we immediately receive visual or auditory feedback, indicating that the appropriate response has been made. The technique is frequently used in conjunction with tangible and social reinforcers that "reward" our having made the desired changes in our physiology.

The most commonly used type of biofeedback is *electromyographic* (EMG). Sensors attached to the skin reveal the electrical activity of nearby muscles, such as that related to muscle tension. By listening to a level of sound, the number of beeps, or by watching a readout screen, we can become aware of the degree of our tension and changes in it as we relax. Other types of biofeedback include *breathing patterns* which records the rhythm, rate, and volume of each breath; *finger pulse* which indicates heart rate; *electrodermal* (EDR) which measures perspiration level; and *thermal* which notes changes in temperature as a function of blood flow.

Biofeedback can be used for many conditions, only a few of which are muscle tension, headache, chronic pain, and teeth grinding. If a body process can be measured, it has the potential of being influenced or controlled by biofeedback mechanisms.

Meditation.   This is an approach of experiencing our "being" or "existing" that is similar to biofeedback but on an internal level. In place of external feedback regarding our physiological functioning, we look to internal feedback through heightened awareness. This awareness of our physiology or other internal processes is not the goal, however. The goal of meditation, in all its hundreds of various forms, is focus on reconnection with "Spirit," God, or Reality - some ultimate or universal symbol that's important to us, that we value.

The process combines physical and cognitive methods and involves a self-mastery of our mental functions. It causes decreased oxygen consumption, increased skin conduction, and alpha brain waves, indicating a state of deep relaxation. At optimum rest, the muscles are relaxed, the mind is clear, alert, and creative. Anxiety decreases as inner control increases.

Find a quiet space without distractions or interruptions. Sit in a comfortable chair or on the floor. Keep your back straight. Select a word or sound to use as a mantra (what you're going to repeat and focus on), such as "Om" or the word "One." Close your eyes and let thoughts drift away. Concentrate on silently saying your mantra. Ignore distractions; you can deal with them later.

Continue for 15-20 minutes then let your mantra fade away. Sit still quietly as the mind resumes its activity. Slowly open your eyes. Make note of physiological changes which have occurred in your breathing and heart rate, muscle tension, or shift in a sense of body boundaries. Note also how time has passed. Practice the technique daily.

Self-hypnosis. Hypnosis is a state of alertness, producing brain-wave patterns which match that of ordinary waking consciousness. Hypnosis has not been demonstrated to be an altered state of consciousness. Rather it appears to be a complex combination of social and psychological factors, such as role-playing, imagination, and social influence. It has three prominent features:

• *Selective attention*
• *Suggestibility*
• *Dissociation.*

Selective attention refers to our narrowly focused attention. We allow ourselves to suspend critical judgment. We see certain things clearly and vividly while excluding all other external stimuli and ignoring context.

Suggestibility is our willingness to adopt the role of subject and be highly responsive to guidance and compliance with suggestions. Approximately 15% of the population is highly hypnotizable and 25% is not hypnotizable at all. Of those who can be hypnotized, only 10-20% achieve a deep trance. Men and women are equally good subjects. Children and adolescents are the best subjects with the capacity for being hypnotized diminishing with age. Higher intelligence gives only a slight advantage. The most important qualification is a willingness to commit our attention fully to the task at hand without concern or distraction.

Dissociation describes an unconscious process by which one group of mental processes (such as knowledge, memory, or voluntary control) is separated from the rest of the thinking processes so they function as individual, independent units instead of as an integrated whole. When this occurs in consciousness, for example, we may not be able to recall our identity and other important information. Our customary sense of reality is lost and replaced by a sense of unreality. We may feel mechanical as if in a dream and perceive ourselves as not in complete control of our actions.

Today the primary uses of self-hypnosis are to allow us to control our lives and encourage us to frame our suggestions to ourselves. Within cognitive-behavioral therapy hypnosis is used to

• *Enhance relaxation;*

• *Generate imagery;*

• *Heighten expectations of success;*

• *Change self-defeating thoughts;*

• *Pair appropriate behavior with a reinforcer in the imagination;*

• *Improve desensitization;*

• *Increase ability to cope with problems of daily living;*

• *Maximize feelings of efficacy and self-control.*

Note: If we're considering having a hypnotist initiate this process for us but are concerned about trusting them, not having control, or giving over some portion of that control to another, we need to remember the following: We can't be hypnotized against our will or forced to do anything we find very objectionable. But if the proposed actions are not in serious conflict with our values and usual standards of behavior, we may perform them. While in a trance, we can't be forced to make unwanted self-revelations. In fact, we're still capable of lying either deliberately or unconsciously.

Self-hypnosis induction is similar to that of progressive relaxation and autogenic training. But other methods, such as concentrating on a spot on the ceiling, swinging pendulum, or flashing light, or pedaling fast on a stationary bicycle, can be used to focus us as we relax ourselves. Once our minds and bodies are feeling calm and fully relaxed, we shift our focus to concentrate on self-suggestions about improving ourselves.

Hypnosis pioneer Theodore X. Barber indicates that self-suggestions are more likely to be effective if we follow a few general guidelines:

1. *Use brief and simple words and phrases to transmit the self-suggestion ideas.*

2. *Word the suggestions "positively" not "negatively." (For example, don't say, "I won't be anxious," say "I will be calm.")*

3. *Self-suggestions should be straightforward, without doubt or qualification of effort involved. (For example, say, "I will speak to one person at the party," not "I will try to speak to one person at the party" or "I would like to speak to one person at the party.")*

4. *Repeat self-suggestions in a manner conveying the feeling behind the statements.*

5. *Use self-suggestions that are specific and sufficiently individualized.*

6. *Create opportunities to try out the suggestions gradually in real-life situations.*

7. *Use a tape recorder to improve wording, phrasing, and methods of hypnotic presentation.*

Physical exercise. As we've seen, when we're anxious, we tend to hold tension in our muscles. When this tension is chronic, we experience constrictions in the muscles, or spasms. These immobilize us and register as pain. Because the neck is a common site for this tension, we speak of tension-inducing situations as "a pain in the neck." While regular, spontaneous movement is necessary to help reduce this tension, it often isn't sufficient. We need, in addition, extended periods of planned physical activity.

Physical exercise has been found to be a powerfully effective method for reducing both anxiety and depression. When we were young, it was a natural outlet for all our arousal. Not only did it reduce all that muscle tension that caused us to feel "uptight," but also it gave us an avenue for discharging pent-up frustrations. It increased metabolism of hormones such as adrenaline, increased oxygen consumption and circulation, and may have stimulated production of endorphins to increase our sense of well-being.

Starting in the late 1980s it has been found that exercise increases concentrations of the neurotransmitter norepinephrine in areas of the brain involved in the body's stress response. More recently some have suggested that exercise thwarts anxiety and depression by enhancing the body's ability to respond to stress. Exercise appears to provide the body with the opportunity to positively, dynamically, and efficiently deal with stress.

It's still a natural outlet for adults and has the dividend of providing health benefits of particular concern to adults. Physical exercise decreases our cholesterol, blood pressure, frustration, and insomnia. It promotes weight loss and improves elimination functions, concentration, and memory. It also creates a sense of control and increased self-esteem.

One reason we don't exercise as much as would be helpful is that we often forget about or ignore it because we tend to regard it as "work." This means that if we're to participate in an exercise program, we have to change how we think about exercise. We need to reframe it in terms of all the benefits it'll provide.

As with our recovery as a whole, we have to feel motivated and committed to making this a part of our program. We have to have physical exercise goals and objectives which become part of our **Daily Progress Notes** and **Recovery Timeline**. It's important to remember that getting started with our exercise program will be difficult until it evolves into a habit for us. Once it's a habit (this generally takes a month), it becomes part of our routine and we simply do it as a matter of course.

How do we know if we need to take up physical exercise? If we generally feel lethargic and tired, out of breath or exhausted after short periods of exercise (even climbing a flight of stairs), our muscles are chronically tense and show poor muscle tone, or we're obese, we need to take it up. (*Warning: If you have any condition for which exercise is contraindicated, or for which there are limits on the type, amount, and intensity of exercise, consult your physician before beginning this or any exercise program.*)

The type of exercise we choose depends upon our goal. We need to ask ourselves what it's for. Is it for

• *Muscle tension*

• *Flexibility*

• *Strength training.*

• *Cardiovascular conditioning*

• *Weight loss*

• *Personal development.*

How do we want to do it? Do we want to do it

• *Alone or with others*

• *Part of a team or as an individual player*

• *Strenuous or gentle*

• *Anaerobic or aerobic.*

The exercise(s) we choose can range from ballroom dancing to bowling, swimming to isometrics, basketball to weight lifting, ping pong to fast walking, tennis to skiing, aerobics to calisthenics, folk dancing to stationary cycling, and all the others in between. Having several types of exercise to do is useful because it reduces the likelihood we'll become bored doing one thing over and over. Having complementary exercises also may provide a needed balance, for example, a competitive sport, like football, with a solitary activity, like running, or an aerobic sport, like swimming, with an anaerobic activity, like isometrics. Exercise which is rewarding unto itself is more likely to be helpful in reducing stress than exercise that isn't.

No matter what exercise program we follow, it'll benefit from the addition of stretching exercises. Stress-reduction therapist L. John Mason cautions that we should never force or strain ourselves in trying to accomplish our goal of loosening and making our muscles more flexible. Slowness and proper breathing are the watchwords. Proper breathing means inhaling deeply and exhaling fully and completely.   Being aware of what we're doing and how our body is responding is half the battle in stress reduction.

Neck rotation. *Drop your head as far forward to the chest as possible then slowly move it to the left or right. See how close you can come to touching your ear to your shoulder. When you feel resistance, stop, take a full breath, and start again. Do it several times and monitor how your neck feels. Rotate the head in the opposite direction.*

Neck flexor. *Drop your head as far forward to the chest as possible then slowly tilt your head backward as far as possible.   Do it several times and note how your neck feels.*

Shoulder rolls. *Let arms your hang loosely and pull down gently on your shoulders. Rotate both shoulders forward very slowly. Lift to feel the tension. Repeat process rotating your shoulders backwards.*

Shoulder stretch. *Lay your forearms on top of your head and grasp your right elbow with your left hand. Slowly pull the elbow behind your head. Don't force it. Hold several seconds, note how it feels, then switch arms and repeat.*

Arm shakes. *Let your arms hang by your sides. Lightly shake your right hand and wrist. Slowly let the movement involve the forearm and elbow. Begin shaking your arm more vigorously and do the entire arm for one minute. Now swing the entire arm back and forth from the shoulder while still shaking it. Let the arm hang still at your side and feel the sensation. Repeat with your left arm.*

Leg shakes. *Balance yourself with a chair or table and begin to rotate your right foot and ankle. Start shaking your foot, ankle, and lower leg. Add the knee then extend to the entire leg. Shake your leg more rapidly. Now swing that leg as you shake it. Stop and notice how it feels. Repeat on your left leg.*

Sitting toe touches. *Sit on the floor with your legs together, extended in front of you. Reach for your toes with both hands and slowly, gently bring your forehead as close to the knees as possible. When you feel the resistance, hold your position for a minute.*

Calf-tendon stretch. *Stand 2-3 feet from a wall, lean forwards, placing your palms on the wall at eye level. Make sure your body is straight. Move your right foot backwards along the floor until you feel your calf muscle stretching. Hold that for one minute then repeat with your left leg.*

Standing leg stretch. *Find a table approximately 3 feet high. Place one leg on the table so that it is extended and parallel to the floor. Slowly extend your fingertips toward your foot on the table and try to touch your knee with your forehead. Hold for one minute, making note of the sensation, then repeat with your other leg.*

Side stretch. *Stand with your feet shoulder-width apart and legs straight. Place your right hand on your right hip and extend your left arm above your head, slowly bending to the right. Hold for one minute, feel the resistance, and repeat on the other side.*

Back stretch. *Stand straight with your feet planted shoulder-width apart. Bend forward from the waist, relaxing arms, shoulders, and neck until you feel stretching in back of your legs. Hold for a minute, bend your knees to take pressure off your lower back before you stand up, then stand up.*

Scalp massage. *With your arms up and elbows out, move your fingers in small circles, pressing gently, around the scalp. Cover your entire head including the nape of neck, your face, particularly around your eyes, and in front of and behind your ears.*

Relaxing with cognitive-affective techniques

Visualization. Once we've relaxed our bodies, with one of the physical techniques, we can make our relaxation more global by bringing in the mind. Since our thoughts and emotions influence not only our anxiety but also our relaxation, we need to address these elements as well. One effective procedure is visualizing ourselves in a scene we find peaceful and comforting. Some place we can look to as a retreat to refresh the soul. It can be real or imaginary, commonplace or fantastical. Whatever we choose, it should be very visual, appealing to all our senses. Perhaps like the Disney nature film.

As we move through the scene, we need to notice every large and minute detail of the environment and describe it vividly: Colors, subtle shadings, light level, temperature, time of day, types of sounds, loudness, movement of objects, their feel, smells, and how we feel about it. As we do this, we should remind ourselves how relaxing this is and how tranquil, comfortable, and secure we feel in this setting. This will be a daytime dream we can choose to enter any time we want to relax and calm our racing mind.

As with relaxation techniques, we need to be in a comfortable position in a quiet, distraction-free environment. The object is to make the images as clear, detailed, and convincing as possible. This may take time and practice. It's important to regard this as an extension of relaxation so we should use relaxation-like affirmations, such as "I'm feeling calm," "I'm letting go of tension," "My body is relaxed." And not as one joker put it, "I have the power to channel my imagination into ever-increasing levels of fear and paranoia." If we choose to try visualization as a replacement for other relaxation techniques, we need to include more direction for our relaxation. When finished, we then need to guide ourselves to an alert state of mind.

As with other relaxation techniques, pre-recording the visualization makes initial sessions easier, though we may wish to simply continue to use the tape indefinitely. To allow ourselves maximum time to visualize we should read the script slowly, with pauses. We can get a sense of how slow that should be by visualizing as we practice reading the script before we record it.

Picture yourself on a wind-swept cliff, surrounded by boulders, looking out over a large expanse of ocean. The beach below is calling to you. It's 11 a.m.

on a glorious summer's day. The sky is pale yellow with fleecy wisps of clouds scudding across it. Everything feels golden and good. You spot a path which gradually switch-backs its way down the cliff face to the beach below. As you gently descend this wide, easy path, you feel yourself becoming more and more relaxed. The farther down you go, the more relaxed you feel. You see red granite rocks covered in orange, yellow, and gray-green lichens lining the trail downward. A squirrel with its cheek pouches filled to capacity, leaps onto a rock to your left, regards you a moment, and scampers away. You smile and you feel more relaxed. A soft breeze caresses your cheek. You see small pink flowers poking their petaled heads between the rocks. Dark green cushions of moss are everywhere, beckoning you to lie down among them.

As you reach the beach, you feel calm and very relaxed. You lean against a rock to take off your shoes and socks so you can paddle across the sand in your bare feet. Fine granules sift through your toes and tickle you. Your legs are feeling heavier. As you reach the water's edge, you spread out your towel in the dry sand and lie down on your back. As you wriggle your body to settle in, you feel yourself melting into the beach, totally relaxed. You listen to the ocean's roar in the background, smell the salt and seaweed, and hear the water's ebb and flow. Waves playfully slap the beach, foam, and withdraw. Rhythmic motion. You can hear your heart beating slowly, evenly, and rhythmically too. The sound is comforting.

An airplane engine drones in the distance and overhead seagulls call and do sweeping sixty-degree turns on wing tips. You feel at one with the universe. You savor the feeling.

Now slowly you're going to return to your waking, alert state of mind. As you count backwards from four to one, you'll become more and more awake and alert. Four - you're becoming awake, feeling alert. Three - you feel more alert and awake, more aware of your surroundings. Two - you can feel your body becoming alert, beginning to move. One - you're wide awake and alert. You can fully move your body. You feel relaxed, refreshed, and revitalized by the peace and solitude.

There are times when we want to do a visualization but don't have time for one this lengthy. At times like this we can do a mini-visualization. Some people picture themselves in the shower, others, soaking in tub, for example. Whatever we choose it has to be something we like.

Picture yourself in a tub in water 103 degrees. You're leaning back with a pillow supporting your head, feeling very comfortable. A single candle is lit, its flame is dancing. You're breathing slowly and evenly as the warm water draws away your cares. With each rhythmic breath you're becoming more and more relaxed. Tension is ebbing. All your worries are evaporating in the rising steam. Your arms are floating gently. The water is soothing, caressing, and massaging your body. As tension releases it hold, your muscles are becoming loose and limp. Your body feels cradled. With every breath you become more and more relaxed.

Visualization also works when we want to keep an image of ourselves in our mind. *Picture yourself in an outfit you associate with a success you've had. This should be an outfit that makes you feel good and confident. Remember that success. Re-experience that confidence. When you're wearing that outfit, you're standing within a large force-field that looks like a cylinder of Plexiglas. It goes wherever you go but others can't see it. It's a shield that is impervious to all the gremlins and trolls who try to attack you: Criticisms bounce off it. Negative evaluations evaporate at its touch. Humiliation melts into a pool in its presence. When the field is on, no one can touch you. No social situation can hurt you. When protected by this shield, you have the power. You command respect. You can do anything you want to and you can do it successfully.*

Relaxation exercises should be practiced often and are best used *before* and *after* an anxiety-provoking situation. During the situation, however, it appears that using abdominal breathing only is best, especially when our arousal is severe. (See Chapter 7)

"Nothing can hurt me so here I come."

CHAPTER **7**

MODIFYING THOUGHTS AND BEHAVIORS

"Out of the whole animal kingdom only humans are endowed with this capacity to make themselves miserable." (Sharon A. Bower & Gordon Bower)

What is cognitive therapy?

Some of us pale at the thought of therapy, with visions dancing in our heads of exchanging thoughts that hurt for a reality that hurts even more. But, what effective cognitive therapy does is target those gut-wrenching, dysfunctional thoughts and beliefs that underlie our feelings of anxiety and our avoidance behavior. It lays bare the process we go through in generating those dysfunctional thoughts. As we discussed in Chapter 4, first, we make negative, anxiety-provoking assumptions about social situations and ourselves. These assumptions then direct us to think anxiously and negatively about ourselves, others, and the situations. Finally, these thoughts, in turn, produce our feelings of anxiety and negativity. It's all in our thinking.

Cognitive therapy allows us to identify our negative and distorted thoughts, evaluate, and modify them. Slowly, gradually this therapy facilitates our altering the biases in our information processing. It's how we think about and interpret information which maintains those cognitive and belief distortions. Once we change the processes, we can begin to function normally again. The goal of cognitive therapy is accurate and rational thinking. The therapy aims to:

- *Determine significant life events and experiences that contributed to development of SA/SP;*
- *Formulate the problem of SA/SP in terms of how our thoughts, feelings, and behaviors interact;*
- *Identify and explore core beliefs about the self, others, and the world;*
- *Recognize and examine maladaptive thoughts, images, and behaviors;*
- *Identify with more realistic and adaptive thoughts;*
- *Accumulate evidence supporting adaptive thoughts;*
- *Modify cognitive responses (mistaken beliefs, distorted thoughts, attentional bias) and behaviors (avoidance, safety behaviors) which interfere with the processing of information which disconfirms our fears and the effects of exposure to fear.*

To achieve these aims cognitive therapy uses the following strategies to:

- *Focus on the importance of maladaptive automatic thoughts, the feelings associated with them, and their consequences;*

- *Determine the antecedents of the factors affecting these automatic thoughts;*
- *Determine the frequency and generalizability of these automatic thoughts;*
- *Determine associations with these automatic thoughts;*
- *Explore problem-solving possibilities;*
- *Question automatic thoughts;*
- *Dispute these automatic thoughts by providing contradictory evidence;*
- *Make different explanations for outcome (reattribution);*
- *Label thinking errors;*
- *Distance yourself from the thought;*
- *Track progress.*

Cognitive therapy focuses on our thoughts associated with the fear of negative evaluation, our expectations of threat in social situations and our poor performance in those situations, and our selective attention to negative information and threat cues.

Expectations. What we expect to happen is based, in part, upon how we explain the world, how we assign causes to what happens to us, how much control we perceive we have, and what our basic assumptions are.

Our *explanatory style* is one important information processing bias. Learned in childhood and adolescence, this is the habitual, automatic way we explain our setbacks. We look at their cause-and-effect, whether it's different in different situations, and if it continues over time. It's the foundation of how we view the world and our place in it. SA/SPers tend to use a *pessimistic* explanatory style. As outlined by Martin Seligman, this style is characterized by our inclination to regard bad events as the result of permanent, universal, and personal causes.

Permanence refers to the consistency with which we see the same bad event happening over time. As pessimists, if we perceive that we do poorly in social situations, we'll tend to see our performance as occurring "all" the time and explain the negative outcome in terms of "never" and "always" ("I never get it right. I always look like a fool"). For us these negative results are practically guaranteed. In addition, the only outcome we're likely to see as temporary in social situations is a positive one. We see it as a fluke, a fleeting, random occurrence, something to dismiss or discount. For us "good news is life's way of keeping us off-balance." These attributions of permanence are the basis of our *all-or-nothing thinking.* If we can see bad events as *temporary*, we help keep pessimism at bay.

Universality is our seeing the aversive event as occurring everywhere. When we think our self-presentation doesn't go well, our pessimism will tend to make us see our failure as likely to occur in all such situations, not just this specific one ("Every time I try I mess up"). Once again, we see any positive outcome for us as occurring specifically, in a particular situation, and not something we can expect to occur in others or in general. If we can see bad events as *situationally-specific*, we can reduce pessimism.

Personalization is where we locate responsibility for the negative outcome, in ourselves or in the environment. In SA/SP we tend to blame ourselves for bad outcomes rather than assign blame to something in the situation ("I failed the test because I'm incompetent," not because the test was hard). If we can see the cause of bad events as *external* to us, we can likewise lessen pessimism's hold.

Those who have a pessimistic explanatory style and suffer bad events are more likely to become depressed. But not all SA/SPers are depressed. So what differentiates SA/SP from depression if they share this pessimistic thinking style? Because SA/SPers use this style only in social situations we fear, we don't see all causes of our misfortune as permanent, universal, and personal. We see as temporary and specific to the situation, creating hope for us. But those suffering from depression see only permanent, universal, and personal cause, leaving them without hope.

Pessimism has other implications for us as well. Seligman found that men who explained bad events in their lives by referring to permanent, universal, and personal attributions had significantly poorer health between ages 45 and 60, even taking into account the physical and mental health of the individual at age 25. He concluded that use of the pessimistic explanatory style in young adulthood seemed to be a risk factor for poor overall health in middle and late adulthood. Specifically, permanent attributions were found to produce longer aversive consequences. Universal attributions produced more generalized negative consequences. Personal attributions predicted increased loss of self-esteem.

Overall, when we use this pessimistic explanatory style, we see desirable outcomes as less likely, specific to certain situations, and the result of luck. But we see undesirable outcomes as more likely, happening across social situations, and the result of our ability level. We see our outcomes, both good and bad, as beyond our control. This perception of lack of control further increases our pessimism about the positive outcome of any situation and leads to emotional consequences. The less control we feel we have to change the negative social situations, the more we'll feel anxious, helpless, depressed, and convinced the world doesn't operate in our favor.

Core beliefs. Core beliefs are our unconditional, fundamental, and central beliefs about ourselves, others, and the world. They're part of our self-concept. These are the standards against which we judge all situations, thoughts, and actions. They reflect our beliefs about our value as humans, our security, and performance. They reflect our sense of our control over the world around us. They tell us how lovable we are and independent we are. They also represent our standards, those of others, and our perception of justice and how it operates. They are the basis of our automatic thoughts.

Our core beliefs trigger in us specific expectations or rules, attitudes, and assumptions about both the situation and how we should play our role in it.

When a core belief is distorted or erroneous, it's considered to be maladaptive. Any thoughts derived from it will likewise be maladaptive.

Core Belief Exercise

*Place a "**T**" if the statement is true or mostly true about your beliefs or an "**F**" if it's false or mostly false. (Exercise adapted from Jeffrey Young's Schema Questionnaire)*

_____1. My needs are legitimate.

_____2. I'm unworthy of love and respect.

_____3. I can take risks.

_____4. I feel unsafe and at risk.

_____5. I do lots of things well.

_____6. My failures are unforgivable.

_____7. I feel pretty much in control of my life.

_____8. I feel threatened by others.

_____9. Others love, appreciate, and care for me.

_____10. Nobody would be interested in me as a partner.

_____11. I'm self-reliant.

_____12. I generally go along with what others do.

_____13. Things generally work out in the end.

_____14. It's an unjust world.

_____15. I strongly feel a part of a family and community.

_____16. I generally feel on the outside looking in.

_____17. Most people are trustworthy.

_____18. People put themselves first.

_____19. My standards for myself are reasonable.

_____20. Trusting my own judgment usually ends up wrong.

*Scoring instructions: Count the number of **Fs** in the **odd**-numbered questions, 1-19. Count the number of **Ts** in the **even**-numbered questions, 2-20. These are your negative core belief which may contribute to your negative, distorted thinking. Add your **Fs** and **Ts**, multiply by 100% and divide by 20. This represents the percentage of your negative beliefs relative to your positive ones.*

From thought to emotion. In general, our emotional response is the result of a chain of activities that we go through when we encounter a situation. Specifically, we (1) *look* at the events and situations which occur in the real world. These may be initially positive, neutral, or negative. Then we (2) *perceive* them (gather information through our eyes and record it in our brain as images). We (3) *think* about the events and situations. We (4) *interpret* them and place our own meanings, from our core beliefs, on them. Finally we (5) *feel* some emotion which we then associate with the images.

(Interpretation)

World Events ⟶ 🔥 ⟶Thoughts ⟶ Emotions

(Evaluation)

RELATIONSHIP BETWEEN EVENTS, THOUGHTS, AND EMOTIONS

Being highly analytical animals, when we enter social situations we implicitly ask ourselves a series of questions to determine what we think about what we see and how we should interpret it. (Adapted from Susan Fiske and Shelley Taylor in **Social Cognition**):

- *"What's the situation here?"*

- *"Who are these people?"*

- *"What's going on and how do I fit in?"*

- *"What are my goals in this situation?"*

- *"Are my goals in conflict with those of others? If there's a choice to make, how do I make it?"*

- *"How do I choose among available strategies to achieve my goals?"*

- *"What happens if I'm wrong? How do I recoup my losses?"*

- *"How will what I choose to do affect others? How do I respond to their reactions?"*

The situation itself doesn't directly determine how we feel. Instead, what we feel is based upon what's going on in our minds as we view a situation. Suppose we saw Joe standing outside a McDonalds' mens' room in his unbuttoned khaki long-sleeve shirt over a black tee, with black Levis, and hiking boots, shifting from one foot to another, continuously looking around. This is a neutral event. There are no interpretations or evaluation initially attached to the behavior. Therefore, we have no emotional response. However, the moment we think about the behavior and add an interpretation or evaluation, our response to the situation changes.

If we interpreted Joe's movements as a sense of urgency to use an occupied bathroom, we'd probably evaluate and label his behavior as reasonable under the circumstances. Our emotional response would follow the evaluation and we'd probably empathize with his distress.

If, however, we interpreted Joe's activities as shifty, anxious, and furtive, that he was likely up to no good, we'd probably evaluate and label his behavior as suspicious and something to be concerned about. Our emotional response would be negative, perhaps fearful. The behavior's the same yet the thoughts, interpretations, and resulting emotions are different.

Negative self-talk. As mentioned in Chapter 4, automatic thoughts are the result of our core beliefs and create our emotional responses to social situations and stimuli. That is, they occur because we think about things which attract our attention and place demands upon us. Thus, the feeling we experience is logically connected to the thought's content. If we believe we're incompetent, we'll feel sad. They're maintained by our misinterpretation of our physiological anxiety symptoms and our use of safety, or avoidance, behaviors. The negative things we automatically say to ourselves generally represent errors in thinking. They are often the result of mistaken or dysfunctional

- *Appraisal of the immediate situation*
- *Perception of long-term consequences*
- *Other associations with the situation.*

They can be experienced as what we say to ourselves or as images we have. They're brief, fleeting, out of awareness, and not based on reflection or deliberation. They may be general perceptions or situation-specific thoughts. When SA/SPers encounter a social situation, we begin to process the information that's available to tell us how to interpret it.

We all (SA/SPers and non-SA/SPers alike) have automatic thoughts, some positive, some negative. They just pop into our heads. But SA/SPers have a multitude of negative, inappropriate, self-defeating, upsetting, and destructive thoughts which constantly magically appear in social situations, creating anxiety for us. It's important to remember that even though we don't choose these thoughts, we're the ones who are responsible for eradicating them.

How do we detect these cognitive errors?

We can evaluate automatic thoughts by their validity. Most will be distorted and contrary to objective evidence. For example, even as Joe was elected to student council, he believed nobody liked him. Some can be accurate but have conclusions which are distorted, as when Sarah says, "I didn't get the video back to the store on time so I'm a totally careless, thoughtless person." Some can be accurate but dysfunctional. For example, Joanna says it'll take her a week to finish her article on the American Cancer Society health fair and thinking about it increases her anxiety and decreases her motivation to do it.

The following are the most common cognitive errors, or categories of negative automatic thoughts (negative self-talk), as identified by Aaron T. Beck and David Burns:

Arbitrary inference is coming to a conclusion when there's insufficient evidence ("The audience will laugh at me if I make a mistake").

Over-generalization is basing conclusions on isolated events then applying them across diverse situations (Our audience which expected us to talk on measles prevention but heard about managed care instead looked bored. We assume that audiences in general will find us boring).

Magnification and **minimization** are a distortion of the importance of events. *Magnification* exaggerates our perceived defects ("I forgot the boss's name and now he'll never give me my pay raise as a result"). *Minimization* inappropriately shrinks our "positive," desirable qualities by discounting or dismissing them ("Yeah, I went to the party and didn't mess up, but it was pure luck"). At the same time it minimizes the "negative," undesirable qualities, or flaws, of the **other** person ("Sure, Charley forgets the boss's name all the time, but he has a lot of important stuff on his mind").

Personalization is arbitrarily and inappropriately seeing ourselves as the cause of negative external events for which we're not responsible ("The teacher was gruff, I must have done something wrong"). It's seeing the event as a reflection of our inadequacies ("Little Jennie wouldn't do Show-and-Tell today. It must be because of my SA/SP. I'm a lousy parent"). It's also seeing ourselves as the specific object of anything negative even when it's obviously aimed at the group instead ("The boss posted a notice to all employees about taking sick-time, but I know she's really talking about me personally because I don't show for meetings").

All-or-nothing thinking is where things are either-or, black or white, with no shades of gray ("If I don't appear perfectly calm as part of the bridal party, then I'm a total failure and will spoil everything" or "At the office party I'm not very social and I can see that my colleagues think I'm either stuck up or I've had to much to drink").

Mental filter is looking for and selectively picking out a single negative detail, ignoring the big picture, and dwelling on it alone until everything seems black ("Even though the editor bought my article, he wanted me to change one sentence. It means he thinks I'm a hack writer" or worrying that the boss didn't like our speech because she whispered in someone's ear while she was applauding enthusiastically).

Disqualifyng the positive is rejecting or dismissing positive experiences by insisting that they don't count. In this way we can maintain our negative belief even though there's contradictory evidence in our everyday experiences ("Even though I haven't been able to stand in store lines for over a month, my trip to the supermarket wasn't any big deal because I needed groceries").

Jumping to conclusions is making negative interpretations even though there are no facts which support this conclusion. There are two types of jumping to conclusions:

Mind reading is arbitrarily concluding that someone is reacting negatively to us and we don't bother to check it out. ("When I posted a message on the social anxiety list and no one responded, it was because they thought what I said was stupid").

Fortune telling error is anticipating things will turn out badly. We feel convinced that our conclusion is already an established fact and we can use it to make predictions. ("Since they didn't care enough about me to respond yesterday when I posted, they obviously don't want me here so I'm leaving the list").

Emotional reasoning is assuming that our negative emotions necessarily reflect how things really are ("I feel it so it must be true").

Should statements represent unrealistically high self-imposed standards of *perfection* that we use to motivate ourselves to do things. We express these unrealistic expectations in terms of *should, shouldn't, must,* and *ought* ("I should be able to use will power alone to overcome my SA/SP" or "I must never show anger to my parents").

Labeling is an extreme form of over-generalization wherein we attach a negative label to ourselves rather than describe our error ("I'm so stupid" rather than "That was a stupid thing to do"). We attach labels to others ("He's such a moron") when they irritate us and describe an event in emotionally-loaded, evaluative language ("He arrogantly shoved my report at me, asking me to do it again").

Rationalization is ascribing justifiable and plausible motives to our thoughts and feelings while real motives go unrecognized because they are unacceptable ("I left the meeting to make an important phone call" rather than "I left because I felt they were all staring at me"). There are two common forms of rationalization:

Sour grapes is a self-deceptive and ego-enhancing device which allows us to avoid anxiety, guilt, and shame. To reduce our disappointment we convince ourselves that the unattained goal wasn't all that desirable in the first place ("Well, I didn't really want the job anyway").

Sweet lemon is similar to sour grapes in that it involves our convincing ourselves that our failure in attaining a previous goal may be a "blessing in disguise" after all ("If I hadn't had that panic attack in the mall in front of the guy I wanted to impress, I might have dated him and then been rejected by him because of my SA/SP").

Our recovery demands that we focus on, recognize, and confront our automatic fear thoughts. We need to differentiate the thought from its interpretation, learn about the situations we associate with them, explore the beliefs underneath them, then counter them with a rational response.

Through assessment we can determine not only our fear but also our underlying thoughts which generate that fear. We can change the underlying thoughts and, thus, change the resulting emotion. According to Richard G. Heimberg's Four Steps to Cognitive Restructuring, this means that in order to counter our fear of negative evaluation, we need to:

1. *Look at the situation in which the fear of the unknown, failure, or rejection occurs;*

2. *Analyze the thoughts attached to the situation;*

3. *Acknowledge the distortion: The interpretations, meanings, labels, and evaluations;*

4. *Respond to the thoughts rationally: Reinterpret, relabel, and re-evaluate.*

This requires our distancing ourselves from the thoughts so their emotion won't entangle us. We can do this by responding as if someone else were presenting the thought to us for our dispassionate, objective analysis.

Sarah's Fear Assessment

Situation: Sarah is a pharmaceutical sales representative. She's looking for suggestions on how to sell to a new market. While she's making inquiries of her contacts, she gets a hot lead on the advice she wants. But to get this information she has to pick up the phone and call a stranger. Sarah assesses her unwillingness to make the call (Format is adapted from David Burns' **Feeling Good: The New Mood Therapy***).*

Fear Thought: I can't call.

Realistic Assessment: I can call, just pick up the phone and dial. I have the person's name, what she can do for me, and I have a reference.

Thought Origin: What is there about calling that bothers me?

Fear Thought: She's busy and doesn't want me to bother her.

Realistic Assessment: She may or may not be busy. Since I am not a mind reader, I have no way of knowing what she will be doing at any given moment. I can't know that she's being bothered unless she says so to me. She might actually enjoy talking to me, taking the opportunity to share. It is her choice how she will respond. I have no right to make her choice for her.

Thought Origin: If she is busy, why is that a problem for me?

Fear Thought: I would be rejected.

Realistic Assessment: If she is not interested in talking to me at that moment or does not have the time to talk, it does not mean that she has rejected me. She has rejected *talking* to me. By chance I would expect a maximum of half of those I call to talk to me. That means half would not.

Thought Origin: If I am rejected, why is that a problem for me?

Fear Thought: I would be shown to be inadequate.

Realistic Assessment: Just because I don't get what I want on one occasion does not mean I am inadequate as a human being. I am adequate in many things I do. I'm OK whether my behavior works or not. If I see a pattern of behavior not working for me, I can consider changing it.

Thought Origin: If I'm shown to be inadequate in this situation, why would that be a problem for me?

In this disputation process we're looking for:

- *Evidence* - Is what we think or believe factually correct? We need to question the evidence for believing specific appraisals. What is the meaning? Where is the logic faulty? Then we need to collect contradictory evidence.

- *Alternatives* - What are the other possible causes? Rarely does anything that happens to us have only one possible cause. We need to generate a list all the possible, rational, and relevant contributing factors. We should focus particularly on those which are *concrete, specific, changeable*, and *non-personal*. (*Non-personal* is especially important because we need to begin externalizing our focus.)

- *Implications* - What is the likelihood of the "terrible" consequences we envision actually occurring (even if the belief or thought were correct)?

- *Usefulness* - Is just holding this thought or belief destructive (whether the thought or belief is true or not)?

Being able to step out of ourselves isn't easy. Neither is figuring out our attitudes, expectations, and beliefs. They're generally hidden from us. However, if we can reach them even superficially or tangentially, we can get a sense of some of the things which trigger and perpetuate our SA/SP.

Your Fear-Thought Assessment

- *Get a pencil and paper and construct your own Fear-Thought Assessment table.*

- *Write down a social situation in which you feel fear of evaluation. Begin by writing down the first fear-thought you have when you think about the situation.*

- *Then, acting as an objective observer, respond realistically and rationally to the thought. Write down your objective response.*

- *Now go back to your thought and analyze it: What is the basis of the problem for you. What are the assumptions, attitudes, expectations, rules, or beliefs on which the problem is based?*

- *Refer to this assessment often, going through your rational responses. Repeat this assessment with other fear thoughts.*

We need to remember that this negative self-talk is really a self-criticism, so we have to talk back to our internal critic with a self-defense. Dissecting fear thoughts helps us get to the heart of the fear which may be many levels removed from the first fear thought we have. Knowing this fundamental, fear-generating thought is useful because it'll show up in many situations in many guises.

We can also recreate our reality by altering the verbal instructions we give to ourselves when we face feared social situations. We can train ourselves to deal with this fear through a simple process: Giving ourselves a pep talk, talking to ourselves as we would to a best friend.

Coping with Fear Exercise

- *Think of a social situation in which you fear being observed, negatively evaluated, or being humiliated publicly.*
- *Visualize yourself in it. As you approach this fear situation in your mind,*
- *Start talking to yourself.*
- *Prepare yourself for the stress that looms ahead.*
- *Confront and handle the stressful situation.*
- *Listen to your negative self-talk.*
- *Cope with the feelings of being overwhelmed by responding with coping self-statements (listed below).*
- *Talk yourself through the problem. Then*
- *Reward yourself for having coped. (See you can be and* **are** *your own best friend!)*
- *Practice these statements often and apply them every time you approach risk taking or any fear situation.*

Fear Defense Statements

(Adapted from Donald Meichenbaum and Roy Cameron in **Self Control**)

1. *Assess the reality of the fear situation:* Is the situation really dangerous so I should be afraid? What is it that I really need to do? I can concentrate on what I have to do; that's more constructive than being afraid.

2. *Control negative, self-defeating, fear-provoking thoughts and images:* I can erase my worry. Worry isn't helpful. Worry is passive, negative, and not constructive.

3. *Relabel fear:* Maybe the feeling I'm calling fear is really eagerness to get the situation over with.

4. *Psych yourself up to perform well:* I know I can confront this situation. One step at a time I'm taking care of it. I'm going to think only about what I have to do and stay relevant. I can relax by taking slow, deep breaths.

5. *Cope with intense fear:* I can focus on what I have to do right now. It cannot and will not last forever. I can wait. I don't need to worry about fear. I can do something else. I feel bad only when I think about it. What's the worst that realistically can happen? How likely is it to occur? Could I cope with it? Yes, I can cope.

6. *Positively reinforce yourself for having coped:* I did it. It worked. It wasn't so bad after all. I blew it out of proportion. It wasn't worth the agony. Every day in every way I'm getting better. I'm proud of myself for my continuing progress.

It's important to remember that concentrating on negative aspects of a situation, whether real or imagined, only serves to promote more negativity and stunt our spirit, growth, and life possibilities. Negative thoughts affect us more deeply than positive thoughts because there's a differential effect of positive and negative. This means we have to work that much harder to keep the positive in the forefront. Concentrating on the positive aspects, whether real or imagined, promotes positive feelings and growth. We can choose to think rationally and feel positive. With effort, we can think our way toward successful recovery. We change ourselves and we change our destiny.

Coping with panic attacks

Not every SA/SPer experiences panic attacks, perhaps less than 50% of us diagnosed with our disorder. But for those who do and those who may, there are some basic things we need to remember when we find ourselves in the throes while in a social encounter or anticipating a social event.

• *Even though your heart is racing and you're sweating and trembling, you're not going to have a heart attack. Your mouth may be dry but you're not going to choke. Your body is simply overreacting to a stressful situation. While the feelings are unpleasant, they're not harmful and will subside quickly if you let them.*

• *Look at what your body is doing. You're hyperventilating which is making your heart race and making you feel dizzy. You need to use your diaphragmatic breathing exercises. Breathing into a paper bag to balance your CO_2 loss may also help reduce your arousal but not as much as your abdominal breathing.*

• *Listen to your thoughts. You're creating worst-case scenarios about what's happening and how others will respond. What you're saying doesn't represent reality. These thoughts create a vicious circle because they engender fear, blame, frustration, and anger which then make you more anxious. You need to talk to yourself, address these negative automatic thoughts, counter them, and then dismiss them.*

• *Trying to escape will make the situation worse. Instead, make yourself as comfortable and secure as possible. Look for ways to distract yourself until your body shortly returns to its normal state.*

• *Recognize that you not only survived the attack but also made it through by maintaining control. You should be proud of yourself. You've demonstrated that you don't have to let the panic control you; you can control it.*

Why we need to control worry

SA/SPers fret endlessly over anticipated negative outcomes. This fretting does nothing to deal with the problem but only makes us feel bad. There are steps we can take to reduce the levels of this ineffective behavior. This method involves recognizing that we're worrying and interrupting the thought before it can build anxiety. By putting aside those things over which we have no control, we reduce the amount of time we spend brooding about what might go wrong. With less time for worry, we have more time and energy to actually solve the problem.

Joe. *The first thing that strikes you about Joe, who is reasonably attractive, is that he rarely smiles. There seems to be a perpetual dark cloud playing across his face. He speaks with a refrain that colors his every conversation on the social phobia online list, echoing like a broken record: "Nothing ever works out the way I want because of this problem. Life is so unfair."*

For Joe life is a series of possible social catastrophes. In fact, he spends his days and nights conjuring up "what ifs" about anticipated situations then plotting strategies to either avoid them or steel himself against their occurrence. He's interested in stunt flying, but thinks, "Even I can make myself go to the air show this weekend, I can't make myself meet that group of pilots Tom said he'd introduce me to. I know meeting them would be my big chance for success. I can't become a stunt pilot if I can't get in with them. But they wouldn't be interested in a dumb kid like me anyway. They wouldn't want me and I'll be stuck forever in my dead-end job. I'll never get into air shows and my life will be ruined."

Most of the time Joe is tense, frustrated, angry, and fearful. He is bombarded by a chain of negative and seemingly uncontrollable thoughts and images. Consequently, he frequently experiences a sinking feeling in his stomach, gastrointestinal distress, tight shoulders, and rapid heart rate. His body speaks of his distorted beliefs: Furrowed brow, hunched shoulders, clenched fists, and furtive glances.

His nonverbal behavior also tends to have a negative impact on those around him. Because he's generally distracted, introspective, and often sullen, his work and relationships suffer. A chronic worrier, Joe spend most of his time each day fretting about things that have little or no substance or likelihood. His untested speculations about the future are inaccurate and unrealistic, yet he feels immobilized by them and the social situations which precipitate them. As a result, he won't assert himself or take risks.

So Joe plays it safe. He avoids these situations but still agonizes over the effects of his avoidance. But his safety measures mean not doing anything. The penalty of his isolation is more acceptable to him than suffering the anxiety of encountering them and any rewards that would be brought by new experiences.

While anxiety about future occurrences which is unrelated to social situations is associated with generalized anxiety disorder (GAD), SA/SPers, like Joe, sometimes experience GAD as a co-morbid condition with SA/SP so that there may be an overlap between the social and non-social things we worry about.

Worry Reduction Exercise

This exercise addresses those non-social future anxieties when they occur (adapted from Thomas Borkovec).

- *Establish a minimum 30-minute "worry session." This should be an uninterrupted period of time in the same place at the same time each day. Scheduling is important. It gives you a sense of control. You're in charge of those otherwise aimless, involuntary, and bothersome thoughts.*

- *Monitor your behavior during the day and identify "worry episodes" by their negative content. They can be a negative thought or negative feeling.*

- *Jot down in your journal the thoughts you consider to be a problem. These are what you'll use in your worry session. Writing down worrisome thoughts or feelings is very reassuring. It gets the problem out of your thoughts, where you'll ruminate upon it, and onto paper. Once you've committed it to paper, you can forget it.*

- *The moment you start to worry, stop yourself. Postpone the worrying until the worry session. You can worry about it at the prescribed time - then and only then.*

- *Substitute something positive for the worrisome thought you just had.*

- *Concentrate on the task at hand in order to distract yourself from worrying.*

- *Make full use of your worry session. This is the time at which you can worry intensely about all those thoughts you jotted down in your journal. Tape and listen to your worries.*

- *Look carefully at each thought and try to figure out what it is you really fear.*

- *Assess how likely it is that such an event would occur.*

- *Discard problems about which you are unable to do anything.*

- *Pinpoint those that are under your control then decide what you can do, want to do, and will do about the situation.*

Safety behaviors

Safety behaviors are those behaviors which we use to protect ourselves from anxiety. Some safety behaviors help us avoid the feared situation altogether. For example, whenever Joanna is invited to a party, she finds an excuse to keep from going so she can't be embarrassed. Other safety behaviors reduce the risk of being negatively evaluated. For example, when Barry goes to the singles' bar, he leans against the bar, bracing himself with his elbow and leg, to prevent anyone from seeing him tremble. The problem with safety behaviors is that in anxiety-provoking situations they not only reduce our fear but also reinforce that fear. That is, they can actually cause or exaggerate some symptoms of SA/SP.

Barry. *When Barry braces himself against the singles' club bar, he's automatically preventing the things he fears from happening. He doesn't allow himself to see what actually would happen if he didn't brace. As a result, he can't unambiguously disconfirm the belief or the expected consequences of his trembling. So he doesn't really know what would happen: If he'd shake, if anyone would notice, and if anyone would negatively evaluate him for it. Instead, he's anxiously preparing for humiliation or rejection which may have a low likelihood of occurring. Furthermore, as he braces himself, he's straining his muscles to keep himself immobile. This strain itself makes the muscles even more likely to tremble.*

Just believing others will negatively evaluate us and mentally preparing for it may make it come true. Studies have shown that when we anticipate a negative interaction, that we'll be disliked, we tend to be rated by the other person in the interaction as less warm, friendly, and disclosing, as compared with when we anticipate a positive interaction. In conversation the behavior of those with SA/SP has been judged to be significantly more negative than that of those with other anxiety disorders or non-patients.

Safety behavior studies conducted by Adrian Wells looked at whether the use of safety behaviors had any effect on the effectiveness of exposure therapy. Two groups of SA/SPers participated in one session of exposure to a feared social situation. One group, however, was instructed to intentionally drop their safety behaviors. The results showed that while exposure alone reduced anxiety and negative belief ratings, exposure plus the dropping of safety behaviors significantly increased this reduction.

What this suggests is that our safety behaviors, so useful in defending against negative evaluation and making us feel in control, can interfere with our recovery. To make cognitive and behavioral strategies more effective, therefore, we need to identify our key safety behaviors. Once we've done that, we need to assess how they're tied to our anxiety-related beliefs. This means discerning how they increase symptoms and/or prevent our disconfirming our mistaken beliefs, examining them, and eliminating them. Safety behaviors include

- *Avoidance of social situations (not going, not accepting engagements or opportunities to interact with others)*
- *Social withdrawal within situations (not speaking, not making eye contact, listening, being outrageous or aggressive, standing apart)*
- *Drinking alcohol*
- *Using recreational drugs.*

These behaviors will be discussed in the section on **cognitive-behavioral therapy** in this chapter.

There are a number of strategies which counter these fear thoughts in the short term.

Thought-stopping. This is a simple but highly effective technique which stops thoughts and interrupts habitual thought patterns. Strategies include:

- *Saying "Stop! I'll think about it later," and scheduling time to think about it*
- *Carrying 3"X 5" card with the word "STOP" in enormous red letters*
- *Writing the thoughts down the moment they occur*
- *Ringing a loud bell*
- *Wearing a rubber band around the wrist and snapping it hard to stop ruminating*
- *Detailing all the ways to change the situation in the future.*

While all these techniques work well individually, they'll be even more effective when used together.

Distraction. We can interfere with our fear thoughts by ignoring or forgetting them, deliberately thinking about something non-arousing or doing something else. We can fantasize or visualize about a favorite subject. However, distraction needs to be used with caution. It's for temporary reduction of symptoms and not for alleviating the disorder itself. Alcohol use, substance abuse, aggressive acts, or sex, for example, should not be employed to take our minds off our anxiety.

Distancing. A belief or thought may or may not represent fact. So our believing or thinking something doesn't make it so. We need to stand back, suspend our judgment, and look objectively and critically at the belief or thought.

Substitution. Substituting a competing emotion for our fear allows us temporarily to go beyond our immobilization or avoidance. When we choose an activating emotion like humor, we focus our attention and energy outward, on the environment. Because we can't respond to humor and fear at the same time, humor affords us a refuge from the perceived danger, as is often seen in life-and-death situations, such as war or medical emergencies. It also provides us a way to respond without fear so we can continue what we're doing.

Barry. *Barry's handwriting totally disintegrated whenever he had to write in front of others. It was a situation that mortified him, leaving him agonizing for days on end about what others thought. So this time, after signing his name to a company blood-drive volunteer list with his colleagues, he made a point of drawing the others' attention to his signature. Chuckling, he said, "Look at that chicken scratch. What does that say? Boy, aren't you glad I'm not your doctor." Everyone laughed and went about their business.*

It's useful to remember that laughter boosts our immune system, lowers our blood pressure, increases our disease-fighting T-cells, and just plain feels good. As we get older, we tend to laugh less. Non-SA/SP children laugh about 400 times a day whereas non-SA/SP adults, only about 15 times a day. While there are no figures on laughter in those of us with SA/SP, we can assume it's, unfortunately, significantly less. To address our laugh-challenged state we can

• *Be more playful;*

• *Surround ourselves with playful, funny, or humorous others;*

• *Do one playful thing a day;*

• *Watch children and/or animals playing;*

• *Collect cartoons to post or jokes to share;*

• *Look for humor in SA/SP and in the absurdity of life;*

• *Listen to humor tapes and/or watch comedies to relieve stress;*

• *Take care not to let humor disguise anger or aggression.*

Anger too may be substituted for fear because it's energizing. But if we use it, we must do so very carefully. Inherent in the use of anger is the question of at whom the anger is really directed. Directing anger at others when we're angry with ourselves only creates more problems for us and others as well. SA/SPers already have more anger than we can handle so this may not be a good first choice for us. If we do use it, we should direct the anger toward the situation and not toward individuals.

Maria. *When Maria thought about not being able to go to church any longer because she felt she'd made a fool of herself with her previously frantic behavior, she became incensed at the whole situation. I can go to church if I want, she snorted. Nothing that's happened can keep me away. No matter what, I won't allow my past performance to spoil everything. The next Sunday she went to church, revved up. She slid into her regular place in the back, noting that no one paid any unusual attention to her. She was glad to be back and her anger disappeared.*

Identification. When we determine that the thought or belief isn't correct, we need to label it as a *thinking error.*

Reframing. Framing is a psycho-linguistic term for how we categorize and perceive our actions, their outcomes, and contingencies. It's our perspective, where we place our emphasis, or the context. As such, it subordinates all other perceptions. For example, do we see social events as a threat or possibility for making friends. Frames are dependent, in part, upon social and cultural norms, our habits, personal characteristics, environmental factors, and, for us SA/SPers, our condition. Like a picture frame, this cognitive device puts boundaries on our thinking and feelings about a subject at a given time, restricting or enhancing our options. It's important to remember that being able to turn negative events around to result in positive outcomes is a characteristic of hardiness.

Joanna. *When Joanna entered her English class, she immediately saw her physiological arousal in terms of her anxiety about giving a speech because she thought she would be humiliated and rejected. She framed her arousal as* *negative and the associated situation as something to be avoided. She could, however, reframe her physiological arousal in view of what she knew to be true about the environment. Her classmates have always been supportive of one another's efforts. A number of students actually look up to her for continuing her education at age 35. She knows her material and has prepared a script from which to read if she has to. So she could legitimately reframe her arousal as eagerness to get the speech over with and finish the requirement for keeping her grade-point average high. By positively relabeling the cause of her arousal, she's allowing herself to respond to the situation in a new, more adaptive way.*

Albert Ellis, the progenitor of Rational-Emotive Behavior Therapy (REBT, formerly RET), says: "People and things do not upset us. Rather we upset ourselves by believing that they can upset us."

Maladaptive Thoughts Record Exercise

You need to spend 15 minutes a day disputing your irrational thoughts and beliefs. Answer the following questions and record both the questions an answers in the Maladaptive Thoughts Record format which follows and put in your journal. (Questions adapted from A New Guide to Rational Living by Albert Ellis and Robert Harper.)

1. *What irrational thought or belief is maladaptive and I want to rid myself of it?*
   (For example, "Everyone *must* evaluate me in positive terms.")

2. *Is this belief or thought correct, factual, or rational?*
   (For example, "No.")

3. *What evidence exists that this thought or belief is incorrect, not factual, or irrational?*
   (For example, "People will judge me based upon their own agendas, biases, values, and experience. I have no control over that. There's no natural law that says they have to regard me positively. If one person doesn't evaluate me positively, there are many others who will. I'm not diminished as a person if any one person doesn't value me as I'd like. If a person values me negatively, it doesn't mean I'm a bad, incompetent, or worthless person. It may mean I have a skill deficit that needs work, but not necessarily.")

4. *What evidence exists that this thought or belief is correct, factual, or rational?*
   (For example, "None really. I'd like everyone to think highly of me. If they don't, it won't be terrible. I can live with it, but I will feel disappointed, frustrated, and maybe deprived.")

5. *What type of maladaptive thinking is this?*
   (For example, "*Should* statements.").

6. *What is the worst thing that could actually happen to me if people don't respond to me as I think they must?*
   (For example, "I could spend all my time trying to make them think well of me. But some people may never think well of me, might even reject me. I

might be alone as a result which would be uncomfortable and unpleasant, but I could survive.")

7. *What positive things can I do for myself if I don't get what I think I must?* (For example, "I can work on my recovery so I can be more comfortable and satisfied with myself and life. I can look for others who might regard me positively. I can devote more time to pleasing those who value me, thereby pleasing myself.")

Maladaptive Thoughts Record

Create a section in your journal for maladaptive thoughts and copy the following table, giving yourself plenty of room in which to respond to each question in the previous exercise.

Date_____

Question	Response
Q#1	R#1
Q#2	R#2
Q#3	R#3
Q#4	R#4
Q#5	R#5
Q#6	R#6
Q#7	R#7

This process, according to rational-emotive behavioral therapy, is as easy as **ABCDE**: (1) **A**dversity - what triggers the anxiety process; (2) **B**elief - what we think about the situation; (3) **C**onsequences - what we expect to result; (4) **D**isputation - what we do to challenge the validity of the thoughts; and (5) **E**nergization - what we experience as a result of countering distorted thoughts.

What is cognitive-behavioral therapy?

Cognitive-behavioral therapy (CBT) is a combination of therapies which works on our fearful thoughts, beliefs, feelings, and our avoidant behaviors. Generally, in CBT we work extensively on the cognitive aspects of our SA/SP first to prepare ourselves for use of the behavioral therapies. The behavioral component is based upon learning theory and is interested in observable behavior, not in thoughts, emotions, conflicts, and motives which we can't observe, measure, and analyze directly.

The behavioral symptoms of SA/SP, for example, are seen as the result of learned patterns of behavior which are not adaptive for us. This behavior, however, can't be considered maladaptive without reference to the (1) social situation in which it takes place and the (2) thoughts and attitudes of the observer (us) who finds it objectionable or unpredictable. The aim of behavioral strategies, then, is to inhibit or remove our maladaptive behavior by directly applying conditioning principles and techniques while using cognitive strategies to restructuring our thoughts.

Assessment is a continuous part of the behavioral approach. It asks:

• *What behavior is maladaptive?* (This is the behavior to be increased or decreased, such as Harry's eating only soft food with lots of liquids because he's afraid of choking.)

• *What in the environment either maintains this undesirable behavior or reduces the likelihood of our performing a more adaptive response?* (When Harry eats soft food and drinks a lot of liquid, he doesn't choke and isn't embarrassed in public.)

• *What environmental factors can be manipulated to alter this behavior?* (Food consistency can be gradually changed to demonstrate that Harry doesn't need to eat soft food to keep himself from being humiliated.)

Behavioral techniques investigate present behavior only. What may have reinforced the behavior in the past is not knowable and may not be the same as what's keeping it going now. The therapy is more interested in "what" behavior needs to be changed than in "why" we're behaving as we do. There's no looking for what happened in the past, whether we were in a wet diaper too long in our crib, suffer from penis envy, or have an overactive superego.

Behavior therapy is aimed at determining where change needs to occur then helping us acquire new, substitute behaviors. This approach uses schedules of positive reinforcement (rewards) which increase the likelihood of our acquiring the new behavior. It also shapes our new responses in social situations, slowly increasing our comfort level in the situation until we can encounter it without anxiety.

Exposure. This is the primary group of behavioral techniques used in CBT with SA/SP. It involves confronting the feared social situation and remaining in it until habituation (arousal reduction) occurs and the stimulus no longer elicits our anxiety. When habituation occurs, our physiological measures of arousal, pulse rate and blood pressure, drop, indicating a decrease in our stress. We'll also tend to rate ourselves as feeling less distressed at that time.

We can encounter our fear in our imagination (**imaginal exposure**) or in the actual fear-provoking social situation (**in vivo exposure**) and we can encounter that fear in either a graduated, step-by-step fashion or at full intensity (**flooding**). Frequently both imaginal and in vivo are used, beginning with imaginal. Once we've adapted to the imaginal scene, we exposure ourselves to the real thing. Flooding therapies elicit a strong anxiety response. The behavioral premise is that encountering the intense anxiety where escape is impossible will decrease or extinguish the anxiety because we're forced to see that our negative thoughts and fears are unfounded.

Another type of flooding is Viktor Frankl's **paradoxical intention.** This is where we intentionally try to bring on our anxiety symptoms in the most full-blown way possible. If we tremble, sweat, or blush when anxious, we try to simulate these feared symptoms. But the harder we try, the harder it is for us to do. So not being able to experience what we expect to experience in a feared situation changes our beliefs about the likelihood of its really happening.

In addition, we can deal with our fear through **intentional errors**. We can force ourselves to confront threatening social situations by purposely creating and acting on those situations. We do this by choosing some minor anxiety-provoking behavior, like dropping papers in front of others or forgetting a colleague's name, then imagining our intentionally doing the behavior, and successfully handling the consequences. To prepare we rehearse this incident in our minds until we feel comfortable doing it up close and personal then we actually initiate the real event.

Since we created the incident and have practiced the action and our response to it, we're the one in control of it. This allows us to step back to objectively observe how others really respond to our behavior and, thus, test our unrealistic expectations. Doing so also allows us to experience ourselves as more confident and successful.

Joanna. *Joanna tried imaginal exposure therapy for her fear of public speaking. She began by imagining herself in her English class when her report was due. Standing at the podium, she should feel her heart racing, her legs tremble, sweat pouring down her back, and her mouth dry. Lost in the role-play, she struggled to envision herself in a near-panic state, on the verge of collapse. But despite generating all the emotion she did, her image was still standing at the podium, unscathed by the anguish she regularly felt in real-life. Joanna made a game of it and she practiced it daily. The next time she was to give a report, she managed not only to stay in the classroom but also to stand up at the podium.*

Harry. *Harry tried paradoxical intention. Before he was scheduled to go on stage, he'd try to make himself anxious enough to vomit. He began the process in his dressing room, carrying the waste basket around with him, willing himself to regurgitate into it, to make the grossest mess possible. He continued as he proceeded into the wings. "I'm an actor," he thought, "surely I can do this." But by the time of his stage cue he hadn't succeeded and was chuckling at the intensity of the silliness of what he was doing. When he walked onstage he felt more comfortable.*

Sarah. *Being in a restaurant paralyzed Sarah, who feared acting like a klutz. Because the possibility of her dropping her silverware and drawing everyone's attention to her lack of social aptitude made her anxious, she decided to become the fork-dropping queen. After practicing her clumsy act in her mind, she tried it out for real at a luncheon with colleagues. As her fork clattered to the tile floor and a good-looking waiter who was passing hurriedly replaced it for her, someone joked that Sarah was just trying to make an impression on the waiter. Sarah smiled and winked, as if they shared a secret, and lunch continued without a hitch.*

While both imaginal and in vivo exposure are useful in reducing fear, real-life exposure has long been acknowledged as a central behavioral component in effective CBT. But real-life exposure has some attendant problems. One is that it's difficult to find natural situations that are repeatable so that we're allowed to do our graduated approaches. Another is they need to be sufficiently long so we can feel the anxiety and habituate to it. Often there's no way to prolong them. Most of these are situations where we have no control, like on a subway or at a party. It's somewhat easier in situations where we have some control over the variables, like in a work or school setting. But there's no way to predict what will happen in a real-life situation, a fact which we may find disturbing.

Furthermore, because of the level of anxiety involved some of us will enter the situation and appear to be engaged in the therapy but be exercising safety behaviors. When we do that, we're really disengaged from the situation and ignoring the cues to which we need to adapt. As a result, we're effectively avoiding the anxiety situation.

Despite these apparent drawbacks, CBT's use of exposure therapies with cognitive restructuring therapies has been shown to decrease anxiety and increase approach behaviors more than relaxation alone or systematic desensitization. In addition, they decrease anticipatory anxiety, anxiety in different situations, and avoidance behavior. Self-ratings for improvement are high. Moreover, the improvements in anticipatory anxiety have been maintained at 6-month follow-up to clinical studies.

To address our anxiety through exposure in a step-by-step fashion we need to construct a hierarchical list for our anxiety-provoking social situation. This hierarchy lists all the relevant factors in our experiencing that anxiety and ranks them by their the severity, from the most disturbing to the least disturbing.

Barry's anxiety hierarchy

Barry doesn't like being scrutinized by others in most situations, but particularly at work. He constructed the following hierarchy of what makes him fearful at work, in descending order from the most disturbing to the least.

Most stressful

Scene #	Scene Description
1.	Being watched working by his boss
2.	Being watched working by ten fellow employees
3.	Being watched working by six fellow employees
4.	Being watched by an expert in his work area
5.	Being watched by three fellow employees
6.	Being watched by one fellow employee

Least stressful

We look at the least disturbing item on our anxiety hierarchy and imagine ourselves in the situation, visualize it in great detail (as we did in our visualization exercise), and monitor our anxiety. The smaller the increments of anxiety, the less intensity we have to experience at each step, and the greater our likelihood of success. It's necessary for us to remain there until we can experience it without anxiety. Once we'd achieved this step, we progress to the next step on our list and repeat the process. It may be better if we address no more than three steps in any one session. Once we can comfortably enter the situation in our minds, we're ready to approach it in real life.

Systematic desensitization.   This is Joseph Wolpe's behavioral therapy which employs both exposure and relaxation exercises. It involves

• *Constructing an anxiety hierarchy*

• *Training in deep muscle relaxation and breathing*

• *Opposing anxiety-provoking elements with relaxation.*

Sometimes difficult to perform, systematic desensitization can be used in our imaginations or real life. Like exposure, it requires being linked with cognitive restructuring and is more effective when we accomplish our hierarchy in our imaginations first then apply it in real life. However, there are few research studies which find systematic desensitization as effective as exposure in CBT for SA/SP. This may be because use of relaxation techniques during exposure may actually interfere with the habituation process, thus rendering the exposure less effective. Or it may be that the process is slow-moving and tedious, making it difficult for SA/SPers to stick with it. This is why it's not recommended that we do relaxation exercises during an anxiety-provoking event. However, if our anxiety is extreme, breathing exercises may help us as we experience the anxiety and see ourselves getting through it without the anticipated social mishaps.

While it may not work for many for SA/SP in general, it may work for some or for co-morbid panic, so let's look at the process. When we've relaxed ourselves, we look at the least disturbing item on our anxiety hierarchy, imagine ourselves in the situation, visualize it, and monitor our anxiety. The moment we begin to feel anxious, we should pause for about 15 seconds then stop imagining the scene. We need to practice these relaxation techniques until we feel calm and relaxed once again then re-enter the situation, repeating the process as often as necessary, and remaining there until we can experience it without anxiety. Once we'd achieved this step, we move to the next step and repeat the process. Once again, when we can address the social situation in our minds without anxiety, we can more easily attempt it in real life.

Virtual reality therapy.   When in vivo exposure is not easily accessible, desensitization may be done via virtual reality. Specifically, we can encounter our fears through a series of computer-generated anxiety-provoking scenes. One advantage of virtual reality therapy (VRT) over in vivo is the freedom it gives to both therapist and client to control the anxiety-provoking situation. Since 1992 VRT has been employed with success in the treatment of psychological disorders, particularly specific phobias such as fear of flying, agoraphobia, fear of heights, spiders, and closed spaces. A recent study conducted at the Virtual Technology Laboratory at Clark Atlanta University looked at fear of public speaking and similarly demonstrated a significant reduction of self-reported anxiety. As yet no studies have been done on generalized SA/SP.

How effective is cognitive-behavioral therapy?

Improvement in our level of SA/SP is the result of a reduction in our fear of negative evaluation which improves our overall level of functioning. Since our fear of negative evaluation is composed of cognitive distortions and supported by avoidance behavior, any therapy to be effective in dealing with SA/SP must address both components. This is borne out in research findings.

Richard Mattick and others have demonstrated that exposure plus cognitive restructuring tends to be more effective than either exposure or cognitive restructuring alone for SA/SP. Independent assessment of individuals' SA/SP after cognitive-behavioral treatment has found that use of an expanded range of cognitive restructuring activities plus exposure led to significant improvement for 89% of the study participants. Approach behaviors increased while self-rated avoidance decreased. SA/SP symptoms interfered less with work, social activities, and family life.

Individual versus group therapy

If CBT is the therapy of choice, what is the most effective way to present it? Is individual therapy better than group therapy? Clinical researcher Richard Heimberg designed a cognitive-behavioral group therapy (CBGT) to assess that question. He developed an approach which maximizes the integration of cognitive and behavioral procedures. Employing two co-therapists (one male and one female), it works with six patients/clients over twelve weekly sessions. Essential to his approach are the following:

- *Training skills in the identification, analysis, and disputation of maladaptive thoughts through structured exercises;*
- *Exposure to simulations of anxiety-provoking situations within the group setting to receive feedback, the opportunity to learn from others' simulations, and the availability of an audience;*
- *Cognitive restructuring procedures used before, during, and after simulated anxiety-situation exposures;*
- *In vivo exposure homework assignments which mirror the in-group exposure simulations;*
- *Self-administered cognitive restructuring test use before and after behavioral homework assignments.*

The "group" element can provide a number of significant benefits. As group participants, we SA/SPers can identify with one another. We can form bonds and share: Ideas, insights, perspectives, feedback, advice, and support. Group therapy is more cost-effective than individual therapy. Moreover, this process has also been adapted for adolescents so that it takes into account their cognitive and developmental levels, behavioral-skills level, and social milieu. However, access to CBGT is more difficult because it tends to be less available than CBT.

But not everyone is comfortable in a group. Some SA/SPers find it difficult enough just to speak with the therapist alone. The presence of other individuals, even those who are SA/SPers like us, may dampen our enthusiasm. We may feel expected to ask or answer questions, make suggestions or comments. We may feel pressured to respond then fear being evaluated in whatever we say or do. However, for those of us who feel we can benefit from the group, CBGT is a good way to go

Comparison of individual CBT and CBGT by Richard Lucas and Michael Telch found that group treatment didn't lead to significantly better outcomes than individual treatment. Both CBGT (61%) and CBT (50%) showed reliable change. However, it's been shown that patients who'd participated in CBGT functioned better than those who had experienced education and support, placebo, or were wait-listed for as along as five years

What really goes on in CBGT?

CBGT for SA/SP typically runs 12-14 weeks with small numbers of SA/SPers (and only SA/SPers) meeting once a week, often in the evening. In between meetings group participants are expected to engage in 20 minutes of therapy practice each day in a peaceful, stress-free, and positive environment at home. Meetings themselves operate on a stress-free rule wherein we're not pressured, not put on display, or asked to do things we don't want to do. However, as we move up our hierarchies, we do voluntarily allow ourselves to be put on display and do things we don't particularly want to do. We do this because this is the only way can get better.

According to clinical psychologist Dr. Thomas A. Richards of The Anxiety Clinic of Arizona, in Phoenix, who conducts CBGT for SA/SP, the group spends a great deal of time practicing cognitive strategies. These include becoming aware of and disputing negative self- talk and participating in behavioral therapy, such as doing presentations or simulations. During these sessions, we watch each other. Afterward, we discuss the presentations. Then to see individually how we're doing, what's right, and what needs work, we also watch a videotape of ourselves. We work on our hierarchies then do practical exposure "experiments" in the real world first with others than on our own. The approach employed in this behavioral therapy is slow and gentle.

Real-world experiments often begin as group exercises where we do those things which make us anxious. We say "hello" first to strangers, raise our voices in public, or drop things in front of others. Each experiment is detailed ahead of time with a handout to follow. Then when we're ready, we can do these actions on our own. Cognitive preparation before and re-interpretation with group members after is one reason this method is especially effective. An ongoing activity is summarizing what we've done to date and what's yet to be done.

CBGT also can be done in an intensive format of four full weeks (with weekends optional). When we follow this course, we need to be ready, willing, and motivated to immerse ourselves deeply in the concentrated material and go at a fast pace. Dr. Richards stresses that a four-week intensive program will not totally alleviate our SA/SP but will get us going along the right path with well-established positive therapeutic habits. While it's important that we continue to use our CBT techniques after termination of regular group sessions, it's absolutely essential that those of us participating in intensive CBGT regularly continue our exercises for several months thereafter. Persistence is the key. Once SA/SPers have returned home following the four-week program, Dr. Richards provides continuing e-mail contact with us to help keep us on track.

Trusting that the solution isn't worse than the problem.

In the words of writer Somerset Maugham, "The common idea that success spoils people by making them vain, egotistic, and self-complacent is erroneous; on the contrary, it makes them, for the most part, humble, tolerant, and kind. Failure makes people cruel and bitter."

CHAPTER 8

BECOMING SOCIALLY EFFECTIVE

"Tiny differences in input could quickly become overwhelming differences in output." (James Gleick, *Chaos*, 1987)

What is social effectiveness?

When we recognize the limitations of our SA/SP-shrink-wrapped lives, we begin to see that social effectiveness is the primary skill area on which we need to work. Social effectiveness skills are aimed at increasing social awareness and interaction. They include a range of cognitive and behavioral abilities, social perception, and information-processing. They address how we select relevant and useful information from social situations and employ it toward reaching our goals. They target our inability to make positively-useful judgments about specific social situations. Furthermore, they zero in on the use of verbal and nonverbal behaviors to maintain our positive relations with others as well as maximize our goal attainment. Thus, to increase our social effectiveness we need to improve our interpersonal skills and social performance and increase our social participation. Doing so decreases our SA/SP.

Interpersonal skills. Interpersonal skills create and maintain relationships and bring us together to influence one another to meet our goals. They include holding conversations, listening, speaking, nonverbal behavior, image, assertiveness, and a sense of what's appropriate for the situation. It's generally thought that most of the skills we need for adult social interaction and successful relationships are learned during our adolescence. This appears to be true even for SA/SPers. If most of us have the skills, then what's our problem? The problem is that if we believe we lack these important skills, as we generally do in threatening social situations, we'll tend to respond inappropriately, if we respond at all. Our resulting communication likely will be less effective. We may also display undesirable mannerisms and seem to have difficulty pulling our conversational weight.

Interestingly, while observers tend to perceive socially anxious individuals as less socially skilled, there are few meaningful behavioral differences between those who are high in social anxiety and those who are low. Yes, SA/SPers tend to speak less about themselves in conversations, ask more questions, and look less at speakers, but they also smile and nod more, interrupt less frequently, and seem more attentive. One could make the case that many of these "socially anxious" behaviors actually socially facilitate conversations, and do so more than behaviors of more "socially confident" individuals.

A low level of social participation, which tends to be characteristic of SA/SP, does not, by itself, indicate poor interpersonal skills. Neither does a low amount of eye contact. What's "appropriate" will necessarily vary with the circumstances. In fact, studies have shown that individuals with high- and low-levels of social anxiety don't differ so much in the frequency or duration of eye contact but in the timing and placement of it. We do it, but we do it differently. Furthermore, whether an individual is perceived to have deficient social skills is more a function of observational bias than the presence of an actual deficit.

But we have the same bias about ourselves. When we're anxious in a social situation, we doubt that we have the social skills to convey the desired message or impression of ourselves to others. Once we believe we lack the necessary skills, we tend to conclude we're unlikely to make that impression or receive a positive evaluation in a situation where those skills are needed.

Yes, it's true that skills we use infrequently may become rusty. It's true that they may suffer from the impact of our continuous negative thinking. But it's also true that sometimes low self-esteem causes us to underestimate our ability to deal effectively with social situations. This means that even when we are socially adept and successfully execute these behaviors, we'll see ourselves as socially deficient. What the central and overriding factor appears to be is not our lack of interpersonal skills, but our perceptions of our own social inadequacy.

We need only to look at ourselves in non-threatening social situations. Generally our self-esteem is high, we feel comfortable and are likely to both feel and appear to be socially skilled. But put us in a threatening social situation and our distorted thoughts and feelings immediately take priority and interfere with our exercising those submerged skills.

Social effectiveness skills training. This is an effective method of both enhancing our social behavior and social effectiveness and reducing our social anxiety. Based on the "Social Effectiveness Therapy" model developed by Samuel Turner, Deborah Beidel, and Michelle Cooley, it uses the techniques of

• *Education about anxiety*

• *Observational learning of a socially-skilled model*

• *Direct instruction in skills*

• *Videotaped evaluation of social behavior*

• *Behavioral rehearsal*

• *Social reinforcement*

• *Corrective feedback*

• *Homework assignments*

• *Flexibility exercises*

• *In vivo exposure.*

Our social anxiety increases in novel, ambiguous, and unstructured situations. It increases in our interactions with strangers. It increases when we're less able to monitor and control our self-presentation. When we don't have a program or script for the encounter, we're likely to feel we can't handle it. Uncertainty takes over.

Social effectiveness skills training helps make us aware of our social environment. It briefs us on what to expect so as to reduce our uncertainty. It teaches us about the formation and termination of interpersonal relationships, the skills necessary to carry on these relationships successfully, and how to speak and present ourselves in public, both formally and informally. It instructs us how to formulate appropriate scripts for these situations then provides us an opportunity to practice our social skills in these scripts. Through exposure it subjects us to feared situations in which we can employ our skills and knowledge and test our readiness. And, perhaps most importantly, it increases our confidence that we'll present ourselves in an acceptable manner, thus decreasing our social anxiety while increasing our social activity.

By improving our social skills, we

• *Improve our self-esteem and self-confidence;*

• *Improve the image we present;*

• *Increase our interactional effectiveness;*

• *Decrease our social anxiety;*

• *Increase the number of interpersonal relationships;*

• *Increase the potential for intimacy.*

How is communication involved?

Communication is the process by which we establish contact with one another. Through symbols we exchange perceptions, knowledge, ideas, and experiences. We share feelings, beliefs, values, and decisions. It's aim is to help us influence each other's behavior, mutually achieve our goals and our understanding. Effective communication is a blend of applied observation, behavioral psychology, and common sense. It relies upon preparation and a combination of verbal and nonverbal skills. Four-fifths of our waking hours are spent communicating. Without effective communication we can't convey our intentions and messages; we can't develop good rapport and relationships; and we can't understand our work. Our self-presentation image, what we want others to see, is rooted in our communication skills.

For most of us SA/SPers, communication feels like a non-starter. The moment we become anxious, we either jabber or become tongue-tied. Our brain selectively erases our memory banks and we blank out. We can't retrieve the words we want when we want them and what falls from our lips often sounds to us like gibberish.

I was giving a presentation at Simmons College in Boston which was going along pretty well until I came to an anecdote I wanted to share. To make a point, I introduced it by saying, "I'll never forget the words of my mentor, Dr. Clara Mayo." No sooner had I uttered those fateful words than my anxiety-attacked brain stopped dead in its cognitive tracks. The "I'll never forget" statement completely severed the connection between my cerebrum and tongue.

A millennial minute passed as I stared blankly at my notes. Finally, I mumbled, "Well, so much for not forgetting her memorable words," and read her quotation to them.

How do we start? One way to make our communication effective is to spell out clearly, in behavioral terms, what we want to achieve. Once again, our objectives must be realistic, concrete, and specific. They must also be achievable, observable, and measurable. Depending upon our objectives, we may want to concentrate on different aspects of communication, such as self-awareness, attitude change, increasing our knowledge, or improving our skills.

Self-awareness means understanding who and what we are, how we think, and how this is likely to affect our communication.

Attitude means developing a more flexible, reality-based and assertive style of communication. It also means a willingness to influence people to behave in desired ways.

Knowledge refers to understanding communication concepts and methods, from definition to analysis to insight. It also means understanding how a message is influenced by the sender's characteristics, the medium through which it's conveyed, and the receiver's characteristics.

Skill refers to learning how to express ourselves, specifically our thoughts and facts, clearly and concisely, and to check that the message has been received and interpreted correctly. It means learning to diagnose, analyze, and solve practical communication problems. It also means learning how to gain such knowledge for the planning, directing, and controlling any project we propose.

While communication is a key part of every interaction, no two people communicate alike. Therefore, there are no specific rules to follow. Rather, there are principles which apply to all situations and people:

- *Think before communicating. Plan what you'll say and how you'll say it.*

- *Decide on the purpose of your communication. Know what is to be achieved.*

- *Take into consideration the situation and circumstances in which the communication is to take place.*

- *Make the message complete, specific, using a frame of reference.*

- *Make verbal and nonverbal behaviors consistent and congruent.*

- *Make the message fit and be appropriate to the receiver.*

- *Describe feelings clearly.*

- *Listen carefully to what is said and how it's said.*

- *Provide feedback to the sender of the message.*

- *Describe behavior without making evaluations or judgments.*

- *Don't jump to conclusions.*

- *Respect the ideas of others.*

- *Acknowledge your feelings and those of others.*

• *Control your emotions.*

• *Use a win/win approach where you and others both get something you want.*

Pinpointing barriers to communication

There are a large number of behaviors and attitudes which prevent communication from taking place.

Assumptions made without any basis in fact. We assume a lot of things about individuals, groups, society, and institutions. For instance, we assume that others understand what we mean and that we understand what they mean. We tend to assume that most people in authority or all people with a college education are good communicators. We may assume that newspapers, magazines, and television provide us with accurate, unbiased, and complete information. One of the most common mistakes we make is assuming that others perceive the world exactly as we do.

Resistance to unfamiliar concepts. Often we prefer to deal with the known and avoid the unknown. This may pertain to new subjects or new ways of thinking about old subjects. Resistance may show up as skepticism about everything.

Use of jargon. Jargon is like a secret code. Its use separates individuals into in-groups and out-groups. Even though each group and profession has its own jargon which is used among insiders, outsiders must use it carefully. While using jargon may show a savvy employer-to-be that we really know what we're talking about, for example, it may also confuse someone not familiar with the professional area. When we're talking with physicians, for example, and are not seen as someone legitimized to use their medical jargon, our use of that jargon may be seen as unacceptable even if we're using it correctly.

Lack of knowledge about the sender, receiver, subject, or medium. When we have inadequate training or knowledge, we can't transmit or receive the message fully or accurately. When we don't understand the communication process, we can't transmit or receive messages adequately. As a result, there may be differences in the interpretation of the sender's and receiver's words and their implications.

Stereotyped thinking. This is generalizing and treating all members of a group (of ideas, objects, or people) as if they were the same. While this short-cut method may be useful in sorting through all the information that bombards us, stereotyping reduces our ability to recognize differences. The same is true when we use evaluative labels based on these generalizations. We close ourselves off to new information. This breeds oversimplification and selective attention and leads to distortion of reality. Moreover, it encourages our jumping to conclusions.

Sender-receiver barriers. These are characteristics and behaviors of both senders and receivers which can interrupt the communication process. One such barrier occurs when the sender lacks a goal or reason for offering the message. Another is lack of communication skills. Incorrect word usage, grammatical errors, or poor delivery, for example, may make it difficult for others to understand what we're trying to say.

Thinking about what we're going to say next. Since we can't concentrate on two things at once (their words and our thoughts), it's better to listen. Similarly, when we're concerned about our role or how we appear, we're not receiving the sender's message. Anything that directs our attention inwards takes it away from what the sender is saying and our understanding of it.

Judging and evaluating others. When we make judgments about the sender or the message, we automatically distort the meaning of the message. If, for example, we don't like the person, it's difficult to hear the message correctly. The same is true for the subject. If we are *pro* or *con,* we'll automatically rally to that mindset. Doing this distorts our understanding.

Not putting ourselves in the other person's place. When we don't see something from the point of view of the sender, we can't hear the message correctly. Likewise, when we listen selectively, we hear only what we want to hear. In doing so, we deny, reject, or distort the message.

Having preconceived notions. When we have already decided what the message will mean, the intended meaning will be lost, obscured, or distorted.

Lack of responsive feedback. A non-responsive or inappropriate response may discourage, frustrate, or insult the sender. For example, if we ask another person with SA/SP who's on the antidepressant Parnate, "How likely do you think it is that Parnate will affect my weight?" (asking if the receiver has experienced weight changes on the drug) and the listener merely grunts or responds, "Ask a psychiatrist," we'll most likely be taken aback and communication will cease.

Lack of trust. When we don't have confidence that the other person will protect our welfare and provide acceptance and support of what we communicate, we may reduce the amount of information we share. This may lead to distortion of our message. Likewise, if we feel the other is disengaged, unreliable, or seems to have ulterior motives, we'll receive what they send with suspicion. Lack of trust is a primary obstacle to effective communication.

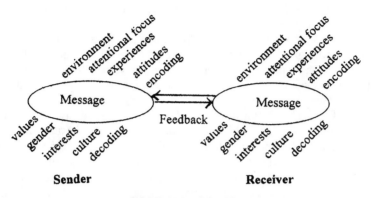

COMMUNICATION

Improving our verbal communication

Language carries communication, but it also interferes with it. What can we do to minimize this interference when we're trying to communicate?

- *Direct your audience's attention to where you want by emphasizing the point, enumerating it, and repeating or restating it.*
- *Convey forcefulness through the use of short, simple words and sentences.*
- *Avoid distracting language, punctuated with fillers, such as "uh," "hey," "like," "I mean," "right," "you know," and "okay." Avoid false stops and starts, sentence fragments, and uncertainties.*
- *Use understandable language, not loaded with ambiguities, technical terminology, acronyms, and abbreviations.*
- *Use appropriate language. This means avoiding profanity, irreverent, discriminatory, or suggestive speech. It also means avoiding political, ethnic, religious subjects, dirty jokes, and derogatory comments in general.*

Spotting thinking preferences

- *Do you ever feel you're on a different wavelength from your audience?*
- *Do people ever look at you blankly when you share information with them?*
- *Do people show frustration when you describe a problem or its solution?*

If your answer is "yes," then you may be a victim of "incompatible hemispheric thinking." You can be limited or liberated by the way you think.

Communication theory has been reborn in the form of a neuro-scientific concept called "whole-brain thinking." Proponents of the left-brain/right-brain approach, such as Ned Herrmann, author of **The Creative Brain,** and numbers of Fortune 500 large corporations, believe that this cerebral training increases skills in communication, problem solving, collaboration, and productivity. They also believe it helps them determine and predict the best use of their abilities and that of their employees.

What is whole-brain thinking? And what can it really do for us? The whole-brain concept states that the hemispheres of the brain process information in different ways. The left hemisphere processes verbal, logical, quantitative, and analytical thought, while the right addresses visual, spatial, creative, and holistic thought.

Each of us has a "brain dominance." This means we favor one cerebral hemisphere over the other. This, in turn, causes us to lean toward one style of thought processing. In practice, however, "dominance" is interpreted to mean not only how we think but also how we *like* to think. The hypothesis is that if we're predominantly left-brained, for example, we're oriented toward logical reasoning, sequences, facts, and conceptual structures. Left-brains, then, are likely to become engineers, accountants, lawyers, or managers.

If we're right-brained, our statements reflect an orientation toward people, feelings, experiences, patterns, and relations. Right-brains, then, are likely to become artists, salespeople, social workers, or entrepreneurs.

Left-brain and right-brain thinking styles are considered equally valid and valuable. Organizational proponents suggest that both styles need to be cultivated at all levels.

Thinking Preference Exercise

Answer the following questions by picking A, B, or C to determine your probable thinking style.

In a conference, where do you prefer to sit?

    A. *Left*
    B. *Right*
    C. *No preference*

How do you prefer to work?

    A. *By myself*
    B. *On a team*

When you're given an assignment, which do you prefer?

    A. *Highly specific instructions*
    B. *Rather flexible instructions*

How do you make your own decisions?

    A. *By careful analysis*
    B. *By gut feeling*

How do you motivate yourself?

    A. *By competing with yourself*
    B. *By competing with others*

Which would you prefer to be married to? Someone who

    A. *Is a thorough planner*
    B. *Has unusual ideas, daring concepts*

How do you shop?

    A. *By reading labels and comparing costs*
    B. *On impulse*

When you meet someone, what do you remember?

    A. *Name*
    B. *Face*
    C. *Both*

Which do you prefer at a meeting?

    A. *Dynamic speaker*
    B. *Imaginative slide presentation*

When driving in a city you don't know well, do you

    A. *Get a map and ask for specific directions*
    B. *Navigate on your own sense of direction*

Mark the word in each line that better describes you.

A. Logical	B. Creative
A. Analytical	B. Intuitive
A Factual	B. Holistic
A. Rational	B. Emotional
A. Linear	B. Spatial

*Scoring: For each **A** give yourself **4** points; for each **B** give yourself **1** point. **C** = **0** points. If your score is **47-60**, you tend towards left-brain thinking. **46-40** you are left-brain and right-brain equally, switching back and forth depending upon the situation. If you score **39-15**, you tend towards right-brain thinking.*

    How we think affects our perception of the best ways to communicate and collaborate. How we communicate can cause people to move toward us or away from us. If, for example, we talk to people who have a preference for right-brain thinking about details, numbers, facts, and sequences, they will tend to turn off. They'll experience actual physiological stress and want to shout, "What is the point you're trying to make?" On the other hand, if we present those with left-brain thinking style with pictures, metaphors, analogies, and the "big picture" first, they'll feel like hopping up and down in frustration, screaming, "How are you going to get there?"

    Individual thinking preferences are important because we all have different styles. We each approach problems differently and describe the problem, the process, and the solution differently.   As a result, collaboration and communication can be difficult if these differences are not acknowledged and addressed.

It's important to note that thinking preferences do not represent skills, intelligence, or level of competence. Rather they are pathways by which we are predisposed, socially and genetically, to solve problems.   Knowing and experiencing them allows us to appreciate how we and others think, learn, and create.

We often don't realize that we and others may have highly disparate thinking styles, that we may use different words, and use the words in different sequences.   As a result, we each try to explain things to the other, using the terms and figures of speech that represent our own thinking style.   But this doesn't necessarily work.   Not in the classroom, on the job, or in a relationship.

When thinking styles collide, we tend to experience a vague sense of conflict or tension.   We don't understand how the other is looking at the situation.   The other person seems, at the very least, obtuse. As a result, we all stop trying. Barry's boss, for example, used to provide Barry with lists of things to which to attend.   "It used to drive me crazy. I don't use lists. I don't need them." Having patience under these circumstances is often very difficult until we realize the thinking styles conflict.   Understanding that lists are very useful for Barry's boss made it easier for Barry not to take personally his being given these lists.

What we must recognize and appreciate is that there are many ways to approach, describe, and process information.   Knowing what differences exist, each person must make an effort to get ideas across in a form the other person can easily grasp.   Until this translation medium is on place, accountants and engineers will throw up their hands and say they can't work with salespeople and artists, and *vice versa*.

The whole-brain approach presents a model for explaining and understanding behavior, for looking at ourselves and others, generating awareness and valuing the perceived diversity.   Classifying thinking styles provides us a point of common reference that can facilitate communication and collaboration. The process fosters creativity and openness to trying new things.

Responding to interpersonal cues

Another approach for developing our communication skills is neuro-linguistic programming (NLP).   Based on the study of linguistics, body language, and communications systems, NLP is a way of increasing our sensitivity to interpersonal cues and learning to respond to them.   It's a way of increasing flexibility and responsiveness to change.   The aim of NLP's behavioral training is mastery of new ways of:

- *Reading another person's internal processes by identifying language patterns and observing nonverbal behavior*

- *Influencing another person's responses.*

According to NLP's observational data, we organize our experiences, our behavior, thoughts, and feelings, through three primary perceptual systems: Visual, auditory, and kinesthetic. There are three basic language patterns which reflect these styles.

Visual people focus on sight. They prefer to read information rather than hear it. When they recall a scene, they do so vividly, in color. They listen for and speak in visual terms: "I see what you mean" and "I get the picture." To make contact with visually-oriented people, it's best to use words related to sight.

Auditory people orient themselves to sound. They prefer to hear information rather than read it. Sounds trigger memories and associations for them. They listen for and speak in hearing terms. For example, "I hear what you're saying" and "Sounds good to me." To establish rapport with auditory individuals, we need to use hearing-related words.

Kinesthetic people relate to how things feel, taste, and smell. The physical world in all its dimensions evokes strong sensations for them. They listen to and speak in body terms. For example, "I have a good grasp on the problem," "It's a pain in the neck," and "I feel we ought to go forward." To communicate with kinesthetically-oriented people, we need to use feeling-oriented words.

How else can we know how others organize their experience and process information? NLP suggests that eye movement is an indicator of our primary perceptual system. Some studies have suggested that we glance in the direction opposite the hemisphere that's most perceptually active at that moment (although it's important to note that there are no empirical data to support the claimed link between eye movement and the brain's sensory-processing mechanism).

Eye movement up and to our right suggests visualizing something new of something which hasn't been seen before (constructed imagery). Up and to the left suggests recalling something which has been seen before (eidetic imagery). Unfocused eyes with pupils dilated, staring into space, suggests we're either recalling or creating something (imagery).

Eye movement horizontally suggests making sense of the sound we hear (internal auditory). Specifically to the right suggests imagining a sound and to the left suggests recalling a sound. Down and to the left suggests talking/listening to ourselves (internal dialogue). In general, however, eye movement down suggests sensing how the body feels (kinesthetic access).

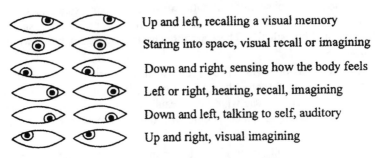

	Up and left, recalling a visual memory
	Staring into space, visual recall or imagining
	Down and right, sensing how the body feels
	Left or right, hearing, recall, imagining
	Down and left, talking to self, auditory
	Up and right, visual imagining

NLP EYE WATCHING

Knowing how our listeners receive information allows us to present it in such a way that they are more likely to attend to it and understand what we're saying. Matching our language style to theirs enables us to more easily gain rapport, a sense of trust and competence.

A form of matching, called *mirroring*, is a method of establishing rapport by doing what the other person does. Mirroring is a behavioral conditioning technique. Specifically, we subtly imitate the nonverbal behavior of others: Their gestures, body rhythm, voice tone and tempo, body postures and orientation, breathing rate, and word choice. We synchronize our behavior with that of the other person so that we're presenting ourselves similarly. Similarity creates attraction and liking.

We can take mirroring one step further to influence the other person's behavior. Through *pacing*, a form of behavior shaping, we gradually change the degree of matching to effect a new behavior. For example, in a meeting with our boss, he becomes angry because of repeated staff interruptions. He begins breathing in a more rapid and shallow fashion. To establish rapport we could assume the same breathing pattern, putting us in synchrony. Then we could gradually decrease the rate. As we do this, our boss likewise will do this, to the point of eventually relaxing and, once again, being in rapport with us.

Perceptual Preference System Exercise

What perceptual systems do you tend to use? Have a partner ask you the following questions then observe the movement of your eyes as you answer. The correctness of the answer is not as important as how you process the question.

1. *What was the name of your best childhood friend?*

2. *What are the three meanings of the word pronounced "2"?*

3. *How many is five times four?*

4. *What did you wear yesterday?*

5. *Which way does Abraham Lincoln's profile face on the penny?*

If your eyes looked to the right, you're left-hemisphere-activated. If your eyes looked to the left, you're right hemisphere-activated. Eyes up, visual. Eyes level, left or right, auditory. Eyes down, kinesthetic.

Why is listening important?

Communication is a shared experience. We listen to understand others' needs. We listen to influence others. We listen to learn. To do this we have to correctly interpret and understand what the other person is saying. Listening is not a character trait but a skill that can be developed. We listen only 25% of the time, while the other 75% we're just hearing.

Listening and hearing aren't the same thing. Hearing is the passive physical process of receiving sound. Listening is the active cognitive process of searching for the meaning of what we hear. The exchange of words and feelings can help us achieve greater productivity and greater group interaction because it encourages action, not passivity. In fact, many corporations, like AT&T, make listening and communication courses mandatory for employees. Some others require similar training for promotion.

Listening Habits Exercise

*How would you rate your listening habits? Which of the following apply to you? In the space provided, put a **Y** for "Yes" or **N** for "No". (Adapted from work by Eugene Raudsepp of Princeton Creative Research.)*

___*I never let others finish their thoughts before interrupting them.*

___*I'm eager for them to finish.*

___*I don't let them explain their problem fully.*

___*I look at them in disbelief when they talk.*

___*I finish sentences for them.*

___*I constantly do other things while they're talking.*

___*I keep trying to get them off the track by making comments and asking questions.*

___*I kid around or am flippant when they're being serious.*

___*I look at them critically while they're speaking.*

___*I rephrase their words, distorting their meaning.*

*Count the number of Ys: **1-2** = Good. **3-4** = Could use improvement. **5-6** = Poor. **7-11** = very poor.*

How to listen effectively

Effective or *active listening* is an art unto itself. We have to train ourselves to listen to receive the messages a speaker is sending to us. This requires that we specifically learn to attend or concentrate on what the speaker is saying. We listen for and note the main points the sender is making. We then begin to analyze what is being said. By the time the sender has completed the message, we have thought through the points made and have reached a tentative conclusion. It's tentative at this point because we still need to check to see if we received the message accurately.

When there is inattentive listening, both the sender and listener suffer. The sender feels frustrated at not being heard, remembered as a unique, identifiable individual, or relegated to the status hearing polluter. The listener too benefits less because the sender is less likely to want to continue to interact under these distressing circumstances.

But words are not all we have to attend to. We must attend to the three parts of the message. Each component communicates important information. Words often do not tell it all:

• *Words (data)*

• *Feeling content (tone)*

• *Nonverbal behavior (delivery).*

Active listening requires that we keep an open mind. This means not trying to second-guess the speaker. Our goal is to understand what is being said, not what we think should be or is likely to be said or meant by this speaker.

To listen actively is to check to see that our impression equals the sender's expression. We do this by giving feedback. Giving feedback is reflecting to the sender what we heard being said. Not the words *per se,* but what they're intended to mean. Feedback is tangible evidence that we have correctly decoded the message. The sender then confirms the accuracy of our impression or corrects it.

For listening to be effective we need to

• *Listen with interest;*

• *Absorb the content;*

• *Actively grasp the facts and feelings we hear;*

• *Listen for total meaning (content and feeling);*

• *Note all subtle cues;*

• *Sense underlying meaning;*

• *Intuit what person is really saying (not saying in words).*

Active listening looks for congruence between what the person is saying in words and communicating through posture, gestures, mannerisms, and voice inflection. We look for the underlying feeling message. While listening, we respond with nodding and expressions of attention, such as, "uh huh" and "I see" (something which SA/SPers are good at). Nodding and other expressions of attention indicate understanding and approval. They encourage the other person to continue speaking. Frequency of these behaviors depends upon what is being said and how it's being said.

When we listen effectively, we communicate:

- *I hear what you're feeling.*
- *I understand how you're seeing things.*
- *I see you as you are right now.*
- *I'm interested and concerned.*
- *I understand where you are now.*
- *I don't judge or evaluate you as a person.*
- *You don't have to be afraid of my censure for speaking out.*

Being a good listener helps us better identify those with common interests, those who can help us, those to whom we can be helpful, and what others really want. Being a good listener creates a good impression and visibility. For a good image being remembered positively is the name of the game.

Acquiring the skills of active listening

Reflecting is feeding back to the speaker the essence of what is being communicated. However, it's not simply repeating verbatim what has been said. If a spouse said, "I really don't want to go to work today. I have a presentation due and I'm freaked out," reflecting would **not** be repeating, "You really don't want to go to work today. You have a presentation due and you're freaked." Instead, a reflective response would be, "You're feeling really anxious about doing the presentation and would rather avoid the situation."

Clarifying focuses on the key underlying issues and sorting out confusing, conflicting feelings. When a school mate says, "I hate this class. I wish I didn't have to be here. Nothing I do satisfies anyone. Even when I do my best writing a report, it's not appreciated," we might respond, "It sounds as though you have questions about the value and acceptance of your work in this class. You'd like to continue the class because it allows you to do what you do well, but feel bad it doesn't reward you for it."

Interpreting offers possible explanations for certain behaviors or symptoms as an hypothesis not a fact. If accurate and well-timed, it can be very useful. For example, "I've noticed that when you say you like living with your parents, you shake your head. Could this indicate that you'd really like to have other living arrangements?" This observation gives the person a chance to consider the validity of the hunch and confirm, deny, or clarify.

Questioning gets us and others in touch with underlying feelings. To do so we need to ask "what" and 'how" questions. They are open-ended and can be responded to in many ways. By not imply that a "right" answer exists, they provide rich and wide-ranging information. As a result, they are more informative than closed questions, such as those requiring a "yes" or "no" answer or those posed by the question "why." "Why" questions imply that some limited numbers of "right" answers exist, that there must be an acceptable "because"-explanation and we need to find it. For example, if we ask, "How do you feel when someone unexpected comes to the door?" we get more and very different information than if we ask, "Why do you feel uncomfortable when someone unexpected comes to the door?"

Empathizing is sensing the subjective world of the other person and being aware of what the other is experiencing. For example, if a friend says, "This week's schedule is very frustrating," we might say, "Juggling family responsibilities, job, and doctor's appointments must be anxiety-provoking and tiring, especially with your new project."

Confronting is challenging some specific behavior. It's done in such a way that the focus is on the behavior and your feelings about it, and not on the person who does the behaving. Thus, we share our feelings, but avoid evaluation, judgment, and labeling the person. For example, "When I asked you about the library hours, you said, 'Shut up' and waved your hand at me as if dismissing me. That made me angry. I felt I wasn't being treated respectfully."

When we confront, we:

• *Present data upon which inferences are based before stating inferences.*

• *Are clear, specific, and concrete.*

• *Present information that is not fact tentatively, as an inference.*

• *Use I-messages throughout confrontation, being careful, caring, and constructive.*

(See Assertivenes Assessment in this chapter for further details)

Why image is essential

Poet W.H. Auden writes, "The image of myself which I try to create in my own mind in order that I may love myself is very different from the image which I try to create in the minds of others in order that they may love me."

Let's take a look at the image we want others to see. A good image is like investment in gold bullion: Highly regarded, valuable, and solid, no matter where we are. But a negative image is like a building situated on quicksand: Doomed from the beginning, sinking fast, and irretrievable. We can't afford not to have a good image.

The saying "You don't get a second chance to make a first impression" is right on the mark as a general rule. The first impression is often the most lasting so we have to give it our best shot the first time around. (This doesn't mean, however, that if we shot ourselves in the foot in our first meeting that there's no hope. There is. We can probable recover from most *faux pas* but will have to work harder and longer to do it.) It gets our foot in the door so we can make our presentation and sell ourselves. These impressions are so important that we can succeed or fail by them even BEFORE we open our mouths to speak.

Take the example of Lt. Colonel Oliver L. North, testifying at the Iran-Contra Congressional Hearings. His full-dress uniform with medals and ribbons set the tone of loyalty and fidelity. When he leaned forward, elbows braced, hands clasped, chin raised, gaze direct, and brow furrowed, he created a Norman Rockwell picture of intense sincerity. He spoke slowly, deliberately, using simple language, liberally peppered with down-home-isms, like "golly gee," "neat idea," and "pray to God." Through energy, passion, and conviction he demonstrated the depth of his beliefs and involved his listeners. Using stories, analogies, and a blow-up of an Abu Nidal newspaper article, he supported each point he made. He controlled the image he wanted to present, what he said, how he said it, and the illustrations used to shape his audience's understanding and response.

Prior to his testifying, North was condemned as a "dangerous loose cannon," the symbol of White House covert intelligence operations run amok. His public favorability rating, 6%. After only one day of testimony, there were billboards proclaiming, "Ollie For President." His public favorability rating, 43%. Regardless of how we may personally feel about him, overnight he had transformed his image from that of "swaggering, messianic crook" to "selfless, flag-wrapped Guardian of the Western World." Skillful image management.

Effectively getting our message across requires our creating a positive and affirmative image. It should engender audience identification with attitudes, values, interests, and background. We need to establish the perception of similarity because it leads to greater attraction and liking. The greater the similarity, the greater the liking. And, interestingly, the more our audience likes us, the more similar to us they perceive themselves to be. It's circular and self-reinforcing.

Our image determines how much power and credibility others perceive us to have. It creates the picture we want others to see and act on. They can see us as a Bill Gates or O.J. Simpson, a Justice Sandra Day O'Connor or Monica Lewinski. We determine which. An effective image helps us accomplish our communication and other interpersonal goals. Image is the basis of our visibility and credibility. Our success in relationships, work, and in life in general depends upon how others see us and feel about us.

The more interested we are in our listener, and the more we tailor ourselves to that listener, the more interpersonally attractive we'll be to them. The more attractive we are, the more socially desirable qualities we'll be perceived to possess (such as, competence, friendliness, intelligence, and influence). The more socially desirable we're perceived to be, the greater our impact in our initial encounters. People want to interact with those whom they believe can provide them with what they want.

Joe. *While Joe wanted to feel unconcerned and tried to present the image of one who was, his presenting himself that way seemed initially to have its drawbacks. It made him feel even more like a fraud, that he was always "on," acting. His everyday life was one big pose whenever he was around anyone, including his family. He spent much of his time and effort trying to look calm and collected in situations which Osterized his gastrointestinal tract. He hated doing it and himself for doing it. Joe's image: Grade-A impostor. But the longer he did it, the more easily he wore his new image.*

It's our image that determines how people value us, to what degree they're attracted to us, trust us, and want to interact with us.

Image assessment.   We need to assess our present image and communication skills by asking ourselves:

- *What image do I want (in concrete, specific terms)?*
- *What image am I currently projecting?*
- *What elements make up the image I want?*
- *What do I need to do to create the image I want?*
- *How am I getting my message across at present?*
- *What do I need to do to project the image I want?*

Fantasize or brainstorm all the different ways you could create the (a) visibility and (b) credibility of a positive image.

- *Do any of these methods create both visibility and credibility for you? Which ones?*
- *Where do you talk informally with individuals, besides your family and office colleagues?*
- *What do you do when you talk with those people?*
- *What results do you get?*
- *What results do you want?*

Now go back over your answers and reduce each to its key words. These words are the basis of planning your image change.

Planning Image Change Exercise

If your image assessment suggests you need to improve your image, answer the following questions as fully as you can. Be specific and concrete.

- *What presentation or image elements do you want to work on?*
- *How do you plan to work on them?*

Now pick five image behaviors you want to work on. Set up a chart like your Recovery Timeline, with "Goal," "Action," "Deadline," and "Results." Under "Goal," list the behaviors that need work. Under "Action," describe how you want to change your behavior. Put down a specific date, "Deadline," by which you want to have this accomplished. When you have met your deadline, note what happened as a result of your actions. Post this chart where you can frequently refer to it and monitor your progress.

Goal	Make eye contact
Action	Write down when I don't. Have friend tell me when I'm not.
Deadline	2 months
Results	Looking at others occasionally in conversations.

Grabbing attention

A first impression is made up of several elements, most of which are nonverbal:

- *Facial expressions*
- *Eye contact*
- *Posture*
- *Gestures*
- *Movements*
- *Tone of voice*
- *Physical appearance*
- *Clothing.*

Remember, whether we're voting for President, buying a dish soap, or looking for a mate, we identify with and relate best to those who present themselves (and are perceived) as likable, warm, sincere, competent, and confident. Of course, perception doesn't necessarily mirror reality. In general, what we want to create is the image of one who is

- *Up/alert/enterprising*
- *Enthusiastic*
- *Interested*
- *Involved*
- *Relaxed (not frantic, frenetic, or frenzied)*
- *Trustworthy.*

We need to create a positive, non-threatening aura. "Looks" and "sounds" communicate over 90% of the meaning of human interaction when people meet for the first time. The words we speak initially, while important, may represent only 7% of the meaning. So we need to look carefully at the specific nonverbal behaviors that contribute to a positive first impression.

Smile. A smile is our most important facial expression, even though it's often difficult for SA/SPers. When it's natural and spontaneous, it warms people. It indicates our interest and willingness to interact. It inspires confidence, trust, and understanding. But, of course, we don't want to look like a Cheshire cat - continuously grinning from ear to ear. This is particularly true for women who have long been socialized to smile all the time. The effect of a "permanent" smile is negative. It creates perceptions of submissiveness, powerlessness, and striving to placate.

Both men and women should smile at strategic points during the conversation. For example, we want to smile before and after our message, making direct eye contact. This establishes sincerity. It emphasizes our point. We want to smile as a reward, when we want to reinforce and encourage positive behaviors, like an interest in what we're saying. Even if SA/SPers can't produce a full smile, we should try at least to get the corners of our mouth to turn up. Often the act of moving our facial muscles into a smile positively affects our desire to smile. Also, while a variety of expression keeps the listener attentive and interested, we must be aware that too much spontaneous facial expression makes us look both overly-dramatic and like an open book which is easy to read.

Eye contact. Eye contact is a very powerful nonverbal behavior. Using the eyes alone, people and lower animals can express emotions, conveying attraction, fear, and aggression. Eye use can open and close the lines of communication. It can also regulate the flow of communication by providing turn-taking signals and monitoring feedback. Furthermore, eye contact can reinforce our other nonverbal as well as verbal behaviors. However, it's important to note that not making eye contact also conveys information. It signals disinterest in or avoidance of an interaction and communicates the nature of the interpersonal relationship. We need to be aware of the eye use of the other person as well. As we SA/SPers know, making eye contact sometimes can be very difficult.

High- and low-status people use their eyes differently. People who perceive themselves to have little power (low-status) tend to look at others a lot, watching for signals. These signals tell them what's going on in the situation and how they should respond. Even when they're speaking, they tend to look at their listeners more often. This is precisely what SA/SPers do time and again. We're hypervigilant, always looking for clues in the encounter that we're being perceived as acceptable, attractive, or interesting, but expecting signs that we're not any of these things.

Confident people and those in authority (high-status), on the other hand, appear not to monitor the behavior of those around them the same way. They look more at the other when they're speaking than when they're listening. They also tend to look at others at strategic moments. When they start to speak, they look at the other person briefly, then look away. They look back when they've finished to signal that it's the other person's turn to speak.

It's better to assume the role of someone in control. When we combine eye contact with appropriate smiling behavior, we create a stronger positive impression. Therefore, we should begin our conversations with direct eye contact to open the communication line then smile to show our friendliness and interest. When we start to speak, we need to look away to maintain our speaking role. As we finish, we look back so that we end with direct eye contact to signal we're done. Then we conclude with a smile.

Obviously, if what we're saying is very lengthy, we'll want to look at our listener occasionally. We do this to make personal contact, to make sure we're being heard, to obtain feedback, and to see if the other will let us continue. Because we're going to be taking turns we want to encourage reciprocity of behavior. But we need to remember not to hold our gaze at the other person too long. Our listener might misinterpret it as a go-ahead to begin talking.

When we assume the role of listener, our eye contact changes to show our interest in what the other is saying. After all, everyone likes to be listened to. Since we gaze more at people we like, we should look at the speaker intently, but short of staring at them. Staring is generally interpreted as aggressiveness and produces considerable discomfort on the part of the recipient - a fact of which SA/SPers are well aware. We try to avoid someone who stares at us. To prevent staring, we need to look away once in awhile.

But what if we can't make direct eye contact? Indirect eye contact will do. We can look at one eye or the bridge of the person's nose. If that's still too uncomfortable, we can catch an eyebrow, tip of the ear or the mouth. Sweeping our eyes over those of the other person, whether we actually look or not, is important to give the impression of eye contact.

Posture. Our posture reveals how we think of ourselves and our listener. If we slouch, with our head down, talking to our feet, as those of us with SA/SP often do, we look as if we don't hold ourselves in very high regard. Whereas if we stand tall, shoulders back, with military bearing, we look confident and competent. We look like someone with whom others would want to interact because of our attitude of self-assurance and pride. Our body orientation also suggests our availability for interaction. If our position is closed with arms and/or legs crossed or close to the body, if we're leaning back, turning away, or looking away, we're not available or interested. If, however, our position is open, with arms and legs apart comfortably, if we're leaning forward, facing the other person, or making eye contact, we're available and interested.   These positions hold equally for our conversation partner.

Voice. Our voice quality conveys enthusiasm, sincerity, informality, and interest in our subject. Our belief in what we're saying will be reflected in our voice. If we believe, are interested and enthusiastic, our listener will follow our lead. If we're not, our listener will pick up on it immediately.   Their eyes will glaze over, and they'll tune us out.

We can regain the listener's attention at any time by pausing for emphasis or speaking softly. When we speak almost in a whisper, we force our listeners to have to strain to hear us. Speaking in a slightly lower register also makes the voice more melodious, authoritative, and relaxed.

Whenever possible we should stand when speaking. Doing this allows us to project our voice better. We can gesture more easily and emphatically when we make a point. This particularly applies to telephone conversations, which many of us SA/SPers hate. On the phone we should stand, smile, and gesture too, speaking at a moderate rate. Better too slow than too fast. If we get a frog in our throat, it's probably a sign of poor breathing, most likely related to tension. If this happens, we should excuse ourselves for a moment to take a sip of a warm drink or take a deep breath or picture ourselves in the most relaxing situation possible. Then humming to lower our voice, we should put on that big smile and resume the phone conversation. This time speaking more slowly.   If necessary, we can tell the other person we'll call back in a hour, giving us time to reduce our mounting anxiety.

Having a phone script may be beneficial, but having a list of points to cover may be more useful because it's less rigid and allows us to wander without guilt or fear of losing our place. Scoping the time available for us to talk limits our anxiety and helps others get to the point. When the time is up, we can then summarize what has been said to confirm understanding. Getting feedback reduces the number of calls needed to correct impressions and information.

Clothing. Our clothing and accessories indicate our status. They also indicate how we care about ourselves. Our attire is the first thing others notice about us after, of course, the basics of race, gender, and age. We want to dress appropriately for the occasion, the people present, the surroundings, and our goal. Some SA/SPers dress to attract attention while others of us dress to blend in with the background. Irrespective of the intention of our attire, we need to look comfortable. If we're uncomfortable, others will be uncomfortable too. If we wanted a job, would we dress for the decision maker at the company the way we would for a beer bash? Probably not. The occasions, people, surroundings, and goals are different.

Our grooming is part of this as well. We need to be meticulous, kept up, and clean (particularly our hands since they tell their own story). Anything flamboyant or "odd," from pierced tongues to chartreuse hair, will generally tend to detract from our positive image, unless we're a SoHo model or punk-rock singer.

Movements. Our walk should look unrushed and purposeful, with no exaggerated motions (I often looked like the White Rabbit in **Alice in Wonderland**). To keep motions to a minimum, we should keep our elbows close to the body and gesture from the elbows down primarily. If we keep our body relaxed and relaxed-looking, we'll tend to feel more relaxed. Aroused behaviors can precipitate arousal. Even facial expressions should be used conservatively so that it's not the expression that carries the thrust of the communication. A pleasant poker face is a good general expression. All movement should appear confident, deliberate, poised, and relaxed, with gestures subtle, minimal, and used sparingly.

What about verbal behavior?

Of course, language is important. It's especially important when we've gotten past the first impression. Powerful language attracts others, as do powerful voices and body language. Verbal behavior conveys ideas - our experience, knowledge, and expertise. Language is powerful when it's direct, assertive, simple, brief-and-to-the-point, and conversational. It's powerful when it's free of fillers, like *um, ah, y'know, I mean, okay*. When it's free of qualifiers and hedges, such as "I may be wrong, but" or "I'm right, aren't I?" (These tend to be more common among females.) When it's free of profanity and prejudice. Powerful speakers don't interrupt. Instead they take turns in conversations to establish and maintain their credibility. This promotes a freer exchange and increased comfort of both partners. Of course, SA/SPers rarely interrupt anyway, though we may when we're anxious to make a point while we have the courage and still remember what we want to say (something I used to do).

Image Behaviors Exercise

Stand in front of a mirror or have yourself videotaped as you respond to interactions with others. If you're doing this by yourself, make a list of questions and comments others are likely to make in an interaction. You can also do this for job interviewing. Assess and make note of your nonverbal behavior.

- *Do you make eye contact?*

- *How do you stand?*

- *How much do you gesture?*

- *How often do you use facial expressions, only for appropriate emphasis or all the time?*

- *Are your expressions appropriate?*

- *Do you frown or wince?*

- *How assured do you look?*

- *How relaxed do you look?*

- *How enthusiastic do you look?*

- *Is there anything you do repeatedly that has no real purpose?*

Creating the 30-second grabber

When making a first impression, we have 30 seconds to grab and hold our listener's attention, to create expectations, and set the tone for the potential interaction. That's 30 seconds to convince and persuade others that they want to talk to us. Thirty seconds to make our point effectively. Why 30 seconds? Because that's the TV generation's sound-bite attention span. People often have a sense of time-urgency, busy schedules, and other things to think about. They're impatient to get to the heart of the matter unless they immediately see it's in their vested interest to listen. In general, they're not willing to wait 10 minutes for us to get around to our point. Conventional wisdom for non-SA/SPers is that "if you can't say it in 30 seconds, you can't say it at all."

In that brief span of time we should give our name, tell something significant and relevant about ourselves, and state what we're interested in and want to achieve in the interaction. The exact subject matter and objective will vary with the circumstances. Then once we've spent our 30 seconds wisely and gotten the listener's attention, we still have only 3-4 minutes in which to effectively tell our story or get our message across. That is

- *Tell them what you're going to tell them* (topics you'll cover, time you'll take, participation by listener, any specific directions).

- *Tell them why they should listen* (reason to give up time, benefit for listening).

- *Tell them the story* (message, examples, evidence, ideas, proposal).
- *Tell them what you told them* (review of most important points and action statement if appropriate).

That's 3-4 minutes to cover the *who, what, where, when, why,* and *how* of your message. Let's look at a clear-cut business example.

Maria wants to open her own travel agency. She needs $10,000, but has only $8,500. She wants to move on this right away and doesn't want to go through a bank. Pat Allen, an acquaintance, invests in small businesses, taking pleasure in watching them grow and prosper. Maria makes an appointment with Pat. After the social amenities, Maria gets to the point. (If you have a clock or watch with a sweep hand, time your reading of the following.)

"Pat, I have a dream. I want to open my own travel agency. You know I have the sales, marketing, and travel agency experience. I have a plan, a location, and am willing to work hard. I'm ready to invest $8,500 of my own money. I need another $1,500. I'm sure you remember someone who helped you make your dreams come true. I need your help to make MY dream come true." (Stop! So how did Maria do with her 30-second grabber?)

Preparation.   Before we start our conversation, we need to prepare. There are seven elements of an effective message which we need to have ready.

Objective.
- *What do we want out of the conversation?*
- *What specifically do we want to achieve?*
- *Do we want information, a referral, a job, a date, or to influence this person to do something?*

We have to know what we want so we can ask the right questions. (Maria wanted $1,500.)

Audience.
- *Who is our listener?* (An investor in Maria's business.)
- *Is this person the decision maker?* (Yes, in Maria's case.)
- *What are their interests? What's important?* (To know that Maria has the essential experience and a good business/marketing plan.)

Right approach.
- *What single, simple, direct sentence best leads to the goal?* (For Maria, "I want to open my own travel agency.")
- *What will build a case around this statement?* ("I have the sales, marketing, travel agency experience and a plan.")
- *How can we find common ground that is related to the interests, needs, and experience of our listener?* ("I need help as you once did.")

We have to know *what* we want, *who* can give it to use, and *how* to get it.

Hook. Whether we're selling ourselves, a product, service, or course of action, we need to capture our listener's attention. The hook is a statement or object used specifically to garner that attention. Finding a hook means looking for something unusual about our subject: Something exciting, dramatic, humorous, or personal. Maria's hook was the personal, 'a la Martin Luther King, Jr., "I have a dream." Questions are also effective, so Maria could have asked, then, answered the question: "What are the key behaviors all successful business people share?" Whatever the hook is, it must relate to our *objective*, our *listener*, and *lead to the point* we want to get across.

Supporting material. Every point we make needs support. It can be documentation, amplification, or clarification. The more personal or visual the better. Facts, figures, examples, testimony, anecdotes, imagery, and visual aids give the points substance and life. It's important to relate to both the rational and emotional.

Asking. Finally we need to ask for what we want. As selling guru Tom Hopkins would say, "Your message without a specific request is a wasted opportunity." We have to know what we want from our listener. We have to know how we want them to respond to us.

Do we want an action or a reaction? If we want an action, depending upon the action, we need to scope it and ask that it be performed within a specific time frame. (Maria might say to Pat: "Give me a list of the documents you want, and I'll have them to you by Thursday.") If we want a reaction, we can use the power of suggestion. (Maria might say, "What I need is someone who believes in me.") We must always decide on our strategy in advance.

What all of this tells us is that if we're going to grab attention, make a positive impression, and "sell" our message, we have to know:

- *What image we want to project*
- *What the communication goals are*
- *Who the target audience is*
- *How we're going to accomplish the goal, then sell the message in 4 minutes maximum.*

Grabber Exercise

- *Create a 30-second grabber for meeting others at a singles' bar.* ("Hi, I'm Barry Ratliff. I heard this place has good pizza, good music, and good company. I'm new in town, from L.A. Since I want to make some friends, I thought I'd give it a try. You seem to be enjoying yourself, what do you think?")

- *Create a 30-second grabber for meeting others at a business conference.* ("I'm Sarah Folsom, sales manager with Nirvana Pharmaceutical. I'm here to introduce "Grinnalot," our new anti-anxiety medication which was just approved by the FDA and has shown 87% improvement in SA/SPers in nation-wide clinical trials.")

- *Create an all-purpose 30-second grabber. Rehearse this daily. Have it on the tip of your tongue. Use it every opportunity you get.* ("My name's Joanna and I'm an aspiring writer. So far I've had four articles on the life of an older college student published in regional papers. When I'm not working on my writing, I'm finishing my B.A. in English at the local college.")

Applying public speaking image tips

When we're giving a speech or presentation, there are a few additional tips which can make it easier to deal with our SA/SP.

- *Make sure your speech has a beginning, middle, and end.*
- *Write it the way you'll speak it. Written and spoken language have a different cadence and tone.*
- *Have no more than 2-3 key points to make.*
- *Put key words, phrases, or concepts for speech on note cards. Using a fully-prepared text may be appropriate for some situations but tends to compel you to read it, become anxious about losing your place, and to lose your place.*
- *Practice in front of a mirror to become comfortable with phrasing, pace, and gestures.*
- *Practice enunciating more clearly.*
- *Use a lectern or podium. It provides a barrier between you and your audience, gives you a resting place for your notes, a place to put your hands, and something to grip if necessary.*
- *Use a microphone and test it well before beginning your speech.*
- *Begin with confidence.*
- *Scan your audience occasionally as if you're including all of them as your listener. If you can see them, look at their foreheads rather than their eyes. If you find a particularly receptive audience member, look at them occasionally for feedback.*
- *Talk to the audience.*
- *Wear comfortable, loose clothing in non-sweat-staining colors, such as black or white.*
- *Wear shoes which don't cause you to teeter.*
- *Have the podium light "on" for your notes and turned in such a way that there's no glare.*
- *Adjust the lighting on you so that it makes it difficult for you to see your audience.*
- *Breathe slowly.*
- *Speak at a slow-to-moderate rate, no rushing, keep a steady pace.*

- *Speak as if talking to friends.*
- *Smile.*
- *Gesture for emphasis, clarification, or expression, but control unneeded movements.*
- *Pause for emphasis.*
- *Involve the audience by asking a question which requires a show of hands, if you can see them, or a vocal "yes "or "no" if you can't.*
- *Have water available.*
- *Wear the glasses that enable you to see your notes.*
- *Consider green-tinted powder to counteract the redness of blushing.*
- *Keep muscles loose. Don't clench fists or lock knees. Muscles under tension tire and tremble. Keep knees slightly bent.*
- *Concentrate on the ideas you want to convey, not on the precise words.*
- *Take any benzodiazepine or beta-blocker you use for specific events before the speech.*
- *Correct and accept mistakes, go on with confidence, forget them. They're bound to occur.*
- *Reframe your "nervousness" as "energy," preparing you to knock 'em dead.*

In the words of Albert Einstein, "Everything should be made as simple as possible, but not simpler."

Picture the audience as clowns, nudes, or nude clowns

CHAPTER 9

SHARPENING PERSONAL EFFECTIVENESS

"If I am not for myself, who will be for me? If I am not for others, who am I for? And if not now, when?" (*Talmud*)

What is assertiveness?

Assertiveness is another name for having standards and limits on what is acceptable and tolerable in our relationships with other people. It's our determination to be firm and enforce those standards and limits. SA/SPers are likely to be less determined and firm (assertive) than those who don't have social anxiety. We're more concerned about getting approval and not being evaluated negatively. This makes setting our boundaries, standing up for ourselves, and asserting our rights in an appropriate manner very difficult. When we're unable to be firm, our behavior tends to create confusion and friction, thus making interactions with others even more arousing, frustrating, and unsatisfactory.

How assertive are you?

*How you feel about the way you handle the following situations indicates how assertive you are. Answer the following questions as honestly as possible. (Adapted from the book **Stand Up, Speak Out, Talk Back!** By Robert Alberti and Michael Emmons.)* **Do you:**

- *Generally express your thoughts and feelings?*
- *Protest verbally when someone takes your place in line?*
- *Often approach people and situations without fear of embarrassment?*
- *Insist your spouse or roommate take their fair share of the household chores?*
- *Speak up in discussions when you want to make a point?*
- *Swallow your anger time after time and later fly off the handle?*
- *Say so when someone is very unfair to you?*
- *Say "no" with ease when a salesperson makes an effort to help you but doesn't have the right merchandise?*
- *Speak up for your own viewpoint when you and a person whom you respect differ?*
- *Refuse unreasonable requests made by friends?*
- *Feel it's unnecessary to justify or make excuses for your not wanting to comply with a friend's wants?*

- *Address issues that bother you rather than just put up with the situation because it's easier?*
- *Ask friends for small favors or help?*
- *Avoid shouting or using bullying tactics to get others to do what you want?*
- *Insist that service people make the repairs, adjustments, or replacements they are responsible for making?*
- *Speak up when you have been waiting in line and a latecomer is served first?*
- *Comfortably accept praise for accomplishment, feeling it's deserved?*
- *Ask the person who continuously kicks your chair in the theater to stop?*
- *Feel comfortable when someone is watching your work?*
- *Have confidence in your own judgment?*
- *Ask the waitperson in a restaurant to correct an improperly prepared or served meal?*
- *Take the first step to introduce yourself to a stranger in a gathering?*
- *Openly express anger without using "You-terms"?*
- *Find it easier to tell family and friends how you feel than to tell strangers?*
- *Find it easy to maintain eye contact when talking with others?*

The more "nos" you answered, the more likely it is that you are acting in a non-assertive or aggressive manner and not feeling good about your actions.

Assertive Scripts Exercise

List situations in which you have experienced discomfort because you didn't do or say what you really wanted to. Or because you felt compelled to justify your behavior. For example, what might you have done if someone standing beside you in the elevator began to smoke which bothered you greatly? As you remember these experiences write an assertive response to each of them:

- *What was the public discomfort?*
- *What I said or did?*
- *What I want to say or do next time?*

How to assess assertiveness

Being assertive requires first that we know what we want to be assertive about. As personal coach Shale Paul suggests, we have to pick our issues then determine what's the minimum that's acceptable and the maximum that's tolerable. What are the factors which brought us to this position? We have to understand and feel comfortable with the logic that brought us to this decision.

Once we know what we want and feel determined to achieve it, we need to start thinking in terms of how to convey our message. This means thinking in "I-messages" rather than "You-messages." "I-messages" indicate that we're speaking for ourselves, describing how we feel about unacceptable behavior, behaviors which exceed our standards, limits, or boundaries. We're taking responsibility for our behavior, but not for the other person's. We're not imputing motives or criticizing. For example, Barry doesn't know what to do about a colleague who continually takes books from his office bookcase without asking. He's angry about his office being invaded, is afraid he won't get his books back, and wants the behavior stopped. If he confronted his colleague, saying, "You took my books again. You're always doing it. You have no consideration for me or my privacy. Don't do it again," what might happen?

His colleague would probably feel angry. There'd be no interest in his complying with Barry's desire for a behavior change because he'd be too busy preparing to retaliate to the attack. Barry's speaking in "you-messages" would most certainly be perceived as threatening and accusatory. It would put the other person on the defensive and make him less likely to even consider negotiating this change.

Instead, if Barry said to his colleague firmly but gently, "When you take my books without asking, I can't find what I need for my work. As a result, I feel really annoyed. I want you to ask me if you can borrow my books," his colleague can then tell Barry how he sees the situation, what his motivation may have been, and what he's willing to do as a result of Barry's request. When it's expressed in terms of Barry, his feelings and his wants, his colleague is less likely to feel criticized and more likely to consider Barry's request.

Specifically, we should:

- *State what you see (describe other's behavior objectively). "When you did... "*
- *State how other's behavior concretely affects you. " The effects are... "*
- *State how you feel about it. "I feel angry... "*
- *State what you want to happen or make a suggestion. "I want...," or "Perhaps... "*

Look back at the incidents you addressed in your assertive scripts. Did you respond in I-messages? If not, rework your responses in the I-message four-stage format. Rehearse the answers at least once a day so they become a natural reaction for you.

Simplifying systematic assertiveness skills

Manuel J. Smith, author of **When I Say No I Feel Guilty**, has designed some simple techniques to help us become more assertive. They're called

- *Broken record*
- *Fogging*
- *Negative assertion*
- *Negative inquiry.*

These are skills which prepare and help us stick to our firmness. They are the basic scripted responses we need so we don't have to solve the problem from scratch each time we encounter the situation. Knowing what to expect and how to respond is everything. They need to be learned and practiced regularly - everyday, at least three times per day.

Broken record is the calm repetition of what we want. The technique teaches persistence in our achieving our goals. Reinforcing our determination, it also allows us to ignore the other person's irrelevant logic, manipulation, or baiting. For example, we're looking for a particular reference book at the library, but the librarian says to us, "You don't really want that one. You won't find it useful." Instead of our normal, socially-anxious "okay," we'd respond calmly and pleasantly, "I'm sure you feel that way, but I want that book." We'd repeat this phrase like a broken record for every argument the librarian might pose.

Fogging is calmly accepting the probability that there may be some truth to what another says about us. At the same time, it allows us to be the ultimate judge of what we do. This suggests that we could say to the librarian, "I understand how you might feel that way, but..." then add the broken record phrase here. This technique shows empathy with the other person while allowing us to receive any criticism without becoming defensive or anxious. Other fogging phrases are" "That may be true, " "I understand that," and "I'm sure you believe that." These phrases acknowledge and reflect what is being said.

Negative assertion is the calm acceptance of our own errors or failings by our agreeing with the criticism, at least in spirit. This allows us to look at our negatives without becoming unduly anxious and defensive. At the same time, our agreeing with this accurate assessment will reduce the critic's hostility and anger.

For example, if Sarah underestimated the amount of time needed to finish a project and her boss is angry because of high-level demands for the final report, her boss might say, "You really messed up royally, and now my butt's in a sling." Using negative assertion, she might respond, "You're right. I really under-estimated the time to finish the project." She acknowledges the element of truth in her own frame of reference, but doesn't buy into the hyperbole.

Negative inquiry is prompting our critics to tell us more of what's bothering them. This allows our critics to be more assertive and express honest negative feelings. It also allows us to seek out critical information more comfortably to open up communication channels. If a spouse says to us, "You spend all your time job hunting," we might respond, "What is there about my spending a lot of time job hunting that bothers you?" Then the spouse may admit frustration, "You're buried in letters and classified ads all the time." Then we could ask, "What is it about my spending so much time with paperwork that's bad?" Each inquiry gets us closer to the underlying problem.

Declaring our personal rights

Assertiveness researchers Robert Alberti, Michael Emmons, Arthur Lange, Patricia Jakubowski, and Manuel Smith have popularized the concept that there are basic personal rights that an individual can choose to defend:

I have the right to

- *Ask for what I want;*
- *Be illogical;*
- *Be the judge of my own behavior, thoughts, and emotions;*
- *Be listened to and taken seriously;*
- *Be treated with respect;*
- *Change my mind;*
- *Choose not to assert myself;*
- *Decide if I'm responsible for finding solutions to other people's problems;*
- *Have and express my own feelings and opinions;*
- *Make mistakes;*
- *Offer no reasons, excuses, or justification for my behavior;*
- *Say "no" without feeling guilty;*
- *Say "I don't care";*
- *Say "I don't know";*
- *Say "I don't understand";*
- *Set my own priorities.*

Dealing with procrastination

According to Christopher Robin in A.A. Milne's **Winnie the Pooh**, "Organizing is what you do before you do something, so that when you do it, it's not all mixed up."

In order to determine and pursue our recovery goals we must become adept at structuring our time. We must be both efficient and effective. Management consultant Peter Drucker says, "Being efficient is doing the job right. Being effective is doing the right job" - those things that really need to be done. This means that the first thing we must do is list and rank the items to be done:

- *What needs to be done first?*
- *Second?*
- *What can wait?*
- *What can be done by someone else just as well, if not better?*
- *What do I do that wastes my time without contributing to my effectiveness?*
- *What can be eliminated?*

For those items we can't do quickly and easily, delegate, or eliminate, we must make a plan. Specifically, we must assess how much time each item we're going to do requires in order to accomplish it. Then we need to chop each item into bite-sized pieces so we can do a little piece each day.

In general, whenever possible, it's better to do a little of each item each day than concentrate our efforts entirely on Item A on Day 1, Item B on Day 2, and so on. Doing a little on each gets all the items closer to completion. This method also keeps our stress level manageable. The necessity for time management applies equally to our personal and work life.

Each morning we need to make out a daily "To-Do" list with approximately eight items on it. All the things on the list should be done in order of priority. Doing the hardest or most important first allows us to avoid spending the day anticipating, dreading, and putting off the task, as SA/SPers are wont to do. In this situation if there's a task we like doing, we can do it after the hard task as a reward.

Rewards are important so we should build them into the list. As we finish a task, we can give ourselves a treat. The larger or harder the task, the larger the reward. This reinforces our accomplishments and keeps our motivation up.

Short-term and repetitive tasks, like planning dinner and paying bills, should take place once a week so we're not continually thinking and obsessing about them. Long-range goals, however, require long-range planning. Knowing where we're going and how we're going to get there makes accomplishing those goals both easier and less overwhelming.

To be most productive we must have a calendar to record the deadlines of tasks to be done. We should also put this in our journal along with ideas on different ways to achieve them and our progress while they're waiting to be done. Reminders are helpful, especially sticking "Post-It" notes everywhere. Our journal should contain not only a listing of our activities but also the time involved. Working consistently and systematically day by day until tasks are completed will allow us feel in control and achieve the success we want.

Part of time management is also ridding ourselves of time wasters. How do we waste time? We have only to think about the times we gave ourselves extra time to do our usual activities. Somehow we managed to fill up all the time with them. Sometimes we wonder, "Where did the time go?" Unfortunately, if we allow ourselves a day to do a task, it'll take a day. If we allow ourselves half a day, it'll take half a day. It's Parkinson's Law: "Work expands so as to fill the time available for its completion."

Procrastination Exercise

To ward off the problems of procrastination you need to:

- *Get your schedule on paper. Prioritize your tasks then break them down. By seeing the task, its pieces, and even diagrams, you'll clarify your thinking.*

- *Eliminate distractions in your work area. Have materials organized and the area uncluttered. Keep temptations to waste time to a minimum. Don't have books, magazines, newspapers, television, radio, or tape players around. Do whatever is necessary to increase your concentration. Use earplugs to cut down extraneous noise if you need to. Some people believe they can concentrate better when they're listening to music. However, in reality, your attention will alternate between the sound and the task to be done. Therefore, it may take you twice as long to complete the task because you are, in essence, trying to do two things at once.*

- *Assemble the tools you need ahead of time. Whatever they are, have them ready first thing in the morning.*

- *Eliminate looking for things. It's easy to waste an entire day looking for misplaced items. Label files and sections of notebooks by topics. Keep and use a 3" X 5" card system to act as a reminder of item replacement. Also keep a Rolodex of telephone numbers, filed alphabetically, available.*

- *Discourage interruptions. Let people know you're working and don't want to be disturbed. Have others screen your calls for you. Find an inaccessible place in which to work. When people want you to chat or do things with or for them, be firm. You have to learn to say, "No," and mean it. To help you do this, cut down on using the telephone or computer (set your e-mail lists to Digest) and holding idle conversations.*

The more we follow time-management suggestions, the more disciplined we'll become. The more disciplined we become, the more we'll accomplish. The more we accomplish, the more confidence we'll gain and the more successful we'll be.

How is self-esteem important?

How we perceive the world and how we are perceived is, in large part, the result of our self-esteem. Self-esteem differs significantly from our *self-concept* which involves our beliefs and thoughts about ourselves. *Self-esteem*, then is our attitude about those thoughts and beliefs. It's our evaluation of ourselves and feelings about our self-worth. It's perceived to be global in scope, representing our self-evaluation across a wide range of different situations. It's based on not only how we compare ourselves to others but also whether or not we believe we meet our own level of aspirations. Derived from perceptions about personal characteristics like IQ and integrity, it tends to be stable over time.

Self-esteem initially comes from

- *What parental figures accepted and respected*

- *What limits they defined and enforced*

- *To what degree they allowed your independent action.*

If our successes match our aspirations and goals..., if they equal those of individuals we use as yardsticks..., if others speak well of us, then we're likely to feel good about ourselves. With high self-esteem we have the conviction that we're worthy of what we want and that our methods are right and appropriate.

Our self-esteem depends on how we evaluate success and failure. We become the label of our actions. If we label failure as "bad" and success as "good," we'll see not achieving our goal as "bad" and ourselves as a failure. This type of thinking has a strong impact on our behavior. It limits what we're willing to try and to what degree we'll be open to growth.

Our self-esteem also appears to be related to how we were given praise as children. Psychologists Carol Dweck and Claudia Mueller have found that children praised for their effort, what they do, tend to maintain their self-confidence more than children praised for their intelligence, what they are. When praise is related to a fixed trait like intelligence and these children meet with difficulty or do poorly, they tend to give up. Perhaps this is because they don't see success as being under their active control.

Thus, our self-esteem may be related to our perceived *self-efficacy*. If we believe we can cope with a threat, control our reactions to it, and accomplish our tasks, we're more likely to feel more successful than not. This sense of worth may relate only to the situation at hand or be generalized to others.

What does low self-esteem mean? It means that we tend to magnify trivial mistakes and imperfections. We make these things symbols of our feelings of inadequacy or worthlessness. We see our self-image as depending upon the approval of others. We have feelings of self-doubt, insecurity, anxiety, and a sense of being unfit. As Groucho Marx wrote, "Please accept my resignation. I don't care to belong to any club that would have me as a member."

Self-Esteem Evaluation

*How do you feel about yourself? Do any of the following statements describe you? If they are true of you, put **T** in the blank next to the item. If the statement is false about you, put **F** in the blank.*

___*I often feel inadequate.*

___*Usually I don't let things bother me.*

___*I like to present my ideas to the group.*

___*It's not easy to be me.*

___*I frequently wish I were someone else.*

___*Often, when I have something to say I don't say it.*

___*My family understands me.*

___*I give in very easily.*

___*There are lots of things I'd change about myself.*

___*I make up my mind without much trouble.*

___*My family expects too much of me.*

___*It takes me a long time to get used to new things.*

___*I often feel upset about the work I do.*

___*My family is pretty considerate of my feelings.*

___*I'm not as well liked as most others.*

___*Generally, I can't be depended upon.*

___*Often I feel like running away from home.*

___*My life is all mixed up.*

___*Others often follow my ideas.*

*Count the numbers of Ts and Fs. **10-13 Fs** = high self-esteem. **10-13 Ts** = low self-esteem.*

Raising self-esteem

- *Make positive statements about yourself:* Compose a list of "I-statements" which reflect how you'd like to describe yourself, such as "I'm confident talking to people I know" or "I do my work well." Read this list aloud to yourself often. Add new ones.

- *Stop making negative statements about yourself:* When you hear yourself saying something negative about yourself, say, "Stop!" Reverse the statement from "I am a failure" to "I can be a success in (name a specific area)." Say the new statement aloud.

- *Punish negative statements:* To reinforce your rejection of negative statements, have a list of boring tasks to perform as punishment when you talk about yourself negatively.

- *Practice imaging:* Design a mental picture of yourself in an actual, positive situation. Run this mental "film" in times of stress and whenever you relax.

- *Reassess your role models:* Are your role models realistic and appropriate? Do you really want to be Cameron Diaz, Whoopi Goldberg, Bruce Willis, Kenneth Starr, Larry King, or Laura Schlessinger? Or do you want to be attractive, assertive, confident, or competent like the characters they portray or their own images. Unrealistic or inappropriate role models are not likely to help you succeed.

- *Check your expectations:* Is your behavior based on your own sense of competence and worth or on your perception of other people's expectations of you? Remember only your own expectations, when grounded in self-love and self-acceptance, can be met.

Self-esteem is our acknowledgment that no matter what we do, whether or not we're successful, we still have intrinsic value and integrity as human beings. In other words, it's self-love. When we truly love ourselves, we can treat ourselves as our own best friend.

High self-esteem means loving, trusting, respecting, and accepting ourselves. It means communicating to others all the good things we are. It also means our willingness to share those qualities with them.

While high self-esteem makes us feel effective, productive, capable, successful, and loving, low self-esteem makes us feel ineffective, worthless, incompetent, and unlovable. Low self-esteem leads to lack of confidence. We feel doomed to failure and, as a result, make little effort toward realizing our goals. While low self-efficacy leads to low self-esteem, low self-esteem leads us down the road to poor performance and a distorted view of both ourselves and others.

When we have low self-esteem, we don't give ourselves credit for the good we accomplish. We see others as doing things better than we do. We see ourselves at the mercy of "fate," not responsible for our behavior and its consequences. Because low self-esteem makes us anxious and unwilling to take the risk of developing close relationships, we are likely to have a lonely, unhappy personal life.

Our feelings of inferiority or low self-esteem are never based upon reality. Instead they're grounded in our negative, self-critical, distorted, and illogical thoughts which make up our self-concept. So we need to look at those negative thoughts, identify the distorted thinking behind them, and dispute them. Self-esteem issues can be addressed as well by the Maladaptive Thought Record.

Self-Esteem Exercise

Joanna has battled feelings of inferiority since childhood. Having her value dependent upon her living up to her parents' high standards of the right grades and the right appearance had convinced her that she was a second-rate human being, totally inadequate. Nothing she did was ever quite right and she savagely criticized herself for it. She wondered why she had ever tried to go back to school and make friends. Sad, discouraged, and frustrated, she was a mental vulture, swooping down on herself, picking her esteem's bones clean of flesh.

To deal with these feelings Joanna talked to her inner critic through a technique called "empty chair." She set up two chairs, facing each other. Sitting in one, she talked to herself as her inner critic, expressing her distorted thoughts. She then changed chairs and took on the role of her defense lawyer. She continued this interchange until her defense lawyer prevailed. Labeling each cognitive distortion, she recorded her basic defense techniques in her journal.

Joanna's inner critic: *"I can't accomplish anything because I just don't have what it takes." (Over-generalization)*

Joanna's defense lawyer: *"That's ridiculous. I do lots of things right."*

Inner critic: *"My parents, teachers, and classmates will see me as a loser." (Over-generalization; Mind reading; All-or-nothing thinking)*

Defense lawyer: *"My parents will think I'm a loser no matter what I do. My teachers may be disappointed if I don't do what they expect, but that's not the end of the world. And my classmates won't really care."*

Inner critic: *"I'm stupid." (Labeling)*

Defense lawyer: *"I am not stupid. I may do 'stupid' things once in a while, but this doesn't make me stupid. Everyone does stupid stuff. It's only human."*

Self-Efficacy Evaluation

Our beliefs concerning our efficacy (our ability to accomplish tasks and achieve goals) affect how we think about difficult situations with which we have to cope.

• *Do you feel you can manage to solve your problems if you try hard enough?*

- *If you're opposed, do you find ways to get what you want?*
- *When confronted with a problem, can you usually find several solutions?*
- *Do you feel resourceful enough to handle unforeseen situations?*

How confident are you that you can manage or cope with the following? (Choose A or B)

1. Your sister has asked you to be part of her wedding party, to be part of the ceremony and on the reception line. Do you

    A. Look forward to making it a positive and memorable day

    B. Start to worry about how you'll appear and what you'll do wrong and have second thoughts

2. Your manager has out-of-town clients coming that she can't pick up at the airport because of a last-minute department meeting so she asks you to collect them, generally acquaint them with your company, and make them comfortable. Do you

    A. See it as a way to make yourself visible in the organization

    B. Know you don't have what it takes to pull it off and will humiliate yourself in the process and look for ways to get out of it

3. The windshield wipers on your new car don't work. Do you

    A. Go back to the local dealership, explain the problem, and ask them to fix it under the warranty

    B. Become angry but hope the malfunction will correct itself so you don't have to deal with the service people

4. You've done a lengthy written report on an historical figure. Your instructor asks you to give a 5-minute presentation to the class on the most significant thing you learned from your research. Do you

    A. Easily prepare the talk

    B. See yourself standing in a pool of sweat, trembling, feeling like a little kid in a dunce cap

If you chose A 3 out of 4 times, you have strong sense of efficacy. You envision success scenarios, expect favorable outcomes, and adopt a problem-solving approach to the difficulties you encounter.

If you chose B 3 out of 4 times, you are riddled with doubt and tend to concentrate on your personal deficiencies. You see failure scenarios and expect unfavorable outcomes. You let this calamitous thinking undermine effective use of your capabilities.

Raising Self-Efficacy

To raise self-efficacy we need to address how to access and interpret information and improve our coping skills. Of the many ways to do it therapeutically performance accomplishment is the single most powerful source of efficacy. This is because it's vivid, self-relevant, and provides first-hand experience with success or failure. Increased self-efficacy leads to success which, in turn, increases self-efficacy.

S. Lloyd Williams' "Guided Mastery Therapy," which uses the assistance of a therapist or "safe" person, has been shown to significantly increase self-efficacy. In fact, six out of eight studies on this approach with agoraphobia have found that it's substantially superior to mere exposure to the perceived threatening situation. The Mastery therapy allows us to

- *See the skills broken down into components and modeled appropriately;*

- *Learn the rules and strategies for applying these skills in different situations;*

- *Put ourselves in a simulated situation we need to manage;*

- *Break the situation into achievable tasks;*

- *Test our capability to consecutively handle each task;*

- *Receive suggestions, encouragement, and reinforcement as we work;*

- *Eliminate safety-, defensive-, and self-restrictive behaviors;*

- *Receive help applying the newly-learned skills in a real situation;*

- *Increase independence, feel confident, and fade out use of the assistant.*

Self-Efficacy Exercise

- *Pick a task that needs to be done or a problem to be solved (e.g. go to Social Security to receiver disability payments).*

- *Set objectives and goals for it (e.g., goal is to get payments. Steps involved: Phone for information; set up appointment; collect information for application; go for interview; follow-through on process; and appeal negative decision).*

- *Make up a list of rewards and punishments.*

- *Write a behavioral contract with yourself that you'll reward yourself for accomplishing each step of the task or punish yourself when you don't (e.g., "I will apply for SSDI. For each step I'll reward my success or punish my failure").*

- *Monitor your progress and record it in your journal.*

- *Administer your behavioral incentives.*

- *Demonstrate how you could apply this process to two other problems.*

Reducing disappointment

To reduce disappointment we need to reduce unrealistic expectations. This means our becoming acquainted with each of these expectations and systematically dealing with them. To do this clinical psychologist David Brandt suggests that we

- *Acknowledge our disappointment* ("I'm not dating");
- *Feel and express our emotions* ("I feel sad and frustrated about not dating");
- *Become aware of and recognize our unrealistic expectations* ("I should be dating");
- *Attain attitude flexibility:*   Separate the wish from the anticipation of its coming true (the wish is "dating"; anticipation is "doing it now");
- *Eliminate:* Expunge rigid, unconditional expectations using *never*, *every*, and *always* ("I'll never date");
- *Gain perspective:* Focus on the implications of the expectation ("If I don't do it now, I'll be devastated" versus "If I don't do it now, it'll be uncomfortable but okay");
- *Reduce attachment:*   Reduce ego identification with the expectation ("I'm okay as a person even if I'm not dating right now");
- *Redefine expectations:*   Do a realistic assessment of capabilities, possibilities, probabilities, and past disappointments to diminish the wish component ("I'll be dating in the future when I'm ready");
- *Prepare for change:* Be willing to give up what we want when we can't have it ("I'd like to date but won't hold it as a realistic goal now");
- *Motivate yourself to change:* ("I want to date and will work toward doing it");
- *Decide to change:* ("I'm going to meet people");
- *Act toward change:* ("I'm working to find people of similar interests");
- *Hope:* Expect some disappointments but maintain a positive belief about the future;
- *Accept:* Reach acceptance of the disappointment and move on.

Disappointment Exercise

Have a pencil and paper handy.   Get comfortable then start your progressive relaxation.

- *Think of a significant disappointment in your life.*
- *Visualize the situation in all its sensory detail and experience the disappointment.*
- *Open your eyes and write down your expectation that was behind the disappointment.*
- *Break the expectation down into the "wish" and the "anticipation" of it.*

- *Write down the ways in which your expectation wasn't met.*
- *Assess the reality of your expectation.*
- *Write down some of the reasons your expectation wasn't met.*
- *Reduce your attachment to the expectation and express the reality.*
- *Assess what would likely happen next time if you kept this expectation.*
- *Redefine this expectation for yourself in realistic terms or eliminate it.*
- *Record your response in your journal.*

Recognizing our anger

Even though anger is a natural response to things perceived to be annoying, frustrating, unjust, or threatening, it can still significantly interfere with our social effectiveness. While it mobilizes our body's resources and defenses, it also distorts our thoughts and actions. It expresses tension but also often leads to aggression. It produces feelings of control but also causes us to defend ourselves when it's unnecessary, often resulting in hurt to others.

A recent study at Duke University found that hostility/anger is correlated with stressfulness. When anger-prone individuals talked about a negative emotional event, their blood pressure and heart rate rose significantly. The results indicate that while the low-hostile participants experienced this stress in their minds, the high-hostile experienced it in their bodies, making repeated anger potentially unhealthy for these people. In these individuals a lifetime of exposure to negatively stressful events could risk damaging their cardiovascular system. While venting anger is an answer, the venting needs to be done within a context of anger-resolution for it to be effective and useful.

Anger Assessment Exercise

In order to see if you need to address your anger as part of your recovery, you have to assess it first. Complete the following inventory, putting a T for generally true or F for generally false in the space provided.

___*My relationships with others are sometimes stormy or unstable.*

___*I seem to have an unusual amount of unnecessary guilt.*

___*I don't like to admit to myself that I'm angry.*

___*I sometimes use humor to avoid facing my feelings.*

___*I tend to be hypercritical about myself and others.*

___*I sometimes use sarcasm as a form of humor.*

___*I feel I'd like to get back at those who've wronged me.*

___*When I feel angry, I find myself doing things I know are wrong.*

___*I usually don't tell others when I'm hurt.*

___*I have physical aches and pains, like headache, stiff neck, stomach problems.*

___Criticism bothers me a great deal.

___I sometimes do things to appear superior to others.

___I often feel inferior to others.

___I'd like to tell people exactly what I think.

___I feel unloved and unappreciated.

___I feel disillusioned with love.

___Sometimes I have difficulty controlling my weight, either losing or gaining.

___At times I feel life owes me more than it has given me.

___I feel that many of my problems can be blamed on others.

___Many of the nice things I do are out of a sense of obligation.

___Many mornings I awaken not feeling refreshed.

___When something irritates me, I find it hard to calm down.

___When people are being unreasonable, I usually take a strong dislike to them.

___I've experienced spouse- or child abuse.

___I'm bothered when things are not done in a predictable way.

___I consider myself possessive in my personal relationships.

___People who know me would say that I'm stubborn.

___Sometimes I could be described as moody.

___I argue or disagree a lot, mostly with family members.

___I've experienced poor interpersonal relationships.

___I can't let go of the past.

___I'm constantly unhappy.

___What I do is often self-defeating.

___I have difficulty resolving conflicts.

___I have difficulty avoiding fights.

___I'm frequently angry with myself.

___I'm constantly disappointed.

___I feel depressed, helpless, and frustrated.

___I resent some people for who they are, what they have, or what they do.

___I can't seem to solve my problems.

Count the number of Ts. This will indicate how important it is for you to confront your anger. If you scored **less than 10**, you control your anger well (or, perhaps, may be unable to admit your anger). If you scored **11 - 20**, you are within normal range, but need to be aware of your anger. Learning how to address it would be useful for you. If you scored between **21 - 30**, you probably have had a lot of problems with which to deal. Life may not be as satisfying as you would like. You would benefit from addressing your anger. If you scored between **31 - 40**, your anger controls your life, prevents you from being fully *functional and achieving a satisfying existence. Your recovery from SA/SP requires you learn how to deal successfully with your anger.*

Controlling anger

Controlling anger requires that we first measure it. We need to know how *frequently* we get angry or demonstrate anger behaviors and *how long* each behavioral incident lasts. We can do this measurement by

• *Keeping track on a pad we carry around for that purpose;*

• *Transferring coins or paper clips from one pocket to another;*

• *Using a golf counter to click-count the incidents as they occur.*

Graphing these data will clarify what's happening. At the end of the first week we should connect the dots from each day's count to form a line. If we've have been conscientious in our spotting and recording anger data, we'd expect to see the line start to slope down toward the end of the week. This shows a reduction in our automatic anger behavior as a result of our awareness of it. This is an accomplishment which we likewise need to acknowledge.

Visualizing our progress as we continue to work on the count is important. We need to see ourselves as feeling more positive and in more control over these thoughts and emotions.

Validating our data is also useful so we'll know whether or not we've picked up most of it. Having a close, trusted friend do spot-checks at some designated period of time each day can provide invaluable information. At the end of each day the two of us would compare counts and data.

Anger therapist Hendrie Weisinger categorizes anger as *just* or *unjust,* *adaptive* or *needless,* depending upon the situation. When someone steals from us, that is "just" anger, but when someone picks up an item we were thinking about purchasing, that's "unjust" anger. When a stranger speaks harshly to us and we feel threatened, that's "adaptive" anger, but when we repeatedly replay perceived parental mistakes in our minds making us angry, that's "needless" anger.

It's unjust, needless anger which creates a problem for us when it

• *Occurs often;*

• *Lasts too long;*

• *Is intense;*

• *Leads to aggression;*

• *Disturbs relationships and work.*

When anger escalates and gets too hot to handle, we have great difficulty thinking and acting effectively. We become prisoners of our own self-perpetuating negative arousal. At times like these we need to isolate ourselves from the anger and the arousing situation. In doing so, we can step back and do an objective appraisal.

Weisinger suggests saying, "I'm beginning to feel angry and I want to take a time-out." The form of this declaration is important. First, it's expressed in I-terms which place no blame. Second, the word "want" suggests choice and control whereas the word "need" would suggest, instead, compulsion.

Time-out.

- *Make the declaration.*

- *Leave the situation.*

- *Cool down via exercise or other constructively physical activity, relaxation, visualization, self-talk, listening to music, driving, etc. Safely discharge the tension so you can think about the situation. If at any point you again begin to feel anger, repeat the declaration, "I'm beginning to feel angry and I want to take a time-out."*

When we return to the situation, we have several options available to us. If there's another involved, we can discuss our feelings at that time. If, however, it's not convenient or the other wishes to postpone it, we two can contract to discuss it at a specific time and place later. Whenever we discuss our feelings, we need to communicate them in I-terms (as described in Assertive Exercise).

Automatic thoughts.   Sometimes distorted self-statements generate anger.   Typical among them are *over-generalization, mind reading, magnification,* and *"shoulds."* (See Cognitive errors in Chapter 7.) Acknowledging, labeling, and disputing these cognitive errors reduces their incidence. The same is true for those other factors which provoke our anger. It's important to pinpoint the specific causes. Generally, provocation can be categorized as the result of:

- *Frustration*

- *Irritation or annoyance*

- *Abuse*

- *Injustice or unfairness.*

Once we've determined what has provoked our unjust-needless anger, we can use cognitive restructuring and exposure to reduce its effect on us.

Saying "goodbye" to anger

In situations where we expect anger may develop, we may want to consider cutting short our exposure to the situation. While this is an "avoidant strategy," it isn't avoidance in the sense that we SA/SPers use it. This doesn't mean not attending the situation or escaping as soon as possible. This means that if it realistically appears that extending the exposure will create anger arousal, we find a way to remove ourselves before it happens. By shortening the exposure to provocation, we decrease the chance of anger.

Embracing anger guidelines

(Adapted from **If You're So Smart, Why Aren't You Happy?** by Mitchell Messer and Linda Dillon)

- *Don't minimize anger by using euphemisms (such as, upset, bothered, ticked off).*
- *Don't invalidate others' anger by saying, "Don't be so sensitive." "You're always angry."*
- *Recognize and validate others' anger. Let them know it's okay to feel that way.*
- *Understand your own feelings before trying to explain and analyze how others feel.*
- *Don't take others' anger personally. It's unpleasant but not a reflection of your worth.*
- *In explosive situations it's best not to argue but to empathize.*
- *Catch yourself as you start getting angry and choose to express yourself appropriately.*
- *Vent your anger in a letter but don't mail it until you've cooled off then read it again.*
- *Catch yourself afraid of expressing your anger out of concern of offending another.*
- *Question who's the proper target of your anger: Another person, a situation, yourself.*
- *Prevent your anger from accumulating, building, and becoming more toxic.*
- *Ask what difference it makes. If it doesn't make a difference in the real world, let it go.*

Forgiving parents and moving on

We must let go of our anger about perceived parental mistakes or it'll eat us alive. Whether they abused us or just seemed too critical, overly protective, or insensitive, they acted as they did because of who they were and what their histories, fears, conflicts, agendas, beliefs, and perceptions dictated. Most of the time they were unaware of the effect of their behaviors on us, as we were of ours on them. But our anger wasn't and isn't the result of their actions alone. It needed our interpretation.

Because we moved every year or so, I was rarely in one place long enough to become part of any well-established groups. And because I was slightly more mature from continual traveling, and therefore, "different," I made only one or two friends on each move. In high school having few friends distressed me greatly, adding further to my loneliness. Still trying to curry favor with my father, I sought his advice. Why, I asked, did I have no friends. Rather than suggesting that I'd had few opportunities because of his work (something over which he no doubt felt guilty), he launched into a catalogue of what he considered to be my faults. When he finished to the sounds of my inconsolable sobbing, he threw in a few suggestions by which I might rescue myself by trying to get people to like me. At that moment, and for many years thereafter, I wondered why I should even bother trying if I was such a mess. I blamed him for my feeling worthless.

"My parents say I'm self-centered and insensitive to their problems. I'M insensitive to THEIR problems?"

Blame and recriminations won't change the "past," but will impact the present and future. We need to say it's over, forgive their humanness, and assertively create what we want now.

"Do not be too timid and squeamish about your actions.
All life is an experiment. The more experiments you make the better."
(Ralph Waldo Emerson)

CHAPTER **10**

NAVIGATING THE MEDICATION MAZE

"When written in Chinese the word 'crisis' is composed of two characters. One
represents danger and the other represents opportunity."
(John F. Kennedy)

SA/SP medications: "Eye of newt and toe of frog"?

Sometimes SA/SPers feel that the treatment we receive for our problem is
really a matter of witchcraft, wishful thinking, or buying a lottery ticket.
Because of the state of mental health care, that may not be far from the truth.
There are four real-world factors which contribute to this. First, primary care
physicians have long been on the front lines of mental health. For example,
surveys have shown that general practitioners prescribe about 80% of all SSRIs.
But they tend not to recognize and to under-treat SA/SP. Second, when they do
recognize and treat it, their first choice of treatment is almost always
psychotropic medications. As psychiatrist R. Bruce Lydiard recently stated at an
American Psychiatric Association symposium, antidepressants are probably
indicated even if there is even a "whiff" of depression in patients with anxiety
disorders. Third, as managed care takes over the mental health area, it's
reducing the number of psychiatric visits we can have. Thus, even if the
physician thinks therapy should be an option, it may not be available or be very
limited and costly. Many managed-care benefits packages only allow up to
three mental health visits. Further therapy, particularly counseling, is often not
reimbursed. Fourth, psychiatrists are doing less and less psychotherapy so they
too are relying even more upon medications.

As a result, psychotropic drugs tend to be given freely and somewhat
indiscriminately. Because of the frequent difficulty matching these drugs to
individual needs and responses, even by professionals knowledgeable in SA/SP,
we as patients are often shuttled from one drug to another to combinations of
them to see what may work for us, frequently obtaining less than optimum relief
in a frustrating process. Then, when these medications work well, they take the
edge off our anxiety and, sometimes, our motivation. Consequently, while we're
on medication, we may have little or no incentive to seek psychotherapy to deal
with our underlying maladaptive cognitions and behavior. We may feel better
but still have the core problem.

Sarah. *When Sarah went to her regular doctor for her fear of answering
the phone and meeting people, the physician gave her a prescription for Inderal,
a beta-blocker, which slowed her heart but did nothing for her fear and
avoidance. Then he gave her Paxil which made her feel jumpy and de-sexed.
Several medications later, she was still looking for relief, wondering if he had*

any idea what SA/SP really was and if she should start prescribing natural supplements, like St. John's Wort, for herself.

From the perspective of many concerned mental health professionals, it would be better if psychopharmacological treatment were used primarily when the intensity and severity of the disorder are such that we can't perform most of our everyday activities and doing even the most basic life tasks is a struggle. Or, when we can't concentrate on psychotherapy because of our level of anxiety. This may be particularly important where onset is early, the disorder is chronic, the impairment extensive, and there exists co-morbidity with other disorders. It's at this point that medication may be more appropriate for getting us on an even keel and reducing

• *Anticipatory anxiety and fear of social situations*

• *Physiological symptoms (trembling, palpitations, e.g.)*

• *Avoidance in social situations*

• *Co-morbid conditions (depression, alcoholism, e.g.)*

• *Overall social-anxiety-induced impairment.*

Allowing us to be back in control, these drugs may help us short-term get through the days so we can work on our necessary long-term coping strategies. While pharmacotherapy may work more rapidly and have more potent effects than CBT, the gains made through CBT tend to be more durable.

Like many other anxiety disorders, SA/SP has been found to be responsive to a number of psychotropic medications. But not everyone responds to any or all of these medications in the same way. What is effective for some us may not be for others. Some of us may experience few sides effects, while others struggle with severe, and occasionally life-threatening, side effects. Some find one drug works well while others may find that nothing works at all or a combination of drugs is best. It's important to remember that drugs are a treatment for SA/SP, not a cure. The goal of this treatment is meaningful improvement toward recovery.

Positive response to treatment will be short-term and long-term. Short-term we should experience symptomatic relief, improved performance, and social relations. Long-term, beginning between three and six months, we should experience greater functionality in all areas of our lives, especially occupational, educational, and interpersonal. However, for some drugs, like the benzodiazepine clonazepam, improvement in functionality may be sooner.

No response to adequate dosages of one medication may mean that a change in the class of medication would be helpful. Partially adequate response may suggest change to another drug in that class may be useful. Or augmentation by another class of drug may be worthwhile to try before making a complete change. For example, benzodiazepines and beta blockers may work to relieve symptoms that antidepressants, such as MAOIs and SSRIs, may not improve. MAOIs and SSRIs are not used together, however. Many SA/SPers use a combination of drugs. In addition, CBT is often combined with drugs, as well as used separately.

How we react to these drugs depends upon a number of criteria. One is correct diagnosis. Because many clinicians misdiagnose our SA/SP as panic attacks, agoraphobia, avoidant personality disorder, generalized anxiety disorder, anxiety accompanying depression, or shyness, we may not be prescribed the medication that's most appropriate for our situation. We need an accurate diagnosis.

Even if we are correctly diagnosed, we may not respond as expected because of our degree of impairment. This too has to be assessed accurately. Then there are individual biochemistries. Each of us responds somewhat differently to drugs. Whether we have discrete or generalized SA/SP also makes a difference. What works for discrete SA/SP (mild performance anxiety) tends not to work for generalized SA/SP (fear of evaluation in social situations, humiliation, and rejection). Furthermore, when we have other disorders which coexist with the SA/SP (and some 69% of us do), the medication may be working well on SA/SP but seem inadequate because it's not addressing the other conditions. Or it may be addressing one or more of the other conditions but bypassing our SA/SP altogether.

Only recently was SA/SP recognized as being treatable by psychopharmacologics. With this recognition of SA/SP as a well-defined psychiatric entity, a growing amount of research data is accumulating as to which drugs are the most effective for it and under what circumstances.

Initially, medical and pharmaceutical groups regarded drugs as more effective than psychotherapy. Studies didn't support this. They then regarded combining drugs with psychotherapy to be clearly better than either treatment alone. Recent findings don't support this either. Now they regard medications to be cheaper than therapy. But a 2-year study of Prozac has shown that treatment with drugs may result in 33%-higher costs than individual therapy. What this suggests is that all the evidence isn't in yet. Medications are not the only answer or necessarily the best answer to treating SA/SP.

There are several categories of medications which are used for SA/SP. Of these some can produce physiological dependence and withdrawal symptoms. There are two drug characteristics which predict likelihood of physiological dependence and withdrawal problems. One is the speed with which the drug enters the blood stream; the other is the speed of its washout. For example, the benzodiazepine aprazolam (Xanax) may cause more withdrawal problems because it's fast-in and fast-out whereas the benzodiazepine clonazepam (Klonopin) is slow to wash out and, therefore, creates fewer withdrawal symptoms. According to SA/SP researcher Suzanne Sutherland, symptoms often occur later and, therefore, aren't always directly connected with discontinuation of the medication. They can, however, be quite severe. *(Important: The following is for information purposes only and should not be used for prescription.)*

MAOIs.   MAOIs are monoamine oxidase inhibitors, a type of antidepressant. As you may recall, monoamines are neurotransmitters which carry signals from the central nervous system to the brain. Oxidase is the enzyme that breaks down the neurotransmitter after it has done its job so it can be reabsorbed. The presence of these amines has a calming effect on us. The hypothesis is that when there's not enough or there's too much present, we may respond by feeling anxious or depressed. One way to keep these amines around longer is to prevent the breakdown and reabsorption. That's what an MAO inhibitor does.

One type of MAOI is irreversible and non-selective. It nonspecifically inhibits both Type A and Type B MAO to block the degradation of norepinephrine, serotonin, and dopamine. Binding irreversibly with the enzyme makes the inhibition more consistent. Phenelzine (Nardil), tranylcypromine (Parnate), and isocarboxazid (Marplan) are the three irreversible MAOIs which are used for SA/SP. Phenelzine reduces both social and performance anxiety and improves social and work functioning. Improvement tends to occur as early as the first four weeks of treatment. Studies have found it to be more effective than apralozam (Xanax), a benzodiazepine, but the same as moclobemide, a reversible MAOI, at eight weeks. MAOIs may benefit as many as two-thirds of all individuals who take them (some studies have response rate of 55-65%). Furthermore, SA/SP tends to respond to phenelzine regardless of the severity of the disorder.

During the first eight weeks of treatment, we may experience various side effects. Some of the more common ones, in order of prevalence, are:

- *Daytime sleepiness*
- *Low blood pressure*
- *Dry mouth*
- *Constipation*
- *Reduced libido*
- *Impaired ejaculation*
- *Vertigo*
- *Headache.*

Even social anxiety which is secondary to medical problems, such as hyperhydrosis (severe sweating), stuttering, muscle twitching, Bell's palsy, Parkinson's, and Charcot-Marie-Tooth disease, may respond to phenelzine.

Tranylcypromine (Parnate) has similar effectiveness but its side-effects may be more difficult to tolerate short term, such as sleep difficulties. But long term, it may be less sedating and not create significant weight gain. In general, phenelzine may be safer, with a lower risk of high blood pressure reactions to tyramine-rich foods, supplements, or medicine. Tranylcypromine also appears to be helpful in situations where phenelzine is poorly tolerated or is unavailable.

Use of Nardil, Parnate, and Marplan may be contraindicated with

- *Congestive heart failure*
- *History of liver disease*
- *Abnormal liver function*

- *Pheochromocytoma.*

Interactions. These drugs can also create reactions of extreme high blood pressure, cerebrovascular accident (stroke), and death when the drugs are combined with certain other drugs (both over-the-counter and prescription, such as bupropion and demerol), foods containing the amino acid tyramine, or alcohol. These reactions can occur while taking these MAOIs and for two weeks after discontinuing use. As a result, phenelzine is rarely considered a first-line treatment for SA/SP. When MAOIs are recommended, it's more likely to be to individuals under the age of 50. (List adapted from 1996 **Journal of Clinical Psychiatry** and the **Physicians' Desk Reference**.)

Foods to avoid:

- *All cheeses, except for cottage and cream cheese*
- *Tofu (fermented soybean curd) and soybean paste*
- *Chianti, vermouth, and beer (including alcohol-free wine, reduced-alcohol beer, tap beer, and wine products). Distilled liquors, such as Scotch, gin, vodka, and rye do not produce hypertensive reaction but increase intoxication.*
- *Whiskey*
- *Yeast or meat extracts used in soups and stews (brewers yeast, Bovril, Marmite, e.g.)*
- *Broad beans, fava beans, Chinese pea pods*
- *Ginseng*
- *Aged, smoked, or cured meat or fish (including corned beef and dry sausages)*
- *Sauerkraut*
- *Pickled fish (herring, lox)*
- *Protein dietary supplements*
- *Any other food which has previously produced reactions or unpleasant symptoms*
- *Any spoiled or improperly refrigerated, -handled, or -stored protein-rich food.*

Foods in moderation - to be eaten with caution:

- *Avocados*
- *Bananas and peels*
- *Caffeinated beverages (coffee, tea, cocoa, colas) and drugs*
- *Cheeses (cottage, cream, processed, mozzarella)*
- *Chicken liver (fresh)*
- *Chocolate*
- *Herring (fresh)*
- *Liver (fresh)*

- *Meat (fresh)*
- *MSG (monosodium glutamate) meat tenderizer*
- *Nuts*
- *Raspberries*
- *Soy sauce*
- *Spinach*
- *Wines (other)*
- *Yogurt.*

Medications to avoid:

- *Cold, hay fever, sinus, and nasal decongestants (pills, drops, or spray), including those with dextromethorphan*
- *Weight-reduction preparations*
- *"Pep" pills*
- *Asthma inhalants*
- *Other antidepressant, especially SSRIs*
- *Demerol*
- *Epinephrine in local anesthesia*
- *L-tryptophan-containing preparations.*

(Note: Symptoms of extreme increase in blood pressure include severe headache, stiff neck, nausea, profuse sweating, palpitations, and confusion.)

We should carry this list with us all the time while taking irreversible MAOIs, even for several weeks after discontinuation of the drug. It's safest not to take any other medication without consultation with a physician. We need to report promptly the occurrence of headache or other unusual symptoms to our physician.

Therapy with MAOIs is generally started with a low dose and adjusted upward or downward over 2-4 weeks according to our response and tolerance. To minimize insomnia dosage may be administered in the morning. Phenelzine therapy usually begins with a dose of 15 mg. and may be increased to a maximum of 90 mg. when necessary. The goal is at least 80% inhibition of the MAO activity. Discontinuation, even after 6-9 months of treatment, may result in substantial loss of gains, at least 50%. Longer treatment and use of CBT may lessen the rate of relapse. When the medication is discontinued, it should be gradually tapered to avoid severe withdrawal symptoms, such as agitation, nightmares, psychosis, and convulsions. Switching to another antidepressant requires a washout period of 14 days.

As of the writing of this book, research is underway to assess the effectiveness of an MAOI patch. Testing going on at McLean Hospital in Belmont, Massachusetts, one of six participating medical centers, indicates that wearing the patch is like getting the antidepressant intravenously, according to Dr. Alexander Bodkin.   Those wearing the patch have shown dramatic improvement in the first week as compared with the 3-6-week response time with oral use.   Moreover, food-related side effects don't seem to occur because the drug bypasses the intestine and possible tyramine interaction.

Reversible MAOIs.   Reversible MAOIs have little chemical similarity to irreversible MAOIs.   Instead, reversible are selective for the Type A MAO and have effects which can be rapidly reversed.   They inhibit the breakdown of serotonin and norepinephrine.   There are two reversible MAOIs that have been studied in SA/SP, only one of which is being marketed.   One is moclobemide (Aurorix, Manerix) and the other is brofaromine.   Brofaromine is no longer commercially available. Because they only weakly respond to oral tyramine, dietary restrictions with their use are, for the most part, unnecessary.   This gives them a considerable safety advantage.   Moreover, the side effects are few, infrequent, and tolerable:

• *Insomnia*

• *Sleepiness*

• *Dry mouth*

• *Headache*

• *Constipation*

• *Low blood pressure*

• *Loss of libido.*

In studies all these side effects either weakened or disappeared by week 16 of treatment.   When treatment is discontinued within four months of starting the drug, there may be relatively high relapse rate.   Dosage for moclobemide is on average 200 mg. twice a day.   While some studies show moclobemide to be as effective as phenelzine for SA/SP, others show it no better than placebo, thus labeling its efficacy equivocal.   Reversible MAOIs have shown promise in studies.   At present moclobemide is available for use in most countries, except for the U.S.

Beta blockers.   Beta blockers (non-selective beta adrenergic blockers) are drugs which reduce the amount of nervous system stimulation and adrenaline to the heart and blood vessels caused by anxiety-induced hyperarousal.   By interrupting the anxiety-arousal feedback mechanism, they diminish our tendency to have rapid heartbeat and trembling. When our heart is not racing, when we're not sweating or trembling during the actual performance, we tend to feel relieved and more confident.

Used widely for treatment of high blood pressure, angina, and migraine, beta blockers are often used in treating SA/SP as well at much lower doses. Their primary use is for performance or test anxiety, the discrete form of SA/SP, though occasionally they are employed for generalized SA/SP in combination with other drugs. In general, beta blockers by themselves are considered to have limited efficacy in the treatment of generalized SA/SP.

Beta blockers include propranolol (Inderal), atenolol (Tenormin), nadolol (Corgard), alprenolol, oxprenolol, and pindolol (Visken). However, propranolol and atenolol are the most widely prescribed. Studies have shown that while beta blockers may reduce sweating and palpitations, these drugs are ineffective at reducing anticipatory anxiety, phobic avoidance, blushing, and cognitive symptoms. Intermittent use for circumscribed performance anxiety, especially for tremor, has been found to be beneficial for some, mostly non-SA/SPers, and long-term use may possibly benefit others.

Propranolol is often prescribed in a dosage of 10-20 mg. to be taken 45-60 minutes before a performance. The effects last approximately four hours. Most healthy individuals tolerate propranolol well although those with a resting heart rate below 60 beats/minute are generally discouraged from taking it. After a test dose, the initial dose usually starts at 10 mg. or lower and builds to 20 mg. if necessary.

Use of beta blockers may be contraindicated with

• *Asthma, and other bronchospastic diseases*

• *Diabetes*

• *Hypoglycemia*

• *Impaired liver function*

• *Hyperthyroidism*

• *Wolff-Parkinson-White Syndrome.*

(Note: There may be drug interactions with Reserpine, calcium-channel blockers, and haloperidol, e.g.)

Benzodiazepines. Benzodiazepines act as a central nervous system depressant. The exact mechanism of action is unknown, although it appears that benzodiazepines increase the activity of gamma-aminobutyric acid (GABA), a neurotransmitter which inhibits the activity of the brain's limbic system. Of those studied, the shorter-acting aprazolam (Xanax) and lorazepam (Ativan), and the longer-acting chlordiazepoxide HCl (Librium) and clonazepam (Klonopin), only the clonazepam was found to be useful in SA/SP. However, while benzodiazepines, in general, tend to have little effect on anticipatory anxiety or avoidant behavior, clonazepam is very effective for them. They're considered medically safe because they don't harm organ systems and can't be used for suicide. However, shorter-acting benzodiazepines, like aprazolam, do have problems with rebound anxiety as the dose wears off. There's also anxious anticipation of next dose availability, severe withdrawal symptoms, potential physical dependence, possible cross-reactivity with alcohol use, and high relapse rate after drug discontinuation.   Longer-acting clonazepam, when dosed appropriately and taken regularly, has none of these problems

Clonazepam may be more effective than aprazolam and has shown the best efficacy in all controlled trials for SA/SP. In one study 42% on clonazepam reported they were very much improved and another 42% reported they were improved. However, there is a high incidence of mostly short-term negative side effects

* *Sleepiness*

* *Loss of libido*

* *Memory problems*

* *Irritability*

* *Incoordination*

* *Weakness*

* *Light-headedness*

* *Insomnia*

* *Weight gain*

* *Blurred vision.*

Dosage with aprazolam may begin at 0.5 mg. three times a day, for a daily total of 1.5 mg. If drowsiness occurs, this dose is often reduced. Dosage may be gradually increased to 4-6 mg. per day total. Aprazolam's shorter half-life necessitates frequent dosing, perhaps up to four times a day. In addition, this drug sometimes has a mood-elevating effect.

Clonazepam usually begins at 0.25 mg. three times a day to keep drowsiness under control, for a daily total in adults not to exceed 1.5 mg. Typical dosage may be increased to 2-4 mg. per day total. Unlike aprazolam, clonazepam can depress mood in approximately 3% of patients. However, the withdrawal symptoms experienced during tapering and withdrawal are less uncomfortable. There are limited data on the use of benzodiazepines, in general, for the treatment of SA/SP.

Benzodiazepines need to be evaluated over a longer period of maintenance therapy than MAOIs. For either drug several weeks are needed to withdraw, especially if the dosage has been substantial. The last 1 mg. has frequently been found to be particularly difficult. Benzodiazepines are contraindicated where there's evidence of liver disease. Furthermore, their action may be synergistically increased by alcohol, MAOIs, tricyclic antidepressants, and other drugs.

SSRIs.   Selective serotonin reuptake inhibitors (SSRIs) are antidepressants which block the reabsorption of serotonin so that it's available longer. The primary ones are fluoxetine (Prozac), paroxetine (Paxil, Seroxat), sertraline (Zoloft), fluvoxamine (Luvox), and citalopram (Celexa, Cipramil). Although not as effective as phenelzine, these are considered an acceptable alternative to MAOIs because of their favorable safety and side-effects profile.

In one study of fluoxetine, 58-71% of SA/SPers showed marked or moderate improvements. In several studies fluvoxamine has been shown to reduce SA/SP symptoms up to 50% with benefits reported as early as three weeks. A recent **Journal of the American Medical Association** article on a 14-

center, randomized, controlled trial on use of paroxetine for generalized SA/SP found that 55% of those taking the drug at 20 mg./day were much improved or very much improved at the end of an 12-week treatment. The conclusion was that these short-term results were substantial and produced clinically meaningful reductions in symptoms and disability. Because of its extensive database for treatment of SA/SP, paroxetine, which was approved by the U.S. Food and Drug Administration (FDA) in May 1999 for the treatment of SA/SP, is considered a first-line treatment for it.

Citalopram, which was also recently approved by the FDA for use as an antidepressant, has been prescribed in Europe since 1989 and has been used by 8 million people worldwide. Studies have shown its usefulness in panic disorder as well. While it shares some of the side effects of other SSRIs, citalopram has several advantages over them. While SSRIs, in general, may interact with other drugs, such as MAOIs, tricyclics, lithium, barbiturates, and theophylline, citalopram interacts only with MAOIs. With a chemical structure unrelated to other SSRIs, it selectively results in fewer sexual side effects, such as decreased libido and ejaculation.

There are two benefits of SSRIs. One is that they are considered "clean" drugs, working primarily on serotonin and not on several other neurotransmitters which may be unrelated to SA/SP. The other is that SSRIs tend not to leave us feeling drugged, although some may feel sedated or draggy.

The usual dose for fluoxetine and citalopram is 20 mg. per day, requiring a 2-3-month trial period. The dose for sertraline and fluvoxamine is generally 70-150 mg./day. SSRIs take 2-4 weeks to take effect, with the mean peak response time around seven weeks. If the drug is working, duration on it is generally six months or longer.

Common initial side effects include

- *Insomnia (trouble falling asleep or frequent awakening during the night, though daytime sedation and insomnia may continue)*

- *Nausea*

- *Diarrhea*

- *Stomachache*

- *Headache*

- *Weight gain*

- *Reduced libido and delayed orgasm*

- *Anxiety.*

Use of SSRIs may be contraindicated with

- *MAOIs*

- *Elevated liver function tests*

- *Severe insomnia which is not due to depression.*

SSRIs should not be combined with other drugs which increase brainstem serotonin activity. Significantly increased serotonin levels can produce *serotonin syndrome*, a potentially life-threatening complication of psychopharmacological therapy. It's often not easily recognized because of its varied and non-specific symptoms, such as tachycardia (rapid heart), hyperactivity, hypertension, high fever, and severe seizures.

Likewise SSRIs should not be combined with MAOIs. If there's to be medication change from an MAOI to an SSRI, the general recommendation is that at least 14 days should elapse between the discontinuation of the MAOI and the initiation of the treatment with the SSRI. If the switch is from the SSRI to MAOI, the recommended washout period is five weeks for fluoxetine, two weeks for others. Abrupt discontinuation of some SSRIs may result in withdrawal symptoms, such as tremor, dizziness, nightmares, muscle aches, crying spells, disorientation, poor coordination, and nausea. Tapering generally requires 7-10 days.

Interactions. Interactions may occur between SSRIs and other drugs. Listed are just a few of the drugs the intensity of which may increase when used with SSRIs. (adapted from a 1996 **Harvard Women's Health Watch**)

- *Prozac/Zoloft*: Anafranil, Clozaril, codeine, Elavil, Haldol, Inderal, lidocaine, Norpramin. Pamelor, Percodan, Risperdal, Talwin, Tofranil

- *Paxil*: Anafranil, codeine, Elavil, Haldol, Norpramin, Pamelor, Percodan, Risperdal, Talwin, theophylline, Tofranil. Warfarin

- *Luvox*: caffeine, Clozaril, codeine, Elavil, Haldol, Inderal, Norpramin, Pamelor, Risperdal, Talwin, Tofranil.

Dual-action agents. Mirtazapine (Remeron), which was approved by the FDA in 1996, is the first agent of this new class of antidepressants. Mirtazapine stimulates the release of both norepinephrine and serotonin while blocking two specific serotonin receptors. The serotonin specificity minimizes common SSRI side effects, such as decreased sexual drive, nervousness, and insomnia, and speeds up improvement. In studies comparing mirtazapine with fluoxetine, citalopram, and paroxetine, mirtazapine was significantly more effective in the treatment of depression, showing greater improvement at the first week. Dosage ranges from 15-60 mg./day. At lower doses it tends to be very sedating but less so at higher doses, unlike other sedating antidepressants. To-date there have been no studies on the use of mirtazapine for SA/SP.

Buspirone. Buspirone (BuSpar) is an atypical anxiety-reducing drug, azaspirone, which appears to act on serotonin and dopamine receptors. While it may act something like a benzodiazepine, it's chemically and pharmacologically unrelated to benzodiazepines, barbiturates, and other sedative - anxiety-reducing drugs. As a result, it has no muscle relaxant or anticonvulsive effects and is less sedating. There's no risk of inducing physical dependency. Unlike benzodiazepines, its anxiety-reducing effects take 2-3 weeks to be noticeable. A buspirone patch is now being tested.

Common side effects include

- *Dizziness*
- *Nausea*
- *Headaches*
- *Nervousness*
- *Light-headedness*
- *Excitement.*

It's used predominately with generalized anxiety disorder and discrete SA/SP, however, those with generalized SA/SP may respond. The general response rate is 53%. When the drug is combined with CBT, the improvement rate climbs to 67%.

Initial dosage is 5 mg. three times per day or less. This can be increased by 0.5 mg. total daily dose over three days. If this is tolerated, it may be increased to four pills and increased every three days until 30 mg. is reached. After four weeks, if this dosage isn't working, it may be increased in 0.5 mg. increments to a total daily dosage of 60 mg. Maximum improvement is around four weeks. Studies have found that these beneficial results may not be dramatic or consistent. Buspirone should not be taken with MAOIs.

Bupropion. Bupropion (Wellbutrin) is an aminoketone which acts as a norepinephrine and dopamine reuptake inhibitor and has a weak serotonergic effect as well.

Side effects, which are less common with use of the "sustained-release" (SR) version of the drug, include

- *Tremors*
- *Agitation*
- *Headaches*
- *Dizziness*
- *Visual disturbances*
- *Palpitations*
- *Insomnia*
- *Dry mouth*
- *Constipation*
- *Nausea.*

Use of "immediate-release" (IR) version of bupropion, particularly at higher than recommended doses, may be contraindicated with

- *History of seizures*
- *History of anorexia nervosa or bulimia (because of higher incidence of seizures).*

Dosage may range from 75 mg. twice a day to 300 mg. per day, divided into three equal doses. With the SR formula dosage is 150-400 mg. total, given once or twice a day, with no more than 200 mg. given at any one time. Bupropion should not be used with MAOIs. Recommended washout period for switching from MAOI to bupropion is ten days. To-date this medication has not proven to have much efficacy for SA/SP.

Tricyclic antidepressants (TCAs).   These medications include imipramine (Tofranil) and clomipramine (Anafranil). They act as serotonin and norepinephrine reuptake inhibitors. As a general rule, they are not effective with SA/SP. This is particularly true about reducing social and interpersonal hypersensitiviy. Clomipramine, however, has shown some improvement in some individuals.

Common side effects include

• *Urinary retention*

• *Dry mouth*

• *Constipation*

• *Blurred vision*

• *Sedation*

• *Weight gain*

• *Sexual dysfunction.*

Average dosage is 75 mg. or more per day. Combining TCAs and MAOIs may over-increase serotonin levels, putting us in jeopardy of serotonin syndrome. As a result, close monitoring is recommended when combining them.

Other medications.   Clonidine (Catapres) is an antihypertensive which has been found to be helpful with panic disorder, generalized anxiety disorder, and severe blushing (one study). Little data are available on the use of clonidine for SA/SP.

Prescribing for children and adolescents

While children and adolescents receive pharmacological treatment for SA/SP, controlled studies on psychopharmaceutical treatment of children are, for the most part, nonexistent. But then again, the same can be said for 80% of all medications listed in the **Physicians Desk Reference**. Even with little scientific evidence supporting their use in children, use of antidepressants in children has been steadily increasing. In 1994, for example, 200,000 prescriptions for Prozac and 300,000 for Zoloft were filled for children ages 5-10 years old. Many view this as alarming and believe that when there's uncertainty and doubt about the safety and efficacy of a treatment, the appropriate action is to test it critically, not to continue to use.

The first large-scale study of children and antidepressants looked at Prozac. Of the 100 child participants 58% did well on the medication versus 33% who did well on placebo. Because of this dearth of information on safety and effectiveness of psychopharmacologics in children, the FDA is urging drug companies to begin studies. In keeping with this goal, NIMH has supported the opening of three child psychopharmacology centers, at Columbia University, Johns Hopkins University, and the University of Pittsburgh, which will look specifically at medications for children with depression and anxiety disorders.

It's important to remember that once a drug is approved by the FDA, physicians can use it for anybody and for any purpose, irrespective of the condition for which it was tested and intended. It's at the discretion of the physician. At present, for those who use or want to use psychotropic drugs with children the suggestion is to start with a low dosage (perhaps the smallest amount per pound of body-weight), go slowly (use only when necessary and increase in small increments), and monitor (watch for side effects, drug interactions, and effectiveness).

Reviewing medications

MAOIs, clonazepam, and SSRIs are considered best for severe SA/SP if there is co-morbid depression. For performance or test anxiety disorder which involves rapid heart rate, short-term use of beta blockers may be appropriate. For severe anticipatory anxiety and frequent panic attacks benzodiazepines are best. Overall, there's little research on the long-term psychopharmacological treatment of SA/SP. Maintenance therapy up to a year may sustain improvement and decrease rate of relapse, as is true for many other psychiatric disorders.

The decision to take psychopharmacologic medications is often not an easy one. We may feel uncomfortable doing so. Perhaps it's because it conflicts with our personal values of avoiding artificial means to effect change. Or it taps into our aversion to the use of anything which interferes with our sense of control. ...We associate it with drug abusers. ...We believe it shows weakness to use them. ...We've tried one medication and didn't like the results or side effects. But if we've tried non-medical strategies first without success and if we're in severe psychic pain and unable to function, we may want to at least consider the use of medications as an adjunct to other strategies until we're up and running again.

Getting hold of psychotropic drugs

Psychiatrist and psychopharmacologist Jack Gorman reminds us in **Essential Guide to Psychotropic Drugs** that there are important guidelines to follow for gaining access to drugs for any psychiatric disorder.

- *Get drugs only from medical doctors (M.D., D.O.) who are authorized to prescribe.*

- *Talk personally with the professional prescribing the drugs. Don't let someone else get them for you.*

- *Consider long-term drug therapy only from a physician well-versed in psychotropic drugs.*

- *Accept treatment designed for your specific needs and situation only.*

- *Get an explanation of and justification for a particular drug for you from the physician.*

- *Learn side effects and any potential interactions.*

- *Get a second opinion from another physician if it's desired.*

- *Make sure there are follow-up visits to monitor the drug's effects and dosage.*

- *Have a support person with you at your appointment.*

Locating drug assistance programs

Many of us find it difficult to afford necessary prescription drugs. In order to have them, we may do without other necessities. Or we may do without the drugs entirely, stopping to take the medication altogether when funds for them run out. However, if we don't have medical insurance or if our medical insurance doesn't cover our antidepressant or anti-anxiety medications, we may be able to obtain help from drug manufacturers.

Some pharmaceutical firms offer special drug assistance programs, often referred to as "indigent patient drug programs." These are not government-sponsored programs. Criteria for qualification will vary from program to program, but the information needed on which to make an evaluation of eligibility includes

- *Combined household income*

- *Assets*

- *Monthly expenses*

- *Number of people in household*

- *Health insurance and co-pay information*

- *Monthly amounts of SSI (Supplemental Security Income)*

- *Monthly amounts of SSDI (Social Security Disability Insurance)*

- *Medicaid eligibility*

- *Prescription drug coverage, if any.*

Some programs may leave the assessment of eligibility up to the physician. If our physician is unwilling to participate, we may look for another physician who will participate or simply enroll ourselves.

The general procedure is that if we think we may be eligible for one of these programs, we should have our physician make the initial contact with the manufacturer. When eligibility is determined, the manufacturer sends the drug directly to the physician's office for appropriate distribution. It's important to remember that not all drugs used for SA/SP will be available through these programs, but many are and new programs and new drugs are continually being developed.

Further resources can be found in the **1997 Directory of Prescription Drug Patient Assistance Programs**, published by the Pharmaceutical Research and Manufacturers of America. It's available free of charge by calling 1-800-762-4636. Online drug assistance program information is available in Chapter 15.

Taking drugs can feel like spinning a wheel of fortune.

Receiving Social Security Disability Insurance

Those of us who are disabled by SA/SP may be entitled to receive benefits as if our disability were the result of a physical condition. *Disability* is defined in terms of our ability to work. According to the National Alliance for the Mentally Ill (NAMI), Social Security Administration (SSA) criteria for claiming disability include

• *Inability to work for a year or more*

• *Inability to do any kind of work*

• *Severity of condition interfering with work-related activities*

• *Condition likely to result in death*

• *Earnings under $500 per month*

• *Disability determined by physicians and disability examiners at state agency-based examinations and clinical evidence*

• *Disabling condition must be on Social Security list or have the same effect as a condition which is on the list.*

Applying for benefits requires our applying in person at our local Social Security Administration office. However, if our SA/SP prevents our doing that, a parent or guardian may apply for us. We'll be interviewed at length and in-depth and have to fill out a number of forms. This may be an anxiety-provoking experience so having a friend or relative along as a support person may help. Our eligibility will be determined by three factors: Medical status, functional status, and financial status. The process takes between three and six months following application and we need to check periodically on the status of our application. As NAMI points out, even if we're rejected, we should persist in seeking funds through the appeals process since 66% of those receiving benefits were initially rejected.

What about Supplemental Security Income?

Twenty-five states now provide additional income to those who are disabled, unable to work, and poor, with benefits up to $407 per month. We can get additional information from the Social Security Hotline at 1-800-772-1213 during regular business hours.

Bumper sticker: "Therapy and drugs are expensive. Popping bubble wrap is cheap. You choose."

CHAPTER **11**

MOVING FROM LONELINESS TO DATING

"All the lonely people, Where do they all come from"
(John Lennon & Paul McCartney, *Eleanor Rigby*, 1968)

How prevalent is loneliness?

In a 1972 study sociologist Robert Weiss found that 50-60 million Americans feel extremely lonely at some time during any given month. Another study showed that one in six Americans don't have a friend in whom they can confide personal problems (in cities it's one in five). Social anxiety is common among all those who are chronically lonely and conversely. SA/SPers in particular experience loneliness, often feeling totally bereft of friends and intimates, without hope of gaining either.

How lonely are you?

*Answer the following questions with **T** for "true" or **F** for "false." (Adapted from David Burns' **Intimate Connections**.)*

___*Nothing I do to improve relationships ever seems to work.*

___*I don't feel very attractive, desirable, or lovable.*

___*It's difficult to tell anyone I feel lonely.*

___*I feel I won't have many relationships because there's something "wrong" with me.*

___*When I'm alone, I'm often bored, restless, or anxious.*

___*I don't know how to meet others.*

___*I don't know what to do when I meet others.*

___*I don't try to get to know others for fear of being rejected.*

___*I'll never have someone to be close to.*

___*Everyone should have someone; it's abnormal to be alone.*

___*The people I'm interested in never seem interested in me in return.*

___*I don't seem to have much in common with others to talk about.*

___*I don't see how anyone could love me.*

___*I feel like a failure, a loser, or inferior because I have no one.*

___*It's difficult for me to become intimate.*

___*I feel helpless and vulnerable when I'm alone.*

___*I often feel empty and unfulfilled.*

___*I'm unhappy doing so many things alone.*

_____*I sometimes think an unhappy relationship would be better than none at all.*

_____*I'm not really connected to any peer groups.*

*Count the number of Ts. 0 - 3 = Minimal or no loneliness. 4 - 6 = Mildly lonely. 7 - 9 = Moderately lonely. **10 or more** = Very lonely.*

Is all loneliness the same?

Loneliness is an unpleasant experience of involuntary isolation which we find distressing. It's that gnawing dissatisfaction with the existing state of our social relations. It's when our social network is deficient in some important way, either quantitatively or qualitatively. It's where some basic human social need isn't being met. For some of us it may be the result of an interpersonal inhibition. But, in general, it appears that loneliness is due to an interaction of relatively stable individual characteristics and our changing social situation. This is why loneliness tends to change as we grow older. We associate loneliness with many things, such as a tendency to avoid social contact, sadness, shyness, anxiety, depression, self-consciousness, self-deprecation, boredom, anger, and marginality.

However we define it, loneliness is not synonymous with "being alone." Solitude, simply being by ourselves, is not necessarily a negative experience. In fact, it actually may be very productive and vivifying. It can let us accomplish tasks with no distraction or let us relax, away from stress, so we can put our life, problems, and priorities into perspective.

Conversely, being with others may be a negative experience, as in hanging around in a bar night after night or being in an "empty-shell marriage." What all this boils down to is that social contact for the sake of social contact offers us no assurance of protection from loneliness. Whether or not we're lonely depends on the type of social contact. We have the quantity and quality of that contact, our expectations, what we want from it, and what it means to us within our life experience.

Weiss describes two forms of loneliness: Social and emotional. *Social loneliness* is a feeling of boredom and marginality because of the absence of meaningful friendships, social network, or a sense of belonging to a community or peer group. It's associated with a lack of trying to make friends as well as a lack of opportunity to do so. It may be either transient, occurring temporarily, or situational, such as the result of specific events, like divorce or death.

Emotional loneliness, on the other hand, is that feeling of anxiety, restlessness, and emptiness which results from the absence of a single, intense, intimate relationship. This is frequently associated with our perceptions of personal unattractiveness. But we also associate it with our fear of rejection, shyness, and lack of social knowledge and social skills. It may include longing for the past, frustration with the present, and fear about the future. When this situation is severe, lasting over two years and having no traumatic event preceding it, it's considered to be chronic loneliness.

Chronic loneliness can be thought of as a loneliness "trait." We have difficulty making social contacts and achieving intimacy even when the conditions are favorable. Contributing to this are three significant factors. One is feeling estranged, excluded, isolated, unloved, misunderstood, or rejected by others. The second is being or feeling deficient in social skills. We believe ourselves to be undesirable because of what we see as unchangeable personality characteristics. The third is having to pass up desired activities because we have no appropriate social partner with whom to participate in them. But irrespective of the factors involved, we feel distressed, dissatisfied, and deprived.

To feel satisfied with our interpersonal relationships, we need two types of interpersonal relationships: (1) Someone to whom we feel attached who'll provide us with emotional intimacy and (2) Social ties which will provide us with a sense of group belonging. Having only one doesn't compensate for not having the other. When we lack either or both of them, we're convinced that there's little or nothing we can do to create these social contacts to improve our condition. As a result, we feel thrust into a tar pit of pessimism, consigned to a perpetual state of unluckiness and despair.

The character of Will Hunting in the movie **Good Will Hunting** is an example. Will has neighborhood buddies but has no one to whom he feels attached. He's lonely, discouraged, insecure, and afraid to try to create intimacy. He doesn't want to be rejected and abandoned again.

Social bonds are considered essential to psychological well being. But when establishing and successfully maintaining them is difficult, we often find ourselves vulnerable to stress, emotional disorders, and impaired physical health. Chronic loneliness has been linked to depression, alcohol abuse, and aggressiveness. It's also been linked to low school grades, a 100%-increase in becoming ill, increased mortality rate, and suicide. The presence of a social network to which we can turn for support is a strong determinant of our predicted degree of overall health.

But as we know, loneliness isn't just the number of social contacts we have. It's partly a matter of our expectations - what we think is "normal" for our age, peer group, and culture. It's partly what we want. Once again our experience is filtered through our assumption-biased evaluation process. Even if we have many contacts, there may be a discrepancy between what we actually have and what we perceive we have. If we perceive the quality of our contacts to be poor, we're likely to feel lonely. If we perceive that the amount of time spent with the other person isn't sufficient, we're likely to feel lonely. If we perceive that our two lives don't intertwine or that the arrangement isn't desirable, we're likely to feel lonely. As the NIMH report, **Preventing the Harmful Consequences of Severe and Persistent Loneliness** suggests, it's "all in the eye of the beholder." This reality is subjective, not objective.

While some of us may avoid social contact because of introversion or depression, the majority of us who are chronically lonely simply find ourselves unable to perform up to our own expectations. When we find our behavior unfulfilling, we avoid the situation. Even when we have a chance to make a social contact, we frequently don't take advantage of it because we don't perceive that the chance really exists. "Deficient" social skills further increase our anxiety which also leads us to avoid social contacts. This, in turn, increases our social skills deficiencies. Like so many other SA/SP situations, this situation creates a vicious circle.

Because we aren't fully participating in social interactions, we don't get the opportunity to learn and practice our social skills: Speaking, listening, conversational sharing, compromising, and cooperating. Our perceived inability to perform these skills comfortably can lead to deleterious effects on our social life. By avoiding social situations, SA/SPers are more likely to experience chronic loneliness.

Role of development and childhood experiences.

Opportunity for social interaction during childhood has been found to have a direct impact on perceived loneliness. Surprisingly, children as young as five years understand the sense of loneliness; 8-year-olds can define and describe it; and feeling lonely is relatively constant at 23% of children between grades 5 and 9. The greater the amount of our involvement with socially cohesive groups, the lesser the degree of our loneliness.

Psychoanalyst Harry Stack Sullivan, renegade student of Freud, who believed that the primary concern of psychiatry should be interpersonal relations, not sexuality, hypothesized that having a preadolescent pal is essential to later social interaction competence. A pal is someone with whom we cooperate, plot and plan, figure out life, share secrets, explore, play, and solve problems. A pal is someone who protects us from pain and whom we protect in return. A pal is someone who teaches us what it means to be a friend.

Lack of an early friendship may then impose lifelong risks for our social development. These friendships prepare the groundwork for having long-term relationships and marriage later on. Studies have linked not having an early friendship with our degree of social competence, drug abuse, chronic anxiety, and depression.

Children need to derive both a sense of emotional intimacy and group solidarity from their early relationships. Group solidarity comes principally from external relationships while emotional intimacy comes initially from the family unit. In many ways the family is the root of loneliness in that it functions as the primary source of our interpersonal involvement. It provides the context for our acquisition of social attitudes and skills. It's the base of security from which we reach out to expand our interpersonal efforts to establish peer relationships. So the nature of the role relationships within the family is important to development of social skills.

As you recall, in Erik Erikson's developmental stages adolescents face the crisis of "intimacy vs. isolation" where we have to deal with establishing relationships. It's at this stage that we become particularly concerned about being unattached. It's also at this time, as Jerome Kagan points out, that we're our most sensitive to social rejection when the rejection potential is very real. We may be rejected for not being seen as acceptable, for having a different appearance, for lacking admired skills, and for being either behind or ahead of others developmentally. In children peer-group acceptance is generally correlated with degree of loneliness across cultures, contexts, settings, age groups, and acquisition of stage-appropriate social skills.

Parents who are supportive and accepting will tend to foster higher levels of self-esteem in their children. This includes supporting children's friendship choices. Specifically, those who socialize their children into positive interpersonal attitudes and skills through modeling and direct teaching will help create higher levels of self-confidence in their children.

Adolescents who have had little opportunity to experience positive social interactions in their early years are likely to feel interpersonal cynicism, mistrust, and loneliness. When parents are cold, rejecting, unsupportive, hinder their children's relationship choices, or are socially withdrawn or anxious, their children will likely have lower self-esteem. Low self-esteem is central to both the onset and persistence of loneliness.

When we experience these feelings of low self-worth, self-consciousness in social interactions, and self-blame for social failures, we employ strategies to try to protect ourselves. We may use compliance, rebellion, or withdrawal.

- *Compliance* is our conforming to the wishes of others in order to avoid criticism or rejection.

- *Rebellion* is our acting against those whom we perceive to be the source of potential negative feedback. We do this internally by our contrary attitudes and beliefs or externally by our appearance and behavior. Our objective is to invalidate the power of the rejecting others over us.

- *Withdrawal* is removing ourselves from social contacts altogether in order to eliminate the criticism or rejection.

Unfortunately these strategies tend to be dysfunctional. By their very nature they don't enhance self-esteem. Instead, they further isolate us or create relationships which are frequently superficial or problematic.

Divorce too has a strong influence on how children perceive interpersonal relationships. Preadolescent and adolescent children often equate divorce with a grab bag of negative feelings. We feel loss, anxiety, a sense of abandonment, social rejection, guilt over being "responsible" for the situation, and fear of being different from our peers. As a result, children of divorce are more likely to be wary of intimacy and its inherent potential for rejection. We are also more likely to choose ending relationships as the solution to our interpersonal problems rather than trying to work things out. However, it's important to note that loneliness may be less stable and persistent in children than it is in adults.

Role of culture. As discussed earlier, cultural trends, such as mobility and the demise of the extended family, often disrupt our family roots and social ties, making continuity of our social bonds difficult at best. What makes the situation often seem nearly insurmountable is the perception that this is a "couples' culture." We're labeled and evaluated by where we fit in on the road to marriage: Working toward it (dating), getting serious (going steady), making a commitment (being engaged), then marriage.

Being alone is looked upon as being deviant. "Being single" is generally referred to as "unmarried" since marriage is assumed to be that standard for interpersonal relationships against which all attachment relationships are judged. So being single represents our failure in the marriage market competition and primes us for loneliness. This notion is reinforced by the fact that married individuals do tend to report less loneliness than their single or divorced cohorts.

The imperative to meet these relationship expectations shows itself in social pressures and rewards associated with being a twosome. We're shamed by parents and friends for not having dates for specific occasions, for sitting home on Saturday night, for not being married yet. "What's the matter with you?" they ask. We're bombarded by advertising which shows that any enjoyment of life, whether it's having a Coke, swimming in the ocean, or going to a movie, requires some form of romantic partner. Those of us who "fail" to measure up to these cultural expectations are left feeling inadequate, dissatisfied, lonely, and totally to blame for our condition.

What it's like to be chronically lonely

One study showed that 13.5% of college students were chronically and severely lonely. They saw themselves as responsible for their loneliness. They blamed it on their shyness, their fear of rejection, lack of social knowledge, experience, and social skills. Of those some exhibited what Carin Rubenstein and Philip Shaver call "sad passivity." These particular students tended to cope with their loneliness by spending their time sleeping, crying, sitting and thinking, doing nothing, overeating, taking tranquilizers, drinking, getting stoned, and watching endless, random television programs "because they were there."

Others coped, instead, by using different, more adaptive strategies. One group was creative in their solitude. They wrote, read, listened selectively to music, exercised, walked, worked on a hobby, and went to a movie. A second group coped through consumerism. They shopped and spent money. A third group coped with the problem directly by making social contacts. They called a friend or visited someone. Those teenagers who experienced a comparatively low amount of loneliness appeared to have a more optimistic viewpoint, better social skills, greater number of attachments, and a perceived connection to at least one peer group.

The lonely students acknowledged having made friends, but they believed their loneliness would continue until they found a romantic partner. Having a romantic partner was an overwhelming concern. But while they desperately wanted this relationship, they felt unable to do what was necessary to establish one. Because of their insecurity, they expressed reluctance to engage in more social-contact strategies and they tended not to get to know new people. But it was forming friendships that was the key to their overcoming their loneliness.

It's the same for SA/SPers. Having a negative, pessimistic view of ourselves, we feel cynicism, mistrust, and often believe new acquaintances dislike us. This perception that others feel negative toward us is not unreasonable from our point of view since we often admit we don't like ourselves very much either. By counter-punching, rejecting others first, we prevent those others from having the opportunity to reject us.

We have a number of strategies to deal with this. One way we protect ourselves and avoid anxiety is to keep our standards of a romantic partner excessively high. In this way when the partner fails to live up to those expectations, we have in place a way of rejecting them before the partner becomes too close. In other words, if the partner is not ideal, they're not "good enough." Likewise, when we don't meet our own perfectionistic standards of attractiveness, we have an excuse for not contacting others or failing in the attempt. Another is idealizing the relationship. This similarly provides us an exit when it doesn't match expectations for infatuation and excitement. If we don't feel what we "should" feel, we obviously don't love each other enough.

Unfortunately we frequently don't realize or understand that part of our problem is the impressions we make on others. Our attitude is generally negative, the result of critical self-evaluation, and this is what we communicate nonverbally. Lonely people tend to be both socially unresponsive and insensitive. Our self-focus tends to make us poor conversational partners. This is particularly true of our reluctance to disclose about ourselves.

It's important to remember that the longer our sad passive coping style persists in the absence of more adaptive strategies, the less likely it is we'll form intimate relationships or allow existing relationships to deepen. This then further removes us from the social relationships we desire. Ultimately, we can end up feeling completely isolated.

Age. It would seem that the longer sad passivity exists, the lonelier the individual becomes, thus making older adults the loneliest of all. But that doesn't seem to be the case. The highest rate of loneliness is between 18 and 25 years of age. Results of surveys by psychologist Daniel Perlman, in fact, suggest that while loneliness peaks in young adulthood, it drops in middle-age and rises again slightly in the older years. This may be due, in part, to our experience of loss in social transitions, such as when we move from home to school or from a life-long married state to singleness.

Gender. While it may appear that loneliness is more common among women than men, because women are more likely to label themselves as "lonely," the opposite may be true. This is because men are less socialized in one-to-one communication than women and, thus, tend to be less effective at it. As a result, those men who are lonely may believe their situation exists because they don't "get along with others," rather than they aren't able to make contact. Because loneliness is associated with social failure and weakness in many people's minds, men tend not to admit their loneliness readily for fear of being stigmatized by it. They may deny or fail to recognize their loneliness, reporting instead vague feelings of dissatisfaction or somatic problems, like headaches and stomachaches.

Whereas loneliness in women seems to be predicted by lack of expressed affection, loneliness in men may be predicted by their lack of expressed inclusion in relationships or groups. This is, perhaps, related to the building and maintenance of social networks. Whether they're married or not, women are more likely to maintain close friendship ties. These ties provide emotional support. Men tend to have close emotional relationships only with their female partners. For both men and women, however, loss of a marital relationship is a greater source of loneliness than the absence of one.

Loneliness vs. depression. Loneliness and depression are not the same thing although chronically lonely people may be depressed. They differ with respect to the focus of our dissatisfaction and the presence of guilt as a symptom. While both loneliness and depression are characterized by a sense of hopelessness with the potential for suicide, that's where the similarity ends. Depression is grounded in our feelings of guilt, shame, and anger. Our dissatisfaction is with our life in general and not specifically with its social aspects. Loneliness, on the contrary, is grounded in anxiety, fear, and low self-esteem. Our dissatisfaction is with our low frequency of initiating social contacts and not with life in general.

Suicidal ideation. Who thinks about suicide? Those who experience depression, alcohol abuse, and panic disorder are not the only ones who think about suicide. Feeling lonely, living alone, and experiencing stressful life events are also important factors. Research by Franklin Schneier and others has demonstrated that those with SA/SP report substantial numbers of thoughts about death and suicide as well as suicide attempts. This is particularly true where we have a co-morbid condition, such as depression. The reasons given by teenagers and adults alike for attempting suicide are wanting to die, to escape from an impossible situation, and to obtain relief. Symptoms associated with our suicidal ideation and suicide attempts include hopelessness, absence of a sense of pleasure (anhedonia), insomnia, impaired concentration, bodily agitation, and panic attacks.

The American Academy of Family Physicians has compiled a list of questions which physicians ask us when we report suicidal thoughts and attempts. We should report all such thoughts to a professional so that they can be addressed appropriately and quickly. Our considering these questions when we're not having suicidal ideation may be useful to us:

• *When did it begin and what precipitated it?*

• *How often do you think about it?*

• *What reasons do you give for it and how do you think about the reasons?*

• *What makes you feel better and what makes you feel worse?*

• *How much control do you have over these thoughts?*

• *What access do you have to the means to commit suicide?*

• *What have you done to set a plan in motion?*

• *How will family and friends respond to your death?*

Chronic loneliness factors. Chronic loneliness is the result of many factors. While our level of self-esteem, social attitudes, knowledge and skills, and loneliness coping techniques are primary factors, we must not ignore the specific circumstances in which we find ourselves. There may be objective obstacles which make our meeting others difficult. They include time, money, and distance. Because of our work and home situations, we may have little time or money to participate in social activities. We may be at a distance from others so travel is difficult. In order for social contact possibilities to exist for us we have to be where the "action" is.

Furthermore, there may be a social mismatch between our social environment and ourselves. A member of People for the Ethical Treatment of Animals might have difficulties finding someone with similar values in a community of hunters. A fan of Smashing Pumpkins might not find someone with similar interests in a work environment of classical music lovers. A globe-trotting travel writer might not find someone with a similar background in an isolated rural area. When we're different from those around us, we have fewer opportunities to initiate relationships and any relationship which we initiate may be very circumscribed.

Rubenstein and Shaver propose that the primary reasons for our being lonely are:

- *Being unattached* (no sexual partner or spouse, or breakup with lover or spouse)
- *Alienation* (having no close friends, not being needed, feeling different or misunderstood)
- *Being alone*
- *Forced isolation* (being house-bound, ill, or without transportation)
- *Dislocation* (being in a new job or school, moving or traveling often, being far from home).

Unfortunately, the opportunities to encounter and interact with those who are similar to us in values, interests, or backgrounds are likely to be haphazard or random. Often we have to carefully calculate the circumstances, like working to locate and attend a chess tournament when we want to meet other chess buffs. Opportunities for making social contacts may be generally more limited than is commonly assumed.

Loneliness Assessment Exercise

*Ask yourself the following questions (Adapted from Ann Van Buskirk and Marshall Duke in the **Journal of Genetic Psychology**):*

- *What does loneliness mean to you?*
- *When have you felt lonely?*
- *Describe how it felt.*
- *What did you do when you felt lonely?*
- *To what degree did doing this ease your loneliness?*

- *What thoughts do you have when you're lonely?*
- *What have you done to improve your situation*

" I can't go in there. They'll think I'm a loser."

Treating loneliness

Clearly, mindlessly staring at the tube, drinking or eating to excess, and hiding out in our room are ineffective ways of coping with loneliness. We need to be active, positive, and goal-oriented. We have to believe we can do something that we can make a change for the better. To increase our desired social contacts and reduce our loneliness we need to do the following:

- *Focus on realistic expectations for yourself, others, and the relationship. Use the disputation method for distorted thoughts.*
- *Develop awareness of defensiveness, self-deprecation, and self-blame.*
- *Modify dysfunctional beliefs.*
- *Determine whether you're depressed because of your loneliness or just depressed.*
- *Differentiate between being alone and being lonely.*
- *Objectively analyze the number, quality, and types of relationships you already have. Decide what's missing and why.*
- *Assess the situational context of your attempts at social contacts and your opportunities for initiating these social contacts.*
- *Attribute your loneliness to its specific components.*
- *Learn appropriate and effective social skills, such as*
  - *Assertiveness (asking for what you want, dealing with criticism)*
  - *Active listening*
  - *Initiating conversations*
  - *Speaking fluently*
  - *Enhancing physical attractiveness*
  - *Handling periods of silence*
  - *Approaching physical intimacy.*
- *Learn more effective strategies for solving interpersonal problems.*

- *Learn to focus on others empathetically.*
- *Look for new opportunities for social contacts.*
- *Cope with aloneness by developing solitary skills.*
  - *Increase number of rewarding solitary activities.*
  - *Become less dependent on others for activities.*
- *Turn loneliness into solitude.*
- *Become comfortable with being alone in order to become comfortable with others.*

Approaching dating

Before discussing the *dos* and *don'ts* of the dating process, we need to look at (1) what factors contribute to our being attracted to others and (2) what factors increase the probability of our initiating a relationship.

Being attracted. A fundamental prerequisite for developing interpersonal relationships is *propinquity*, or closeness. The smaller the physical distance between two people, the greater the attraction, liking, and friendship. The same applies to repeated exposure. The more frequently we see someone, the more positive our recognition of that person and the less uncertainty we feel. Therefore, those who are close to us by virtue of our frequent interaction with them or seeing them where we work or live, for example, are more likely to become our friends. Propinquity creates familiarity which we prefer. The greater the familiarity, the greater the liking.

Seeking similarity. As noted earlier, similarity tends to create positive feelings as well. We like people whom we believe are similar and those who actually are similar. We like those who agree with us and dislike those who don't. Similarities to which we resonate include family, background, age, religion, politics, values, interests, education, jobs, and attitudes.

We particularly like those who hold similar attitudes. But it's not the total number of similar attitudes that matters, but the proportion of similar to dissimilar attitudes which creates greater liking. Interestingly, physical similarity is likewise a factor. We tend to seek out those who appear similar to us, but "better." In other words, we look for an ideal version of ourselves. When we find both attitudinal and physical similarity, our attraction to the other person increases even more. It's important to note that when we're attracted, even before we've had a chance to check out similarities, we assume similarities exist.

However, since we SA/SPers evaluate ourselves negatively, we may not respond to attitudinal similarities in such a strong fashion. We may not make note of them or may interpret them negatively. Moreover, we may react more negatively to those who disagree with us, shutting off further exploration of similarities. What we may respond positively to are those who have positive qualities we admire but believe we lack.

Lusting after physical attractiveness. Physical attractiveness plays a major role in determining interpersonal attraction. Attraction is an attitude toward another person; it's an evaluation of the positiveness or negativeness of what we're feeling at the time. It too is determined by the proportion of positive to negative feelings. In general, we believe that "what is beautiful is good." That is, we tend to see those who are physically attractive as possessing many positive characteristics. We're likely to see those individuals as more socially skilled, strong, positive, outgoing, kind, poised, exciting, sociable, nurturant, with better characters, and having increased sexual activity, warmth, and responsiveness. Moreover, we see their futures as brighter, that they'll have greater prestige, social and professional success, fulfilling lives, and happier marriages. Because of this we feel being with them is rewarding. As a result of our associating with, some of their status and power does rub off on us.

Developing appearance preferences. Through our family and cultural history we've all acquired a set of preferences for physical appearance, which include facial features, weight, height, hair, eye, and skin color, hair length, facial hair, anatomy shape and dimensions, and clothing type. There's an assumption that those who look a particular way will correspond to our stereotypes. In the 1960s, for example, males with long hair were assumed to be drug users, anti-democratic, nonproductive members of society while those with short hair were thought to be clean-living, productive defenders of country, motherhood, and apple pie.

"Beauty" varies with the time and culture, with some cultures being mammary-obsessed, for example, while others concentrate on tattoos or filed teeth. Within each culture at any given time there's fairly good agreement about what is beautiful. Our Western culture places a great deal of value on this superficial attribution and striving toward some arbitrary standard of perfection, ranging from anorexic to muscle-bound, and building entire industries around it.

Importance of expectations. Because we like those whom we expect will like us, our expectations of others are important in the formation of interpersonal relationships. When we expect to be attracted to someone, we act in ways to elicit attractive behavior from the other person. We're friendlier, showing more socially desirable personality characteristics when with the person. As a result of our being friendly, positive, and upbeat, the other person is likely to respond to us in kind. This then becomes a self-fulfilling prophecy. Unfortunately, it's the same when we expect we won't be attracted. Our expectations reveal themselves in our behavior and we send and receive negativity.

When we expect a relationship to develop but perceive external threats to it, we're often motivated to re-establish our freedom to secure it. Irrespective of our initial level of attraction, when we believe obstacles are being thrown in our relationship path, we'll react strongly. This is known as the "Romeo and Juliet effect." We're even more attracted to what we think we can't have.

Looking longingly. Gaze, or eye contact, is one of the first nonverbal behaviors to signal involvement. In general, when we look frequently and longer (1-7 seconds) at those with whom we're interacting, that person will tend to evaluate us positively. Gazing behavior does differ by gender. Women tend to look more when they're speaking, but men tend to look more when they're listening. Frequently women, because of lower status or for the purpose of affiliation, tend to spend more time gazing into the face of the man than the other way around. Men rate these high-gazing women as most attractive because their gaze shows their focused attention on them. Women, on the other hand, rate low-gazing men as most attractive. Women's low-gaze preference may be related to men's long gazes being perceived as sexual, domineering, and threatening.

Joanna's contact. *Joanna felt stuck at the crowded, noisy Christmas office party. She had wanted to leave as soon as she had arrived. Anxious, tired, and bored, she just didn't want to hear another inane discussion about the weather, stock prices, racket ball scores, or daycare costs. She had made her appearance, had a drink, hung around the outer fringes of a few conversations, nodding and smiling on cue, and now she was looking for ways to escape gracefully. As her eyes scanned for her boss and the exit, another pair of eyes caught hers, and held them for a heartbeat longer than a glance.*

Joanna looked away, shifted her position, and forgot for a moment what she was doing. She surreptitiously looked back and his eyes clasped hers again. He smiled. Slowly, almost imperceptibly, Joanna returned his smile. Then before she knew what had happened, he had threaded his way through the crowd and was standing beside her. Without either one having said a word, their mutual attraction was confirmed. With a touch on her arm, he said quietly, "Let's go somewhere and talk."

Distance. Distance between participants in interpersonal relationships is the result of mutual agreement about use of personal space. *Personal space*, a term coined by sociologist Robert Sommer, is the invisible boundary we maintain between ourselves and others wherever we go. It represents spatial zones, defined as *proxemics* by anthropologist Edward T. Hall, through which most other people should not pass.

Our personal space expands and contracts depending upon the situation and serves two primary purposes. One is to act as a buffer against real or perceived threats. These threats may be physical or emotional. Emotional threats may result from too much intimacy, too much stimulation, or not enough privacy. Having a buffer zone enables us to control the intensity of interpersonal relationships and protect ourselves. The other purpose is to facilitate interpersonal communication which depends upon maintenance of comfortable personal space.

Preference for interpersonal distances in different situations appears to be developed early in life. It remains relatively stable over time. It's important to remember that both individual and situational differences affect our personal space.

According to Hall, there are four ranges of personal space in interaction with others:

- *Intimate (0 - 1 ½ feet)* - in intimate contact, physical sports, and aggression. Smell and touch are more important than verbalization for communication.

- *Personal (1 ½+ - 4 feet)* - with close friends and acquaintants. Vision and verbalization more important for communication, though touch is still possible.

- *Social (4+ - 12 feet)* - for impersonal, businesslike contact. Vision and verbalization most important.

- *Public (12+ feet)* - for formal contact between individuals and the public, such as performers, speakers, politicians. Exaggerated nonverbal behaviors supplement verbalization.

We selectively attend best and most easily recall information at a distance of 5 feet although attraction affects the size of our personal space. The greater the attraction, the smaller the personal space between individuals. Women interact more closely with women as the relationship becomes stronger than men do with men. Women, likewise, tend to stand closer to men in initial interaction than men do with women.

Invasion of personal space. When we assume an inappropriately close distance from another, we're likely to decrease attraction as well as increase negative inferences. We often respond to such invasions by turning away, avoiding eye contact, trying to put an object between ourselves and the other. Or we may mumble, stammer, stutter, fidget, become restless and uncomfortable. As a result, we need to be exquisitely aware of people's personal space and avoid invasion. Of course, as we all know, this isn't easy to do.

Closer distances may be tolerated by individuals of a similar age, race, status, or members of our own group, except for SA/SPers. We tend to keep larger buffer zones in general, irrespective of our group affiliation. Even accidental touching may make SA/SPers uncomfortable. Violation of our personal space tends to make all of us angry and hostile. The English, Swiss, and Swedish, for example, interact at distances similar to those of Americans. But Latin Americans, French, Greeks, and Arabs, for example, use smaller interaction distances. They also tend to be less rigid in their use of space. In the U.S. socioeconomic status is an indicator of spatial behavior, showing that lower-class African Americans and Northern European Americans interact at closer distances while middle-class African Americans and Northern European Americans interact at greater distances.

When we differ in our preferred interpersonal distances, we inadvertently create problems. We sometimes find that the person with whom we're speaking keeps stepping closer or farther away, causing us, in turn, to try to adjust our own preferred personal space. The phenomenon, called the "diplomats' waltz" because it often happens between representatives of different cultures, demonstrates how sensitive we are to perceived invasions and our need to re-establish a comfortable distance between ourselves and the other. When we're not aware of personal space issues, we may misinterpret the spatial behavior of others. Someone coming too close may be perceived as threatening or dominating while someone too far away may be seen as aloof or disinterested.

Sequence. Our motivation to interact with others reflects our need for affiliation and our levels of self-esteem and adjustment. The greater our need for connecting with others and the higher our levels of self-esteem and adjustment, the greater our motivation for a close relationship. But before we interact, we look to visible characteristics that will guide us toward or away from the interaction. They suggest the degree of attraction and the likelihood of meeting our expectations. To do this we first match the other person to our cultural norms of attractiveness. Then we initiate a conversation which will probably involve a series of attitudinal and interest comparisons. While we're generally looking for similarities, sometimes dissimilar characteristics are attractive because they reward us in some way. Perhaps the person is outspoken and we wish we were. Our emotional state at the time also influences our judgment, wherein positive begets positive.

Once we then reach the stage of "just good friends," we're able to discuss ourselves to some degree, our fears, embarrassments, and fantasies. As a general rule, we are most attracted to those who match us on **what** we disclose and **how much** we disclose about ourselves. Our attraction increases also if the other person with whom we're interacting seems moderately selective and discriminating in their relationship choices. Specifically, we're attracted to someone who plays hard-to-get with others but not with us.

What keeps the budding relationship going is perceived reciprocal and equitable social exchange. In wanting the best relationship we can get, we're looking for one that's the most rewarding and the least costly, presenting us with the best value available as compared with others. Our rewards may be the intrinsic characteristics of the other person that we value (such as beauty, intelligence, or sense of humor), directly rewarding behavior (such as attention or empathy), and access to external resources (such as prestige, money, and other people).

Costs are determined relative to rewards and represent how much we're willing to pay for the relationship. Satisfaction with the relationship is based on a comparison of the perceived rewards to perceived costs. If the rewards outweigh the costs, we're satisfied. Instrumental rewards (such as physical attractiveness and sexuality) appear to be more important to men in relationships while expressive rewards (emotional support and affection) appear to be more important to women. Happy couples tend to act in less negative and costly ways and emphasize rewards.

Equity. In any relationship we need to feel that what we put into it is balanced by what we get out of it. We pay attention to our inputs and outcomes as well as those of our partner. Both are important in determining how we feel about the relationship. An equitable relationship is one in which both parties perceive they get about the same amount of benefit from the relationship relative to what they put in to maintain the relationship. Equity is subjective and qualitative. Once again, it's not the total number of inputs and outcomes that's important. It's the proportion of our individual outcomes to our inputs.

Equitable relationships are expected to last longer, be more satisfying, stable, and mutually responsive, foster security and trust as well as sexual expression and satisfaction than inequitable relationships. This doesn't mean, however, that **equality** is unimportant. On the contrary, as partners we tend to want to benefit equally from external and tangible rewards to the relationship. We may also want both partners to equally bear relationship burdens, such as expenses, transportation, chores, children, and aging parents. Equality is more objective and quantitative. If we buy a car or sell the house, we want to benefit equally. And when we don't, we're likely to feel dissatisfaction. Thus, the most successful relationships will emphasize both equity and equality.

Where to meet people

When seeking to find and meet others, we need to look in all the usual places:

art galleries or exhibits, bars, banks, beaches, bicycle paths, blind dates, bookstores, bulletin boards (online), buses, chat rooms (online), church, classes, clothing stores, club meetings, coffeehouses, coffee shops, community meetings, computer dating, concerts, conventions, dances, e-mail lists, elevators, fairs, gyms, hiking, hotels, laundromats, lectures, movies, museums, news groups (online), outdoor markets, parks, parties, pen-pal lists, personal ads, planes, plays, political rallies, pubs, resorts, restaurants, running, seminars, sports events, supermarket, support groups, tennis courts, trains, work.

Unless we're very isolated, most of us have a large territory available to us to scour for potential partners. That being the case, why aren't more of us successful with our territory? For one thing, as couples therapist Stephen Johnson points out, most of us don't really cover the available territory. We dismiss out of hand many of the ways to meet others as illegitimate, or, at least, as being "superficial," "cheap," and "beneath our dignity." As a result, we meet only a small percentage of the numbers of people we could if we were more open to these different possibilities.

Added to that is our fear. We all experience a fear of the unknown and being embarrassed. But women have the additional fear of being hassled, while men are concerned about being rejected. Our distorted and irrational thinking takes over, pointing out all the false starts, disappointments, and inconveniences we'll encounter. Wishful thinking intrudes, suggesting that maybe we'll stumble over a truly wonderful person without having to endure the search-and-sweep operation. Before long inertia sets in, we do next to nothing, and we're sitting on a bench in the park, feeding pigeons, just as lonely as before.

In truth, finding a partner requires hard work - very hard, persistent work. It means finding out where people gather and being there. It's all a probability game. The larger the number of people we encounter, the greater the probability of our finding someone. The more people we encounter, the more frequently we can try out and practice our social skills. The more we can deal with rejection, the more desensitized we'll become to it, and the better we can determine what we're really looking for.

I tried computer dating but most of the men I met were either desperate for a mother for their children or just plain desperate. One who didn't come across that way was a dentist. After several telephone conversations, I decided to meet him. All courtesy and enthusiasm, he wanted to show me his newly decorated home and office. Click. While his office was aseptic-looking, his home above it was a Moroccan movie set. Unfortunately, it didn't take long before the pro forma pleasantries were replaced by wrestlemania. And when he saw I wasn't going to be "cooperative," things turned ugly. Rape was a heartbeat away as I tried to calmly reason with him. After 45 minutes of my verbal anesthesia, he began to talk about the trip we would take the next day to the Rocky Mountains on his motorcycle named "Sexy Sarah" where we'd find a cabin and live. Then he unplugged the phone, locked all the doors, and curled up in a fetal position on his bed, hugging the phone to his breast. In the morning he took me to breakfast, talked animatedly about what a great time he'd had the night before, made suggestions for our next date, and escorted me back to my car.

When my next computer-date called, I nearly blew him off until he mentioned he worked with an old friend of mine who had encouraged him to call me. Two years later I married this guy.

Singles' bar. The singles' bar is one of the places many of us tend to discount because of its superficiality. While we may believe that only the terminally-desperate and losers frequent these establishments, they do provide us with several benefits in our search. For one thing, they are teeming with warm bodies and people-to-meet. The environment is casual, relatively protected, and allows rapid learning of what works and doesn't. (It was in singles' bars that I discovered after being inundated with astrologically-challenged, hairy-chested gold chain wearers that maybe I wasn't as pathetic as I thought I was.)

Because of its pervasive careless and indifferent attitude, everyone is approaching everyone else, with each encounter having less significance than it might elsewhere. Since there tends to be little personal investment in these often half-hearted meeting attempts, we can learn to assertively say "no." Our sense of personal worth isn't riding on each encounter. Threat of criticism or other negative reaction to our "no" is reduced. We get to talk with many we don't want to know as well as some we do. Going to a singles' bar is like doing an CBT assignment. It teaches us a lot, gets us incrementally closer to our goal, and may even be enjoyable (as when a self-professed pool sharp tore up the green felt trying to impress me then I countered by running the table).

What we do in meeting others and dating is the basis of contact making which we'll discuss in the next chapter. Specifically, we're working to develop a fulfilling social network of people through activities we find interesting and enjoyable. We do this by knowing our goals and how to present ourselves to get what we want to achieve them. What's important is our being willing to explore and test. As we become more involved in activities and interests in general, we give ourselves more creative outlets for when we're not actively engaged with another person. As we move from loneliness, we move toward a more enriching solitude and beyond, to satisfying relationships.

Image.   Being seen as positive, independent, self-sufficient, and with many interests is attractive to others. When we appear to be in desperate need of others for companionship, love, or fulfillment, we're perceived, charitably, as "less attractive." Our efforts, as a result, will be less effective. Consumed by our own needs, we can offer very little to others. What we do offer may be seen as a strangling dependency, causing others to run, not walk, away from us.

If we appear depressed, cynical, angry, or sarcastic, others may be reluctant to even consider getting close. Use of sarcasm is particularly troublesome because while it often passes for "humor," its presentation is cutting and critical. Both those with and without SA/SP may laugh when someone else is the object of sarcastic derision, but, at the same time, we may secretly fear we could be next.

Humor that works best in most situations is that which is light, nondiscriminatory, and self-deprecating. For example, when *I was crossing a busy city intersection, I saw a long, lean, nicely-muscled cop standing on the curb, talking to his pudgy partner. His angular facial planes and quick smile further piqued my interest. He was, you should pardon the expression, a "stud muffin." Fortunately, I was walking on a long walk-light because I couldn't keep my eyes off him. Then... whomp! I walked straight into a large metal sign on a pedestal in the middle of the thoroughfare which threw me unceremoniously onto my butt.*

As I raised my bruised body from the asphalt, I saw that the object of my affection was staring at me with his mouth open. A woman on the other side of the street rushed to my aid, dusting me off, checking the lump on my temple, making my faux pas even more obvious to all now assembled on both sides of the street. Then the light changed and there we were, abandoned. We darted into traffic, dodging and weaving the unforgiving oncoming vehicles. By now the exasperated stud muffin had insinuated himself in the fray, busily directing traffic around us so he wouldn't have a fatality on his watch. Once safely on the sidewalk, I glanced back at him and sighed. After going through all that, I never even got a smile from his sweet lips.

As pianist-humorist Victor Borge says, "A laugh is the shortest distance between two people."

People Meeting Exercise

*(Adapted from Stephen Johnson's **First-Person Singular**.)*

• *Make a list of all your interests. Include not only avocational but also vocational.*

- *Make a second list of all the possible places (using the **where to meet people** list as a base) where people who share these interests might gather or frequent.*

- *Analyze the list and rate each activity by (1) your level of interest and (2) how likely it will lead to dating partners.   Use a 5-star scale, with 5 the highest, and 1 the lowest.*

- *Activities which are rated 5-5 are your "definitely will pursue" list while those rated 1-1 are your "only for practice" list. Don't discard any possibilities but concentrate on the more likely ones first.*

Process orientation. It's essential that we focus on the process and not on the outcome. We have to be comfortable actively working to seek out others. We want to know what characteristics, attitudes, and values we want in them. We want to develop our skills in approaching and speaking with them. We want to be capable both verbally or nonverbally of asking for our desire for further contact. This is a trial-and-error learning process. There is no other way to do it. Once we learn to become more adept at initiating contact, we'll be better prepared to develop our ability to evaluate each person as a relationship potential. We want to systematically make and follow a plan to cover all the possible locations and activities now and in the future.

Initiation strategies. The best way to initiate a conversation is to

- *Make a comment;*

- *Ask a question (open-ended whenever possible);*

- *End a comment with a question (to put the ball in the other's court).*

The basic topics for the comment or question are:

- *Environment (location, situation, activity, event, weather)*

- *Other person (attire, non-sexual physical attribute, skill, environment-related interests, movies, music)*

- *Yourself (feelings, interests, activities, skills, attributes, current situation, occupation, movies, music).*

If we choose the other person as our topic, irrespective of whether we ask a question or make a personal comment, we have to make sure that it's not *too* personal. There's plenty of time for us to get beyond superficialities once we get the conversation up on its feet and trotting along. Until then a light touch is desirable.

As soon as we hear the other person's name, we need to repeat it aloud. Others like to hear their names and this also gives them a chance to correct the pronunciation if necessary. Moreover, our saying it helps embed it in our memory. As we all know, it's so annoying to have someone either not hear our name at all or mishear it and keep calling us by something erroneous, even when we try to correct them. I pronounce my name, Signe, as "sig-nuh" But after I introduce myself, I'm regularly called "sig-nee," "sin-yuh," "sid-nee," sig-net", and "son-yuh." Also we should never assume that it's acceptable for us to arbitrarily choose to employ a nickname or shortened form of a name for another person. Names are an important part of our identity and are very personal. Frequently people trying to be friendly decide to call me "Sig," much to my chagrin. And because asking them to call me by my full name is often awkward, I don't always do it. Not the best way to initiate a relationship.

Wherever we go to meet others, we need to have a short list of boilerplate initiators with us which we can tailor to the situation and person. For variety we should have both questions and comments, representing the three topic areas. In this way we won't be struggling to create something even remotely intelligible to say when we anxiously need it.

Here are some typical examples. They're varied by topic and format so we can see how they can change accordingly.

Environment

Comments: "They have a good band here." "The speaker has a new book out on the topic." "This building used to be a roller rink." "This bank's tellers seem very new." "The weather forecast didn't say anything about this torrential downpour."

Questions: "How long has this band played here?" "What is the title of the speaker's new book?" "How long has it been since this place was a roller rink?" "What's triggered the turnover in tellers lately?" "What's the latest about when this deluge will end?"

Other Person

Comments: "You really seem to enjoy the band here." "You remind me of the successful lawyer in the speaker's new book." "You move like a skater. I'll bet you used to skate here when this place was a roller rink." "You handled that dispute with the new teller so well." "That shawl you're wearing is beautiful."

Questions: "What do you think of the band?" "How often do you attend these lectures?" "What do you think of the roller rink motif?" "How did you ever get that teller to change his mind?" "Would you tell me about that Irish lace shawl you're wearing?"

Yourself

Comments: "I come here frequently to hear this band." "I've just purchased the speaker's new book." "I used to skate here when this place was a roller rink." "I never handle disputes with the tellers very well." "I gave my mother a shawl like that for her birthday." "I'm a paramedic with the fire department here in the city."

It doesn't matter that the question or comment isn't brilliant or witty. It doesn't have to be. All it has to do is (2) Let the person know we're interested and (2) Let us know if the potential partner is open to having a conversation with us. If we deliver our question or comment positively and respectfully, we enhance our chances that the person will be receptive. Once the person responds, we need to share some information about ourselves in return.

Comments: (I come here frequently to hear this band.) "I think it's the best they've had so far." (I've just purchased the speaker's new book) "I like his style and can't wait to read this one." (I used to skate here when this place was a roller rink) "but that was years ago. Now I run." (I never handle disputes with the tellers very well.) "It's a skill I've been wanting to develop." (I gave my mother a shawl like that for her birthday.) "I searched all over for it. It was her prized possession." (I'm a paramedic with the fire department here in the city.) "I really feel I'm doing something important helping others in emergencies."

Note: SA/SPers often regard small talk as too empty, tedious, boring, or stressful to participate in. If given our choice, we'd prefer to sit drenched in honey in the path of a battalion of marauding fire ants to having to think of anything casual to say and keep the inanity going. But since small talk is a social lubricant, something like petroleum jelly to grease the skids to keep interactions moving along, we need to pay particular attention to it. We need to think of it in positive terms. Small talk is our stargate to real, connection-making conversations and developing relationships.

We need to think of initiating conversations as a treasure hunt, searching for subjects to use as a springboard. Similarly, in preparation for conversations we need to look for topics. Conversational gems, such as fascinating, funny, unusual, or informative tidbits, are lying everywhere for us to collect, store, and share in an exchange.

Each time we draw out the other person and make self-disclosures in response, we provide more fuel for the conversational flame. We should think of these conversations as a casual game of tennis. The goal is to keep the conversational ball in the air and make sure everyone has an equal opportunity to hit the ball. For the best results, we need to strive for a comfortable rhythm. For SA/SPers a good strategy is to keep playing to the other player's strengths, rather than concentrating on demonstrating our own strengths. Making fancy shots or acing out the other brings the conversational game to its conclusion all too quickly. The objective of our game should be everyone's satisfaction, a good workout, and mutual desire for another game.

Our opening conversational gambit needs to be not only situation-specific and non-threatening but also without assumptions. As pointed out in Chapter 8, we carry around a garbage bag full of assumptions which we also project onto each new interaction. We assume that others understand what we think, feel, and want. We assume they understand our motivations and intentions. We also assume they know what we mean by our specific questions, comments, or disclosure. If people who really know us have great difficulty figuring this out, how can a stranger possibly be expected to. This suggests that as much as we'd like others to be able to read our minds on these occasions, they aren't psychic.

As a result, we have to look for indications that our messages are being received as sent. When in doubt, we need to use feedback to check. A word to the wise: If others can't read our mind, we can't read theirs either. To have even an inkling of what they mean and intend, we have to pay attention to what they say and how they say it. Then we have to look for congruence among all their verbal and nonverbal behaviors: Do their behaviors support the meaning of their words? As a general rule, when in doubt, we should rely upon nonverbal behaviors.

What we're all striving for in conversations is to find some common ground so we have some basis for continuing the interpersonal interaction. This requires that we look for areas of interest, knowledge, or experience to which the other person can relate. Politics, religion, sexual practices, and our struggle with SA/SP definitely don't qualify as neutral subjects and, in general, should be avoided. While partners in established relationships may differ on philosophical approach or views on controversial topics and survive, embryonic relationships aren't likely to. Instead, we're likely to reject the other out of hand as being dissimilar.

We find common ground by drawing others out with casual questions, not a police grilling. As we listen for and offer information, we learn what to pursue. Maintaining conversations means carefully attending to and remembering information. Conversations don't require that we hold precisely the same views or agree on everything, but some commonality helps. Two big no-nos are (1) trying to change the other person's mind and (2) telling them what to do. Those behaviors are perceived as controlling and are not conducive to further relationship exploration. Our ability to hold up our end of the conversation and appear socially adept is of primary importance.

However, no matter how carefully we listen, share information, and hold up our end, not every interaction will be successful. It's essential we view this in its proper perspective. Sometimes things just don't work out no matter how hard we try, how assertive, polished, positive, or clever we are. We have no control over the circumstances or the other person. This is **not** a personal failure. It's the way things sometimes work out in life. In the dating process, in particular, we should expect to experience this more often than not, reframe it as an opportunity to grow and a learning experience, and move on.

Fail-safe mechanism. We can also approach others in a way that further minimizes the potential for personal rejection. Stephen Johnson suggests the business card method. When we see someone of interest, we can send or pass that individual our business card with a message on it. He suggests that the note on the back of the card might read:

"I find you very attractive and would like to take you for drinks (or lunch). Please check one : ___(1)Yes, my phone number is_____. ___(2) No, thank you."

Making progress. How do we know we're making progress? The best way is to be aware of the nonverbal behavior of the other person. Upon our physical approach, if the person makes eye contact, smiles (perhaps coyly), nods, makes room for us to sit or stand, and/or allows us into their personal space, they're probably showing interest or acceptance. Women tend to have a smaller personal space than men. A woman may also cock her head to one side, look, glance away, then look again, whereas a man may simply look with a smile playing upon his lips. Sexual interest is often signaled by stares, winks, blinks, lip wetting, chest- and hip accentuation, touching self or other, flipping the hair or head, crossing and uncrossing legs, looking the person up and down, a swaggering or wiggling walk, whispering, and primping.

If the person isn't interested, they may make no eye contact, clench teeth/jaw/lips, look away, pull away, turn their body away, cross their body with their arms, cross their legs or ankles, or put an obstacle, person or object, in our path. *My first and only meeting with a computer-date physician was over dinner in a nice restaurant. Throughout the hour's conversation of, by, and for him, he kept his eyes closed, looking only occasionally to spear another hunk of steak and lobster. My attempted contributions tended to be ignored or dismissed. I didn't know whether his anxiety was worse than mine or he thought I'd be so honored by his presence that paying attention to me was unnecessary.*

It's important to note that sometimes when others quit listening to us or just seem bored, it has nothing to do with how scintillating we are. Instead, it may indicate their arrogance. Arrogance isn't just preening, glancing at one's reflection, and being boastful or flamboyant. It's also showing us that they believe we're not as important, fascinating, or worthy as they are and, thus, are less deserving of their valuable attention.

As the conversation continues, we and our companion will begin to turn toward one another, showing increased interest and blocking entrance by outsiders. Perhaps we touch briefly and casually. But remember, touch is "touchy" because it breaches personal space, suggests intimacy, and has sexual connotations. Also, one of the things SA/SPers have mentioned in our two years of conversations is that we may fear or dislike being touched by others, particularly strangers (although as relationship intimacy increases, discomfort with touching may decrease). Being touched may make us feel self-conscious, uneasy, startled, angry, or trapped. We agonize over it: What does it mean? Is it a signal? What should I do?

Since this area hasn't been investigated as yet, it's difficult to say why we may tend to respond this way. Perhaps it's a response to invasion of our personal space. Perhaps it's our anxious expectation about having to reciprocate and not knowing what to do. Perhaps it's our fearing we'll misinterpret the message. Or, perhaps if we interpret it correctly, we'll perform clumsily and be rejected.

As a result, if touch takes place initially, it should be done very cautiously. In opposite-sex encounters men touch women twice as much as women do men. It appears to be related to dominance. As a result, it's often better if it's the woman who makes the first touch, as in a slight brushing of hands or a hand to an arm, to signal a developing rapport. As a general rule, heterosexual men are well-advised not to take this touching as a sexual come on.

In same-sex encounters touching may tend to occur less frequently because it has the potential to draw public attention to the individuals involved and, thus, to their sexual orientation. In addition, because of the negative implications of misperceiving the receptivity of the other person to a same-sex relationship, gays and lesbians may be more reticent initially about touching. In established relationships lesbians may engage in non-sexual touching as a communication device in a manner similar to that found in non-lesbian same-sex relationships. Gays, on the other hand, may be more likely to have their touch represent both sexual and non-sexual messages, depending upon the circumstances.

At this point, whether in opposite-sex or same-sex encounters, eye contact and smiling become more frequent. Voices show enthusiasm and a behavioral *synchrony* may develop. Specifically, we're imperceptibly mirroring each other's movements. As we saw earlier, this neuro-linguistic technique improves communication and builds rapport.

Same-sex dating.
While gays and lesbians face many of the same challenges as straights in the dating game, they also have to deal with pressures not encountered by straights. While a heterosexual male, for example, may rightly assume that most females are potential partners, homosexual males and females can't make that same assumption about others of their own sex. To heterosexuals the potential dating partner is easily recognizable by gender. Not so with homosexuals. Each individual of their sex may be heterosexual and probably not interested, bisexual and possibly interested, or homosexual and potentially interested. This means that gays and lesbians have to meet a great many more people in order to identify the same number of potential partners as straights do. The more people they meet the greater is the risk of exposure of their sexual identity and resulting risk of stigmatization.

Because homosexual children are generally born to heterosexual parents, they'll tend to lack role models for sexual relations, dating behavior, and social rules. Thus, they likely won't have a clear idea what a same-sex relationship looks like, how it functions, or how to initiate one. What is recognized and considered socially acceptable in general will not be the same for the two sexual orientations, witness laws which prohibit same-sex hand-holding or kissing in public.

If gays and lesbians have a smaller potential partner pool by virtue of their sexual orientation, their situation is made worse when they have SA/SP. This restricts their circle of acquaintances even further. To minimize the threat of being rejected by heterosexuals some may seek out same-sex social settings. However, doing so may become an obstacle to the widening of their social circle and meeting desirable partners.

Reframing dating.
Putting dating in another, less anxiety-ridden context may be helpful. When we see dating, love, or fulfillment as the end-all and be-all of the process, we're likely to invest too much emotion in each interaction and each potential partner. This leads to desperation which can make initiating contacts sheer torture, a matter of life or death, and, thus, reduce our willingness to even try. If we reframe the process in terms of looking for others with whom to share understanding, recreational activities, and companionship, we may remove some of the burden. If those relationships develop further and deepen, so much the better if that's what we want. Placing less emphasis on them and less pressure on ourselves to perfectly perform this mating dance, to find someone right now, is likely to make the process more enjoyable. It allows us to expand our interests, our activities, resources, and network of contacts to

enrich our lives. We need to use all our cognitive-behavioral skills to allow ourselves to be natural, relaxed, and confident in this process.

Who asks? Today it's acceptable, in general, for the woman to ask the man since both women and men tend to be flattered by being asked for a date. The conventional wisdom used to be that the older the individuals the more traditional they'd be with respect to sex-role behavior. However, Baby Boomers will likely run the gamut. Irrespective, asking is conflictful for both those on the sending and receiving ends. Asking means we put ourselves on the line for rejection. Being asked means we have to be able to say, "no" as honestly and kindly as possible: "I'm flattered you asked but I don't feel we have much in common."

Telephoning. Once we're able as SA/SPers to use the telephone, we can start using this instrument to further our interpersonal relationships. When we place the call, the first thing we should do is identify ourselves as quickly and completely as possible. If at the start we leave the person on the other end of the line puzzling over who this is, where we met, and why we're calling, we've already dropped the ball. For example, if we say, "Hi, Sarah, this is Barry. How are you doing tonight," the other person feels awkward not remembering who we are and where we met, and wonders how they should feel or relate to us as a consequence. They're likely to feel wary and one-down because we know something they don't. And we're both probably going to feel embarrassed as a result.

Unfortunately for us, the easiest and quickest way for them to relieve this feeling of defensiveness is to get us off the phone as soon as possible. This means they won't care very much why we called. They won't be listening to whatever proposal we want to make. At the very least we've created a negative impression.

If Barry had identified himself better, he'd have put himself in a better position. For example, "Hi, Sarah, this is Barry Ratliff. We met last night at Planet Hollywood when I found your handbag for you near the ladies' room." Before moving on to his reason for calling, Barry needs to wait for recognition from Sarah. "Oh, yes, you're the man in the L.L. Bean soccer shirt." At this point, Barry can broach the subject of his call. His call is really a request that Sarah respond positively to him in some way, such as talking on the phone or agreeing to go out with him.

But it's here that everything may become a tangle of confusion if the person called resorts to *polite code* to avoid saying "no." While it's meant to be a kinder, gentler way of letting the other down, saying, "I can't do it tonight." "No, Saturday's not good either." "Monday through next January, I don't know right now." And "I may have to wash my hair" leads to misinterpretation. What is it they or we really want to say? Is it "yes" or "no"? If the answer's "yes" but the night specified is the problem for us, we need to say so. "I'd like to go to the movies with you sometime, but Monday night is a problem for me." We can then supply an alternate night for consideration.

If the answer's "no," we need to communicate that clearly but not harshly. It's not easy to put oneself on the line, risking rejection, to ask for a date. The response needs to acknowledge that we perceive that the person is doing something positive. It needs to provide a reason we aren't complying with the request, one that is both generally true and protective of the other person's ego. We might say, "It very nice of you to ask me, but I can't right now" then supply a plausible excuse. The excuse might be recently having broken up with a significant other, dating one person steadily, or not adding new people to the list of those we date at the present. Being kind and gentle doesn't mean, however, we have to explain our feelings or behavior or justify our decisions. It also doesn't mean we have to put up with arguments about it.

Going out. We want everything about the interaction to be as settled and comfortable as possible. If we confer with our partner about what we'd both like to do, we can arrive at some acceptable compromise. When we don't yet know one another, it's best to pick activities which allow us some quiet time to talk to actually become acquainted. Until we know the other's interests, women's mud wrestling, monster-truck rally, or astrophysics lecture shouldn't be our first choice for a date activity.

There are other guidelines for first dates as well. As a general rule,

- *Shorter dates are better than longer because they create less pressure.*

- *Less expensive is better than expensive because it creates less obligation.*

- *Use of two cars is better than one because it creates less threat.*

- *Meeting in a neutral place is better than on someone's turf because it creates less threat.*

- *Meeting in a public place is better because it creates less threat.*

- *Single dates are better than double dates because they allow more opportunity to get acquainted.*

- *Deciding right away on who pays and when is better because it reduces conflict.*

- *Learning what the other does for a living and fun, as well as about friends, lifestyle, standards, and values is better sooner because it provides a basis for information to share.*

- *Learning about the other's personal relationship history is better sooner because it tells their current status (single, going steady, separated, divorced, or married).*

Establishing intimacy. Once we've begun to find out information about the other person, we can self-disclose and share. Disclosure is a form of confiding about ourselves, our background, our feelings and thoughts about ourselves and others. Carefully-controlled openness begets openness. Controlling the depth and amount of the information we disclose initially is important for everyone, but especially for us SA/SPers.

When we feel we've found a kindred spirit, we tend to want to share everything with them all at once. We often get a bad case of verbal diarrhea. This can be overwhelming for the other person and even more overwhelming when that confidence includes information about our SA/SP. We don't want the person to turn off, look for the nearest exit, saying to themselves, "Oh, no, what have I gotten into." We need to measure out our honesty in level teaspoons not heaping tablespoons. While we have to gauge each individual situation, in general it's better to postpone the subject of SA/SP until much later.

So we need to disclose slowly, somewhat superficially at first, keeping the topics relatively neutral. As we explore the quality of the relationship, we begin to talk more about our hopes and fears as well as those of our companion. Being sensitive to our companion and ourselves will guide us as to what level is appropriate and comfortable for us both. The sooner we begin building verbal intimacy into the relationship, the more comfortable we'll be in seeing whether the relationship meets our needs.

When we talk about past or ongoing relationships, we need both not to dwell on them and to take care how we present them. Specifically, we don't want to make paragons of virtue of them, an image no one could live up to, but we don't want to say negative things about past partners either. Sometimes it seems that if we show how terrible the former companion was, it'll make the new companion feel better by comparison. Unfortunately, the opposite tends to happen. The negativity itself will make the person on the receiving end feel bad. They'll begin to wonder if we'll talk about them too, either behind their back now or later if things don't work out with the relationship. They may wonder what all this negativity says about us for saying it. How did we treat our last partner and will they be treated the same way? It's similar to what girls used to be told by their parents, frequently fathers, "If you want to see how he'll treat you, look to see how he treats his mother." Instead of criticizing a former partner, we need to be kind. The more charitable we are the more likely we are to reassure our new partner.

As we work to create positive first impressions, we need to be mindful of falling into the *pretender trap*. The pretender trap occurs when we're trying so hard to accentuate all those aspects of ourselves that we think will be attractive that we exaggerate or lie about our interests and tastes in certain areas. First impressions are lasting impressions so we need to create an honest, positive impression we can live with.

Presenting ourselves as something we're not is likely to come back to haunt us. On the one hand, we're going to be stuck doing things we dislike or don't really want to do very often because we've convinced our companion we do. On the other, we may be rejected when our new partner discovers we've been sailing under false colors: We're not the person they thought we were. If we weren't honest about this, what else is there we haven't been honest about. Uncertainty, doubt, and suspicion can quickly become emotional hazardous waste material.

Etiquette. The rules by which we date are very ambiguous at this point in time. Some people adhere to traditional prescriptions about male and female dating roles. These traditional expectations are that the man gets the doors and coats, orders food, pays for meals and entertainment, and is generally in charge. Some subscribe to looser behavioral roles where each person gets their own coat, whoever is at the door first gets the door for the other, cost of meals and entertainment is divided, and both are in charge. Others approach dating behavior from somewhere in between, choosing this from column A and that from column B.

Since there's no way to know initially, it may be best to do three things:

- *Think of etiquette in terms of courtesy, doing something thoughtful and kind for the other person, and be prepared to act in ways to demonstrate that courtesy.*

- *Watch for nonverbal behavior which may suggest the expectations of your partner. For example, if you pull into a parking space and your female companion makes no move to open the door, she may be expecting you to open it. If your male companion asks you what you're going to have as the waiter approaches, he may be preparing to order for you.*

- *When in doubt, it's best to inquire: "May I get your door (or coat) for you?" "Is it okay if I order for you?" or bring it up for discussion: "We haven't discussed expenses, but I'd like to pay half."*

Mutual consideration is the goal. We don't need rigid rules to enforce it. Despite the fact that knowing for sure what's generally expected from encounter to encounter makes dating a lot easier, we can establish our own guidelines within each relationship.

Who pays? Part of the guidelines we mutually devise will concern money. We need to remember that money isn't neutral. It's symbolic of power, status, and dominance. As a result, we need to address it early before misunderstandings and conflicts result from unmet expectations and hard feelings.

One rule of thumb is that the one who initiates the occasion is acting as host and, therefore, is responsible for the expense. But initiation is all in how the subject is presented. When it isn't crystal clear, it's better to inquire than find we've made an erroneous and awkward assumption. We can't assume that the man is the only one with resources and should, as a result, pay for everything. Sensibilities today more openly acknowledge that this perceived obligation to pay is burdensome. The woman may feel she's being bought and the man may feel he has to purchase companionship. This leaves both partners uncomfortable. Wherever possible, sharing of expenses may reduce the discomfort. Where activities simply come about or are the result of partner negotiation, equitable or equal sharing is fair. Where one partner has more resources than the other, the two can pay proportionately. Or they can participate only in activities that both can afford.

Since money is for some, mostly men, a greater taboo than sex, it's often easier if the woman addresses it first. She can suggest that they pay their own expenses. But if, as time passes, she doesn't, the man may introduce the topic. For example, "I'd feel more comfortable if we could share expenses for these activities in some way because I have a budget to stick to. There are lots of things we can do together, some expensive, some not. How do you feel about it?" However it's addressed, we need to negotiate something with which we're both comfortable.

Ending the date. For most people this is probably almost as awkward as asking for a date. The cardinal rule is be honest but be kind. If we enjoyed ourselves, we should say so, suggest that we get together again, and ask our companion how they feel about that. If we didn't, we should still say we enjoyed ourselves but don't feel we have enough in common to continue dating. If we like the person more as a friend than as a date, we should say so and suggest some friendship activity.

Then there's the question of intimacy. Should I try to kiss her? What will she think if I do? What will she think if I don't? What should I do if he tries to kiss me? What if he doesn't try? While we may want our companion to be attracted enough to want intimacy, we SA/SPers may not want our companion to act on it just yet. It's taken a tremendous amount of courage for us to get this far. We're not sure of the "rules" or if our social skills are up to it. And trust may be a big issue for us. Afraid of messing it up, and/or being exploited and rejected, we're torn between approach and avoidance.

Coded signals in the best of situations are often ambiguous. And even if they weren't, we tend to be lousy cryptographers. One way to address this issue is to discuss it **before** the end of the date. For example, "I've really enjoyed your company this evening and would like to kiss you." A response, other than an affirmative, might be, "I've really enjoyed this evening too, but because of my last relationship I'd like to take this a little slow" or one of the "no" responses we used for telephone calls. Having this settled already as the date ends means there's less probability of having to deal with the embarrassment of the "unwanted kiss" or grope situation.

But what about S-E-X? If we decide to have sexual intimacy, it's best that we know that that's what we really want. That our motivation isn't an anxious response to what we think is expected. Or a counter-phobic reaction to our fear of intimacy, to show ourselves we're not really afraid so we go hog wild. Or a confusion of our fear with attraction and excitement.

SA/SPers are particularly anxious about doing "it" and being rejected as well as not doing "it" and being rejected. Damned if we do and damned if we don't. Of course, anxiety in such a situation is quite natural and is likely to be experienced, to some degree, by the other person as well. Everyone is concerned about appearing clumsy or gauche, doing the right thing and doing it well, having bad breath, love handles, mammography-challenged breasts, flatulence, and sweaty feet. And SA/SPers have the additional concern about blushing.

My concern was post-nasal drip. Convinced my breath could stop velociraptor at fifty paces, I sucked on Clorets until my mouth looked algae-fied. It didn't matter that treating my tongue was unlikely to have any effect on my sinuses or that perhaps I didn't really have a bad breath problem, I felt compelled to do something to keep from being embarrassed, just in case. But when there was even a remote possibility of anything romantic, I switched to Chanel No.5 since a green oral cavity doesn't whisper "Come hither." This meant that before and during the date I surreptitiously gargled with the eau de toilette. Did it work? Well, I did get kissed, and sometimes more. I don't know if it was the Chanel No.5 or I would have been kissed (etc.) anyway. But what I do know is it was a very expensive mouthwash and humiliation-preventive.

Most people are self-conscious about their bodies and feel uncomfortable about being nude.   We associate nudity with exposure, powerlessness, deficiency, and vulnerability. Without clothes we lose our specialness. Without clothes our excessive sweating is obvious.   Moreover, some of us just don't want to be looked at, scrutinized, and evaluated.

One reason SA/SPers are anxious about sex is that we tend to feel that the other person knows exactly what to do, how, and when. We see them as calm, cool, collected, and sexually savvy - all the things we're not. We don't have the knowledge or experience. In fact, many of us may still be virgins in our 30s and beyond. We're not prepared. Our minds are a welter of questions: Am I doing this right? What if they don't like it? Should I lead or follow? How do I decide what to say "yes" or "no" to? Should I go ahead and do it or ask permission first?

Another reason for anxiety is our ambivalence. We want to but we don't. We're concerned about what's expected: Women, for example, are expected to be experienced but not "too" experienced. Men are expected to be smooth and in control. Unfortunately, sometimes "in control" translates to "controlling," which may be problematic, particularly when our self-esteem increases. We're both expected to graceful, arousing, and aroused. But are we expected to replay the noisy, athletic sex scenes from **Fatal Attraction** in all their wild, primal Hollywood-style abandon? If we could do this without nervous giggling, would we really want to?

A third reason is that sexual situations trigger all sorts of memories, thoughts, and feelings. We may think of past relationships, sexual associations, parental admonitions, guilt, past failures, and unfulfilled dreams. We may remember hearing our parents having sex when we were small or think about the sounds of sex and someone hearing. Or we may fear someone walking in on us.

Unfortunately, when we're anxious and inexperienced, we may feel compelled to appear more worldly than we really are. This deception is hard to maintain and creates confusion for our partner when we slip. We are likely to feel guilty and fear being found out. As a result, the charade makes us even more tense.

As a general rule, in any situation, sexual or otherwise, when we have questions, concerns, and uneasiness, the best thing to do is bring it out into the open to discuss it. If we're unsure what to do next, we need to say so. Our honestly addressing the situation is far better than sending inaccurate signals to the other person as well as being untrue to ourselves. It may be a little awkward to do so, but a little awkwardness at this stage is better than a lot of awkwardness as passions escalate and panting, sweaty bodies intertwine.

No matter how things go, SA/SPers can expect personal recriminations to follow a sexual encounter as they do our other encounters. We'll start imagining what we did wrong: "I was too _____ (fill in the blank: Desperate, eager, aggressive, passive, disclosing, non-disclosing, personal, impersonal, quiet, noisy, clinging, independent, tense, shy, talkative)." Then we'll decide that we'll be rejected as a result. We'll continually replay the episode, analyzing every negatively-filtered aspect we remember. This is where it's essential that we use our disputation methods for negative self-talk and assess the reality of our expectations.

As psychiatrist Herbert J. Freudenberger suggests, sex is like walking onto a stage where we must throw ourselves into the part, concentrate on technique, timing, dialogue, movement, blocking, and control while simultaneously summoning up some authentic emotion. How we handle it and the degree to which we enjoy it will depend upon how prepared we are for it.

What do we really want on a date? Richard Sides and Pat McChristie writing about singles on the Internet suggest that men and women want different things from a date. According to Sides, **men** want

- *Conversations in which their female companion can speak to subjects and issues in which they're interested, whether it's sports, health, business, or social issues*

- *Conversations which have a beginning, middle, and end. Talking about feelings doesn't achieve closure for them so they're less comfortable talking about feelings*

- *Confirmation that they have unique strengths which are needed. Not being secure about their appeal, they can't tell what the woman wants unless she says so.*

According to McChristie, **women** want

- *Advance notice for dates of two to four days in general. Last-minute date requests more often than not receive "no" responses*

- *Conversations that are more about the present than the past or future glories at the beginning of relationship, which don't drone on about previous relationships, work or career, children, grandchildren, pets, relatives, financial problems, or the man himself*

- *Conversations in which she's not asked excessive questions about her past loves but is asked about herself*

- *Not being interrupted when she talks*

- *Cooperation not competition.*

The object of dating is to see what the possibilities and options are, to meet people, and enjoy ourselves. One important principle to remember in the dating process is that we're more likely to be successful if we accept those we meet for what they are and not for what we want them to be. We can't let our unrealistic expectations creep into the process. Wishful thinking will result in disappointment and disillusionment. Our trying to make them change to fit our ideal is doomed to failure. Moreover, their worth is not dependent upon their ability to meet our needs any more than our worth is dependent upon meeting theirs.

Dating Exercise

- *Identify three activities you enjoy. Compose a brief speech (several sentences) on each, highlighting (1) what you like about the activity, (2) how you became interested, and (3) how often you participate in it.*
- *Initiate two conversations a week for three weeks on the topics (one per week).*
- *Over the next three weeks invite someone to join you in the activity.*

SA/SPER'S IDEAL

Coming out

Paraphrasing Hamlet, "To tell or not to tell. That is the question." We SA/SPers all have grappled with the conflict of revealing our condition to friends, relatives, dates, colleagues, teachers, and employers. Part of us desperately wants to share this, our darkest secret. We want to release some of the pressure, to stop feeling like a liar, and make our sometimes-odd behavior understandable. But as much as we feel compelled to "come out," we feel equally compelled to stay silent because we fear how others will respond to this disclosure.

Joanna. *Joanna wanted to tell her parents but feared more of the same criticism she'd always received from them. Having SA/SP would be equivalent to receiving a "D" on a test. She wouldn't meet their standards of acceptance. Her condition would be seen as her fault, something easily remedied if she'd only try harder. While she might feel better saying the words, the relief would be short-lived. She knew she didn't need to provide her parents with more* *fodder for their demonstrating their disappointment in her. So she decided not to tell them about it.*

Parents and family. Reactions to disclosure can be diverse. Some parents may respond with guilt, making our condition their problem. In doing so, they make themselves, not us, the focus of the situation. Some parents may respond with denial, making our claim invisible. Some may blame us for it, as Joanna fears her parents will, tell us not to exaggerate and to "shape up," making our problem even worse. Other parents may be relieved that there's a name for "it" and be supportive.

Siblings may worry that the condition is hereditary and that they're at-risk. Some may feel guilt that they were spared while others may not want to be associated with this stigmatization. Our condition may strengthen or weaken family bonds.

Barry. *Barry and his childhood friend Chaz had weathered many storms over the years and were always there for one another even though they lived 500 miles apart. When Chaz came to town on business trips, Barry and he always spent time together. Much to Barry's chagrin, Chaz generally suggested they end their evening at a singles' bar where they could pick up women. Barry could never bring himself to address his extreme discomfiture participating in this activity, leaving him to suffer in literal silence.*

But on Chaz's latest trip Barry blurted out how anxious he felt and why. To Barry's surprise, Chaz, after assuring himself Barry wasn't kidding around, clapped his friend on the back. "Hey, that's okay. I was only suggesting we meet some women 'cause you don't seem to know any and look as if you could use a little diversion. Myself, I'd rather play pool or go to a night game with you."

Friends. Depending upon their relationship with us, friends may be glad we shared with them or wish we hadn't, feeling uncomfortable with our "psychiatric disorder." They may start analyzing everything we do and have done in the past in terms of our SA/SP rather than accepting it as an aspect of us. Some may take it personally, feeling insulted and betrayed that we didn't trust them enough to confide in them, thus creating a new interpersonal conflict.

How to come out

If we choose to come out, what should we say and how should we say it? In general, we need to frame our anxiety in terms others can understand and identify with. Few will be able to relate to "social anxiety disorder" or "social phobia." The terms are too clinical and psychiatric. They're not only meaningless, a semantic blab, but also overwhelming and frightening for most people. What we need is something which is user-friendly like "shyness" or "anxiety when giving speeches or meeting strangers." Something which talks about behavior not negative labels. It's definitely a K.I.S.S. situation: "Keep it simple, stupid" (or, if you prefer, "Keep it super-simple"). If we start small, we can elaborate later as the situation allows. If we start big, we have no place to retreat if the announcement doesn't play well.

Dates. As mentioned earlier in this chapter, since dates are generally new people in a new relationship, we have to ask ourselves if there's a compelling reason to lay something as heavy as SA/SP on them. If we feel we must say something and the timing feels appropriate, we should make reference to its being like "shyness" but do it as positively as possible. This actually may be seen as endearing rather than frightening. Then as we get to know the person, they will see examples of our "shyness" and this may be a basis for a discussion of it. However, we're the ones who decide if we'll disclose, what we'll disclose, and when.

Teachers. When our class work and attendance suffer because of our SA/SP, we have to decide how we're going to communicate our underlying problem to the teacher(s) involved. While some SA/SPers may just drop out of class or school rather than address it with teachers, that isn't a viable option for many of us. One possibility is for us to approach the teacher during their office hours to explain our no-doubt confusing and "incomprehensible" behavior. Unfortunately our best efforts may be thwarted by the very thing we want to discuss. It may prevent us from ever getting to the topic ("Nice trophy... and photos of your family") or make our presentation unintelligible and further the misunderstanding. Another possibility is to compose and send a letter or e-mail explaining the problem, thus eliminating the face-to-face freeze-up we invariably experience.

When counseling is available at the school, our speaking with a counselor may provide another avenue of communication. The counselor may speak on our behalf to the teachers in question. Having a credible third-party intervene may add substance and weight to our plight.

If we're already in therapy, we could get a letter from our therapist, explaining our "shy," anxious, or phobic behavior and inability to participate in class discussions or do presentations. We could then show it to each teacher at the beginning of the year. Even if we're not in therapy, we could talk with each teacher at the beginning of the school year about our problem to prepare them. While communicating the severity and seriousness of our condition is essential, we still need to describe SA/SP in behavioral terms they're going to understand, that are relevant to class participation.

How individual teachers may respond to this information is unknowable. They may well respond as do parents or friends, with some being put off and others being supportive and understanding. Our making the effort, however, will likely be perceived favorably, particularly if we do it early before any misunderstandings occur.

Employers. As a general rule, disclosing our SA/SP to employers is not useful. We want them to see us in a positive light. Psychiatric labels or anything which suggests a "problem" recasts who we are, what we do, our corporate value, and our potential contribution to the smooth running of business in a negative light. Only if our avoidance behaviors and anxiety are measurably interfering with our work should we consider saying anything. Then, what we do say is best couched in the behavior that is problematic.

Our trying to present the context of the problem as well the manifestation of it will likely overwhelm the employer and send their anxiety soaring. For example, if we're asked to give a speech, we don't want to vomit our social anxiety life history all over the employer: "Oh, I can't talk before a group; I sweat like a pig. I've never been able to do that or answer the door or go the grocery store or even make friends without a stiff drink. That's why I'm still a virgin at 30. I'd spend my days in my room, crying, if I could."

What we might disclose when asked to give a speech is that we're not comfortable doing any kind of public speaking and are concerned we wouldn't do a good enough job for the company. If pressed on it, we might further volunteer that we tend to stammer and go blank under those circumstances. These are commonplace difficulties others can relate to. In other words, we should disclose only what's necessary and sufficient about the specific *behavior* and present it in the most *non-clinical* and *identifiable* way possible.

Before my writing this book, the only people to whom I'd disclosed my SA/SP were subscribers to the "Social Phobia e-mail list." Specifically, I'd never told my family, friends, teachers, colleagues, or employers. My reasons were twofold. One was the concerns elucidated above. The other was that most of my adult life I've worn the mask of an extrovert. Rarely have I let it slip to allow anyone to see a sustained pattern of underlying SA/SP, for them to puzzle about. As a result, I've doubted anyone would believe it existed in me.

Before I started the book, I tested this hypothesis. I told several friends, family, and colleagues I was researching shyness and social anxiety, gave them defining characteristics, and asked if they thought any of the above applied to me. To a person they laughed, shook their heads in mock disbelief, and gave me a resounding, "no!" How do you argue with that? And what, you may ask, will they say when they read this book's disclosure? Will they resolve their cognitive dissonance by believing my SA/SP was so minor that it was unobservable? Well, any port in a storm. But, then again, maybe from the outside world's perspective they'd be right.

"Far away there in the sunshine are my highest aspirations. I may not reach them, but I can look up and see their beauty, believe in them, and follow where they lead." (Louisa May Alcott)

CHAPTER **12**

MAKING CONTACTS FOR FRIENDS AND PROFIT

"The people who get on in this world are the people who get up and look for the
circumstances they want, and if they can't find them, make them"
(George Bernard Shaw, *Mrs. Warren's Profession*)

Once we're more comfortable with approaching others, we need to start
using our social effectiveness skills to make contacts, to network, to help us
achieve our goals.

Why network?

One of the most important characteristic of self-made millionaires and other
successful people is that they meet as many people as they can. They network
everywhere, all the time. Networking is an active process of information
exchange which usually leads to other human interaction. Networking is the
primary way that we gain access to tips, leads, and referrals for jobs, hobbies,
health information, and making friends. Whether we're aware of it or not, we
all, even SA/SPers, have a basic network of contacts. Even if we never
consciously created it, it evolved all the same.

Our existing network, or the circle of people with whom we can get in
touch, consists of a primary and secondary group. Our *primary* group is made
up of our family and close friends. This group tends to be homogeneous,
sharing values, attitudes, beliefs, and friends. Because the members of this
group often know one another, the network is considered to be "closed." The
social circles represented by the members overlap to a great degree.

Our *secondary* group is made up of acquaintances. This groups tends to be
heterogeneous, composed of individuals of different values, attitudes, and
beliefs. Because the members of this group usually do not know one another,
the network is considered to be "open." The social circles represented by the
members tend to overlap very little. The casual contacts who make up our
secondary group come from:

- *Work, past and present, including former bosses, subordinates, peers,
  prospects, customers, competitors, consultants, suppliers, trainers, department
  heads*

- *Service providers, including doctor, dentist, clothiers, accountant, lawyer,
  insurance agent, banker, hair stylist, real estate agent, therapist*

- *Social contacts, including sports and hobby friends, present and past
  neighbors, parents of children's friends and children's teachers*

- *School, including former teachers, classmates, students, seminar peers*

- *Religious, including clergy, church friends*
- *Civic, including politicians, bureaucrats*
- *Organizational, associational, club, professional, fraternal, sororal, alumni, alumnae, and volunteer groups.*

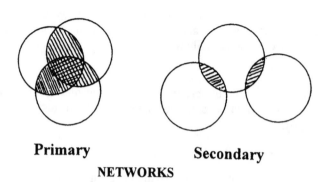

Primary   **Secondary**
NETWORKS

How important are contacts? We locate health care professionals, schools, accountants, lawyers, hairdressers, civic groups, opportunities, service people, and entertainment through contacts. Significantly, of all jobs, from the highest to the lowest, eight out of ten are found through contacts. The percentage is even higher at managerial levels. When Premac Associates queried 520 executives in various executive programs at Columbia University's Graduate Business School about their experience with personal helping relationships, 90% of them said they had had that kind of help. Three-quarters said that helpers had contributed substantially to their career development. There are few things we do that don't result from information passed on to us by contacts.

Benefits of having contacts. What are some of the things contacts can do for us?

In our **personal life** contacts can help us

- *Share and help solve common problems;*
- *Provide emotional support by listening, reflecting thoughts and feelings, and being there;*
- *Relieve stress because of the number of people to count on;*
- *Enhance our personal growth, expand our horizons, and help us become part of the larger community;*
- *Increase our self-esteem by helping us find that we know more than we previously believed;*
- *Increase our self-esteem by helping us find that we're a unique combination of talents, information, and experiences;*

- *Increase our self-esteem by helping us find that we're needed and wanted for what we have;*
- *Allow us to act with others as a unified force in accomplishing a common goal;*
- *Present opportunities.*

In our **work life** they can help us

- *Find a job;*
- *Obtain guidance and direction;*
- *Get problem-solving assistance;*
- *Find a new business;*
- *Market and sell a service or product;*
- *Obtain information;*
- *Obtain advice, support, and counsel;*
- *Obtain sponsorship;*
- *Find opportunities.*

Proof that it works. Contacts provide us with many job and career benefits. For example, a survey of 399 men aged 20 to 60 found that job seekers needed two things to reach people of influence: (1) Personal resources (most importantly educational and occupational achievements) and (2) Contacts. An estimated six out of ten of the survey respondents had used contacts to get their present job. The remaining four out of ten had used contacts in combination with going directly to the employer and formal agencies. This points out the necessity of our having access to social resources. The greater our social resources, the greater the occupational status we can attain.

When we're seeking a higher-level or executive position, *personal contacts* (old friends and family) are the most useful. They significantly increase our ability to get our foot in the door. Even when we're seeking a lower-level position, contacts are important. At this level *impersonal contacts* (associates) are the most useful. Irrespective of job level, the study found that those respondents who said they'd gotten their last job through contacts had a mean income of $2,500 (in 1980 dollars, or $8,000-10,000 in today's dollars) more than those who hadn't used contacts.

What is a contact? Whether we want technical information, experience, advice, or support, we can get it most effectively and efficiently through contacts. A *contact* is someone with whom we can meet and talk, an individual who is available to listen and give feedback. A contact is someone who can do something for us and for whom we can do something in return. This relationship is a variation on the barter system. It's based on fair exchange.

Our relationship with a contact may be personal or impersonal, depending upon what each participant wants from the interaction. *Impersonal* contacts provide a superficial exchange of information and resources, such as where to find the technical data we want or the right person to see about CBT for SA/SP or a particular job. *Personal* contacts provide assistance over a period of time, such as helping with our problem-solving abilities or grooming us for a new position.

Why are contacts important?   Information from contacts is considered to be *inside information*. It's often up-to-the-minute rather than old from sitting on the shelf. It's also considered the most reliable because it's often firsthand. Primary source information is always more credible and, therefore, more valuable.

"The most successful man [sic] in life," said Benjamin Disraeli, nineteenth-century Prime Minister of England, "is the man who had the best information." Contacts are said to have *information power*. Information power is not having every fact and detail on the tip of our tongue, rather it's knowing where to find the facts and details we want when we want them. As a result, knowing how to make the right contacts is power. Specifically, knowing whom to call is everything.

For those of us who are old enough to remember, we need to think about when Lee Iacocca was out of a job, fired from Ford Motor Company. What did he do? Did he dust off his résumé and head on down to his local unemployment office or executive placement agency? No, he talked to his associates and cronies. Over lunch. On the phone. On the golf links. He talked with two close friends, George Bennett of State Street Investment Corporation and Claude Kirk, former-governor of Florida.

As a result, Bennett and Kirk together talked with Richard Dilworth, a Board Member of Chrysler Corporation. Bennett and Kirk suggested that since the financially-embarrassed Chrysler had a leadership problem and they knew of a leadership solution in Iacocca, they should all get together to discuss the possibilities. Over a quiet lunch at the Hotel Pontchartrain, Chrysler offered Iacocca its presidency.

The process is as straightforward and simple as it sounds. First, Iacocca had to know what he wanted to achieve. When he chose his goals, he then figured out how to accomplish them. Next, he acted by approaching his contacts who, in turn, acted as sponsors and cheerleaders for him. They persuasively presented his qualifications to Chrysler decision makers. In no time at all, the former head of Ford was in a new position, one that was of his choosing and befitting his status and bank account.

This networking process also works in reverse. What worked for Iacocca would work similarly for his associates, friends, and cronies, in that Iacocca would act as a contact for them. It's important to remember that the heart of this relationship is *mutuality*. While the other person is a contact for us, we're also a contact for them. The contact does something for us and we do something for them in return. This is the underlying assumption of *reciprocity*. Reciprocity is a powerful norm in our Western culture. Participants in the relationship share and expect to give as well as receive. If they don't, the interaction will feel dissatisfying and incomplete.

Barry's resource seeking exchange

It may be more than a little difficult for us to identify with auto magnate Lee Iacocca. However, Barry has used this process in a situation a little closer to home.

Barry grudgingly had come to the realization that his interpersonal skills in general, not just with women, needed help. It had become increasingly obvious that both his direct and indirect behaviors were antagonizing others. Barry wanted desperately to change jobs but knew that this negative behavior and its history would follow him wherever he went. The consequences would likely be worse than trying to address it in his present job.

Through a personnel counselor, Barry heard that Tom, a sales manager with his company, had a similar problem and resolved it. Barry wondered how Tom found help so he did several trial runs then screwed up his courage and asked Tom what worked for him. Tom told him about a low-key assertiveness training class at a local college and psychological guidance in that area. Feeling he had accomplished something himself, Tom volunteered to give Barry a hand. Later that month Tom asked Barry for assistance with a marketing problem he was having and Barry reciprocated.

It's important to remember: What we're doing is tapping what's available and using what's offered. We aren't taking away someone's resources or gifts; we're asking if they're willing to share them with us in an exchange. Contrary to the concerns of some, there's no exploitation. Both of us can choose whether or not to enter into the relationship, knowing that with choice comes responsibility.

Contact Exercise

Take a minute to think about your own experience with contacts. Ask yourself what you have looked for and received from others:

- *Hints on how to do something?*
- *Where to find certain expertise?*
- *Single piece of needed information?*
- *Ready ear for your problem?*
- *Guidance in learning something new?*

In your journal write down your answers.   See, you already have benefited from contacts. When you finish that, ask yourself what are some of the things that you have given to others:

- *Information?*
- *Emotional support?*

- *Hints?*
- *Leads?*
- *Advice?*
- *Development?*

See, we do have resources of value to others.

Ascertaining our existing network

How great is our existing network of contacts? It's probably a lot larger than we think. We all know the expression, "It's a small world." Psychologist Stanley Milgram wondered how quickly a letter (snail mail - this was pre-e-mail) could be passed from one randomly selected individual in Nebraska to another randomly selected in Boston. It typically took only five or six people to complete the communication chain then. The play, later made into a movie, **Six Degrees of Separation** was based on this premise. Just think how quickly it could be done now via the Internet. A couple of clicks and there we are.

It has been suggested that if we know fifty people on a first-name basis and so do all the people we know, we have available to us 2,500 friends of friends. The more friends we have, the exponentially greater is that number. Unless we have focused on this issue before and systematically documented the contacts we have, we're unlikely to have a clear idea of the number. If fact, we're likely to underestimate it. Good self- and job-marketing strategies require that we have a clear idea of what resources are available to us. Consequently, we need to document our existing network for:

- *Who they are;*
- *What they do;*
- *What they know;*
- *Whom they know.*

Everyone we know is a potential resource.

Documenting Existing Network Exercise

Construct your own table of contacts using the following list, giving yourself plenty of space. Name as many individuals as possible in each of the categories. Add additional categories as necessary. Then detail: What they do; What you know they know; and Any of their contacts of whom you're aware.

- *Family*
- *Close friends*
- *Work associates (past/present)*
- *Civic*
- *Religious*
- *School (teachers/students)*

- *Fraternities/sororities*

- *Professional*

- *Volunteer.*

Although defining and determining contacts is difficult at first, it tends to become increasingly easier as we document them. We begin to remember more and more people. Chances are we have found that we already know a great many people who represent diverse resources. Anyone we can contact by phone, mail, fax, e-mail, or in person is a potential source of information and other resources. These are resources which can be useful in many aspects of personal and professional growth.

Cultivating contacts

Once we're aware of our existing network, we need to start cultivating it. Our network is like a garden. We need to prepare the ground before we can sow the seeds and reap the harvest. To the networker every stranger represents an opportunity. This is a chance to meet new friends, reach goals, find SA/SP information, support groups, treatment, and jobs. We've already determined our recovery goals and what we need to achieve them. This means we're ready to match what we need with what our network contacts can provide.

Contact Matching Exercise

Make three columns length-wise on a page in your journal.

- *List your goals and the specifics you need to achieve them on the left.*

- *List the names of contacts in the middle with the resources that match your needs.*

- *Record interactions with contacts and the results on the right.*

This list will change as you accomplish objectives leading up to your goals. It'll change with achievement of each objective, goal, your awareness of new resources, or acquisition of new contacts. When you're done, it's important that you refer to it and update it often.

W. Clement Stone, founder of **Success!** Magazine, crystallizes this networking need by saying, "To achieve your mission in life, you must seek out and work with other talented, dedicated, experienced people...in harmony... ."

When we seek advice and suggestions from others who can help, we're really paying those individuals a compliment. We're telling them that we value what they have to offer. Advice is a commodity that others like to share. It's also a commodity seldom in short supply. Sometimes identifying the right person for what we need is a challenge because that person won't necessarily be obvious. But finding that person will make all the difference.

To use our existing network to achieve our goals requires attitudinal and behavioral tools. The effective use of contacts requires our being committed to sharing our resources. It requires our acknowledging ourselves as a valued resource to others, something which takes SA/SPers awhile to recognize. But this knowing and accepting our strengths has to occur *before* we interact with contacts. It also requires our appearing confident, competent, and comfortable presenting ourselves as strong in the areas we want to promote: Our abilities, skills, and experiences. This is particularly important in the area of job- and promotion seeking. So we'll focus on that. This means we have to be willing to deliver on what we advertise. In the immortal words of Flip Wilson's "Geraldine," "Don't write a check with your mouth your body can't cash!"

Pursuing job-related networking

Once we're familiar with our strengths, we need to make important others familiar with them too. These "others" may be potential contacts, decision makers in our present organization, or potential employers. For them to feel the weight and worth of our resources we have to both hone and tout our skills.

Cultivation of contacts demands we make ourselves visible. This is because it's not just "what you know" or "whom you know." It's "who knows you" that counts. This means we have to make ourselves known to others in our areas of interest. Get their attention. Show them that we value their specific resources and are interested in an exchange relationship. Show them that we too have resources that we're willing to share.

Making others aware of our resources is necessary but not sufficient. That is, we have to reinforce that association of the resource with us. It's imperative that when they think of that strength or resource, our face comes to mind. We need to keep reminding them because making that connection takes repetition. Also, the more people who see us as a specific available resource the greater our contact base, and the greater our job-related opportunities, for example.

As we've seen, the image we project has to be one of experience, competence, interest, and involvement. People want to interact with those who are both interested in them and who'll follow through on the promises they make. This means we have to present ourselves as serious about resource-sharing and demonstrate it consistently from exchange to exchange. When our contacts mention us to others as a possible contact, we don't want there to be any reservations about our commitment to participate fully and appropriately.

Cultivating contacts is an active process. We can't sit back to wait for contacts to seek us out. Instead, we have to approach potential contacts and introduce ourselves to them. We have to take the first step. However, while we have the right to let others know that we're interested in them as a resource, and that we have resources to offer in exchange, others have the right to either accept or reject our interest, offer, and resources as well. It's important that we see that this possible "rejection" is not personal and, thus, should not be taken personally, despite the fact that we SA/SPers are inclined to do so.

Contact information. When we introduce ourselves to potential contacts, we should offer our business card and ask for theirs in return. Even though many of us don't have business cards, every job holder and job seeker should have them. We can think of them as introduction cards. They create an immediate impression that we're professional, we know who we are, and accessible. Moreover, they provide a convenient way for others to remember us. As such, they contribute to our visibility. (By shopping around at business supply stores and stationery houses we can find bargains as low as 500 cards for $25. A small price to pay for recognition.)

When we receive someone's card, it's often useful to record pertinent information we gather from the conversation on the back of the card. This can include date and location of meeting, subjects discussed, and contact's background, interests, abilities, or areas of expertise. Transferring this data to a small notebook designated for "Contacts" will keep this information in one place. Specifically spelled out should be how this contact can help us and how we can help them in return. Indexing these resources makes retrieving the information faster and easier. Of course, we need to keep this notebook handy, use it often, and keep it up-to-date.

Prospecting at work. As we continue to expand our circle of contacts, we need to focus on our organization. (If we're self-employed, we should begin with the organizations and individuals with whom we do business.) At work it's always safer to be cautious about talking with people about our interest in changing jobs or seeking promotions. It may be advantageous to couch our information-seeking in the guise of developing ourselves in our career. We should approach anyone we believe may be useful because of who they are, what they do, and whom they know. The best time to approach company associates is during non-work moments, such as when they're on a break, at lunch, before or after work, at company cocktail parties, picnics, or outings.

Discussing personal issues on company time may make the contact feel uncomfortable, concerned about others, especially superiors, being displeased by this social activity. After all, the organizational expectation for us job holders is that we should be devoting our energy and time to work issues. So it may make us look bad, potentially leaving a lingering negative impression. Furthermore, for the interaction to be productive, both participants need to be interested and involved. If either person is distracted, thinking about work issues or time conflicts, the meeting will likely be a waste of time. Non-work time allows our contacts not only to think about the issues but also to act on them if they choose.

Another benefit of non-work time, such as company picnics, is that it may allow individuals of different status and job levels to interact as equals. For example, a senior finance officer may be uncomfortable if a junior finance person tries to discuss personal career goals during business hours. However, that same person may feel complimented by the junior person's interest if that person approaches after the company softball game.

Many large organizations, like AT&T, IBM, General Electric, and Digital Equipment Corporation, for example, have offered formal channels through which their employees can develop contacts. Two such avenues are special projects and corporate task forces. There are special-interest clubs. Another is company bulletin boards and newsletters which identify people from other areas of the company, their interests, and pet projects. Company-wide events and activities, such as blood drives, awards dinners, and incentive planning committees, are often volunteer-staffed and -directed. Within each of these individuals from many levels work together for a common cause. The number of channels open to us within a large organization may be limited only by our imagination.

Conducting business. Business meetings, particularly if they are cross-organizational, offer opportunities for new connections. They allow us to address those in our company as well as those in other companies. While those in our organization can provide us with inside information, socialization, and sponsorship, those on the outside can provide us with diverse perspectives and competitor intelligence.

Social occasions. There are many locations that are particularly useful for creating new contacts. One unique site in the 1980s was the Business Networking Salons held in Manhattan's then-trendy Studio 54 Discotheque. Weekly 2,000 people paid $8 a piece to meet, exchange business cards and telephone numbers, and promote themselves. The club was the invention of former-anti-Vietnam War Yippie-turned-entrepreneur Jerry Rubin. Rubin's philosophy was, "You can meet anyone you want to know through one or two people. And don't be surprised if you meet someone who changes your life."

Commonplace locations include seminars, workshops, lectures, courses, community and political meetings, conferences, professional gatherings, conventions, and trade shows. Some of these are useful in multiple ways. Trade shows and conventions, for example, offer us a chance to both learn about the "guts" of our industry and to broaden our professional perspective. In one place we find all aspects of the industry, from suppliers who serve the business to trade publications describing it. Each trade show is a forum in which to expand our knowledge of how the business operates. The people to which we're exposed are often movers and shakers in the industry and are the people we should know.

When we attend any function where participants have a common interest or goal, we immediately share a common bond. This provides an entree into conversations and acts as a basic relationship link which can be strengthened. It's essential that we talk with as many people as possible at these functions. The byword is "socialize." But as we socialize, we must never lose track of (1) our networking goals, which may vary with time and place, and (2) what we need to achieve them.

If we know that people of interest are present, we need to seek them out. This is a priority so we need to manage our time accordingly. Without fail, we must likewise introduce ourselves to the leaders, hosts, and speakers of the function. It's important not to let their "celebrity" be a barrier, to prevent us from letting them know we have an interest in them and their work, then, disclosing something about ourselves to enhance our interpersonal connection.

But introducing ourselves to a potential contact is not enough to achieve our goals. It's like promoting the Pet Rock. Talking about the Pet Rock only tests for interest. "Let's run it up the flagpole and see who salutes it." We need to take it a step further. We need to indicate our desire to work on some particular activity or project and to get together on it. This is what creates the opportunity for promotion. Since these gatherings are often noisy and hectic, with people milling around, laughing, talking, eating, and drinking, it's often difficult to talk in detail and at length. To overcome these obstacles we can set a specific time and date or arrange to call later.

After the gathering, it's usually a good idea to send a follow-up note to those individuals with whom we've spoken we believe can be helpful. Reminding them of the circumstances of our meeting, we let them know that we enjoyed talking with them about a specific topic. We emphasize that we want to learn more about their areas of expertise or other resources. If the contact is a psychologist doing research, we need to know what kind of psychologist they are (e.g., social psychologist). We need to know the subject of the research (effect of social effectiveness training on SA/SP). We need to indicate our related interest (promoting social skills training for anxious school children). Then we need to tell them what we want to pursue in a relationship (ways to implement this training program in our community). Specificity is important.

These follow-up notes should be like thank-you notes or fan letters. They should show appreciation, thoughtfulness, and interest. In doing so, they enhance our visibility and predispose the recipient to think kindly of us. This same type of letter can be directed to those we have not as yet met but whose accomplishments we admire or whose activities relate to our goals. Explaining our interest, we can show how it overlaps or differs with theirs. We can also introduce another perspective on the topic that may generate a response. (As a result of such a letter, I was asked to do a project for the national headquarters of the American Red Cross.)

At this point we should ask for a luncheon engagement or appointment. If we're seeking an appointment, it's important that we make it crystal-clear what we want so they will not mistakenly think we're looking for a job from them. Asking for 15 minutes is usually comfortable for the other person who'll extend the time if they feel it's necessary. Since we perpetually need to be looking for new avenues to explore, we should always ask each new contact, at an appropriate time in our interaction with them, "Can you suggest anyone else with whom I might talk about other aspects of this as well?"

Taking care of contacts. Part of the process of cultivating contacts is extending ourselves to the other person. This means going beyond what is expected in the simple exchange. In between exchanges our doing favors, such as sending articles of interest, or extending courtesies lets contacts know we're thinking about them and value them. In this way we keep live contact warm and rekindle cooling ones. If someone seems to have forgotten a promise to us, we need to remind them gently after a reasonable period of time has elapsed, and re-emphasize our eagerness to follow their advice.

An important part of the care and feeding of contacts is always giving them feedback. When we receive a tip or help, we have to follow through with it in some fashion - not only do what the contact suggests but also report on the results. This may include preliminary, intermediate, and final results. Contacts expect feedback. They need to know that we value their time, effort, and advice enough to pursue their suggestions.

The information provided by contacts usually has been given some thought. Often it's been tailored to meet our specific needs and not some triviality tossed our way to placate us. As a result, we need to be careful not to dismiss this help lightly, but instead give it the consideration we'd want others to give our advice.

There have been times when someone asked us for our advice. We discussed the situation with that person and gave it serious thought. Then we offered our considered opinion. Sometimes we received no feedback on what happened as a result of our suggestions. Sometimes when we inquired, we learned the person hadn't pursued any of our suggestions. In that situation most of us likely felt annoyed and vowed, "That's the last time I offer them any help!"

Contacts want to know how useful any particular piece of information is. Knowing this helps them determine if it's worthwhile to pass it on to others as well. It tells them how accurate and useful the source of that information is. As a contact, we likewise will need this feedback.

If the contact suggests a course of action we've already tried, we might say the idea sounds interesting then later report our results as a matter of courtesy and diplomacy. If the contact suggests something about which we have strong negative feelings, we should pursue it far enough to get preliminary information, report on what happened and the decision whether or not to pursue it further. While it's important to be diplomatic with the contact, it's also important that we be honest with ourselves. If the contact is someone with whom we interact often, discussing a host of ideas, we can more readily say, "Yes, that suggestion does sound good. I've tried it, but it doesn't work that well."

After expressing gratitude to a contact, we should say words to the effect that, "You've been helping me. Now what can I do for you?" This further acknowledges that was has been done on our behalf is perceived as helpful. This reminds the contact that we know an exchange is in order. Shifting the focus from our needs which are being met to theirs which haven't gives a feeling of balance.

There's an old saying we should heed: "If you do something good, three people will hear about it. If you do something bad, ten people will hear about it." This applies to the "goodness' of providing feedback and the "badness" of not providing it. A telephone call. An e-mail. A fax. A note. Each requires only a few minutes of our time, yet the importance is incalculable. Our job-seeking and other successes may well depend upon it.

Practice does it. To make it more likely we'll communicate what we want to potential contacts, we need to prepare a short description of ourselves, our relevant interests, and what information we're seeking. This means keeping in mind the 30-second grabber rule to seize others' attention, with the 3-4-minute follow-up if we succeed. All contact-making behaviors need to be scripted, rehearsed, visualized, and practiced. Trying different behaviors on different people is necessary for our trial-and-error learning process. We need to see what suits us specifically and seems most appropriate for us in different situations. Contact-making is an individualized approach. We have to tailor these strategies to our style and personality, while keeping the essence of the recommendation. It's a matter of degree, not omission

Valuing personal assistance

Contact relationships fall along a support continuum, ranging from impersonal (peers/networks) on the low-power end to the personal (sponsors/mentors) on the high-power end. Different supportive roles can be placed along this continuum, representing increasing degrees of power and involvement. My research has shown that the contact and assistance scales are correlated: Certain dimensions go together. Specifically, instrumental functions (providing information) occur with *impersonal contacts* (networks) and support functions (guiding) occur with *personal contacts* (mentors).

Some who provide support may be called a teacher, coach, developer, guru, guide, counselor, advisor, patron, rabbi, model, uncle, sponsor, or mentor. Where the supportive contact would be seen along this continuum is individually determined by the recipient of the support. Therefore, labels are somewhat interchangeable.

Carl R. Boll, former Placement Director for Harvard University's Business School Alumni Association, says that for taking advantage of promotion and executive job opportunities, personal contacts are the most effective technique. This suggests that while impersonal contacts most effectively provide information and discrete resources, personal contacts most effectively provide counseling, grooming, advice, influence, and continuing support. Depending upon our goals, impersonal contacts may not be able to provide us with everything we want. That's when personal contacts may be able to fill in the gaps and further provide us with what we need for seeking or enhancing the job or other activity.

Personal contacts have been seen as so beneficial that Wheaton College designed a program to help undergraduates plan their careers through these helpers. Each Junior was assigned a personal contact from the college who worked in the student's field of interest. The aim was to ease the transition from college to full-time work and help the students assess working conditions in their fields. Eighty percent of the pairings, at the time of evaluation, were successful.

Career development. As a career vehicle, a personal contact can provide us with exposure, recognition, and the visibility we need to advance. The contact can distinguish us from the crowd of competitors, argue our virtues against those of others, as well as defend and fight for us in conflict and promotion situations. If our contacts are persons of influence, they may be in a position to help us bypass hierarchical obstacles and short-cut cumbersome procedures. In essence, a personal contact can put us on the fast track.

Interpersonal benefits.   A personal contact can also act as an exemplar - a role model with whom to identify within or without the organizational context. The contact may be a quasi-parent figure whose values, approach, and career moves can be imitated. Most socialization into life and organizations is through models. In this way the contact may aid us by giving us a sense of competence by helping clarify our organizational identity and effectiveness as a job holder. This can further increase our self-esteem.

The contact can act as counselor, providing us with emotional support and encouragement and expressing recognition and caring. The contact may guide and instruct us in various aspects of our career development. As such, the contact may evolve and function as a friend. In the relationship, we and the contact may interact socially and come to regard one another as intimates.

Organizations tend to regard personal contact as sponsorship or mentoring which influences job opportunity. Sociologist Robert Turner has found that among those qualified for a position based on ability and past performance, the individual selected is most likely to be one who has the most extensive degree of sponsorship, because sponsorship provides recognition and visibility. Sponsorship or being mentored is generally considered to be an important way an organization can assist and develop individuals within their work setting. Having access to such assistance tends to be associated with higher prestige, influence, and organizational status than not having it.

What about being liked?   We need not be particularly concerned about whether or not potential personal contacts are attracted to us. It's no longer believed that mentoring relationships are based only on interpersonal attraction. While physical attractiveness is a factor in the forming of some social relationships, it has relatively little bearing on the formation of a business exchange. In a social exchange, however, degree of attractiveness has its greatest impact on initial encounters, wherein individuals are first establishing an awareness of each other. In a business exchange, the initial impact of degree of attractiveness tends to be suppressed or put aside so that the agendas which prompted the encounter can be addressed.

The same applies to being perceived as similar to the mentor. While historically mentors have chosen protégés and chosen them for their similarity, having similar attitudes, values, personalities, social characteristics, and affiliations isn't required for having a business exchange. Neither is belonging to the same gender, race, religion, or ethnic background. Identifying with and having an interest in the potential contact generally creates sufficient similarity between the contact and us to initiate a business discussion. *What is **necessary** is that (1) the contact have the interpersonal skill or quality we want **and** (2) the two of us can work together so we can gain access to our desired resources.*

Disadvantages of personal assistance.   While personal contacts are generally perceived as positive and beneficial, liabilities do exist. One cost is dependency which we may find in a personal relationship where there is a power differential between us the person on whom we rely for help. In these situations we may feel obligated to do whatever the mentor wants because of what they are doing for us. Because the contact probably doesn't feel equally obligated to us, dependency makes the relationship unbalanced. So while this dependence may provide us with prime resources, it may also make it difficult for us to disengage ourselves from the relationship, to assume responsibility, and function autonomously.

Personal contacts may become too invested in us and our dependence on them. This emotional investment parallels that which is seen in courtship relationships. These mentors may have difficulty acknowledging, accepting, and dealing with separation as the relationship naturally ends. Excessive investment by either party may result in vulnerability within the organization. If our personal contact becomes angry with us, they could sabotage us.

What this indicates is that the costs of the relationship may be greater for us than for our mentor. This is because we may be perceived by those outside the relationship as being weak, needing a personal contact in order to make it. The suggestion might be that we must ingratiate ourselves with a powerful, high-status person in order to succeed.

Renting a mentor. Another way we can get what we want from personal contacts and still maintain our independence is to "hire" help. In essence, we can offer to pay our personal contact as a consultant. This is particularly appropriate if our personal contact doesn't perceive our resources to be useful at the time. Offering payment equalizes the relationship. It shows that we place an economic value on the contact's time and resources. If the exchange is not resource-for-resource, it can be resource-for-fee. If the contact refuses payment, we should insist on a token payment because it's important we don't get help for nothing. That only fosters dependency.

Maximizing contact advantages

There is good news. We can maximize the advantages and minimize the disadvantages of having personal and impersonal contact relationships. My research has found ways for us to get the good without all the bad.

Impersonal contacts are the best source of instrumental functions:

- *Diverse individuals*
- *Dissimilar attitudes, influence, resources*
- *All kinds of information*
- *Experience*
- *Work - career advice*
- *Diverse perspectives*
- *Problem-solving assistance*

- *Sales and marketing leads*
- *Job change leads.*

Personal contacts are the best source of support functions:

- *Counseling*
- *Interpersonal feedback*
- *Personal advice*
- *Sponsorship*
- *Development and grooming*
- *Instruction and coaching*
- *Role models*
- *Guidance and direction*
- *Assessment of worth*
- *Feeling of organizational connectedness*
- *Order, stability, and emotional security*
- *Support.*

A series of large-scale studies I conducted with people in business demonstrated that there are specific conditions which make career development the most likely. Participants in these studies were females and males, age 23 to 59 years, from different social, racial, ethnic, and economic backgrounds, performing diverse types of work. What the studies found was that if we're using *impersonal contacts* at work, the more of those contacts we have the better, with **four** being a minimum number. For these contacts to be most effective for us the relationships should be known. Therefore, when we have four people who provide us with help in highly visible relationships, we tend to be seen by others as successful, effective, productive, and upwardly mobile.

With **impersonal contacts**

- *There doesn't have to be intimate rapport for us to get access to the things we want.*
- *We don't have to be similar to the contact.*
- *Contact doesn't have to really like us.*
- *Contact doesn't have to be attracted to us.*
- *We don't necessarily have to know the person to get help.*

But when we're using *personal contacts* at work, the fewer the better, with **one** in any organization being the best. For the contact to be effective in that specific environment, the relationship should **not** be known generally but to higher-ups only. Therefore, when we have one person who provides support functions in a low-visibility relationship, we tend to be seen as more successful and likely to advance.

With **personal contacts**

- *We know the person.*
- *We may be attracted to one another.*
- *We may like one another.*
- *We may see ourselves as similar in some ways.*

Whenever possible we must enter into a relationship with a personal contact as equals, each giving as well as receiving. Mentoring is based on this social exchange model. The interaction is regarded as desirable by both participants when the behavior that each shares with the other is rewarding. This requires that we believe that while our respective resources are different, they are of comparable value. To believe that our contact's resources are worth more than ours creates that status- or power differential which introduces dependence. By being autonomous and independent, we gain control over our outcomes.

To make the most of all contacts within the organization we must:

- *Create all contact relationships, personal or impersonal, as a function of the behaviors or resources we want;*
- *Control the number of contacts within the organization who provide us with specific types of help;*
- *Control the visibility of our contact relationships within the organization, depending upon whether they're personal or impersonal;*
- *Treat all contact relationships as a business exchange.*

Outside the organization. We need to create as many different personal and impersonal contacts as possible both inside and outside our organization. As sociologist Mark Granovetter found when he asked a random sample of recent professional, technical, and managerial job-changers about their use of contacts, the majority used *impersonal* contacts for job change: 55.6% saw their contacts occasionally and 27.8% saw them once a year. However, 16.7% used *personal* contacts and saw them at least twice a week. What Granovetter's study demonstrates is that we don't receive all our benefits from one type of contact. For us to be maximally effective in achieving our goal, we need to be both interpersonally adept (through the use of personal contacts) and instrumentally knowledgeable (through the use of impersonal contacts).

Using role models

Successful people are exciting to be around. Like Oprah Winfrey, they seem to vibrate with energy, inspiring others in their midst to think and act with renewed vigor, to stretch themselves to greater accomplishments. When we look for people to help us, we should not overlook role models. These are individuals with whom we can identify. These are people with whom we feel we share something: Goals, obstacles, values, or background. These are people whose behavior or achievement we wish to emulate. Role models let us know we're not alone. They demonstrate that others have made it so there's a chance for us too. They can make all the difference in what goals we set for ourselves and in how successful we are in achieving them. The role model can be a composite ideal of traits we admire in different individuals. However we create them, role models are considered important ingredients in development of our personal and professional identities.

Dr. Clara Mayo at Boston University took me aside as I started my doctoral program and said, "You're an individual with great resources. That's called 'ability.' But you're unhappy leading a life you feel lacks direction. That's called 'frustration.' You want to be a success, to have fame and comfort. That's called 'desire.' But you want these without having to do the things necessary to achieve them. That's called 'normal.' But," she added, " 'normal' doesn't get you anywhere." Then she introduced me to the concepts and practice of networking and mentoring.

"Would you like Donald Trump, Steven Spielberg, or Hillary Clinton?"

CHAPTER **13**

MARKETING YOURSELF IN THE JOB MARKET

"Having control over ourselves can be nearly as good as having control over others" (Fortune cookie)

Becoming a marketer

Whether we realize it or not, when we communicate, date, and network, we're marketing ourselves. We're promoting our good qualities, our positive image to important others. Our image says who we are and what we do well. This is no different from when we're trying to improve our present job, move up in our company, find a new job, or develop our career.

In today's highly competitive market we need to think of ourselves as both marketers and their product. So when we're engaged in job-getting or job-enhancement, we're engaged in the exercise of marketing psychology. This means we need to know our *customers* (the companies and decision makers) and *what they need* so we can tailor our *product* (us) to meet that need. This means putting ourselves in the shoes of our customers and thinking like them. It means doing marketing research, networking, and the communications necessary to achieve our desired result. It also means demonstrating to the customer that our product is the solution to their problem. While this approach is important to all those in the job market, it's especially important to SA/SPers who need all the advantages we can get.

Overall our efforts need to be directed toward that end. The information we present must motivate the customer to draw specific conclusions about us, to make appropriate inferences, and create positive associations. Our words and actions must demonstrate our compatibility with the job, the decision maker, and the organization. Everything we do and communicate intentionally and unintentionally must contribute to the customers' positive attitude and warm feeling about us. We want them to like, respect, and trust us. Our goal is to influence our customers so that when they need the product, they'll automatically think of us. Job-getting and/or job-enhancement is a marketing game.

The market. Marketing is very other-oriented. To market ourselves we have to get outside ourselves to know our customers, understand their business situation, attitudes and characteristics, and what they want in a product. We need to ask customer-centered questions:

• *What is the customer's problem?*

• *How does the customer want to solve the problem?*

• *Why?*

• *When?*

Only when we know what customers are seeking can we show them how our product is exactly what they want. As marketers, we don't create customer needs and wants. They already exist. We only influence the direction customers take to satisfy them.

To do this we need to point out the primary and secondary benefits of our product. *Primary benefits* are the psychological rewards that satisfy the basic needs of Maslow's Hierarchy: Health, security, safety, self-esteem, belonging, prestige, affiliation, friendship, freedom, and self-actualization. The drive to satisfy these needs is what gives us direction in our lives.

Secondary benefits are the processes by which primary needs are satisfied. These are the perceived qualities of particular products or services. Customers buy them because they are warmer, less expensive, cleaner, more protective, stronger, gentler, etc. These suggest to customers how a particular product can more efficiently and effectively satisfy their needs and wants to the degree that they want to buy the product.

Who is our market? It's all the potential customers for our product. The size of the market depends on the number of individuals who:

• *Have an interest in the product;*

• *Have the necessary resources for an exchange (to buy it);*

• *Are willing to offer those resources to obtain the product.*

We SA/SP marketers have to know what the external factors are affecting the market and how they're doing it. We must know the impact of *social change*, such as what the increasing numbers of women joining middle management and executive ranks means. We must know how *economic factors* are affecting both the economy in general and that of the industry, region, and company in particular. In a slow-growth economy one company may look for "generalists" who can perform a variety of tasks. Another may look for risk-taking, crisis-intervention-oriented people.

We must also know where there is a *scarcity of certain resources*. If the customer wants decision-making expertise, the marketer needs to show that resource. We also need to know the status of the *human resource pool* of other individuals possessing similar skills and experience. If, for example, there's a shortage of software engineers in an area where a software company is expanding rapidly, we marketers with the appropriate credentials have a greater opportunity. If, conversely, there's a glut of secondary school teachers, we marketers must know that competition for each and every such position will be particularly intense and the chances of getting what we want are reduced.

Because marketing is customer-oriented, it's predicated on two behavioral assumptions. First, customers will favor those products that offer the most benefits and quality for the best price. Second, unless products are thought of as essential, customers will resist buying them. Therefore, to get the customer to desire and buy our product, we marketers have to make a substantial effort to stimulate the customer's interest.

While all customers are not created equal, they can be grouped into different market segments, based upon customer needs and wants. Our task as marketers is to research and choose specific market segments and then develop a marketing program that has a high probability of attracting and holding customers within these segments.

The essence of our marketing program should be *dynamic positioning*. We focus on a particular segment of customers and their needs. Targeting everyone is a shotgun approach, wastes time and energy, and invariably fails. For example, if we were selling coaching services, we might decide to facilitate individuals in their growth and development rather than help business executives become more effective leaders. As much as SA/SPers may want to, we can't be all things to all people. We then distinguish our product from its competitors, demonstrating what makes us better or more valuable to the customer. For example, perhaps we have a psychotherapeutic background. While coaching and therapy aren't same thing, they do share some important interpersonal characteristics so we could use our skills and experience in motivating and guiding people quickly as a way to position ourselves.

Positioning is psychological. We determine what specific attitudes we want the customer to hold about our product then find ways to foster them. We can position ourselves by pointing out the benefits of our product to customers, how it meets their needs, and how it's better than other products. Thus, we create and occupy a special niche. In job-seeking, for example, we can emphasize our creativity, risk-taking approach, computer graphics background, or generalist experience in sales as what makes us better than the average job seeker.

Strategic personal marketing then means:

- *Finding what the customers want*
- *Researching and assessing the market*
- *Showing how you and only you can fill all those needs.*

The product. Seeing ourselves as a product that is apart from others requires our presenting ourselves in a way that clearly demonstrates what we can do for the customer, what benefits we can provide to the employer for hiring or promoting us. It's important to bear in mind that we ourselves don't buy from logic. As a general rule, we buy from emotion. Our customers are no different. They're not buying the steak. They're buying the sizzle.

Calvin Klein's perfume "Obsession" doesn't sell fragrance; it sells the promise of sexual encounters. BMW doesn't sell cars; it sells status, luxury, comfort, and dependability. And Mrs. Fields doesn't sell cookies. As Debbi Fields says, she sells a "feeling-good experience...chocolate chip cookies coming out of the oven...home and Grandma."

Marketing Approach Exercise

Answer the following questions as completely and specifically as possible. They will give you a baseline for developing your personal marketing strategies.

- *Exactly what are you marketing and selling?*
- *To whom are you marketing and selling? (Who needs what you have?)*
- *Why do they need it?*
- *How will the customer benefit from buying this product?*
- *What factors are most important to the customer?*
- *How do you position your product? (Specialize so you target a particular audience.)*
- *What is the focus of your marketing effort? (How are you planning to achieve your goal?)*

Product value. It's easier to promote and sell a product in which we believe and value than one in which we don't. Chances are that if we could see our own resources in another person, we'd be favorably impressed. There's expertness, depth, intensity, and diversity - qualities perceived positively by employers.

We need to be as good to ourselves as we would to someone else whom we considered worthy. It's not egotistical to appreciate those attributes, skills, abilities, and experience that just happen to belong to us. They're valuable no matter to whom they belong. We're not impostors when we promote ourselves as a unique and valuable asset. That's what we are. If we don't appreciate ourselves for what we have to offer, no one else will either. We have to keep this central to our thinking because we all unconsciously project our degree of self-appreciation in our look, approach, words, and behavior. For good or ill, SA/SPers are very easy to read. If we believe we're the solution to the employer's problem, if we make it known to the employer that we want to share our solution with them, we'll see positive results.

To be successful in the job market we have to learn to accept challenges, to try new things, and take risks. In doing so we grow, enriching our lives as we open ourselves to new concepts, people, and relationships. We have to create and maintain self-confidence because believing we can do it is half the battle. We also have to remain flexible, accepting change even though change may trigger our anxiety. This is how we enrich our lives.

As Martina Horner, past president of Radcliffe Colleges says, "Success isn't the money or the privilege. It isn't the might and the mighty. It's being able to do things you deeply care about." Success is:

- *Self-confidence*
- *Positive self-image*
- *Goal-achievement motivation*
- *Career enthusiasm*
- *Assertive and effective communication*
- *Growth-oriented thinking*
- *Positive visualization*

• Feeling in control.

Martin Seligman believes that "Optimism for success is management's best predictor of actual on-the-job success." He's found that the way we explain life events can predict and determine our future. If we believe we're masters of our fate, we're far more likely to succeed than those who attribute their fate to forces beyond their control. In effect, how we view our success becomes a self-fulfilling prophecy.

Seligman has also shown that when we have a positive attitude, we shrug off the bad and internalize the good. We're persistent, take risks, and regularly surpass expectations. This makes positive thinkers, or optimists, valued commodities in the job market. We not only perform better but also positively influence those around us.

The more positive we feel about ourselves, the more positive others will feel about us because others mirror our feelings, perceptions, and attitudes. Our goal needs to be to create a perception that we're a model of success. We want to show that we're the ideal representative of the employer's organization. In other words, if the company were to commission a poster to recruit bright up-and-comers, we'd be the model for it.

What does the organization look for in a success model? They want someone who is "one of us," acts like "most of us," and becomes the "best of us." To be seen as "one of us," we need to show we're a team member and willing to work cooperatively with others to achieve company goals. Employers want to be sure we'll be loyal and supportive.

To be seen as "most of us," we need to appear to uphold the organization's values, attitudes, and goals. When we're lined up with the organization's means and ends, we're operating as most employees are expected to function. This doesn't mean, however, that we have to conform to some organizational stereotype. In general, organizations aren't expecting us to be corporate clones. But they are expecting a good fit between us and the organizational culture.

To be seen as the "best of us," we must be perceived as more that just another cog in the organizational machine. We must be perceived to be special, not interchangeable with other people in our job category. We are more than the sum of our present job experience, daily performance, skills, and aptitudes. This is what we need to project and demonstrate to employers. We need to show that what we do we do well. We need to show them that what we bring to the organization is unique and valuable. We need to be perceived as not just "competent" but "competent-plus." We can express these qualities by demonstrating that we have:

• Taken on undesirable but necessary assignments;

• Had and used specialized knowledge and skills;

• Brought others along in the organization;

• Developed ourselves for advancement;

• Shared our resources.

While in the past organizations valued and rewarded those employees who did exactly what their job description dictated, organizations today, like Mary Kay Cosmetics, look for and reward those who go that extra mile for the company. They look for and reward those who

• *Are willing to do more than is required;*

• *Show high aspiration;*

• *Show a strong work commitment.*

Choosing goals. Before we approach employers, we need to know two things:

• *What are our goals?*

• *What do we need to achieve our goals?*

As discussed earlier, our goals must be based on an understanding of ourselves. Before we can begin to hunt for or enhance a job or seek a promotion, we have to determine what we have and what we want to market. Goals to be meaningful must be realistic and achievable. This means we need to assess and record information about our interests, abilities, values, strengths and weaknesses, ranking the information to determine what is most important for each situation. Making a wise job-related decision requires a thorough self-examination, as does every other aspect of our recovery.

Fortunately there are guidelines for evaluating our needs and the relative merits of job alternatives. One basic question we need to ask ourselves is, "Should I work for a big or small company?" Either choice has many important implications for us. We need to consider a few of them.

Risk versus security. A medium-sized company with $400 million in annual sales, in business for thirty years, will offer more security than an entrepreneurial startup. We need to ask ourselves where we function better. Do we prefer the security of a large, established firm or the risk and challenge of a small, innovative company?

Overall industry outlook. If the industry as a whole is on the decline, it won't make much difference what size organization we choose. But if the industry is healthy or growing, we need to orient on the company. What is the company's standing in the marketplace? Is it developing new products, increasing its annual sales, and receiving a reasonable return on investment?

Again size won't mean much if the organization is stagnating, standing still, relying on tried-and-true products rather than engaging in active research and development for future products or services. Is the company likely to be part of a merger or the object of a takeover attempt? These two scenarios create instability and dramatic change. They're areas to be avoided by all but thrill-seeking crisis managers.

Exposure and opportunity. In a small company we're likely to have greater exposure to senior management and, as a result, have greater opportunity for involvement in strategy and diverse aspects of the company. This means greater likelihood for recognition of our efforts. It also increases our chances to be creative.

In big companies, however, our role is likely to be more specialized and focused. Our responsibility will tend to be for one type of activity. Having this circumscribed position, one more distant from decision makers, makes both our efforts and accomplishments less recognizable and may render us relatively anonymous. We have to assess whether we can feel fulfilled in a job where we function more as a cog than as a driving force. As we get our SA/SP under control, we may be surprised at our preferences for visibility and activity.

Personality and work style. Do we like working with a variety of tasks? Do we like the broad exposure afforded when we're seen as a generalist? Can we function effectively under the pressure inherent in the multiple-task, multiple-responsibility environment? Can we accept autonomy? Can we take the initiative? If so, a small, recently-established company or our own company may be for us.

Or, do we prefer a more structured environment with clearly defined tasks and responsibilities? Would we prefer to work at a slower pace, with more supervision? Do we see ourselves as more of a specialist, doing one thing very well rather than many things passably? If so, a large company may be for us.

As SA/SPers we have to decide how much interpersonal interaction we prefer and can handle at our stage of recovery. However, *none* is not an option since no one will pay us to be a hermit. Occupations which have less interaction usually involve being given a task, our going off and doing it, then presenting the final product. In general, jobs which require social skills pay better than those that don't. Lower-interaction jobs may include: Bookkeeping, accounting, data entry, drafting, computer programming, medical transcription, typing, inventory, gardening, writing, illustration, landscaping, direct mail sales, online services, furniture making, house cleaning, assembly-line work, copy writing, editing, and delivery. Degree of interaction will vary with time, location, and company. This is not an exhaustive list. As our SA/SP improves, so should our willingness to pick a job because of what benefits it has rather than what costs it doesn't have.

Long- and short-term goals. Before we decide on pursuing only large or small companies, we need to ask ourselves about our goals. Do we want to progress at a steady rate over the years, slowly collecting salary increases, and, perhaps, promotions? Or do we want to be on the fast track, rapidly moving up in title, power, and financial remuneration?

Where do we want to be in five years? In ten years? If we want to be doing pretty much what we're doing now, but with more pay and/or responsibility, the large company may be our environment. If, however, we want to be in control, shaping strategy and policy, influencing profit, and reaping the free-climbing benefits, a small, innovative company may be our milieu.

By realistically assessing ourselves and our goals in terms of our values, needs, abilities, and experience, we should be able to determine what organizational structure best meets our requirements. We can then set our sights on potential companies which match our preferred profile.

Values.   Our values are those qualities in ourselves, others, and the situation which we find most attractive and meaningful.   Some values are recognition, security, affection, approval, popularity, achievement, power, belongingness, and wealth. We need to see how our values relate to the goals we're trying to achieve.

Work/Life Values Exercise

Answer each of the following fully on a sheet of paper entitled, "Values Important to Me," and place it somewhere in plain view, such as on the refrigerator, as a constant reminder:

• *What do you value in life? (List all that are important.)*

• *What are your three most important personal values?*

• *What do you value in a job?*

• *What are your three most important job values?*

• *What conflicts, if any, exist between job and personal values?*

• *Describe your ideal job.*

• *Describe your ideal work day.*

• *Describe your ideal boss.*

• *Describe the ideal work/personal life balance.*

• *List in order of priority the following job values: Achievement, approval, fringe benefits, independence, leadership, leisure, money, popularity, power, prestige, recognition, relationships, rewards, security, self-expression, service, time, variety.*

Experience and abilities.   Since we're probably unaware of the diversity and extent of our skills, abilities, and information, we need also to make a careful examination of them.   Specifically, we need to determine our organizational strengths, areas of expertise, and the types of information and experience we possess.

Assessing What We Offer Exercise

• *Specify and describe as many areas as possible of information and/or expertise you have (such as software, health supplements, teaching, manufacturing, advertising, etc.)*

• *Look at all you've listed and described. List the ten you consider the strongest in terms of special knowledge and/or experience.*

• *Rank-order these strengths by their level of importance and list the five most important. These are what you want to market to an employer.*

- *Specify and describe as many areas as possible of skills and abilities you have (such as identifying problems that exist, listening to what is said, following detailed instructions, selling ideas to decision makers, etc.).*

- *Look at all you've listed and described. List the ten you consider the strongest in terms of skills and abilities.*

- *Rank-order these strengths by their level of importance and list the five most important. These two lists of five items represent the primary strengths you can offer to an employer. These are what you want to market.*

Assessing What We're Marketing Exercise

Using the two lists of your five most important strengths, write down situations in which you demonstrated those strengths. Indicate how you used the strength and the result of its use. For each strength, prepare a vignette such as:

Strength: "Sell idea to decision maker."

Situation: "Sold boss on using new filter supplier."

Result: "Effected a 20% cost reduction."

Whenever possible, quantify the result and relate it to the bottom-line. Everything you do in your job has a result and implications associated with it. You may need step back to see it. This bottom-line orientation has more meaning and impact for employers. So that you can continually remind yourself what it is you're marketing, commit these vignettes to paper. Entitle it, **"What I'm Marketing,"** *and keep it in plain view.*

Strength Preferences Exercise

Of all the skills you have and have demonstrated, ask yourself the following:

- *What skills do I particularly enjoy?*

- *Where have I used these skills?*

- *Toward what purposes have I used these skills?*

Knowing our strengths also gives us a better sense of ourselves. It bolsters our self-confidence. It prepares us for making decisions, setting goals, writing job-getting letters, and handling interviews.

Strength Visualization Exercise

Visualize yourself in these skills situations in your vignettes. See yourself as an individual who is demonstrating abilities and experience. See yourself as effecting something that is valued by the organization. The more clearly you see yourself as an **active bottom-line results-producer***, the better you'll project and promote this image to others, particularly present or future employers.*

Job values. When we think about job targets, we need to think about what's important to us in a job. What's *primary*? Is it commuting? Opportunity for advancement? Responsibility? Money? What's *secondary*? Location? Company? Title? Being invisible? We have to break it down for ourselves.

Job-Value Assessment Exercise

Answer the following as fully as possible:

- *What do you do or are you trained to do for a living?*

- *What kind of company or organization do you want to work for? (Check all that apply)*
___*big* ___*little* ___*family-owned* ___*multi-national* ___*profit* ___*non-profit*
___*college* ___*association* ___*foundation* ___*government*

- *How do you want the organization to relate to employees? (Check one)*
___*care about employees*
___*not care about employees*

- *Which is more important to you?*
___*quick advancement with no security*
___*slow advancement with security*

- *Which would you prefer?*
___*large national company with possibility of relocation*
___*small local company with little possibility of relocation*

- *What kinds of hours do you prefer?*
___*high-involvement - arrive early, leave late*
___*low-involvement - essentially 9-to-5*

- *What kind of environment would you prefer?*
___*very competitive with opportunity for advancement*
___*less competitive with less opportunity for advancement*

- *How important is it for a company to have a social conscience? (Check all that apply)*
___*concern for the environment*
___*concern about discrimination (race, gender, sexual orientation, age, religion)*
___*concern about product quality*

- *Which stability situation is more important?*
___*rapid expansion with instability*
___*slow expansion with stability*

- *Which do you prefer to work with?*
___*product*
___*service*

- *What do you prefer to work with?*

___*people*
___*data*

• *Which work situation do you prefer?*
___*work alone*
___*work with group*

• *What is the preferred maximum number of employees in company?*

• *What salary do you want in a new position?*

• *Would you settle for less salary to gain greater responsibility, challenge, or fringe benefits?*

• *How much pressure are you willing to experience?*

• *What do you want to accomplish through your job?*

• *How willing are you to engage in company politics?*

In today's competitive world, it's not true that good things come to those who wait. We can't sit back, hoping employers will guess what we've accomplished in each job then come looking for us. We can't assume that employers will give us the job of a lifetime just because they like our looks. There's only one way these things happen for us. We have to make them happen. We have to know what we want and what we have to offer. We have to communicate those qualities to an employer in such a way that the company will see us as the profit-maker or cost-reducer they need to solve their problems. In other words, we have to create our own career opportunities.

Goal Setting Exercise

The same way you set goals for your recovery you have to set goals for your job situation. With a pencil and paper look at your short- and long-term goals and ask yourself:

• *What do I want to do or achieve now?*

• *What do I want to do or achieve in the future?*

*Write down your responses then spell out the **whats** and **whens** of those goals in concrete and specific terms:*

• *Exactly what do I want?*

• *By what date do I want it?*

We have to be as descriptive as we can in order to clarify things for ourselves. Jay W. Lorsch of Harvard Business School's Advanced Management Program says, "You develop your inner vision by identifying short- and long-term goals. You must design your business strategies to achieve all your objectives. Understand that realizing the vision means following through on all your plans."

Once we're satisfied that we know exactly what we want to achieve, we need to specify how long it'll reasonably take to accomplish these goals. Detail is important. Having done that, we need to go back once more to distill each goal into a sentence, or sentence fragment, of key words. Lastly, we need to make two lists: One of all our prioritized goals; the other of our goals chronologically, with short-term goals first with assigned deadlines.

Goal Visualization Exercise

You're going to use your visualization technique to envision yourself working on your goals. See yourself in your new position or functioning more fully in your present position. Picture yourself working on your goals:

- *See yourself writing down your values, your wants, and your experience, assessing each of them with your goal in mind.*
- *See yourself successfully setting up and navigating interviews.*
- *Actually imagine yourself going through the motions of accomplishing each objective (short-term goal), feeling what it will be like: The challenge. The accomplishment.*
- *See yourself meeting the final goal you set.*
- *See yourself where you want to be, doing what you want to do the way you want to do it.*
- *Ask yourself what it means to you: Satisfaction? Power? Responsibility? Challenge? Money?*
- *Ask yourself how you feel: Excited? Eager? Scared? Describe your emotion.*
- *Where precisely will you be when it happens? Describe your physical surroundings.*
- *What will you be doing when it happens?*

Repeat your visualizations daily. Each time start the sequence with the next objective to be accomplished. In this way you work your way toward your final goal.

Visualizing our goal achievement makes the process and result more concrete. When we can see each step as tangible, climbing them is easier. Repeated visualization of these steps is a rehearsal for their actual achievement. Visualization reinforces our confidence that we'll make it. As a result, we'll feel comfortable with the process because it's familiar and achievement becomes more likely.

Researching the market

What impresses executives the most is individuals who present themselves as professionals. In this case, it's job-seekers who indicate they want the job, are willing to be versatile and flexible, and who'll adapt to change as required. The only way we're going to know if a match exists between a company and us is to research the company. If we don't, we'll hurt our chances in as many as 75% of the interviews we encounter. Researching the market shows us the common ground with a potential employer so we can credibly demonstrate that we're a match.

There are all kinds of matches. It can be that we're

• *In the same or similar business*

• *Handling the same or similar products or services*

• *In a very similar position requiring similar skills and experience.*

As mentioned earlier, perception of similarity is exceedingly important in interpersonal relationships. This applies to employer and employee as well. It's really useful to think of work as a series of interpersonal relationships. The greater the perceived similarity in these relationships, the greater the attraction and liking.

Marketing research takes a lot of the risk out of the job-seeking gamble. It allows us to position ourselves in keeping with industry and company trends, needs, and characteristics. Understanding the customer's problems enables us to identify and promote ourselves as the solver of their specific problems. It also clarifies our goals and creates confidence. Knowing where we're going, why we're going, and how we're going to get there is everything. Knowledge is power. Anything less is wishful thinking. To focus and direct our job-search efforts we need to ask:

• *What are the main trends, opportunities, and threats within the industry and company?*

• *What is the current and future size of the market?*

• *What are the operating characteristics of this market?*

• *What do these customers buy?*

To identify companies and executives in a particular industry, area, or profession, we need to consult the most recent volume of business reference books such as

• **Standard & Poor's Register of Corporations, Directors, and Executives** (publicly-held companies)

• **Thomas Register of American Manufacturers** (product descriptions)

• **Dun & Bradstreet's Million Dollar Directory** (alphabetical and geographical)

• **Dun & Bradstreet's Billion Dollar Directory** (corporate families)

• **Dun & Bradstreet's Middle Market Directory** (privately-held, smaller companies)

• **Dun & Bradstreet's Directory of Corporate Executives** (biographies)

• **Moody's Manuals of Public Utilities and Industrials** (sales and growth trends).

Each profession has its own "who's who" and each state has its own directories of business, industries, and manufacturers. Since changes happen rapidly in corporate American, it's necessary to verify the names, titles, and addresses of decision makers by phone.   For companies in our geographic region, we need to also check area employer directories, directories for area employment and executive search agencies, city business magazines, trade papers, Chamber of Commerce publications, and city industrial directory.

Once we've decided on specific companies of interest, we need to locate those companies' annual reports which specify what they do, how well they're doing it, and their philosophy.   These are available at business college libraries or directly from the companies themselves.   Annual reports are reports to stockholders issued by publicly-held companies.   We can also receive considerable information from the companies' public affairs (public information or public relations) department, including copies of articles about the company as well as a description of the company, its products or services.

Knowing what's been published about them is useful.   It gives us information from a different perspective.   We can find articles referenced in

- *Business Periodicals Index*
- *Funk & Scott Index to Corporations and Industries*
- *New York Times Index*
- *Wall Street Index* (which includes *Barrons Index*)
- *Public Affairs Information Services Index*
- *Readers Guide to Periodical Literature.*

Other helpful miscellaneous resources include newspaper libraries, advertising and public relations firms, stock brokers, management consultants, bankers, attorneys, Fortune 500 listing, and government agencies.   These often reveal inside information about:

- *Problems*
- *Changes*
- *Crises*
- *Growth*
- *Sales*
- *Trends*
- *New products*
- *Decision makers*
- *Company philosophy.*

Having and using this information shows companies that we know not only about the field in general but also about their company in particular.

Hidden agendas. All these resources are important because we need to know the hidden agendas of the companies. This is the way things are actually accomplished within the organization.   It's the real operating procedures for dealing with people.   This is not information we'd find in employee manuals, the company policy manual, or as part of orientation. Some hidden agendas encourage workaholism, some prescribe how we'll learn what the company expects of us, some dictate who can provide mentoring, while others define the company's perception of usefulness or how to access and use inside information.

Some questions to be answered.

- *What do employers want?* Each employer will be looking for specific characteristics which they believe produces the best person for the job available.

- *How important is having experience in the specific business with a specific product or service?* This is often the most important criterion for an employer because it implies understanding of the existing situation and immediate productivity.

- *How important is having experience and expertise in a specific type of work?* Employers look for a performance record. They want to see not only that we've done a particular type of work but also that we've done it well. If we've done it well in the past in that area, the assumption is that we'll do it well again in the future in that area.

- *How important is having a specific educational background?* Employers may feel more comfortable with knowing we've had schooling or training in the area of interest. Hands-on learning in some form is, of course, essential. However, knowing the history and theoretical concepts of advertising, for example, as well as all the different possible approaches to an advertising campaign one may take may make all the difference between our being perceived as a professional and a technician.

Informational interviews. Having all the factual information we need to rank companies in order of their fit with our criteria for the "ideal" company isn't quite enough. We still need to get the personal slant of specific decision makers. These decision makers are in our area of interest at the companies of interest. Getting their input gives us their perspective on the market in general and their company's place in it. However, getting this information can be difficult to do, particularly in large cities or in highly visible, large or unique organizations where decision makers may be too busy to talk with us. But elsewhere it may be less so.

One way to get this is through an informational interview (by phone or in person). To get what we want requires in-depth preparation. We need to know the company's background, what facts we're seeking, and the precise questions to ask to get the information we want. Our best bet is to locate this decision maker through our networking efforts, but if that's not possible, we can approach them without an introduction. This interview is designed to fill in the gaps, clarify specifics, and pick up any hints of the decision maker's philosophy and interests. Asking the right questions, such as how the company is responding to particular industry trends or about a new product or service, for example, shows that we're savvy. If our questions are policy-oriented, organizationally-complex, or technical enough, the decision maker's secretary, who screens the decision maker's calls will likely choose not to answer them and refer us to the decision maker. It's important to note that secretaries, however, can be very knowledgeable and may provide us with useful information and needed insights.

We need an acceptable premise for the call - and saying we're unemployed and "researching the ideal job" isn't it. We're **not** calling to hustle the decision maker for a job and we definitely don't want them to think so. We can be honest and tell them that we've been researching the company, following its progress in the market, liking what we see, and we're interested in where the decision maker thinks the company, product, or service is going next: What do they see on their organizational horizon. The premise for our research on the topic could be for a class paper, discussion in class or business group, column in an organizational newsletter, or newspaper article - whatever is closest to the truth. Lying is not a viable option because it'll likely come back to bite us. We must remember that, in general, decision makers like to be acknowledged as important informational resources.

Once we actually reach the decision maker, we need to introduce ourselves. If we're been referred by a contact, mention the contact's name. Then we need to explain why we're calling, that we have a couple of questions to ask, and then assure them that it'll only take a few minutes. Starting with a general questions allows us to follow up on specifics. Questions which begin with *what, how,* and *to what degree* are open-ended and are likely to provide us greater quantity and quality of information. When we're done, we should thank the decision maker and later send a thank-you note.

This telephone process is a little easier for SA/SPers than our meeting the decision maker face-to-face. It allows us to write a script, rehearse the call, have all our research notes available, not worry about eye contact, blushing, trembling, and sweating. We can also practice abdominal breathing or some relaxation technique while on the phone.

Tooting your own horn

Another way for us to create our image and market ourselves is self-promotion. We need to get our name and our area of expertise before our customers in general and targeted employers in particular. This creates visibility and credibility for us. The following are a few of the number of ways to do this:

• *Give a formal or informal talk, speech or lecture in your area.*

• *Conduct a discussion, class, seminar, or workshop in your area.*

• *Speak to an issue at a meeting (associational, organizational, or town) in your area.*

• *Write an article in your area of expertise for a newspaper, association or company newsletter, company web site, or trade periodical.*

• *Write letters to the editor of newspapers, newsletters, and magazines on topics and issues to which your skills and experience apply.*

• *Appear on radio and television as an expert or representative of your field.*

• *Make decision makers in your chosen field aware that you're available for writing assignments and/or public speaking engagements.*

Joe. *When Joe saw an article featuring a stunt pilot he admired, he wrote to the pilot, in care of the newspaper, about the Piper Cub Super Cruiser he used and compared it to the stunt pilot's plane. As a result, Joe received an invitation to take a short fight in the pilot's plane and meet some of the stunt team.*

Doing these activities allows us to practice our interpersonal skills and gain confidence as we make ourselves available to others to learn about us. It makes us known to the people who matter. We see others responding to us because of who we are and what we do. One big advantage of this approach is that we reach larger numbers of potential contacts and potential employers per hour of our time and get interpersonal practice as well.

To résumé or not to résumé

A résumé is a resource document only - an inventory of all we've done that may be relevant to particular areas. But it doesn't market us or represent us. It's merely the foundation of our job-seeking campaign. It's the general document to which we refer when we're creating and tailoring a targeted response to specific job opportunities.

While a résumé lists elements of our background and experience, it doesn't give the measurable results or implications of what we've done. It doesn't show the benefits that would be derived from hiring or promoting us. The traditional résumé simply can't relate our efforts to the company's bottom line or emphasize those factors that the particular employer is looking for. It doesn't tailor our image to that of the company, the position, or decision maker and does nothing to create their desire in us or encourage them to take a specific action relative to us.

To market ourselves we need a marketing document. A marketing document immediately grabs the reader by the collar and rivets their attention. To be a successful job-getting vehicle, it must show how closely we fit with the customer's needs, the specific job requirements, and the company's image and philosophy. It has to sell us as **the** solution to their problem.

We need to think in terms of the functions we've performed and the results we've achieved. We need to think in terms which reflect *profit-consciousness*:

• *Increased sales*

• *Increased profits*

• *Increased productivity*

• *Increased efficiency*

• *Saved money*

• *Reduced turnover*

• *Reduced costs.*

Each of these must be quantified, made specific and concrete. Such as, "Designed three-year marketing plan for software firm to increase sales 45%" or "Created layout and copy for 10,000-physician national direct-mail pharmaceuticals package" or "Operated home-cleaning services for six years at 21% profit."

Action verbs are important because they can:

• *Reveal your management ability;*

• *Create a positive impact;*

• *Stress your competence;*

• *Indicate your ability to handle details;*

• *Reflect your intelligence;*

• *Show you're profit-directed;*

• *Bring out your specialist or generalist ability;*

• *Emphasize your action-orientation.*

When applying for a job, we need to use our market research and write directly to the decision maker. We need to write a personal, action-oriented letter which highlights four or five accomplishments (what we've done, the results, and implications), in bulleted form. This tells the recipient why we're a particularly good match for them. This action letter is a marketing tool to pique their interest, to sell us to them enough to get us an interview. At some point we'll be asked to hand over a résumé because that's *pro forma*. We should postpone handing it over until we know enough about the job that we can tailor the document to the position, emphasizing some areas of our background, de-emphasizing or eliminating others. It's important to remember that a résumé for a job shouldn't be *everything* we've ever done. It's *only* those things which establish a pattern of success and consistency and are relevant to the employer. A two-page document is maximum for non-academic jobs.

We should also, whenever possible, avoid personnel departments until the decision maker has read our marketing documents. In general, the decision maker, the person who initiated the search, is the only one who really knows what is needed and acceptable for the job. Too often personnel people can't know what factors which are not part of a specifications' list might be acceptable to the decision maker when presented in the right context. For example, a decision maker for a managed care company looking for someone to do psychotherapy may list acceptable credentials as M.S., M.A., M.S.W., L.C.S.W., leaving out the higher-priced professionals, such as Ph.D., Psy.D., M.D., psychiatric nurse, or Ed.D. These individuals who also have relevant experience and demonstrated skills may be willing to take a pay cut for other considerations.

Also we need to remember that only 17% of jobs are gotten through newspaper ads. Nothing works like contacts and inside information for finding a job.

Finessing the interview

As we who have SA/SP are especially aware, how we handle ourselves in a job interview can either make or break us. According to Challenger, Gray, and Christmas, a Chicago-based out-placement consulting firm, 60% of job seekers don't get the offer they want simply because they fail to "sell themselves."

Being prepared to carry the conversational ball, knowing our company research, what we want to sell, and how we want to sell it is what's required when we step over the threshold of the interviewer's door. The object of our self-presentation is to be a "successful interviewee" **not** a "successful job-getter." The distinction is to make the point that no matter how brilliant our marketing campaign, compelling our action letter, or successful our interview, we still may not get the job. Although we may be able to control many variables in the job-hunt and -promotion process, we can't guarantee the behavior of the other people involved or predict changes in the environment. All we can do is present our best case as persuasively as possible.

What to wear. Our attire is important. In fact, it's 90% of what people notice first when we walk in. It suggests our goal and how we see ourselves, so we should dress to emphasize our skills, competence, and experience. Even if the organization itself is laid-back, we should go to the interview dressed formally, in conservative business attire.

Entrance. Since we'll be viewed and treated as we expect to be, we should enter the interviewer's office and present ourselves with assurance and assertiveness. If the interviewer is seated behind a desk, we should walk to the side to shake their hand, rather than lean over the desk. Facing the other person directly, we should shake firmly, pulling the interviewer toward us slightly, holding the grip just a heartbeat longer that they do. This enhances the perception of our confidence and control.

When we sit, if we have a choice, we should pick a chair that's at the side of the desk, thus eliminating the desk as a barrier between us. The desk is a symbol of power and authority. The person sitting behind the desk is automatically one-up, leaving the interviewee one-down. Sitting at the side allows us to equalize the power somewhat. When we can talk as equals, we'll feel more comfortable, confident, and come across better.

Of course, we have to be careful about coming on too strong. Being too dynamic or intelligent can intimidate an interviewer (as I found out after an interview for a clinical internship. My supervisor, who couldn't understand why I wasn't accepted, was told that I was too "positive" sounding and that they worried about my flexibility). However, our demonstrating that we're aware that the interviewer knows more about the job and the company than we do, and then "deferring" to that "superior" knowledge, makes us more likable.

Don'ts. No matter what the interviewer does

- *Don't drink alcohol, even if the interview is conducted in a restaurant, everyone else is hoisting a few, or the chat becomes very chummy.*

- *Don't smoke because it signals nervousness and pollutes the enclosed space.*

- *Don't fidget (excessive body movements, wringing hands, clenching fists, gripping chair arms, tapping fingers or toes, jiggling a foot, scratching or rubbing yourself or an object, fingering hair or objects, licking lips, crossing and uncrossing arms or legs, bobbing head, chewing gum, pencil, eyeglasses, hands, nails, or pacing).*

- *Don't name drop.* Even if you know the person well, it'll sound phony, arrogant, and superficial. Interviewers will tend to think you can't sell yourself on your merits alone and have to rely on your associations with some well-known person to pick up the slack. For example, at a group interview for a position of curriculum developer at a local college, I mentioned working with Dr. Robert Chin, internationally-known organizational development consultant who was also my dissertation advisor and who had promised to send a letter of reference on my behalf. No sooner had I said his name, than one of the interviewers announced that she thought it was inappropriate for me to name-drop. At that very moment, the interview ended...with a resounding thud.

- *Don't get into an argument even if you disagree. Use active listening and assertiveness techniques.*

- *Don't tell jokes unless it's very mild self-deprecating humor. Showing you're fallible can make you more likable.*

- *Don't introduce the topic of money first. You're supposed to be there to show them what you can do for them. Besides, you should have gathered this information prior to the interview. Generally look for a 20%-increase over last salary if your previous salary was on par with industry average.*

Dos. No matter what else is going on we must

- *Carry the ball. About 80% of interviews start with "Tell me about yourself," so you have to be ready with at least five accomplishments, elaboration of which was highlighted in your action letter. Time will be short so you have to know what you want to say.*

- *Use your 30-second grabber to sell your message.*

- *Develop brief anecdotes about your experience. In each emphasize your strong points. Follow the T-Bar format: Topic sentence; Background; Action; Results. For example, if asked about your "creativity," you could respond:*

- *T - "I've done a number of things I consider creative."*

- *B - "One example is when I worked on the automobile advertising campaign. The company's promotional material had failed to increase product share."*

- *A - "I researched the car market, ran focus groups, and discovered that half the expected market wasn't buying because the ads didn't appeal to their thinking style. So I developed ads which presented the car graphically for those who respond emotionally, and verbally for those who respond intellectually."*

- **R** - *"Within six months sales increased 18% and market share gained five share points."*

- **Know what the interviewer will ask** and be prepared with answers.

- **Prepare your own questions** *about the job in advance (such as, scope and details of job; areas of responsibility; what specific skills/experience would help someone do this job; to whom report; with whom be working; typical day; growth potential; why is there an opening; chance to meet co-workers before accept position; when is first job performance evaluation, etc.)*

Riding out stress interviews

Sometimes interviewers will try to unnerve us by creating a stressful situation, firing questions at us, grilling us, or shooting down our answers. The rationale most frequently given for this sadistic exercise is that our response to this stress demonstrates how we'll handle stress on the job. Why any individual interviewer does it is hard to say, but there are no data to support the contention that how we handle extreme stress in the unnatural situation of a job interview has any correlation with our performance on the job. In an interview we're already nervous and perhaps a little desperate. We feel all the power is on the interviewer's side. All we want to do is put our best foot forward just to be considered for the job. Thus, pressure on us even before we're in the door is enormous, whether we have SA/SP or not. Very few people, however bright and competent, will handle a stress interview well **unless** they're prepared for it. As Martin Yate points out in **Knock 'Em Dead**, typical questions include

- *Why should I hire you when I can hire someone already in the company?* (Ask what strengths they need [it's why they're going outside the company] and reiterate yours that match.)

- *What are your greatest shortcomings?* (Pick non-lethal faults [ideas] or ones that can be turned into virtues.)

- *Why haven't you moved up very rapidly in your present company?* (Minimal-growth company, no promotions in your area, you're acting now.)

- *Why are there big gaps in your work history?* (Provide sound reasons, minimize problems, and emphasize looking for a long-term match.)

- *"Convince me to buy this pen" ploy.* (Emphasize benefits and features, showing quick thinking and good verbal communication.)

Knowing that this approach may be used allows us to further prepare to meet the additional stress. While having a friend feed interview questions to us is always a good idea, having that person also employ attack-dog tactics can help us become accustomed to the threatening effect. As with other anxiety-provoking situations, use of systematic exposure, positive coping statements, negative self-talk disputation, diaphragmatic breathing, and assertiveness training will be of great assistance. Whatever the outcome of the interview or how we feel about working for a company which would treat us so shabbily, we want to feel we've done our best.

Becoming self-employed

Sometimes SA/SPers wish we were working for ourselves so we wouldn't have to put up with job seeking, employers, and fellow workers. But being self-employed isn't a panacea for our work problems. In fact, it's a tough road to take with or without SA/SP. This is because it requires our imposing an internal structure and discipline on ourselves and being responsible, moment to moment, for every aspect of our business. Having a business doesn't eliminate our having to deal with others, but it may allow us to control the circumstances, frequency, and duration of those interactions at least to some degree.

To create a business we have to (1) find something we like to do and know something about, and (2) carefully research the market to see if there's really a perceived *need* out there for what we want to sell. Market research is essential, whether we want to sell a product or service. We can't just assume there's a market or that "everyone" will want what we have. Rarely is this so. We have to target our market properly and accurately because not having a market means not having any sales.

Next we need to construct a detailed business plan which will tell us precisely

• *What you're going to do;*

• *How you're going to do it;*

• *When you're going to do it (now or a year from now etc.);*

• *Where you're going to do it (store front, direct mail sales, distributor, web site etc.);*

• *To whom specifically you're doing it;*

• *How much it'll cost to start and run the business;*

• *How much you'll need to charge per unit to make a profit;*

• *By what date you should show a profit;*

• *How you'll market the business (marketing is a full-time activity);*

• *What assistance you'll need (computer programmer, lawyer, accountant, marketer, advertiser).*

Because the self-employed need specialized help, we need to seek experts in relevant areas to help us. Small business marketing master and mentor Jeffrey Lant, for example, has produced a series of books (several of which I've already cited), reports, and services which cover the full range of issues encountered by the self-employed. His **Sure-Fire Business Success Catalogue** and online marketing newsletter are available *free* by writing him at *drjlant@worldprofit.com.*

Working for ourselves requires high motivation, pragmatism, and hard work.   But as Daniel Goleman points out **in Working with Emotional Intelligence**, doing well in any job is predicated upon not only our expertise but also, perhaps more importantly, our ability to manage our feelings, interact, and communicate.   As in most aspects of life, success gravitates toward those who are self-aware and optimistic; who possess self-control, initiative, motivation, empathy, altruism, and social and communication skills; and who build bonds, manage conflict, and lead.   Yes, we SA/SPers CAN do that.

Affirmation: "I no longer need to punish, deceive, or compromise myself...unless I want to stay employed."

"Interview? We don't need no stinkin' interview!"

CHAPTER 14

OVERCOMING SWEATING, BLUSHING, AND BB

"Thou are not for the fashion of these times, When none will sweat but for promotion." (William Shakespeare, *As You Like It*)

Excessive sweating (hyperhidrosis), severe facial blushing, and bashful bladder (avoidant paruresis) are three conditions which create embarrassment and anxiety in social situations which can add to the discomfort we already experience in SA/SP. Although hyperhidrosis and severe blushing may occur with SA/SP as specific phobias, they are not necessarily a part of it. In fact, those without DSM-IV-defined SA/SP appear to be the majority of sufferers.

What causes excessive sweating?

Hyperhidrosis is due to over-activity of the sweat glands primarily of the palms (palmar), soles of the feet (plantar), armpits (axillae), face, and groin. Sweating is an involuntary activity which regulates our body temperature by sending signals to the body surface where two types of sweat glands (apocrine and eccrine) are located to produce sweat. There are 5 million eccrine glands in the body, 2 million of which are in the hands. The sympathetic nervous system controls these glands by way of two chains of knots of nerves (ganglia). Referred to as the "sympathetic chain," they run on either side of and parallel to the spinal column, with each ganglion above a rib where the ribs meet the vertebrae.

There are two types of this excessive sweating: Generalized and localized. Generalized sweating may accompany fever, a dysfunctional thyroid gland, cardiac infarction or insufficiency, or neurological disorder. Localized sweating, however, particularly of the palms and soles, may be caused by other factors, most of which are as yet unknown. This localized sweating may be sudden or continuous. It's always worse at higher temperatures, improving during cooler months, and doesn't seem to be related to strenuous exercise. Sweating generally ceases during sleep. Psychological factors are thought to play a part for many individuals. In addition, for a minority sweating appears to run in our families.

The social impact of excessive sweating can be enormous. When we have palmar hyperhidrosis and our hands are soaking wet most of the time, some of us are too embarrassed to shake hands, hold hands, or dance, making us appear disinterested, standoffish, or anti-social. We're unable to play musical instruments, work with electrical devices, type on computer keyboards, tie knots, or handle papers. We won't participate in sports which require holding or catching objects, such as basketball, football, baseball, bowling, tennis, or pool; or play games, such as cards, video games, or chess. Our hands slip on the steering wheel of the car making the situation dangerous. Because this sweating generally can't be obscured by our clothing, we feel particularly helpless.

Some of us who have facial or axillary hyperhidrosis find ourselves continuously anxious about whether others are noticing the constant drip, drip, drip off our faces or clothing stains under our arms. We know the sweating makes us look unprepared, soggy and unkempt, tense, and perhaps a little bit suspect. What we can wear is limited by color and roominess, making us less a fashion statement or dress-for-success model. As a result, we're ill-at-ease most of the time and preoccupied with how we look and ways to stay dry. All the while watching our self-esteem drip into puddles before our very eyes.

The first-line therapeutic measures to be tried for sweating are aluminum chloride hexahydrate antiperspirants, sedatives and anticholinergic drugs, iontophoresis (electric current in electrolyte solution), botulinum toxin, acupuncture, and classical conditioning. In general, these methods have met with variable success. (I used to keep the Mitchum Antiperspirant Company in business as I unsuccessfully tried to control wetness and acrid odor.)

AREAS OF SWEATING

What causes severe blushing?

Likewise, excessive and persistent facial blushing creates social and work obstacles in our paths. When our faces flush, we become a beacon toward which all others direct their attention. They assume we're embarrassed, tense, and uncomfortable and that this is the cause of our blushing. As a result, they may see us as socially inept.   While this may be true, it isn't always or necessarily so. We may also blush spontaneously, registering a range of colors from light pink to deep red. (My face, neck, and upper chest often turned dark red when I least expected it.)

Blushing is the result of dilatation of blood vessels in the face and upper torso and may result from a hyper-reactivity, early conditioning, or both. It's primarily controlled by the sympathetic nervous system at the thoracic (T2 ganglion) level.   It represents an atypical sympathetic response.   This relationship between blushing and the sympathetic nervous system is important for the potential of surgical control.

It's important to note that persistent redness of the face may be due to an underlying medical condition.   One such condition is rosacea, a chronic inflammatory disease which usually begins in middle age or later and occurs generally in the central area of the face. It's characterized by visible dilated blood vessels, redness, and lesions. Other causes of facial redness are exposure to sun, wind, and cold, excessive alcohol, reactions to drugs, food, environmental or chemical allergens, and carbon monoxide toxicity.

Are fear of blushing and/or sweating SA/SP? As mentioned earlier, generally both fear of blushing and fear of sweating are thought of as specific phobias which stand alone, are secondary to SA/SP, or are the result of an underlying medical condition. The reason they are not considered to be synonymous with SA/SP is that SA/SP is defined as "an extreme and irrational anxiety in social situations." The anxiety and avoidance associated with excessive blushing and sweating, on the other hand, may be considered rational and quite understandable given the embarrassing nature of the symptoms (although the severity of anxiety may vary from person to person). As Richard Heimberg points out, "solving" a problem such as SA/SP by removing the stimulus doesn't change our view of ourselves, any more than having plastic surgery provides an effective fix for body dysmorphism. What this suggests is that while elimination of blushing and/or sweating will likely eliminate the fear of blushing and/or sweating, there's no reason to believe that eliminating those specific fears will eliminate SA/SP.

Curing sweating and blushing with ETS

Virtually the only effective way to "cure" moderate to severe primary hyperhidrosis and significantly diminish severe facial blushing appears to be ETS. This procedure is contraindicated for hyperhidrosis resulting from a medical condition, however. ETS stands for **E**ndoscopic **T**ransthoracic **S**ympathectomy, a surgical procedure which blocks the upper thoracic sympathetic nervous system ganglia which control the sweating and blushing.

Procedure. The surgery ("keyhole" surgery) is performed under total-body anesthesia through a ¼-inch incision made in the armpit area while we're lying on our back with that arm outstretched at approximately a 70-degree angle from the body. After the lung on the side of the incision is deflated by a small amount of CO_2 to make visualization easier, an endoscope is inserted into the chest cavity. This instrument contains a fiber-optic video camera on a catheter and an electric wire to ablate, or destroy, the specific nerves. Surgery may also be done through two tiny slits, with the second access to the chest for placement of 8 mm. clamps on the offending nerves, to compress rather than damage them.

As the surgeon navigates around blood vessels and other nerves, locating anatomical landmarks as they seek the "trouble-making" ganglia, the surgeon can view the progress on a television monitor. Once the individual nerve (or nerves) is found and separated from the surrounding tissue of the ganglion, it's then cauterized with radio frequency or clamped. This may occur from just above the T2 (*T* for thoracic) ganglion to just below the T4 ganglion. Some surgeons, however, do not include T3 and T4. By not treating axillary sweating, they avoid compensatory sweating.   What nerves are ablated or clamped depends upon the specific areas of sweating.   For the face and hands, the T2 nerve is made non-functional, although some surgeons may destroy the total T2 ganglion for severe palmar sweating.   For severe hyperhidrosis of the axillae, it's the T2 and T3, and perhaps T4.   It's important to note that for some surgeons facial sweating alone is not the target of this surgery.

Where the nerve is destroyed, it may or may not be retracted from the underlying tissue.   When the nerve (or nerves) has been done, that lung is reinflated, the CO_2 removed, and a pneumothorax tube inserted to allow excess air in the chest cavity to escape.   This takes approximately 20 minutes.   There are no stitches to be removed.

At this point the surgeon performs the same procedure on the opposite side of our body.   Some surgeons, however, prefer to do the two sides on separate occasions.   Following surgery, we are monitored in recovery, the pneumothorax catheter removed, and the chest x-rayed.   Procedures vary from clinic to clinic. In some facilities we can leave that day, in others we're discharged the next day. Mild soreness may be expected to persist for a minimum of four days but we can resume our normal activities within 48 hours and sports activities within two weeks after surgery.

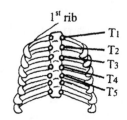

1st rib

T1
T2
T3
T4
T5

THORACIC GANGLIA

Results.   When ETS is performed by a surgeon skilled and experienced in this procedure, the results are definitive.   As we awaken from the anesthesia, our upper extremities and armpits are dry and warm. Statistically, palmar hyperhidrosis is cured in 99% of the cases and facial sweating, 90%.   Where there was severe sweating of the soles of the feet too, this is generally addressed. Spontaneous blushing likewise is corrected about 95% of the time.

Isolated plantar hyperhydrosis can be addressed by a lumbar sympathectomy, done as an open abdominal procedure.   However, this procedure is not recommended for men.   One distressing side-effect is retrograde ejaculation into the bladder which may cause impotence.   It may also cause postural hypotension (low blood pressure) in which we may feel dizzy or faint upon standing from a sitting or lying position. Plantar hyperhydrosis generally doesn't occur by itself.

If the patient with axillary hyperhidrosis isn't responsive to medical therapy, the condition may be treated by removal of axillary sweat glands. Diffuse sweating of the trunk or general sweating is not treated by surgery.

Side effects. There may be complications and/or side effects to the surgery. One common side effect, occurring in approximately 47% of patients, is called *compensatory hyperhidrosis*. This is where other parts of the body, such as chest and the back of the legs begin to sweat more. We become more sensitive to thermal stimuli. It appears that compensatory sweating occurs more frequently in those who are operated upon for axillary hyperhydrosis because more ganglia have to be divided to cure the underarm problem. For most of us this will be tolerable and may even improve over time. Another side effect is *gustatory sweating* which occurs while smelling or eating certain foods (especially those which are strong, spicy, or sour). It may show up as actual sweating or as the sensation of sweating, occurring in up to 2% of patients.

These side effects are generally mild to moderate. There appears to be a direct relationship between the number of ganglia treated and the incidence and intensity of compensatory sweating. The more ganglia treated or the more damage inflicted, the greater the likelihood of compensatory sweating. But, at this point in time, there's no clinical way to definitively predict the appearance or intensity of compensatory sweating. When it appears, however, it tends to decrease within the first 6-12 months. There's no reliable treatment for compensatory sweating on the torso.

Complications.

- *Horner's syndrome*, found in 0.3% of patients, occurs when there has been damage to the T1 nerve (stellate ganglion), resulting in constriction of the pupil and drooping of the eyelid (ptosis) on the affected side of the body. These are cosmetic symptoms and do not impair vision. The eyelid can be repaired through reconstructive surgery called blepharoplasty, but the condition may correct itself over time. T1 damage may also cause a slowing of the resting and/or exercise heart rate.

- *Excessive bleeding*

- *Infection*

- *Lung injury*

- *Pneumothorax* occurs where air remains within the chest wall.

Contraindications. ETS is a treatment for excessive sweating which doesn't occur secondarily to other conditions, such as

- *Hyperthyroidism (untreated)*

- *Fever*

- *Skin diseases*

- *Severe cardiac, vascular, or pulmonary insufficiency*

- *Severe pleural diseases, such as tuberculosis, pleuritis, empyema, and emphysema*

- *Menopause*

- *Hormone treatments*

- *Central nervous system disorders*
- *Psychiatric disorders*
- *Cancer treatments*
- *Other medications.*

All other causes for hyperhidrosis must be ruled out before ETS can be considered as a treatment. All underlying conditions need to be treated first.

Results preview. A few surgeons offer us the opportunity to preview the effects of surgery through a procedure called a *stellate block.* This is a reversible process in which 10 ml. of an anesthesia solution are injected into the left side of the neck so the solution flows into the muscular area near the stellate ganglion (T1).

While this temporary procedure doesn't affect blushing, it does block sweating on the left side of the upper torso so we can experience ourselves in the non-sweating state which will result from surgery. The duration of this block is 2-6 hours and we as patients are encouraged to put ourselves in situations, during that time period, in which we might expect to experience excessive sweating in order to make the comparison. Thus, we can experience what it's like to be free of sweating-associated embarrassment.

Because the block affects the T1 nerve, we experience Horner's syndrome while the block is in effect. Blood pressure and heart rate may drop during this period. It's important to note that the stellate block doesn't predict but suggests surgical outcome. There's no way to make an accurate prognosis.

Cost. The costs of having ETS will vary internationally from approximately $4,000 in Italy and Canada and $6,000 in Sweden to $7,500 in Finland and the U.S., not including air fare and hotel accommodations. Whether the procedure is covered by our health insurance depends upon our policy: (1) If the procedure is classified as experimental or standard procedure and (2) if the referring physician will stipulate that it's necessary, not elective, surgery.

Addressing the bashful bladder

Bashful bladder (BB), also known as shy bladder, shy kidney, shy voiding, pee-shy, phobia of urination, avoidant paruresis, psychogenic urinary retention, sphincteric phobia, and urophobia, is a common problem among SA/SPers (from 0.2-7% of us), where we're afraid, embarrassed, or unable to urinate in *public* places. Here "public" may mean any place where strangers are present, others are in close proximity to us, or we lack visual or auditory privacy. Though BB is common to both men and women, it appears that men are more concerned about lack of visual privacy whereas women are more concerned about auditory. *I used to wait in a stall in a restroom until others left then try to convince myself to go as fast as possible, as if I could control the rate. When others were within ear shot and I had no choice, I'd wad yards of toilet paper to damp the sound, try to avoid hitting the water directly, or repeatedly flush... all of which no doubt damned my conservationist's soul to perdition.*

While BB may even occur in our own homes, the most common locations in which it's experienced are public restrooms, restrooms on moving vehicles (planes, trains, boats, and buses), and bathrooms in other people's homes. As with our SA/SP in general, BB occurs when we feel anxious. Specifically, we experience urinary urgency in other than a "secure" environment. Our autonomic arousal kicks in, our bodies prepare for fight-or-flight, and our muscles tense. This involuntary muscle contraction includes the muscles which control voiding (bladder and urethral sphincters), thus making voiding impossible. When BB is severe, it can further interfere with our every day activities, relationships, and career- and job choices.

Treatment. The first thing we should do if we feel we suffer from BB is see a physician to make sure that our urinary retention isn't the result of a physical, medical, or medication problem. If, instead, the problem appears to be anxiety-related, we can then see a knowledgeable physician, urologist, or psychologist to deal with it. Some of the treatments which have been tried include cognitive-behavioral therapy, medications, and mechanical means.

The two most useful behavioral methods appear to be systematic exposure and flooding (no pun intended). Paradoxical intention may likewise be effective. Even though cognitive factors are strong in this condition and CBT has been recommended as treatment, little attention has been paid to-date to those cognitive aspects. One study demonstrated that CBT produced positive results which were maintained at least six months. Additional methods include having a "pee-buddy" may help. This is someone with whom to practice our desensitization, accompany us to the restroom to make the area more secure, and to give support. Making noise when we're trying to urinate can make us more comfortable that our urine stream won't be heard. Covering our ears and listening to music likewise can distract us enough so we can relax our muscles.

While some try drugs to assist BB, pharmacological results have been disappointing and don't look promising. Studies have looked at the full-range of medications from antidepressants, anxiety-reducers, sedatives, to urinary-releasers without much success. Drugs which some BBers have found useful, to some degree, include alcohol, which acts as a disinhibitor, benzodiazepines, and a post-surgery medication for urinary retention, bethanechol. Any drug, however, should be thought of as a temporary measure only. It's important that BBers be aware of the urinary-retaining or dehydrating properties of any drug we take, whether prescribed, over-the-counter, or recreational. When in doubt, we should consult a pharmacist or physician.

The primary mechanical means available to BBers is urinary self-catheterization. This is suggested by some urologists as a way to handle severe BB resulting when we're away from home for extended periods of time or in emergencies. Carrying a "Catheter Pack," consisting of two catheters, water-based lubricant, and topical anesthetic lidocaine, allows us to feel more secure that we can void when we absolutely need to. However, it's important to remember that self-catheterization poses several potential problems. One is possible infection from an unsterile catheter or its handling, urethral irritation from catheterization, and long-term reliance on mechanical management. The goal is short-term usage as an adjunct to CBT to deal with any underlying SA/SP problem.

For web sites on hyperhydrosis, facial blushing, ETS, and BB see Chapter 15.

Treating with supplements and natural products

According to the **Journal of American College Health**, over the last fifteen years there's been a heightened interest in "going back to Nature" to treat health problems. This is due, in part, to the fact that many of us feel misunderstood, ignored, or excluded from the medical decision-making process. We have turned to these substances to treat ourselves, to demonstrate our control over our health and our independence from the medical system. While the prevalence of natural supplement use as "therapy" is unknown, one study found that one in three individuals had used at least one such natural therapy in the past year.

This may be particularly true for those suffering from psychiatric conditions such as SA/SP. The stigma of mental illness makes it difficult to seek treatment in the first place. Often the medical system is impersonal and off-putting. Health care professionals tend to be ignorant about not only our condition but also treatment for it. This makes natural supplements and personally-designed and -controlled treatment very attractive. And in our desperation we may be willing to try almost anything.

As a result, natural products have become abundant. Being heavily marketed as the *real* answer to our health concerns, natural products or supplements have taken on a cachet. Because they're not supposed to be synthesized in a laboratory out of beakers of chemicals but rather taken from plants and other living organisms, we tend to perceive them to be good, safe, and wholesome.

The reason we're able to look to natural supplements for help is the Dietary Supplement Health and Education Act passed by the U.S. Congress in 1994. This law allows supplements, such as herbs and hormones, to be advertised and sold without the oversight of the FDA *as long as these substances are not represented as treatments or cures for disease.* Once a product claims to treat or cure, however, it's automatically reclassified as a *drug* and put under the jurisdiction of the FDA.

Note: Information is provided for educational purposes only and should not be used for prescription.

St. John's Wort. St. John's Wort (*Hypericum perforatum*) is a perennial herb which has been used for centuries to treat such maladies as depression, insomnia, and nervous conditions. Clinical studies have repeatedly demonstrated that the herb is useful for depression. A meta-analysis of 23 studies, involving a total of 1,757 individuals, showed that hypericum extract was significantly superior to placebo and as effective as standard antidepressants for mild to moderately severe depression.

Because research needs to be done on SJW's effect on severe or major depression, NIMH has collaborated with National Institutes of Medicine's Office of Alternative Medicine and Office of Dietary Supplements to do just that. As a result, in 1998 NIMH began the first U.S. large-scale controlled clinical trial on it. A 3-year study at Duke University will include 336 individuals with major depression. Patients will be randomly assigned to one of three treatments for an 8-week trial. One group will receive a uniform dosage of 900 mg. daily of hypericum. One group will receive a placebo. And the third group will receive an SSRI commonly prescribed for depression.

Just how hypericum works and how long it stays in our system are not yet known. Some studies suggest that it's a serotonin reuptake inhibitor, like fluoxetine (Prozac). But others studies hypothesize that its pharmacological properties are more like that of a low-grade MAOI, heavy on the norepinephrine and serotonin reuptake blockers.

Clinical studies have found that side effects exist though they tend to be mild.

- *Gastrointestinal irritation (relieved by intake of food and a large glass of water)*
- *Dry mouth*
- *Dizziness*
- *Skin rashes and itching*
- *Fatigue*
- *Restlessness*
- *Photosensitivity (usually from high doses).*

Dosage of hypericum extract is usually 300 to 900 mg. for a daily total, divided into 2 or 3 doses. Actual dosage is difficult to calculate since many kinds of hypericum exist. Some more potent than others. As of this writing, there's no standardization from manufacturer to manufacturer.

Hypericum should not be mixed with antidepressants or diet drugs because any drug which operates on neurotransmitter levels in the brain, particularly serotonin, is likely to interact with similar-acting drugs. If we were to mix hypericum with fluoxetine, for example, we could over-increase our serotonin, leading to possible central nervous system imbalances, resulting in anxiety, depression, and sleep disorders. But being short-term ill effects, they would disappear rapidly once the drugs were removed. Combining hypericum with MAOIs likewise creates the possibility of adverse reactions. Substitution of hypericum for a prescribed antidepressant should be done only under the supervision of a physician.

Important to note: As a rule of thumb, anyone who's depressed should consult an appropriate health care or mental health care professional. When we're depressed, we're not necessarily the best judge of the degree of our condition. This is especially true if we're severely depressed and/or suicidal. We need a knowledgeable, objective opinion. St. John's Wort may not help everyone who's depressed. While it helped most people in the studies who were mildly or moderately depressed, it didn't help everyone. Furthermore, depression may require psychotherapy as well as medication.

Valerian. Valerian (*Valeriana officinalis*) is obtained from the root of the plant commonly called garden heliotrope, all heal, amantilla, and setwall. Having a sedative and hypnotic effect, it's thought to enhance sleep quality, reduce anxiety and nervousness. Few studies have been done on valerian and most of those assessed sleep which may be of interest since SA/SPers frequently suffer from insomnia. While the root extract didn't alter sleep onset time, time awake before sleep, or REM (rapid eye movement) sleep, it did increase the perception of sleep quality. In one study 44% reported perfect sleep while 89% reported sleep improvement.

Little is known about the root's pharmacologic properties or how long it stays in the body. There are no reports of adverse effects. Dosage can range from 500 mg. to 12 grams before bedtime.

Kava-Kava. Kava-kava (*Piper mesthysicum*) is the root of a pepper plant found in Polynesia and the surrounding area. It acts as a central nervous system depressant and anxiety-reducer. Several studies have looked at its effect on anxiety syndromes, such as agoraphobia, generalized anxiety disorder, specific phobia, and adjustment disorder with anxiety, and found significant improvement. Just how it works is not yet known, though there's some evidence that it has a weak effect on benzodiazepine-binding sites but doesn't have any significant effect on gamma-aminobutyric acid (GABA). Because of this, Kava may interact negatively with benzodiazepines to produce lethargy and disorientation.

Dosage in one study was 100 mg. three times a day. While no adverse effects have been reported at this dosage level, increased usage may result in a yellow scaly rash referred to as *Kava dermopathy*. Heavy usage may cause metabolic abnormalities, such as increased liver enzymes and cholesterol, and decreased albumin and plasma protein.

Melatonin. Melatonin is a hormone secreted by the pineal gland in the brain which acts on sleep disturbances. The highest level of secretion is at night when we're sleeping. Production decreases with age from a level of 5-25 micrograms in young adults, a fact which may shed some light on the high incidence of insomnia in older adults.

Its most frequent usage has been for alleviating jet lag and altering circadian rhythms (sleep-wake cycles) for those doing shift work. It hasn't been used as a "sleeping pill" in the classical sense and its usefulness for those with chronic insomnia has not yet been determined. It appears that oral administration of melatonin doesn't precisely duplicate the hormone's effect when it's produced by our body. Moreover, while the hormone generally clears the body overnight, when we use it in excess of two weeks, it begins to store in fat tissue.

Short-term studies suggest low-toxicity, but long-term studies have not been done to determine the effect of fat-storage of the hormone. Safety data do not exist. Precise dosage likewise has not been determined, though studies have shown effect between 0.3 mg. and 80 mg. In addition, timing of dosage is important, but correct timing is unavailable.

What does "natural" really mean? Most natural products or supplements are, in fact, potent drugs. Referring to them as "natural," doesn't mean they're effective or safe. It doesn't mean they can't have medicinal or drug-like properties. As nutrition expert Jane Brody, author of the **New York Times Book of Health**, states, most of these products lack necessary and sufficient information on

• *Safety*

• *Purity*

• *Dose-response relationship*

• *Drug interactions.*

We need to inform our health care professionals about any supplements or natural products we're taking so they can evaluate our health status and concerns more accurately. In that survey of individuals taking supplements as therapy, only 28% who were being treated by a physician for a medical condition informed their health care provider of their simultaneous use of natural products for the condition. SA/SPers are even more likely to do this, fearing negative and critical responses. It's easy to envision their rolling their eyes, shaking their heads, and clucking at us. When using natural products or supplements, we should also document that usage since we can't assume safety alone or in combination with other medications. Furthermore, drug interactions are, for the most part, still unknown.

Is the answer to SA/SP in the inner ear?

According to psychiatrist Harold Levinson in his book **Phobia Free**, 90% of all phobias, anxiety, and panic attacks are the result of a hidden inner-ear dysfunction (a cerebellar-vestibular disorder, or CVD). His hypothesis is based on his research with individuals with dyslexia and learning disorders who manifested CVD and phobias. Levinson then generalized his conclusions about dyslexics to non-dyslexics.

While inner-ear disorders may cause anxiety, this anxiety is generally associated with dizziness, disorientation, unsteadiness, ringing in the ears, and/or blurred vision, as is often seen in panic disorder or agoraphobia with panic attacks. Studies of agoraphobia and panic disorder have suggested that vestibular dysfunction and impaired balance may occur in individuals with these disorders particularly in those who report space and motion discomfort, such as fear of small spaces or moving vehicles. To-date there are no findings to link SA/SP with CVD.

Levinson's approach to treatment of "CVD-induced" anxiety, phobias, and panic is medication, antioxidants, behavior modification, and psychotherapy. His medication recommendation differs from the general psychopharmacological prescription in that it has two levels. The primary level consists of motion sickness drugs and antihistamines, such as

• *Dramamine (dimenhydrinate)*

• *Benadryl (diphenhydramine HCl)*

• *Antivert (meclizine HCl)*

• *Sudafed (pseudoephedrine HCl; brompheniramine maleate)*

• *Dimitapp (chlorpheniramine)*

• *Hydergine (ergoloid mesylate)*

• *Transderm scop (scopolamine).*

The secondary, to be used in conjunction with the primary if the primary alone doesn't resolve the problem, consists of antidepressants and anti-anxiety medications. Because of possible drug interactions, we shouldn't combine primary- and secondary-level drugs on our own. What this line of inquiry suggests is that if we experience both anxiety and balance impairment symptoms, we should contact a physician.

Is the answer in the eyes?

EMDR (eye-movement desensitization and reprocessing) is a technique introduced in 1989 by Francine Shapiro, to treat post-traumatic stress disorder. According to the EMDR Institute, the technique "accelerates the treatment of a wide range of pathologies and self-esteem issues relative to both upsetting past events and present life conditions." Its goal is to rapidly desensitize traumatic memories, cognitively restructure memories, and significantly reduce emotional distress, intrusive thoughts, flashbacks, and nightmares. Studies on EMDR have also included persons with phobias and panic disorder, but the technique in these studies appears to be least effective with generalized negative themes.

Over the years EMDR has come to consist of a great many elements besides eye movements: Imagery, cognitive assessment and restructuring, sensory input alignment, targeting information, exposure, free association, and sensation awareness. In EMDR therapy the therapist asks us to remember and rate disturbing memories on a subjective distress scale. Focusing on our body sensations, thoughts, and the emotions attendant to our memories, we are to vividly picture and hold the traumatic scene in our mind while the therapist waves two fingers before our eyes, taps, or produces tones. We perform these eye-tracking movements in repeated sets with only short intervals in between. Proponents claim that symptomatic relief may occur in one 30-minute session or may require three such sessions.

This procedure is controversial and has divided the psychological community. This is because research results on EMDR are mixed. Some studies show superior results; some show results equivalent to that of other therapies for trauma and simple phobias; and others show no effect. What concerns many of its critics is what they see as the lack of sufficient control groups and use of standard measures, thus resulting in inadequate valid scientific support for it. Where the studies are carefully controlled, the technique has no effect or resulting improvement is similar to that of existing therapies.

No one knows how this technique works for those who report feeling symptomatic relief. Nathan R. Denny, Ph.D., hypothesized it's based upon classical conditioning. In Pavlov's classical conditioning we can take any reflexive response to a stimulus and pair it with a neutral object so that the neutral object takes on the ability to stimulate the reflexive response. For example, Pavlov's dog salivates (unconditioned response, or UCR) to the smell of meat powder (unconditioned stimulus, or UCS). A bell is rung when the meat powder is presented. The sound becomes associated with the food (conditioned stimulus, or CS) which produces salivation in the dog (conditioned response, or CR). Similarly for EMDR, the traumatic memory would be the CS and our emotional/cognitive/physiological response to it the CR.

EMDR could elicit what's called our *orienting reflex* (OR) in a repetitive, learning trial-like manner. The orienting reflex is the automatic movement of our eyes in the direction of a light or our heads in the direction of a sound. One property of this reflex is called *external inhibition* because when we orient, the orientation tends to suppress or inhibit conditioned responses. So the reflex could compel us to stop our routine behavior and immediately shift our attention to the novel or salient stimulus. When this happens, we have a tendency to act on one and only one activity at a time, to the exclusion of all other acts. This is called the *exclusion principle*.

Thus, when we elicit the traumatic memory and simultaneously elicit the orienting reflex by waving fingers, alternating sounds in each ear, or other distracting strategies, the OR suppresses or inhibits the distress associated with our memory. We can then turn our attention to the memory which we can comfortably evaluate and reinterpret. For example, we conjure up feeling mortified when a colleague grimaced during our presentation then reinterpret the scowl as having to do with personal bad news and not with our competence.

This opportunity for cognitive restructuring, or reframing, allows us to modify our emotional, cognitive, and physiological response to the memory and permits a new meaning to emerge. It's important to note that memory reprocessing can occur spontaneously, without the use of EMDR. We reprocess sub-traumatic memories all the time. Also, memories change over time. Whether they're very unpleasant, intense, tenacious, persistent, or important, they continuously and almost imperceptibly shift in character, organization, and clarity.

While this makes sense, research on the components of EMDR suggests something else may be going on. One study in the 1997 **Journal of Consulting and Clinical Psychology** found little difference between EMDR with eye-movement procedures and EMDR without it. It concluded that the data failed to support the usefulness of eye-movement in EMDR. Another study in the 1999 **Journal of Anxiety Disorders** found that when EMDR was compared with a modified version of itself which eliminated its cognitive elements, they had the same effect. This suggested that what creates EMDR's effectiveness is EMDR's central "imaginal exposure" component. While research on EMDR for fear of public speaking supports this hypothesis, studies are ongoing to determine what factors in EMDR are effective and for what.

As of the writing of this book, there have been no data on the use of EMDR for SA/SP.

Interacting with pets

Owning and caring for a pet has long been hailed as therapeutic for those who were old or ill, under stress, dealing with grief, anxious or depressed. This is because it provides companionship, security, bonding, and affection. Recent research has further suggested that pet ownership positively influences most human beings' emotional state and health. For example, it's been found that interacting with an animal can lower blood pressure, while conversing with a human will likely raise it. Interacting with a pet interrupts stressful thoughts. Individuals who have a pet recover more quickly from cardiac surgery than those who don't have a pet. In fact, having a pet has been found to be the strongest predictor of survival in these cases. However, what makes pets therapeutic for SA/SPers is more subjective than that. A pet can meet so many of our everyday psychological needs that simply aren't being met by humans.

A pet will love us even if we can't bring ourselves to give a speech, if we skip class to avoid people, or if we think of ourselves as stupid, ugly, incompetent, or a failure. A pet won't judge us, criticize us, lie to us, or betray our trust. Instead, it'll offer us unconditional love and acceptance. This is sincere affection, unsullied by hidden agendas, manipulation, and desire for control. In exchange for proper care and returned affection, a pet will provide companionship, loyalty, openness, and a friendly welcome home each time it sees us.

When there's no one else to listen to us, a pet will. We can always talk to a pet, confide in it, reveal our feelings, and share our secrets, even the most embarrassing or humiliating. And, unlike humans, the pet will act as an attentive and empathetic listener. When we're lonely, it'll be a playful and intelligent companion. Its humorous antics will distract us from our pain. Its nonverbal messages of love and attachment will comfort us when no one else seems to understand. Because it cares about us, it physically touches us and wants to be touched in return. This offers us the opportunity for the most basic, necessary, and nurturing form of communication. It gladly gives and receives this kind of affection.

Having "someone" to care about and for gives meaning to our life. A regular schedule of pet care provides structure to our time and lives and fosters a sense of purpose, something we particularly need when our SA/SP makes the world seem bleak and futureless. Reflecting a sympathetic resonance, pets give us the chance to nurture and feel needed.

For eight years one gray and white amber-eyed feline made me feel loved, appreciated, and needed. Found wandering the streets, this lung-scarred, ear-infected furry ball of optimism named "Faust" quickly became my steady companion. When he wasn't draping himself around my neck, he was sitting on his special chair at the dinner table or walking with me down the sidewalk in his harness and leash, greeting passersby. Unlike most cats, he loved riding in the car, sitting on my lap, looking out the window. But his favorite activity was Hollywood-style training. It was here that he could put both Babe and Lassie to shame. On cue he would sit up, stand up, walk across the room on his hind legs, waltz in a circle, roll over, climb a ladder, and talk. All for a good scritch between the shoulder blades or piece of chicken, but especially the chicken. Despite the fact he was frequently ill, he never faltered in his attention to our relationship which was short but oh so sweet.

Pet ownership influences us positively in social situations as well. People with animals are thought by others to be friendlier, happier, more hardworking, and intelligent, thus tempering the anxious vibes we sometimes send out. People walking their dogs, for instance, experience more social contact and longer conversations than those walking alone. People are attracted to other people's pets. As a result, pets provide a simple and casual method for us to make contact with others and for others to do the same with us. They also make available an ever-ready topic of conversation, hobby and interest possibilities, as well as a reason and opportunity to get out of the house to be with people, to have fun, to play, and relax.

"Hmmm. Cute dog....cute owner."

Overcoming insomnia

About one-third of all American adults experience bothersome insomnia. When we have a sleepless night, this elevates our stress hormones and deteriorates our ability to focus our attention and make decisions, making us tense and anxious about getting sleep. The more anxious we are, the more likely we are to have insomnia. At this rate, it's a wonder SA/SPers get any sleep at all.

However, it's important to remember that insomnia is a symptom of many conditions and not, in fact, a disorder in itself, although there are more than 80 known sleep disorders. While it may result from underlying medical or psychological problems, insomnia is often related to taking medication. For example, some antidepressants, anxiety-reducers, anti-inflammatories, such as prednisone, antihypertensives, and alcohol affect sleep quality and quantity. We need to consult with our physician or pharmacist to see if any of the drugs we take contribute to our sleep problem.

Once we determine our insomnia isn't likely related to a drug or medical condition, there are numerous steps we can take to beat our sleeplessness. These steps are based on dealing effectively with what keeps our insomnia going rather than on what originally may have started the process.

- *Keep a sleep diary. You need to know what your sleep patterns are and how much sleep you really need. For one week record when you go to bed, how often you awaken, for how long, and when you rise in the morning. If you take alcohol or any medication during this time to help you sleep, record that also.*

- *Keep regular hours. Go to bed and get up the same time each day. Make it earlier rather than later so you don't get over-tired. If you get to bed late one night, don't try to make up for it the next. Keep to your strict schedule.*

- *Go to bed only when it's time to sleep. Don't read or watch TV in bed. It's best not to associate these attention-focusing activities with where you sleep. Watch TV or read sitting in a chair or do it elsewhere.*

- *Don't take naps or allow yourself to doze off earlier than your scheduled sleep time. Keep moderately active. If necessary, ask a friend or spouse to help you keep awake.*

- *Start each day with at least 20 minute of sun. It helps wake you up, energizes you, and tells your internal clock that it's daytime.*

- *Take carbohydrates before bed. Milk or tryptophan-rich food, like turkey, before bed will not make you drowsy. A light meal of carbohydrates, such as dry cereal or toast and jelly, will however. When insulin is released to metabolize the carbohydrates, it metabolizes other amino acids as well, leaving the tryptophan in your blood stream to make its way to the brain to calm you. Don't eat a heavy meal within 4-5 hours of bedtime.*

- *Restrict your intake of caffeine, nicotine, alcohol, and MSG (monosodium glutamate) late in the day. Caffeine (in coffee, tea, cocoa, chocolate, some soft drinks, over-the-counter medications) takes six hours to leave your system. While alcohol may initially allow you to drift off, it tends to make it harder for you to stay asleep when it leaves your blood stream within several hours.*

- *Restrict your liquid intake after 6 p.m. If you tend to use the bathroom multiple times a night, drinking less in the evening may help. When thirsty, try sucking an ice cube.*

- *Eat a light breakfast and lunch.*

- *Exercise daily (at least 30 minutes) during the day, preferably late afternoon or early evening, but not within two hours of bedtime. Being inactive is considered one of the worst things an insomniac can do.*

- *Prepare your mind and body for sleep by doing relaxation exercises, meditation, yoga, mild stretching, taking a hot bath, or listening to soothing music before bedtime.*

- *Make your bedroom very dark. Don't allow moonlight, light from other rooms of the house or outside to penetrate.*

- *Sleep at a comfortable temperature. Keep the temperature and other environmental factors consistent from night to night.*

- *Use a white noise generator to block out outside sounds.*

- *Beware of nonprescription sleep aids. Most of these products consist primarily of antihistamines which are slow to take effect and slow to leave the body. They may leave you feeling drowsy. Aspirin may work for some.*

- *If you awaken during the night and can't get back to sleep, don't toss and turn. Get up and go to another room to read, watch TV, or do chores until you feel sleepy again, then return to bed.*

- *Use sleeping pills only as a last resort for "transient" insomnia. Transient insomnia results from a temporary situation, such as jet lag or personal loss. These should be used for only a week or two at a time. If you need something more, consult your physician.*

"Like cure, rehabilitation implies participation of the mind as well as of the body, integrated through volition for a creative process of adaptive changes." (Réné Dubos)

CHAPTER **15**

ACCESSING PROFESSIONALS AND RESOURCES

"Life shrinks or expands in proportion to one's courage." (Anais Nin)

How can we tell if it's time to seek help?

- *You feel you can't do it alone.*
- *You feel stuck or trapped with no way to turn.*
- *You anticipate and worry all the time.*
- *Everyday life is being affected negatively.*
- *It's not getting better.*

Looking for a clinician

As pointed out earlier, before we can successfully look for help we need to

- *Recognize that a problem exists;*
- *Feel the need for help;*
- *Clarify and concretize the problem so that it's specific, current, and solvable;*
- *Decide what you want to be the result;*
- *Learn all you can about your condition and treatment;*
- *Be motivated to act and be responsible for the outcome of therapy;*
- *Find out what's available.*

To solve our problem we need to put it in terms of its effect on us. Its seriousness depends upon its production of the three **Ds**: **D**isorganization; **D**ysfunction in everyday habits or living; and some degree of **D**isruption. We also need to choose a problem-solving process which contributes to the development of habits which will help solve subsequent problems. Problem-solving success in one area often generalizes to other areas and increases our sense of self-efficacy.

Unstructured self-help. Self-knowledge is almost always useful. But, unfortunately, self-knowledge is no guarantee of effective problem solving and, in fact, may not even be necessary for it. For example, through talk therapy, Maria discovered that she had had a love-hate relationship with her deceased mother, wanting to please her yet never measuring up to her standards for acceptance. While this explained a lot about the dynamics of her relationship with her parent and the guilt Maria felt, it did nothing to help her cope with feelings of not measuring up in the present day to others around her.

Furthermore, when we follow the self-help path outside a structured approach, we run the risk of going in circles, trying one thing then another, never fully doing what's necessary to achieve progress. Many of us, for example, have been thrown into social situations which exposed us to our greatest fears. But this "exposure" didn't "cure" our SA/SP. Because of this we may believe that exposure is useless. After all, it never worked for us before. But the exposure of which we speak wasn't presented to us systematically in graduated steps of slowly increasing anxiety. It didn't come with cognitive restructuring to be practiced throughout the exposure. Often, too, lack of structure in our self-help efforts never gets us outside of our impressions of the problem, either to test the validity of our assumptions or to shape a constructive solution.

Support groups. These are groups of individuals who share the problem and offer the opportunity for

* *Compassion*
* *Emotional support*
* *Information*
* *Advice*
* *Sharing experience*
* *Identification*
* *Resources*
* *Access to networks.*

Professional help. There are four primary types of professionals from whom we can receive help with SA/SP: Clinical psychologists, clinical social workers, psychiatric clinical nurses, and psychiatrists.

Clinical psychologists generally have a bachelor's degree plus six years of psychological education plus two years of clinical training (one year doctoral-level clinical internship and one year post-doctoral direct supervision, equaling 3,500 hours). On average that's 7.2 years of graduate education and training beyond an undergraduate degree. They may hold a Ph.D. or Psy.D., are psychotherapy-oriented, and, at this writing, don't have prescription privileges. There's a strong movement for clinical psychologists to receive several years of additional training so they can prescribe. Similarly, counseling psychologists who hold an Ed.D. may also provide therapy. To practice independently they must be licensed by the state in which they practice. Other state requirements for practice of psychotherapy may vary. Clinical psychologists may be a member of the American Psychological Association and/or American Psychological Society.

Clinical social workers generally have a master's degree in psychology or social work plus two years of direct supervised training. Not all social workers do clinical work. They may hold an M.S.W. or L.C.S.W., are psychotherapy-oriented, and do not have prescription privileges. They must be licensed or certified by the state in which they practice, except in states which don't offer or require licensing or certification. State requirements may vary. Masters-level professionals generally have a master's degree from a mental health field (M.A., M.S., M.S.W., M.Ed. or Ed.M.) plus one year of supervised training (1,750 hours). They may be a member of the National Association of Social Workers, American Psychological Association, and/or American Psychological Society.

Psychiatric clinical nurses have an R.N. plus a master's degree in a mental health specialty plus 800 hours of psychiatric practice (direct patient contact). They receive certification for this from the American Nurses Association. This specialty certification may be referred to as C.N.S. (clinical nursing specialist), C.N.S./N.P. (clinical nursing specialist/nurse practitioner), P.N.P. (psychiatric nurse practitioner), or A.N.P.-M.H. (adult nurse practitioner - mental health). Because of their medical training, psychiatric nurses are qualified to do physical exams and order tests. They must be licensed as registered nurses by the state in which they practice. They may be a member of the American Nurses Association and/or American Psychiatric Nurse Association.

Psychiatrists have an M.D. plus four years of residency/supervised training in psychiatry. They are generally oriented toward medication but a dwindling few may do psychotherapy as well. Some may further specialize. Because of the impact of managed care, it has been suggested that psychiatrists in the future may likely be doing even less direct psychotherapy and more primary care work. They have prescription privileges, can diagnose, and admit patients to the hospital. Because of their medical training, they are qualified to distinguish between physical and psychological causes of both physical and mental distress. They must be licensed in the state in which they practice. They may be a member of the American Psychiatric Association and/or the American Medical Association.

What to look for. Looking for a therapist is a project all by itself. We can't assume Blanche DuBois's approach in **A Streetcar Named Desire** and "depend upon the kindness of strangers." We must know what we're looking for. We want to find professionals

• *Familiar with SA/SP diagnosis and treatment*

• *Experienced in dealing with it and dealing with it successfully*

• *Philosophically congruent with you in the approach used, whether it's medication, talk therapy, cognitive, behavioral, CBT alone, CBT-plus-medication; whether it's individual or group sessions.*

On a more personal level we also want to find professionals who are

• *Comfortable with our checking out different therapists before deciding on one*

• *Warm, accepting, and non-judgmental*

• *Respectful and not arrogant*

• *Comfortable with therapy participants being equal partners in the process*

- *At ease, friendly, not anxious or depressed*
- *Open to your explanations, views, and values*
- *Actively engaged in helping you with your concerns*
- *Mindful that the message received needs to be checked against what was sent*
- *Open to your questions and flexible about what may be helpful*
- *Clear about the therapy process, what it entails, your rights, responsibilities of both parties, and confidentiality*
- *Oriented toward present life pressures, concerns, and daily functioning*
- *Conscious of the need for regular progress evaluation.*

Thus, a good therapist must do three essential things: (1) Know SA/SP and appropriate techniques; (2) Motivate us; and (3) Provide us with emotional support. Anything less and we risk failing to make our SA/SP life changes.

To find these professionals we can ask a trusted friend, our physician, a member of the clergy, the Employees Assistance Program (EAP) at work, or check directly with known treatment centers. We can get a referral from community mental health agencies, the local United Way, or a crisis hotline. Sometimes we can find professionals by their reputation in the community or with their peers (do others refer to them). Mostly, since SA/SPers may not want to talk to others about this, we'll find them by checking out the phone book Yellow Pages under "psychotherapists," "psychologists," or "psychiatrists" listed under "physicians." If this doesn't pan out, however, we can check with the Anxiety Disorders Association of America (ADAA), our local professional societies for clinical psychologists, clinical social workers, clinical psychiatric nurses, or psychiatrists, medical schools in the state, hospitals, university psychology departments, and major research and clinical centers.

According to the ADAA, once we have some names, we should speak with several therapists before deciding on one in order to see the range of possibilities available to us. The specific information we need to know is

- *What is the basic approach?*
- *Is it individual (one-to-one) or group?*
- *Are additional treatments available? If so, what?*
- *If necessary, will the therapist come to your house?*
- *Does the standard treatment have a fixed length? How long is it?*
- *What if more time is needed?*
- *Is there a provision for follow-up?*
- *How is treatment success measured?*
- *What is the background of the therapist: Training, credentialing (in-field degrees, accrediting agencies, licensure), experience with SA/SP?*
- *How long has the therapist been treating SA/SP?*

• *What is the cost of the treatment? Is there a sliding scale? Is any part of the fee reimbursable by insurance?*

• *Is it possible to speak with someone who has been through the program?*

What to do for the first visit

Before our first visit, it's essential that we be as fully informed and prepared as possible. This means learning all we can about SA/SP and its treatments. Since talking about ourselves is often so difficult, we should make up a description of our symptoms to share with the therapist (a copy for them and a copy for us). It's imperative that the two of us have a common understanding of what has initiated this visit and work from common definitions. Clarifications are easier when we're sharing our information.

The description of our SA/SP symptoms should include

• *Thoughts and Behaviors you have*

• *When and Where you have them*

• *Antecedents (what precedes) and Consequents (what follows)*

• *Frequency of your experiencing them*

• *How SA/SP impacts your daily functioning and life satisfaction.*

It's particularly important to emphasize SA/SP's consequences. A recent study of how physicians responded to descriptions of headache pain showed that descriptions of the pain itself led to reassurance whereas descriptions of how the pain disrupted the patient's life quickly led to development of a treatment plan to bring the headache under control.

It's very useful for both ourselves and the therapist for us to keep a journal. It will often reveal the *what, when, where, how,* and *to what degree* of our SA/SP as well as its patterns. These patterns provide the therapist with hints about the specific cognitive distortions, safety mechanisms, and avoidance behaviors we employ. It suggests the types of social situations where anxiety is greatest. And it indicates where additional therapeutic exercises may be useful, such as for self-esteem, self-efficacy, and social skills.

When we're not sure the therapist is really well-acquainted with SA/SP, we may find it useful to have a photocopy of "frequently asked questions" (FAQ) about the disorder. Hopefully, the therapist will willingly accept this information, but responses may vary. Some may resent what they perceive to be "presumptuousness" on our part. They may be insulted or embarrassed. This doesn't mean that if they seem to know less than we do, we shouldn't share with them to help bring them up to speed. After all, we're really not there to make them feel good, even though we may act as though we are. We're there to make ourselves feel better.

The part of therapy that most of us dislike, specifically because of our SA/SP, is being expected to speak. We need to be prepared for all kinds of questioning. If we don't force ourselves to provide requested information, we're hindering the therapist's role and, therefore, our progress. Because of our reluctance to speak, we'll find there may be silences in the conversation. While silence may be a therapeutic prompt to urge us to be forthcoming, sometimes it can seem too much and push us to avoid the situation. Though therapists well-acquainted with SA/SP will tend to keep the conversation casually moving along. In addition, when the therapist does something with which we're not comfortable, it's best to bring it up for discussion to see if the difficulty can be resolved by mutual agreement. While this may be difficult for us, it is essential.

When we have questions, it's best to bring them up directly.

Sarah. *Sarah noticed that her therapist looked too young to have had a lot of experience. Sarah felt ill at ease about this and needed reassurance. At her next session, she couldn't bring herself to ask so she commented on how young the therapist looked. The therapist looked quizzical, "Why are you commenting on my age?" "I wasn't...I was just making an observation," Sarah replied with trepidation, quickly changing the subject. She felt stupid, angry, and embarrassed. What she had really wanted to know was whether her therapist had the credentials and experience necessary for dealing with herSA/SP. Asking specifically for what she wanted would likely have answered her concerns and not left her anxious about the possibility of having jeopardized her relationship with the therapist.*

It's important for us to make our wishes and concerns known and to get the therapist to listen. But we may be concerned that asking questions, correcting, or disagreeing with the therapist's perception may make waves. We don't want to risk making the therapist unhappy with us because we fear rejection and abandonment. But when we act on these fears, we tend to accede to whatever is said or done, irrespective of how it represents the situation or makes us feel. This frequently leaves us frustrated and angry.

When we feel this way, we're likely to act on it indirectly. We may not follow the therapist's suggestions or simply choose not to return. If we're receiving medication from that individual, we may start prescribing for ourselves, by increasing, decreasing, or dropping the medication or by adding a new "natural medication" to it. And even if we continue with therapy, we may not inform the therapist of our self-imposed changes and/or alternative medications.

It's important to remember that nearly everyone (both those with **and** without SA/SP) has some trouble confronting medical establishment authority figures. We know they're "the only game in town." There are no viable alternatives so we need them. Since they're the experts and hold the resources, we feel at their mercy. Everyone is a little concerned and fearful about possible rejection and abandonment by them.

There are no two ways about it. Initially dealing with a therapist is extremely hard for SA/SPers since it encompasses all the situations that we fear and want to avoid. It requires us to talk with strangers on the phone, assert ourselves to ask them probing questions about therapy and qualifications, and meet the new therapist in person. And once we're in the therapist's office, we become the center of attention. We're questioned. We have to talk about ourselves and divulge personal information under circumstances which sometimes seem like the third-degree. We may be afraid we'll choke up, forget what we want to say, and blank out on questions we're asked. Fearful of being tested and evaluated, we may anticipate feeling criticized and misunderstood.

However, if we know what to expect and prepare for it, we're more likely to survive the "ordeal" more or less unscathed. It may be useful to ask if we can bring a tape recorder at least for the initial visit when our anxiety is sky-high and we're unlikely to remember, or recall accurately, anything that is said to us. Use of a recorder also allows us to hear how we really sound, what we really said, to confirm or deny our perceptions.

What to expect on the first visit

What happens on the first visit can vary dramatically from profession to profession, from setting to setting, so the following includes all the possible scenarios. However, most of us are unlikely to experience all of them.

Interview is a series of open-ended questions, such as "What's the nature of your difficulty?" "What problem are you having?," and "How can I help you?" Since answering questions is awkward for us because it puts us on the spot, we can have answers prepared, written down, to take with us. The therapist is really asking *what is your chief complaint?* Specifically, what are the salient thoughts, feelings, behaviors, and sensations that occur in social situations which make us anxious and avoidant. The SA/SP-acquainted therapist may say, instead, "Tell me what your life is life."

History will likely cover not only the disorder's history but also our medical, psychiatric, developmental, family, social, marital, educational, and occupational histories. The therapist will look for co-morbid conditions, like depression and substance abuse. Some of this information may appear inconsistent so the therapist may challenge specific aspects. While this may seem aggressive, it's intended as clarification.

Physical examination may be done or recommended to rule out any underlying medical problem.

Anxiety inventories and/or observation of behavior may be used to determine the manifestation, intensity, and severity of our SA/SP.

Depending upon what's done during the interview, the therapist may then begin to work with us to formulate our goals for therapy and a plan to meet them. This plan will be the basis of all we do in therapy and will be amended over time as we try different strategies and achieve specific objectives. Ideally, this plan will be a collaboration between the therapist and us, even if treatment consists only of medication.

Characteristics of effective therapists

• *Effective at attempting to understand your SA/SP behavior*

- *Effective at identifying self-defeating patterns and helping change them positively*
- *Effective at knowing what to do about SA/SP*
- *Effective at helping you look at yourself to ask, "Who am I?"*
- *Effective at reasoning systematically and thinking in systems' terms*
- *Effective at reaching out*
- *Effective at caring, respecting you, and inspiring trust*
- *Effective at being contemporary with world view of events*
- *Effective at being accessible to you by phone or e-mail.*

How does therapy work?

The goal of therapy is to help us look objectively at our feelings, thoughts, and behaviors in social situations. In doing so, we learn more effective ways to handle those situations. Together, the therapist and we, the client, will identify goals and agree on the process to achieve them and assess our progress. Psychotherapy requires strict attention to the client's welfare, goals, and confidentiality.

Dealing with a therapist or a best friend?

Even though we're seeing a professional because that person is an expert in our area of need, we want that person to be warm, accessible, honest, open, and friendly. We want to feel as comfortable as we can laying bare our secrets and feelings to this person. We're telling them thoughts and feelings we may not even share with a spouse or close friend.

However, it's important that we not expect therapists to be our best friends or chums, to reveal intimate aspects of their lives to us, or see us outside the therapist-client relationship. Yes, they can be approachable, sharing, and somewhat disclosing of themselves to us. They can talk with us in a more natural and casual way. But for them to do their job as psychotherapists most effectively, they must keep the roles and boundaries of the therapist-client relationship clear.

They're the professional, the expert, whose professionalism and expertise we're purchasing. If they let us regard them as a bosom buddy too, that very frequently changes the dynamics of the relationship. We respond differently (cognitively, emotionally, and behaviorally) to a close friend than we do to an authority figure. For example, in a business setting if our boss tells us to do something we don't like, we'll probably do it without much of an argument. But if we're intimate with the boss and they tell us to do something we don't like, we might well balk, argue, and dig in our heels. The roles of superior-subordinate, professional-client, and friend-friend would be in conflict.

We've come to therapy because we're vulnerable. We need help. We need to be able to depend on and put our trust in someone who'll help us and not betray that trust. This means having a therapist who'll do only what's best for us. But a therapist who is also a pal may have difficulty doing what's best for us. Their personal involvement tends to shift the focus off us and our needs and desires onto them and theirs.   According to the American Psychological Association code of ethics for practitioners, the client should always be the focus and first consideration of therapy.   Therapists should never use their clients to help satisfy their own needs.   Multiple relationships, or emotional involvement, can cloud objectivity and interfere with the psychologist's effectively performing their functions as a psychologist, and/or possibly harm or exploit us.   It can create misperceptions for us that the friendship will continue when therapy is finished.   Our believing that they will always be there for us to depend on can lead to a sense of betrayal and rejection when they aren't.

Researching insurance coverage

Many insurance- and government-sponsored plans provide some coverage for psychological or behavioral services; but they are not required to.   Without coverage we have to pay out of pocket.   However, some therapists will have a sliding scale of fees or payment plans.   An alternative to a private therapist would be help at a community mental health center.

The federal 1996 Mental Health Parity Act stipulated that health plans (except for those exempted by ERISA - the Employee Retirement Insurance Security Act) which offer medical, surgical, and mental health benefits must provide these benefits equally.   But treatment of mental disorders is limited to so-called "severe biologically-based mental illness" (such as, schizophrenia, schizoaffective disorder, bipolar disorder, paranoia, and other psychotic disorders).   Because of this a total of 19 states (as of 1998) have passed some degree of mental health parity to lessen this mental health discrimination. Degree of parity and the disorders covered by this legislation, however, will vary from state to state.

To determine if health insurance covers psychological or behavioral services, the American Psychological Association suggests that we should call our insurance plan representative for our level of coverage.   Coverage may include outpatient therapy, inpatient treatment, or only "medically necessary" treatment.   We need to inquire what percentage of treatment is covered and what limits may exist.   Specifically, we need to know about the co-payment, the total number of visits and if this is for a year or a lifetime, and what to do if coverage is denied or cut off.   It's also useful to determine what credentials therapists must have for reimbursement.

If we have coverage, it's important to remember that under most for-profit managed care organizations we need to get "prior authorization" before making an appointment with a psychotherapist.   If our primary care professional doesn't authorize it, we'll likely need to contact the plan's customer service people ourselves, tell them we want to access our psychological or behavioral (or whatever the plan labels it) benefits, and request a "prior authorization number." Having our plan member number available is necessary.   Once we have the authorization number, we can make our appointment with a therapist to whom we have to give the number. Even if the therapist doesn't think they need to take it, we should give it to them anyway.

We have to be guardians of this number because it's what determines whether or not we're going to be financially liable for the service. We need to keep the number safe and some suggest writing it on the checks paid to the therapist. Also, as a precaution, if the plan's customer representative tells us we don't need a prior authorization number, we have to double-check that they understand what specifically we want and we, in turn, have to understand their reply: "You're saying I don't need prior authorization to see a psychotherapist?" Those who have been given misinformation suggest that we protect ourselves by getting the representative's name, recording it, the date, and time of the interaction. In the end, the money we save will be our own.

Locating professional organizations and others

If we have difficulty locating mental health professionals, we can contact their professional organizations for names. (Adapted from NIMH resource list and Franklin Schneier and Lawrence Welkowitz's **The Hidden Face of Shyness**.)

American Academy of Child and Adolescent Psychiatry
3615 Wisconsin Avenue, NW
Washington, DC 20016-2891
(202) 966-7300 (voice) or (202) 966-2891 (fax)
http://www.aacap.org/

American Counseling Association
801 N. Fairfax Street, Suite 304
Alexandria, VA 22314
(800) 326-2642
http://www.counseling.org/

American Psychiatric Association
Public Affairs Office, Suite 501
1400 K Street, NW
Washington, DC 20005
(202) 682-6220
http://www.psych.org/

American Psychiatric Nurses Association
1200 Nineteenth Street, NW, Suite 300
Washington, DC 20036-2422
(202) 857-1133 (voice) or (202) 223-4579 (fax)
info@apna.org
http://www.apna.org/

American Psychological Association
750 First Street, NE
Washington, DC 20002
800-964-2000 or (202) 336-5800
http://helping.apa.org/apahelp .htm
http://www.apa.org/about/contact.html

Canadian Mental Health Association
National Office 2160 Yonge Street, 3rd Floor
Toronto, Ontario M4S 2Z3
(416) 484-7750 (voice) or (416) 484-4617 (fax)
cmhnat@interlog.com
http://www.cmha.ca/

Canadian Mental Health Association - BC Division
1111 Melville Street, Suite 1200
Vancouver, BC V6E 3V6
(604) 688-3234 (voice) or (604)688-3236 (fax)
office@cmha-bc.org

http://www.cmha-bc.org/

Canadian Psychiatric Association
260-441 MacLaren Street
Ottawa, Ontario K2P 2H3
(800) 267-1555 or
(613) 234-9857 (fax)
http://cpa.medical.org/

Canadian Psychological Association
151 Slater Street, Suite 205
Ottawa, Ontario K1P 5H3
(888) 472-0657 toll-free in Canada or
(613) 237-1674 (voice) or (613) 237-2144 (fax)

National Association of Social Workers
750 First Street, NE, Suite 700
Washington, DC 20002-4241
(800) 638-8799
http://www.naswdc.org/

Using other organizations

Agoraphobia Foundation of Canada
Box 132
Chomedey Laval, Quebec
H7W 4K2
(450) 688-4726

American Self-Help Clearinghouse
Northwest Covenant Medical Center
25 Pocono Road
Denville, NJ 07834
(800) 367-6724 (in NJ)
http://www.cmhc.com/selfhelp/clrnghse .htm#states (US and Canada)
http://www.cmhc.com/selfhelp/ clrnghse.htm#international
(International)

Association for Advancement of Behavior Therapy
305 Seventh Avenue, 16th Floor
New York, NY 10001-6008
(212) 647-1890 (voice) or
(212) 647-1865 (fax)
http://server.psyc.vt.edu/aabt/

Anxiety Disorders Association of America
11900 Parklawn Drive, Suite 100
Rockville, MD 29852-2624

(301) 231-9350 (voice) or
(301) 231-7392 (fax)
http://www.adaa.org/
(To search in a particular city or state.
Go to ADAA Web site, click on
"Consumers Resources," then "ADAA
Professional Therapists," then "Search
the Therapist List.")

**Council of the National Register of
Health Service Providers in
Psychology**
1120 G Street, NW, Suite 330
Washington, DC 20005
(202) 783-763 (voice) or
(202) 347-0555 (fax)
natlregstr@aol.com
*http://www.nationalregister.com/memp
ubl.html*

Freedom from Fear
308 Seaview Avenue
Staten Island, NY 10305
(718) 351-1717 (voice) or
(718) 667-8893 (fax)
FFFNADSDaol.com
http://www.freedomfromfear.org/

International Paruresis Association
P.O. Box 26255
Baltimore, MD 21210
(800) 247-3864
ssooifer@ssw02.umaryland.edu

**National Depressive and Manic-
Depressive Association**
730 N. Franklin, Suite 501
Chicago, IL 60610
(800) 826-3632
http://www.ndma.org/

National Alliance for the Mentally Ill
200 North Glebe Road, Suite 1015
Arlington, VA 22201
(800) 950-NAMI (6264) or (703) 524-
7600 (voice) or (703) 524-9094 (fax);
TDD 703-516-7227
helpline@nami.org
http://www.nami.org/

National Institute of Mental Health
Information and Inquiries
Room 15C-05
5600 Fishers Lane

Rockville, MD 20857
(800) 647-2642 or
(301) 443-4513
*http://www.nimh.nih.gov/
anxiety/*

National Mental Health Association
102 Prince Street
Alexandria, VA 22314-2971
(800) 969-NMHA (6642)
(703) 684-7722 (voice) or
(703) 684-5968 (fax)
http://www.nmha.org/

**National Mental Health Consumers'
Self-Help Clearinghouse**
1211 Chestnut Street, Suite 1000
Philadelphia, PA 19107
(800) 553-4539 or
(215) 735-6082
THEKEY@delphi.com
*http:www.libertynet.org/~mha/
cl_house.html*

**National Panic/Anxiety Disorder
News, Inc.**
1718 Burgundy Place
Santa Rosa, CA 95403
(707) 527-5738
npadnews@ap.net
http://www.npadnews.com/

Online Psych Therapist Locator
*http://onlinepsych.com/
locator/*

Phobics Anonymous
P.O. Box 1180
Palm Springs, CA 92263
(619) 322-COPE (2673)

**PsychScapes World Wide Therapist
Locator**
*http://www.mental-
health.com/PsychScapes/tin.html*

Toastmasters International
P.O. Box 9052
Mission Viejo, CA 92690
(949) 858-8255 (voice) or (949) 858-
1207 (fax)
tminfo@toastmasters.org
http://www.toastmasters.org/

http://www.foundersdistrict.web2010.c
om/facdocs/faq0.html (covering US,
Canada, Australia, United Kingdom,
South Africa, Philippines, and Europe)

Tapping into research programs

The following are centers which are
conducting research on and/or provide
treatment for social anxiety, social
phobia, and anxiety (Adapted from list
prepared by Anxiety Disorders
Education Program of NIMH)

California
San Diego State University
Psychology Clinic
6363 Alvarado Court, #103
San Diego, CA 92120
(619) 594-5134

University of California, Los Angeles
Anxiety Disorders Behavioral Program
Department of Psychology
 Franz Hall, Room A225
405 Hilgard Avenue
Los Angeles, CA 90095-1368
(310) 206-9191

Anxiety/Panic/Phobias Program
Neuropsychiatric Institute and Hospital
300 UCLA Medical Plaza Bldg.
Los Angeles, CA 90095
(310) 206-5133
http://www.npi.ucla.edu/anxiety/
Anx_Panic_Phobia/default.htm

University of California, San Diego
Psychopharmacology Program
8950 Villa La Jolla Drive #2243
La Jolla, CA 92037
(619) 622-6111

Palo Alto Shyness Clinic
407 Burgess Drive
Menlo Park, CA 94025
(415) 328-6115
http://www.shyness.com/shyness-
institute.html

Connecticut
Yale Anxiety Disorder Research
Connecticut Mental Health Ctr.

34 Park Street, Room 269
New Haven, CT 06519
(800) 538-0284 (in CT) or
(203) 789-9610

Yale University School of Medicine
West Haven VA Medical Center -
Psychiatry
116A2 950 Campbell Avenue
West Haven, CT 06516
(203) 932-5711

Florida
University of Florida
Center for Emotion and Attention
P.O. Box 100165HSC
Gainesville, FL 32610
(352) 392-2439

Indiana
*Indiana University Anxiety Disorders
Clinic*
550 University Boulevard,
Suite 3124
Indianapolis, IN 46202-5111
(317) 274-7422

Iowa
University of Iowa
Psychiatry Department
University of Iowa Hospitals and
Clinics
200 Hawkins Drive
Iowa City, IA 52242-1000
(319) 353-6314

Maryland
The Johns Hopkins University
Anxiety Disorders Clinic
600 N. Wolfe Street,
 Meyer Room 115
Baltimore, MD 21287
(419) 955-5653
http://ww2.med.jhu/anxietyclinic/
index.html

*National Institute of Mental Health
Anxiety Disorders Clinic*
NIMH Clinical Center, Bldg.10
4th Floor Outpatient Clinic
Bethesda, MD 20892-1368
(301) 496-4874

Massachusetts
Boston University
Center for Anxiety and Related
Disorders
648 Beacon Street, 6th Floor
Boston, MA 02215-2015
(617) 353-9610
http://www.bu.edu/anxiety/

Massachusetts General Hospital
Anxiety Clinic and Research
15 Parkman Street #815
Boston, MA 02114
(617) 726-3488

Michigan
University of Michigan
Anxiety Disorders Clinic -
Med Inn C435
1500 E. Medical Center Drive
Ann Arbor, MI 48109-0840
(313) 764-5348

University Psychiatric Centers
Warren Anxiety Disorders Clinic
28800 Ryan Road, Suite 300
Warren, MI 48092
(810) 558-8900
http://www.neuron.med.wayne.edu/anx dicl.html

Wayne State University
Depression/Schizophrenia/
Anxiety Studies
2751 E. Jefferson, Suite 200
Detroit, MI 48207
(313) 993-3426

Missouri
St. Louis University
Anxiety Disorders Clinic
St. Louis University Medical Sciences
Center
1221 South Grand Boulevard
St. Louis, MO 63104
(314) 577-8718

Nebraska
University of Nebraska, Lincoln
Psychological Consultation Ctr.
Department of Psychology
116 Lyman
Lincoln, NE 68588-0308
(402) 472-2351

New York
Albert Einstein College of Medicine
Phobia, Stress, and Anxiety Clinic
Long Island Jewish Medical Center
Hillside Hospital
75-79 263rd Street
Glen Oaks, NY 11004
(718) 470-8442

Columbia University
Anxiety Disorders Clinic
New York State Psychiatric Institute
722 West 168th Street
New York, NY 10032
(212) 960-2438, (212) 960-2442, (212) 960-2367

State University of New York, Buffalo
Anxiety Disorders Clinic
Park Hall, SUNYAB
Amherst, NY 14260
(716) 645-3697

White Plains Hospital
Anxiety and Phobia Center
Davis Avenue at East Post Road
White Plains, NY 10601
(914) 681-2284
http://www.phobia-anxiety.com/

North Carolina
Duke University
Anxiety and Traumatic Stress
Duke University Medical Center
Box 3812
Durham, NC 27710
(919) 684-2880

University of North Carolina, Chapel Hill
Department of Psychology
Davie Hall CB3270
Chapel Hill, NC 27599-3270
(919) 962-5082
tlr3@isis.unc.sedu
http://www.unc.edu/depts/clinpsy/anx1. html

Ohio
Kent State University
Department of Psychology
107A Kent Hall
Kent, OH 44242-0001
(330) 672-2266

Wright State University School of Medicine
Anxiety and Affective Disorders
4100 W. Third Street
Dayton, OH 45428
(513) 267-5319

Oklahoma
Oklahoma University Health Sciences Center
Psychiatric Clinic
3223 E. 31st Street
Tulsa, OK
(918) 744-9669
http://www.tulsa.uokhsc.edu/ clinics/psych.htm

Pennsylvania
Allegheny University of Health Sciences
Social Phobia Program
Broad and Vine Streets -
Mail Stop 988
Philadelphia, PA 19102-1192
(215) 762-3327
http://www.geocities.com/ HotSprings/5388/

Medical College of Pennsylvania
Department of Psychiatry
Center for Anxiety Treatment
3200 Henry Avenue
Philadelphia, PA 19129
(215) 842-4010

Pennsylvania State University
Department of Psychology
Stress and Anxiety Disorders
541 Moore Building
University Park, PA 16802
(814) 863-6019

University of Pittsburgh
Western Psychiatric Institute
Anxiety Disorders Clinic
3811 O'Hara Street
Pittsburgh, PA 15213-2593
(412) 624-1000

Temple University
Department of Psychology
Weiss Hall
Philadelphia, PA 19140
(215) 204-1575

Rhode Island
Brown University/Butler Hospital
700 Butler Drive, Duncan Building,
Box G-BH
Providence, RI 02906
(401) 444-1900

South Carolina
Medical University of South Carolina
Department of Psychiatry and
Behavioral Sciences
Clinical Research Division
171 Ashley Avenue
Charleston, SC 29425
(800) 369-5472

Texas
University of Texas, Austin
Center for Cognitive-Behavioral
Therapy
2914 Kassarine Pass
Austin, TX 78704
(512) 404-9308

University of Texas Medical Branch
Department of Psychiatry and
Behavioral Sciences
301 University Boulevard
Galveston, TX 77555-0429
(409) 772-7378

Washington
University of Washington
Department of Psychiatry
Harborview Medical Center
325 9th Avenue,
Mail Stop 359911
Seattle, WA 98104
(206) 731-3404

Wisconsin
Dean Foundation for Health, Education and Research
8000 Excelsior Drive, Suite 302
Madison, WI 52717
(608) 836-8030

University of Wisconsin Hospitals and Clinic
Anxiety Disorders Clinic
600 Highland Avenue
Madison, WI 53792
(608) 263-6056

Canada
The Clarke Institute of Psychiatry
250 College Street
Toronto, Ontario M5T 1R 8
(416) 595-6878
http://www.clarke-
inst.on.ca/mood_anxiety/bipolar_clinic.
html

Chedoke-McMaster Hospital
Anxiety Disorders Clinic
McMaster Division
1200 Main Street West
Hamilton, Ontario L8N 3Z5
(905) 521-5018

Douglas Hospital
6875 Lasalle Blvd.
Verdun, Quebec H4H 1R3
(514) 761-613

St. Mary's Hospital
3820 Lacomb Avenue
Montreal, Quebex H3T 1M5
(514) 345-3584 or
(514) 345-3511

Royal University Hospital Anxiety and
Mood Disorders
Department of Psychiatry
Ellis Hall, Room #111
Saskatoon, Saskatchewan
 S7N 0X0
(306) 966-8226

St. Boniface Hospital
Anxiety Disorders Clinic
Winnipeg, Manitoba
R2H 2A6
(204) 237-2606

Western Canada Behavior Research
Center for
Depression and Anxiety
#210, 320-23 Avenue SW
Calgary, AB, Canada T2S OJ2
(403) 671-6058
http://www.depressionanxiety
.com/

Providing family help and support

While those of us who are working to recover from SA/SP need help from friends and family, their providing this assistance isn't always easy. One of the primary reasons is that there's an existing relationship built around certain thoughts, beliefs, values, emotions, behaviors, expectations, and history which may be in conflict with our recovery change. For example, there may be issues of dependence, ambivalence, disappointment, anger, resentment, guilt, and neediness. These may intrude upon their successfully providing help and support to us.

There are two ways in which family members or friends can assist us with our SA/SP. They can help us with exercises and/or they can make room in which we can change and grow into more fully functioning persons. Helping, however, means their not taking over, telling us what to do, or trying to make decisions for us. It means stepping out of the relationship's roles for the two of us. It means offering reassurance and encouragement and allowing us to work at our own pace.

Frederic Newman, M.D., director of The Anxiety and Phobia Treatment Center at White Plains Hospital (NY), advises families and friends to:

- *Become familiar with aspects of SA/SP treatment and encourage the family member or friend to give it a fair trial;*

- *Help where necessary in executing exercises, especially exposure, and tracking progress;*

- *Provide support and minimize acute stresses which aggravate SA/SP;*

- *Avoid ridiculing social fears, anxious feelings and thoughts because they're real to us;*

- *Avoid belittling our attempts to address our SA/SP because progress is made in baby steps, which are often hard for the outsider to see;*

- *Avoid trying to convince us that we can do what we feel we can't. Those of us with SA/SP will do it when we feel ready;*

- *Avoid using guilt as a motivator because we already carry a heavy satchel of it and don't need any more;*

- *Avoid scolding, coaxing, cajoling, bargaining, and tricking us into doing more than we planned to do. We're the best judges of how far to go;*

- *Keep promises and don't betray our trust. Trust is a big issue for us and we have few people we're comfortable relying upon;*

- *Avoid trying to protect us from the world by making things "safe." We need to meet challenges in order to resolve our SA/SP and develop confidence and independence.*

Accessing online resources

Having access to the Internet has opened up a world full of opportunities for SA/SPers. Online we can find:

- *Information*, both general and specific, about our disorder, cognitive-behavioral therapy, medications, and co-morbid conditions;
- *Support*
- *Referrals*
- *Shared experiences*
- *Friendship (and sometimes romance)*
- *Links to other sites of interest.*

There are pros and cons to online use. On the negative side there's less of a sense of social presence and less sensory feedback. In Chapter 1 we talked about some of the perceived disadvantages of online use. Online use tends to decrease real-life social interaction and may lead to loneliness and/or depression. A 2-year study conducted by Robert Kraut at Carnegie Mellon's Human-Computer Interaction Institute seems to indicate that like television viewing interactive computer usage tends to reduce social involvement. Study participants reported a decline in interaction with family members and a reduction in their circle of friends as computer online usage increased. Even one hour a week had the potential to lead to depression and loneliness. The hypothesis is that relationships maintained over long distances with no face-to-face contact ultimately do not provide the kind of support and reciprocity that typically contribute to a sense of psychological security and happiness.

A heads up. While SA/SPers gain a great deal from these online relationships, particularly because of our "real-life" social deprivation, we need to consider that excessive computer use may indeed cut us off from initiating and maintaining so-called "real" relationships. For this reason we need to look objectively at our online use. Are we

- *Using online every day?*
- *Losing track of time when online?*
- *Spending less time with others or doing other things?*
- *Denying the time you spend online?*
- *Checking our mailbox repeatedly throughout the day?*
- *Getting complaints from others that you're on too long?*

"Yes" answers to these questions suggest excessive usage which, in turn, indicates possible Internet addiction.

On the positive side, according to psychologist Storm King, it's online that we're able to find peers no matter what topic is of interest to us. We don't have to search long and hard to find a compatriot. Online provides us with an enhanced opportunity to feel at ease with others. We don't have to worry how we look and we can take our time in creating the impression we want others to see. Because we're generally in the privacy of our own homes, we're at less interpersonal risk than we'd be in a face-to-face encounter. Rude intrusions can be handled easily, unlike someone unexpectedly coming to the front door. Because this medium offers us control of the interaction, we feel a greater sense of autonomy as well.

Since we can't see one another, our communication is more an exchange of ideas, thoughts, feelings, and impressions. Factors such as gender, race, and age don't matter because they don't come into play directly. This leads to an increased opportunity for us all to share and be heard. With this equal opportunity for participation comes an empowering sense of membership and community.

We can locate these resources via

- *Web sites*

- *News groups*

- *Chat rooms*

- *E-mail*

- *Lists*

- *Forums.*

Web sites. A web site is any computer on the Internet which is running a World Wide Web server process. My web site, for example, is *http://www.effectiveness-plus.com/.* This is its URL (Uniform Resource Locator). In the URL the site is identified by the site name "effectiveness-plus" and the domain is identified by the site name plus ".com," designating a commercial site. Some of the following selected web sites deal with SA/SP and its treatment; hyperhydrosis, severe blushing, ETS; and drug assistance programs:

http://www.anxietynetwork.com/
(Dr. Thomas Richards, Anxiety Clinic of Arizona)

http://www.colba.net/~audiotex/
(Social Phobia Mailing List and Resource Site)

http://uhs.bsd.uchicago.edu/~bhsiung/tips/social.html#English (Medications)

http://www.rxlist.com/
(Medications)

http://www.algy.com/anxiety/
(The Anxiety Panic Internet Resource)

http://www.keirsey.com/
(Keirsey Temperament Sorter & Theory [Introversion])

http://www.merck.com/
(**Merck Manual** of Diagnosis and Therapy [Medical Disorders])

http://mentalhealth.miningco.com/msub6.htm
(Mental Health Resources: Depression)

http://www.handsweat.com/overview.html
(Center for Hyperhydrosis)

http://www.parsec.it/summit/hyper1.e.htm
(Hyperhydrosis - Ivo Tarfusser, M.D.)

http://www.angelfire.com/mi/blushinglobster/
(The Blushing Phobia Homepage)

http://www.endoscopic-surgery.com/thoracos.htm
(ETS - Jim S. Garza, M.D. [Texas])

http://www.parsec.it/summit/sympath1e.htm
(ETS - Ivo Tarfusser, M.D. [Italy])

http://www.privatix.fi/home.html
(ETS - Timo Telaranta, M.D. [Finland])

http://www.carlanderska.se/cont.htm
(ETS - Contacts in Sweden, Norway, England, Denmark, Lithuania, Yugoslavia, USA)

http://www.geocities/HotSprings/Villa/7781/
(You're in Control - Avoidant Paruresis)

http://www2.cy-net.net/~richardz/ajw4598.html
(Pee Shy and Bashful Bladder)

http://www.goodnet.com/%7Eee72478/enable/medications.htm   (Information paper by U.S. Senate's Special Committee on Aging re: Drug Manufacturers' Programs)

http://www.westworld.com/~mhcrept/medicine.html
(Medication Assistance Programs)

http://omhs.mhd.hr.state.or.us/presdrap.htm
(Prescription Drug Assistance Programs).

News groups (Usenet). These are public discussion groups where we access the group, read, and add messages. Topics are presented in an hierarchical fashion so that we can easily follow the conversational thread. Messages to the news group are distributed to every computer connected to the Internet where they are stored for a short time. The news groups to which we have access depends upon what groups are supported by our server.

News groups may be moderated or unmoderated. In a *moderated* news group every message sent to the group is reviewed by a moderator, who can edit, filter, reject, or post the message. If it's considered appropriate to the news group's topic, it'll be published. But if it's not, the moderator will notify the author that the message is being returned. Messages may be returned for flaming (attacking), spamming (sending unsolicited e-mail), harassment, use of obscenity, or length. An *unmoderated* group has no such constraints.

There are pluses and minuses to news groups which vary from group to group:

Plus side

- *Don't need to subscribe;*
- *Drop in any time;*
- *Can ask questions;*
- *Have access to FAQs, specific and general information;*
- *Have access to links, references, and other resources.*

Minus side

- *Frequently not moderated;*
- *Spawn spammers, crusaders, troublemakers (trolls);*
- *Posts are archived and open to the public;*
- *Need to be careful with personal information;*
- *News servers may not receive all posts so may be difficult to follow conversations;*
- *Some servers don't carry all groups.*

Some news groups dealing with aspects of SA/SP are:

- *alt.support.anxiety-panic* (Anxiety and Panic)
- *alt.support.depression* (Depression and Mood Disorders)
- *alt.support.shyness* (Shyness)
- *alt.support.social-phobia* (SA/SP)
- *alt.recovery.panic-anxiety.self-help* (Cognitive Approaches to Anxiety)
- *soc.support.depression* (Depression and Treatment)
- *soc.support.depression.misc* (Depression and Treatment).

Mailing lists. These are public discussion groups designed around a particular topic where messages are sent and received by e-mail. To participate we have to become a *subscriber* to the list. Messages received by the list are distributed by the listserver to all subscribers. Message archives are not available to non-subscribers. Lists may be moderated or unmoderated. Some relevant lists are:

- ***Social Anxiety.*** Send e-mail to *listserv@maelstrom.stjohns.edu*. No subject line. Message: *sub soc-phob your name* . For instructions regarding this list send to *soc-phob-request@maelstrom.stjohns.edu*

- ***Anxiety.*** Send e-mail to *listproc@frank.mtsu.edu*. No subject line. Message: *subscribe anxiety-L your name*

- ***Depression.*** Send e-mail to *listserv@soundpoint.brandywine.american.edu*. No subject line. Message: *subscribe depression your name* .

Chats (IRC - Internet Relay Chat). This is one of the more popular interactive services because we can talk in real-time with people from around the world. Some chats have specific topics and provide the ability to have both public and private conversations. Many are available 24 hours a day seven days a week. "Secret" channels also exist and are tagged by "+s." These won't show up on the list of channels when we do a */LIST* command.

Programs for IRC include mIRC, Pirch, Virc for Windows, and Ircle for Macs. The particular program doesn't matter since they all connect to the same chat networks. After loading the program, we need to read up on the basic IRC commands, netiquette, use of emoticons and abbreviations before jumping in. A *#beginners channel* may be provided to bring us up to speed before joining a chat. It's important to be aware that some chat channels will have sex talk, garbage, sleaze, and obscenity For assistance check out *http://www.irchelp.org/.* Two chat rooms dealing with aspects of SA/SP are:

- */join #social phobia* (connect to the Undernet then type address)

- */join #shyness* (connect to the AfterNet Network then type address).

Forums. Forums are like message- or bulletin boards where we post questions, offers, or comments for others to scan. Two such forums are:

- Anxiety Network Forum for Panic, Social Phobia, and Generalized Anxiety Disorder
- *http://www.delphi.com/anxiety.co.uk/*

- Panic Forum
- *http://www.panic.smithkline-beecham.co.uk/*

Ten commandments for overcoming SA/SP

As Darrell L. Hill, of Diverse Solutions, suggests, our recovery is predicated upon developing both new ways of looking at the world and new skills with which to deal with it. There are ten areas which we need to continuously address to alleviate our SA/SP. Hill calls these the "Ten Comandments" (*http://www.ncpsych.com/*):

1. Thou Shalt Not Let the Evaluation of Others Drag Thee Down.

2. Thou Shalt Not Be Perfect.

3. Thou Shalt Learn to Argue With Faulty Logic.

4. Thou Shalt Know Thyself and Appreciate Thy Gifts.

5. Thou Shalt Learn to Relaxxxxx.

6. Thou Shalt Learn the Art of Conversing.

7. Thou Shalt Rehearse, Rehearse, Rehearse.

8. Thou Shalt Expose Thyself (no trenchcoats need apply).

9. Thou Shalt Be Assertive.

10. Thou Shalt Roam the Social Wilderness.

To derive the maximum benefit from this book you need to embrace it, live with it, read and re-read it, fully immerse yourself in the concepts, do all the exercises, apply the cognitive skills, behavioral strategies, and life techniques every single day. You need to practice until your positive and appropriate responses become automatic. Only in this way can you reach toward your recovery and enjoy the satisfying, productive life you deserve.

As Eleanor Roosevelt wrote in **You Learn by Living** (1960), "You gain strength, courage, and confidence by every experience in which you really stop to look fear in the face. You are able to say to yourself, 'I lived through this horror. I can take the next thing that comes along.'...You must do the thing you think you cannot do."

Then, and only then, can you do what Tom Robbins urges in **Even Cowgirls Get the Blues:** "Be your own master! ...Rescue yourself! ...and Free the Heart!"

BIBLIOGRAPHY

Chapter 1

Abrams, G. (1992). Cheaters do prosper, young feel; Dishonesty rotting U.S. "moral zone." *Los Angeles Times*, November 13, 17.

American Psychiatric Association. (1994). *Diagnostic and Statistical Manual of Mental Disorders (DSM-IV)*, *4th ed.* Washington, DC: Author.

Barlow, D.H. (1988). *Anxiety and Its Disorders: The nature and treatment of anxiety and panic.* New York: Guilford Press.

Beck, A.T., Emery, G. (1985). *Anxiety Disorders and Phobias.* New York: Basic Books.

Borkovec, T. (1985). What's the use of worrying? *Psychology Today* (Dec.), 59-64.

Dayhoff, S.A. (1991). Experiencing stress? You're not alone. *Salt Lake Tribune* (March 3).

Dayhoff, S.A. (1988). Worry too much? You're not alone. *Wellesley Townsman* (October 20).

Hofmann, S.G., Albano, A.M., Heimberg, R.G., Tracey, S., Chorpita, B.F., Barlow, D.H. (1999). Subtypes of social phobia in adolescents. *Depression and Anxiety, 9,* 15-18.

Holt, C.S., Heimberg, R.G., Hope, D.A., Liebowitz, M.R. (1992). Situational domains of social phobia. *Journal of Anxiety Disorders, 6,* 63-77.

Ihenga, K., Kiriike, N., Matasuyama, M., Oichi, S., Kaneko, K., Yamagami, S. (1996, August) *Phobia and anxiety symptoms in preadolescent and adolescent children.* Paper presented at the World Congress of Psychiatry, Madrid, Spain.

Kessler. R.C., McGonagle, K.A., Zhao, S., Nelson, C.B., Hughes, M., Eshelman, S. et al. (1994). Lifetime and 12-month prevalence of DSM-III-R psychiatric disorders in the United States. *Archives of General Psychiatry, 51,* 8-19.

Kessler, R.C., Stein, M.B., Berglund, P. (1998). Social phobia subtypes in the National Comorbidity Survey. *American Journal of Psychiatry, 155,* 613-619.

Kobasa, S.C. (1979). Stressful life events, personality and health: An inquiry into hardiness. *Journal of Personality and Social Psychology, 37,* 1-11.

May, R. (1996). *The Meaning of Anxiety.* New York: W.W. Norton.

McLuhan, M. (1967). *The Medium is the Massage.* Cambridge, MA: M.I.T. Press.

Rubin, T.I. (1975). *Compassion and Self-Hate.* New York: McKay.

Schachter, S., Singer, J. (1962). Cognition, social, and physiological determinants of emotional states. *Psychological Review, 10,* 264-273.

SunAmerican Financial. (1998). *National women's retirement survey.* September. Washington, DC: Women's Institute for Secure Retirement.

Turner, S.M., Beidel, D.C., Cooley, M. (1994). *Social Effectiveness Therapy: A program for overcoming social anxiety and social phobia.* Mt. Pleasant, SC: Turndel.

Zimbardo, P., Ebbesen, E.B., Maslach, C. (1977). *Influence, Attitude, and Changing Behavior.* Reading, MA: Addison-Wesley.

Chapter 2

American Psychiatric Association. (1980) *Diagnostic and Statistical Manual for Mental Disorders (DSM-III). 3rd ed.* Washington, DC: Author.

American Psychiatric Association. (1987) *Diagnostic and Statistical Manual for Mental Disorders (DSM-III-R). 3rd ed., rev.* Washington, DC: Author.

American Psychiatric Association. (1994) *Diagnostic and Statistical Manual for Mental Disorders (DSM-IV). 4th ed.* Washington, DC: Author.

Aron, E. (1996*). The Highly Sensitive Person: How to thrive when the world overwhelms you.* New York: Broadway Books.

Black, B., Uhde, T.W. (1995). Psychiatric characteristics of children with selective mutism: A pilot study. *Journal of the American Academy of Child and Adolescent Psychiatry, 34,* 847-856.

Buss, A.H. (1980). *Self-Consciousness and Social Anxiety.* San Francisco: W.H. Freeman.

Butler, G., Culligan, A., Munby, M., Amies, P., Gelder, M. (1984). Exposure and anxiety management in the treatment of social phobia. *Journal of Consulting and Clinical Psychology, 52,* 642-650.

Caspi, A., Elder, G.H., Bem, D.J. (1988). Moving away from the world: Life-course pattern of shy children. *Developmental Psychology, 24,* 824-831.

Herbert, J.D., Hope, D.A., Bellack, A.S. (1992) Validity of the distinction between generalized social phobia and avoidant personality disorders. *Journal of Abnormal Psychology, 101,* 332-339.

Hofmann, S.G., Ehlers, A., Roth, W.T. (1995). Conditioning theory: A model for the etiology of public speaking anxiety? *Behaviour Research and Therapy, 33,* 567-571.

Hofmann, S.G., Gerlach, A., Wender, A., Roth, W.T. (1997). Speech disturbances and gaze behavior during public speaking in subtypes of social phobia. *Journal of Abnormal Psychology, 104,* 224-231.

Hofmann, S.G., Roth, W.T. (1996). Issues related to social anxiety among controls in social phobia research. *Behavior Therapy, 27,* 79-91.

Jones, W.H., Briggs, S.R., Smith, T.G. (1986). Shyness: Conceptualization and measurement. *Journal of Personality and Social Psychology, 51,* 629-639.

Kagan, J., Resnick, S.J., Snidman, N. (1987). Physiology and psychology of behavioral inhibition in children. *Child Development, 58,* 1459-1473.

Kagan, J., Snidman, N., Arcus, D. (1993). On the temperamental categories of inhibited and uninhibited children. In K.H. Rubin and J.B.Asendorpf (Eds.), *Social Withdrawal, Inhibition, and Shyness in Childhood* (pp. 19-28). Hillsdale, NJ: Erlbaum.

Keirsey, D., Montgomery, S. (Ed.) (1998). *Please Understand Me II: Temperament, character, intelligence.* New York: Prometheus Books.

Last, C.E., Hersen, M., Kazdin, A.E., Finklestein, R., Strauss, C.C. (1987). Comparison of DSM-III separation anxiety and overanxious disorders: Demographic characteristics and patterns of comorbidity. *Journal of the American Academy of Child and Adolescent Psychiatry, 26,* 527-531.

Lecrubier, Y., Weiller, E. (1997). Comorbidities in social phobia. *International Clinical Psychopharmacology,12* (Supplement 6), 17-21.

Mannuzza, S., Schneier, F.R., Chapman, T.F., Liebowitz, M.R., Klein, D.F., Fyer, A.J. (1995). Generalized social phobia: Reliability and validity. *Archives of General Psychiatry, 52,* 230-237.

Marks, I.M. (1970). The classification of phobic disorders. *British Journal of Psychiatry, 116,* 377-386.

Miller, R.S, (1996). *Embarrassment: Poise and peril in everyday life.* New York: Guilford Press.

Miller, R.S., Leary, M.R. (1992). Social sources and interactive functions of emotions: The case of embarrassment. In M. Clark (Ed.), *Emotion and Social Behavior* (pp. 202-211). Beverly Hills, CA: Sage.

Mills, R.S., Rubin, K.H. (1993). Socialization factors in the development of social withdrawal. In K.H. Rubin and J.B. Asendorpf (Eds.), *Social Withdrawal, Inhibition, and Shyness in Childhood.* Hillsdale, NJ: Erlbaum.

Rogers, C.R. (1960). *On Becoming a Person: A therapist's view of psychotherapy.* Boston: Houghton Mifflin.

Schneier, F.R., Johnson, J., Hornig, C.D., Liebowitz, M.R., Weissman, M.M. (1992). Social phobia: Comorbidity and morbidity in an epidemiologic sample. *Archives of General Psychiatry, 49,* 282-288.

Schuckit, M.A. (1986). Genetic and clinical implications of alcoholism and affective disorders. *American Journal of Psychiatry, 143,* 140-147.

Solyom, L., Ledwidge, B., Solyom, C. (1986). Delineating social phobia. *British Journal of Psychiatry, 149,* 464-470.

Stopa, L., Clark, D.M. (1993). Cognitive processes in social phobia. *Behavior Research and Therapy, 31,* 255-267.

Turner, S.M., Beidel, D.C., Larkin, K.T. (1986). Situational determinants of social anxiety in clinic and non-clinic samples: Physiological and cognitive correlates. *Journal of Consulting and Clinical Psychology, 54,* 523-527.

Turner, S.M., Beidel, D.C., Townsley, R.M. (1990). Social phobia: Relationship to shyness. *Behavior Research and Therapy, 28,* 497-505.

Weiller, E., Bisserbe, T.C., Boyer, P. et al. (1996). Social phobia in general health care: An unrecognized, undertreated disabling disorder. *British Journal of Psychiatry, 168,* 169-174.

Weinshenker, N.J., Goldenberg, I., Rogers, M.P., Goisman, R.M., Warshaw, M.G. et al. (1996-97). Profile of a large sample of patients with social phobia: Comparison between generalized and specific social disorder. *Depression and Anxiety, 4:5,* 209-216.

Wittchem, H.V., Belloch, E. (1996). The impact of social phobia on quality of life. *International Clinical Psychopharmacology, 11* (Supplement 3), 5-23.

Zimbardo, P. (1977). *Shyness: What is it? What to do about it?* Reading, MA: Addison-Wesley.

Zimbardo, P., Carducci, B. (1995). Are you shy? The problem of shyness. *Psychology Today, 28,* November 21, 34-48.

Chapter 3

Arrindell, W.A., Emmelkemp, P.M.G, Monsma, A., Brilman, E. (1983). The role of perceived parental rearing practices in the aetiology of phobic disorders: A controlled study. *British Journal of Psychiatry, 143,* 183-187.

Bandura, A. (1977). Self-efficacy: Toward a unifying theory of behavioral change. *Psychological Review, 84,* 191-215.

Bandura, A. (1988). Perceived self-efficacy: Exercise of control through self-belief. In J.P. Dauwalder, M. Perrez, V. Hobi (Eds.), *Annual Series of European Research in Behavior Therapy (Vol.2,* 27-59). Lisse, Holland: Swets and Zeitlinger.

Bandura, A. (1988). Self-efficacy: Conception of anxiety. *Anxiety Research, 1,* 77-98.

Baumeister, R.F., Leary, M.R. (1995). The need to belong: Desire for interpersonal attachments as a fundamental human motivation. *Psychological Bulletin, 117,* 497-529.

Baumeister, R.F., Tice, D.M. (1990). Anxiety and social exclusion. *Journal of Social and Clinical Psychology, 9,* 165-195.

Baumeister, R.F., Tice, D.M., Hutton, D.G. (1989). Self-presentation motivations and personality differences in self-esteem. *Journal of Personality, 57,* 547-579.

Bourne, E.J. (1995).The Anxiety and Phobia Workbook. New York: New Harbinger Publishers.

Bruch, M.A., Gorsky, J.M., Collins, T.M., Berger, P.A. (1989). Shyness and sociability revisited: A multicomponent analysis. *Journal of Personality and Social Psychology, 57,* 1216-1221.

Eastburg, H., Johnson, W.B. (1990). Shyness and perceptions of parental behavior. *Psychological Reports, 66*, 915-921.

Engfer, A. (1993). Antecedents and consequents of shyness in boys and girls: A 6-year longitudinal study. In K.H. Rubin and J.B. Asendorpf (Eds.), *Social Withdrawal, Inhibition, and Shyness in Childhood* (pp. 49-79). Hillsdale, NJ: Erlbaum.

Erikson, E.H. (1959). Identity and the life cycle: Selected papers. In *Psychological Issues Monograph Series 1*. New York: International Universities Press.

Fyer, A.J., Mannuzza, S., Chapman, T.F., Liebowitz, M.R., Klein, D.F. (1993). A direct interview family study of social phobia. *Archives of General Psychiatry, 50*, 286-293.

Goldman, D. (1996). High Anxiety. *Science, 274* (5292), November 29, 1483.

Holmes, T.H., Rahe, R.H. (1967). Social adjustment rating scale. *Journal of Psychosomatic Research, 11*, 213-218.

Kushner, M.G., Sher, K.J., Beitman, B.D. (1990). The relation between alcohol problems and anxiety disorders. *American Journal of Psychiatry, 147*, 685-695.

Leary, M.R., Kowalski, R. (1995). *Social Anxiety*. New York: Guilford Press.

Lesch, K-P., Bengel, D., Heils, A., Sabols, S., Greenberg, B. et al. (1996). Association of anxiety-related traits with polymorphism in the serotonin transporter gene regulatory receptor. *Science, 274*, November 29, 1527-1531.

Mannuzza, S., Schneier, F.R., Chapman, T.F., Liebowitz, M.R., Klein, D.F., Fyer, A.J. (1995). Generalized social phobia: Reliability and validity. *Archives of General Psychiatry, 52*, 230-237.

Maslow, A.H. (1970). *Motivation and Personality*. 2nd Ed. NewYork: Harper & Row.

McEwan, K.L., Devins, G.M. (1983). Is increased arousal in social anxiety noticed by others? *Journal of Abnormal Psychology, 92*, 417-421.

Merck Sharp & Dohme Research Laboratories. (1992). *Merck Manual of Diagnosis and Treatment (16th ed.)* Rahway, NJ: Author.

Mills, R.S., Rubin, K.H. (1993). Socialization factors in the development of social withdrawal. In K.H. Rubin and J.B. Asendorpf (Eds.), *Social Withdrawal, Inhibition, and Shyness in Childhood*. Hillsdale, NJ: Erlbaum.

Mineka, S., Gunnar, M., Champoux, M. (1986). Control and early socioemotional development: Infant rhesus monkeys reared in controllable versus uncontrollable environment. *Child Development, 57*, 1241-1256.

Ng, S. (1980). *The Social Psychology of Power*. London: Academic Press.

National Institute of Mental Heath. (1998). *Genetics and Mental Disorders: Report of the NIMH genetic workgroup*, #4268. Washington, DC: Author.

O'Banion, K., Arkowitz, H. (1977). Social anxiety and selective memory for affective information about the self. *Social Behavior and Personality, 5*, 321-328.

Ohman, A., Dimberg, U., Ost, L-G. (1985). Animal and social phobias: Biological constraints on the learned fear response. In S. Reiss and R. Bootzin (Eds.), *Theoretical Issues in Behavior Therapy* (pp. 125-175). New York: Academic Press.

Olweus, D. (1993). Victimization by peers: Antecedent and long-term outcomes. In K.H. Rubin and J.B. Asendorpf (Eds.), *Social Withdrawal, Inhibition, and Shyness in Childhood* (pp. 315-341). Hillsdale, NJ: Erlbaum.

O'Neill, J.M. (1981). Patterns of gender role conflict and strain: Sexism and fear of femininity in men's lives. *Personnel and Guidance Journal, 59*, 203-210.

Ost, L-G., Hugdahl, K. (1981). Acquisition of phobias and anxiety response patterns in clinical patients. *Behavior Research and Therapy, 16*, 439-447.

Plomin, R., Daniels, D. (1986). Genetics and shyness. In W.H. Jones, J.M. Cheek, S.R. Briggs (Eds.), *Shyness: Perspectives on research and treatment* (pp. 63-80). New York: Plenum Press.

Raab, A., Oswald, R. (1980). Coping with social conflict: Impact on the activity of tyrosine hydroxylase in the limbic system and adrenals. *Physiology and Behavior, 24*, 387-394.

Rapee, R.M., Lim, L. (1992). Discrepancy between self and observer ratings of performances in social phobics. *Journal of Abnormal Psychology, 101*, 728-731.

Reich, J.H., Yates, W. (1988). Family history of psychiatric disorders in social phobia. *Comprehensive Psychiatry, 29*, 72-75.

Rosenbaum, J.F., Biederman, J. Hirshfeld, D.R., Bolduc, E.A., Faraone, S.V. et al. (1991). Further evidence of an association between behavior inhibition and anxiety disorders. Results from a family study of children in a non-clinical sample. *Journal of Psychiatric Research, 25*, 49-65.

Scott, J.P., Marston, M. (1953). Nonadaptive behavior resulting from a series of defeats in fighting mice. *Journal of Abnormal and Social Psychology, 48*, 417-428.

Stein, M. (1998). A direct interview family study of generalized social phobia. *American Journal of Psychiatry, 155*, 90-97.

Turner, S.M., Beidel, D.C., Dancu, C.V., Keyes, D.J. (1986). Psychopathology of social phobia and comparison to avoidance personality disorder. *Journal of Abnormal Psychology, 95*, 389-394.

Chapter 4

Albrecht, K.(1979). *Stress and the Manager: Making it work for you.* New York: Simon and Schuster.

Beck, A.T., Emery, G. (1985). *Anxiety Disorders and Phobias.* New York: Basic Books.

Beck, J. (1995). *Cognitive Therapy: Basics and beyond.* New York: Guilford Press.

Burns, D. (1980). *Feeling Good: The new mood therapy.* New York: William Morrow.

Clark, D.M., Welles, A. (1995). A cognitive model of social phobia. In R.G. Heimberg, M.R. Liebowitz, D.A. Hope, F.R. Schneier (Eds.), *Social Phobia: Diagnosis, assessment, and treatment.* New York: Guilford Press.

Clemes, H., Bean, R. (1981). *Self-Esteem: The key to your child's well-being.* New York: G.P. Putnam's Sons.

DeRosis, H. (1979). *Women and Anxiety.* New York: Delacorte Press.

Duval, S., Wicklund, R.A. (1972). *A Theory of Objective Self-Awareness.* New York: Academic Press.

Ellis, A., Harper, R. A (1975). *New Guide to Rational Living.* No. Hollywood, CA: Wilshire Book Company.

Ellis, A., Knaus, W. (1977). *Overcoming Procrastination: How to think and act rationally in spite of life's inevitable hassles.* New York: New American Library.

Frankl, V.E. (1962) *Man's Search For Meaning: An introduction to logotherapy.* Boston: Beacon Press.

Friedman, M., Rosenman, R. (1974). *Type A Behavior and Your Heart.* New York: Fawcett-Crest Books.

Gold, M. (1989). *The Good News About Panic, Anxiety, and Phobias.* New York: Villard Books.

Horney, K. (1950). *Neurosis and Human Growth: The struggle toward self-realization.* New York: W.W. Norton.

Lange, A.J., Jakubowski, P. (1976). *Responsible Assertive Behavior: Cognitive/behavioral procedures for trainers.* Champaign, IL: Research Press.

Leary, M.R. (1986). The impact of interactional impediments on social anxiety and self-presentation. *Journal of Experimental Social Psychology, 22,* 122-135.

Leary, M.R., Haupt, A.L., Strausser, K.S., Chokel, J.T. (1998). Calibrating the sociometer: The relationship between interpersonal appraisals and state of self-esteem. *Journal of Personality and Social Psychology, 74,* 1290-1299.

Leary, M.R., Knight, P.D., Johnson, S.A. (1987). Social anxiety and dyadic conversation: a verbal response analysis. *Journal of Social and Clinical Psychology, 5,* 34-50.

Leary, M.R., Kowalski, R.M. (1995). *Social Anxiety.* New York: Guilford Press.

Leary, M.R., Kowalski, R.M., Campbell, C. (1989). Self-presentational concerns and social anxiety: The role of generalized impression expectancies. *Journal of Research in Personality, 22,* 308-321.

Morrison, J. (1997). *When Psychological Problems Mask Medical Disorders: A guide for psychotherapists.* New York: Guilford Press.

Tavris, C. (1982). *Anger: The misunderstood emotion.* New York: Touchstone Books.

Young, J. (1990). *Cognitive Therapy for Personality Disorders: A schema-focused approach*. Sarasota, FL: Professional Resource Exchange.

Chapter 5

Aleksiuk, M. (1996). *Power Therapy: Maximizing health through self-efficacy*. Seattle, WA: Hogrefe & Huber Publishers.

Bandura, A. (1991). Self-efficacy concepts of anxiety. In R. Schwarzer and R.A. Wicklund (Eds.), *Anxiety and Self-Focused Attention*. New York: Harwood Academic Publishers.

Babior, S., Goldman, C. (1996). *Overcoming Panic, Anxiety, and Phobias*. Duluth, MN: Whole Person Associates.

Baugh, J.R. (1988). Gaining control by giving up control: Strategies for coping with powerlessness. In W.R. Tiller and J.E. Martin (Eds.), *Behavior Therapy and Religion: Integrating spiritual and behavioral approaches to change* (pp. 125-138). Newbury Park, CA: Sage.

Bourne, E.J. (1995). *The Anxiety and Phobia Workbook*. New York: New Harbinger Publications.

Chakravarthy, B., (O'Donnell-)Dayhoff, S.A., Marecki, S. (1975). *Decision Making For Managers*. Boston: Education for Management (AMACOM).

Garfield, C. (1986). *Peak Performers: The new heroes of American business*. New York: William Morrow.

Hill, G.J. (1989). An unwillingness to act: Behavioral appropriateness, situational constraints, and self-efficacy in shyness. *Journal of Personality, 57*, 871-890.

Lazarus, R.S. (1984). The trivialization of distress. In B.L. Hammond and C.J. Scheier (Eds.), *Psychology and Health*. Washington, DC: American Psychological Association Press.

MacCrimmon, K., Wehrung, D. (1985). *Risk-Taking*. New York: The Free Press.

Maddux, J.E., Norton, L.W., Leary, M.R. (1988). Cognitive components of social anxiety: An investigation of the integration of self-presentation theory and self-efficacy theory. *Journal of Social and Clinical Psychology, 6*, 180-190.

Mamries, L.M., O'Connor, C., Cheek, J.M. (1983, April). *Vocational certainty as a dimension of self-esteem in college women*. Paper presented at a meeting of the Eastern Psychological Association, Philadelphia, PA.

Miller, W., Rollnick, S. (1991). *Motivational Interviewing: Preparing people to change addictive behavior*. New York: Guilford Press.

Rogers, C.R. (1951). *Client-Centered Therapy: The current practice, implications, and theory*. Boston: Houghton Mifflin.

Rogers, C.R. (1960). *On Becoming a Person: A therapist's view of psychotherapy*. Boston: Houghton Mifflin.

Schlesinger, S., Horberg, L. (1988). *Taking Charge*. New York: Simon and Schuster.

Schwarz, J. (1992). *The Path of Action*. New York: Aletheia Foundation Book.

Viscott, D. (1977). *Risking*. New York: Pocket Books.

Chapter 6

Barber, T.X. (1979). Training students to use self-suggestion for personal growth: Methods and word-by-word instructions. *Journal of Accelerated Learning and Teaching, 4* (2), 111-128.

Benson, H., Klopper, M. (1975). *The Relaxation Response*. New York: William Morrow.

Collinge, W., Duhl, L. (1997). *American Holistic Health Association's Complete Guide to Alternative Medicine*. New York: Warner Books.

Jacobson, E. (1938). *Progressive Relaxation*. Chicago: University of Chicago Press.

Kuntzleman, C.T. (1979). *Consumers Guide to a Flatter Stomach*. New York: Pocket Books.

Luthe, W. (1969). *Autogenic Therapy*. New York: Grune and Stratton.

Mason, L.J. (1980). *Guide to Stress Reduction*. Culver City, CA: Peace Books.

Melamed, B., Siegel, L. (1980). *Behavioral Medicine: Practical applications in health care*. New York: Spring Publishing Company.

Wolpe, J. (1973). *The Practice of Behavior Therapy*. New York: Pergamon Press.

Wolpe, J. (1986). *Psychotherapy By Reciprocal Inhibition*. Stanford, CA: Stanford University Press.

Chapter 7

Albano, A.M., Martin, P.A., Holt, C.S., Heimberg, R.G., Barlow, D.H. (1995). Cognitive-behavioral group treatment for social phobia in adolescents. *Journal of Nervous and Mental Disease, 183*, 649-656.

Beck, A.T., Emery, G. (1985). *Anxiety Disorders and Phobias*. New York: Basic Books.

Borkovec, T. (1985). What's the use of worrying? *Psychology Today* (Dec.), 59-64.

Burns, D. (1980). *Feeling Good: The new mood therapy*. New York: William Morrow.

Clark, D.M., Wells, A. (1995). A cognitive model of social phobia. In R.G. Heimberg, M.R. Liebowitz, D.A. Hope, and F.R. Schneier (Eds.), *Social Phobia: Diagnosis, assessment, and treatment*. New York: Guilford Press.

Clark, H.H., Clark, E.V. (1977). *Psychology and Language: Introduction to psycholinguistics*. New York: Harcourt Brace Jovanovich.

Dayhoff, S.A. (1988). Worry too much? You're not alone. *Wellesley Townsman*, October 20.

Ellis, A., Harper, R. (1975). *A New Guide to Rational Living*. No. Hollywood, CA: Wilshire Books.

Fiske, S. Taylor, S. (1991). *Social Cognition*. New York: McGraw-Hill.

Frankl, V. (1960). Paradoxical intention: A new logotherapeutic technique. *American Journal of Psychotherapy*, 14, 520.

Glasser, W. (1984). *Control Theory: A new exploration of how we control our lives*. New York: Harper & Row.

Heimberg, R.G., (1990). Cognitive behavior therapy (for social phobia). In A.S. Bellack and M.Hersen (Eds.), *Comparative handbook for treatments for adult disorders* (pp.203-218). New York: John Wiley & Sons.

Heimberg, R.G., Barlow, D.H. (1991). New developments in cognitive-behavioral therapy for social phobia. *Journal of Clinical Psychiatry, 52* (11 Supplement), 21-30.

Heimberg, R.G., Becker, R.E., Goldfinger, K., Vermilyea, J.A. (1985). Treatment of social phobia by exposure, cognitive restructuring, and homework assignments. *Journal of Nervous and Mental Disease, 173*, 236-245.

Heimberg, R.G., Salzman, D.G., Holt, C.S., Blendell, K. (1993). Cognitive-behavioral group treatment for social phobia: Effectiveness at five-year follow-up. *Cognitive Therapy and Research, 17*, 325-339.

Hope, D.A., Holt, C.S., Heimberg, R.G. (1993). Social phobia. In T.R. Giles (Ed.), *Handbook of Effective Psychotherapy* (pp. 227-251). New York: Plenum.

Lucas, R.A., Telch, M.J. (1993, Nov.). *Group versus individual treatment of social phobia*. Paper presented at the annual meeting of the Association for the Advancement of Behavior Therapy, Atlanta, GA.

Marzillier, J.S., Lambert, C., Kellet, J. (1976). A controlled evaluation of systematic desensitization and social skills for socially inadequate psychiatric patients. *Behaviuor Research and Therapy, 14*, 225-238.

Mattick, R.P., Peters, L., Clark, J.C. (1989). Exposure and cognitive restructuring for social phobia: A controlled study. *Behavior Therapy, 20*, 3-23.

Meichenbaum, D., Cameron, R. (1974). Modifying what clients say to themselves. In M. Mahoney and C. Thorsen (Eds.), *Self-Control: Power to the Person*. Belmont, CA: Wadsworth.

Mersch, P.P.A., Emmelkemp, P.M.G., Lips, C. (1991). Social phobia: Individual response patterns and the long-term effects of behavioral and cognitive interventions: A follow-up study. *Behaviuor Research and Therapy, 29*, 357-362.

North, M.M., North, S.M., Cobb, J.R. (1998). Virtual reality: An effective treatment for fear of public speaking. *International Journal of Virtual Reality, 3* (3).

Rothbaum, B.U., Hodges, L.F., Kooper, R., Opdyke, D., Willeford, J., North, M.M. (1995). Effectiveness of computer-generated (virtual reality) graded exposure in the treatment of acrophobia. *American Journal of Psychiatry, 152* (4), 626-628.

Seligman, M.E.P. (1991). *Learned Optimism.* New York: Alfred A. Knopf.

Trower, P. Yardley, K., Bryant, B., Shaw, P. (1978). Treatment of social failure: A comparison of anxiety-reduction and skills-acquisition procedures on two social problems. *Behavior Modification, 2,* 41-60.

Wells, A., Clark, D.M., Salkovskis, P.M.S., Ludgate. J., Hackmann, A., Gelder, M.G. (1995). Social phobia: The role of in-situation safety behaviors in maintaining anxiety and negative beliefs. *Behavior Therapy, 26,* 153-161.

Young, J.E. (1990). Cognitive therapy for personality disorders: A schema focused approached. Sarasota, FL: Professional Resource Exchange.

Chapter 8

Bedell, J., Lennox, S. (1997). *Handbook for Communication and Problem-Solving Skills Training: A cognitive-behavioral approach.* New York: John Wiley and Sons.

Bruch, M.A., Gorsky, J.M., Collins, T.M., Berger, P.A. (1989). Shyness and sociability revisited: A multicomponent analysis. *Journal of Personality and Social Psychology, 57,* 1216-1221.

Dayhoff, S.A. (1987). *Create Your Own Career Opportunities.* Andover, MA: Brick House Publishing.

Dayhoff, S.A. (1987). *Creating Visibility and Credibility Through Speaking: Seminar series 2.* Wellesley, MA: The Mentoring Network.

Dayhoff, S.A. (1989). How to succeed in getting your message across. *Wellesley Townsman,* July 13.

Dayhoff, S.A. (1990). Hype Yourself. *Entrepreneurial Woman,* May/June, 60-62.

Dayhoff, S.A. (1989). Thinking styles can be barriers or opportunities. *Mass High Tech,* February 27.

Dayhoff, S.A. (1988). Whole-brain thinking gives you the inside track. *Wellesley Townsman,* November 10.

Delmar, K. (1984). *Winning Moves: The body language of selling.* New York: Warner Books.

Dilts, R., Grinder, J., Bandler, R., Delozier, J. (1980). *Neuro-Linguistic Programming - Volume I: The study of the structure of subjective experience.* Cupertino, CA: Meta Publications.

Egan, G. (1982). *The Skilled Helper: Models, skills, and methods for effective helping*. Monterey, CA: Brooks/Cole.

Elsea, J. (1984). *First Impression, Best Impression*. New York: Simon and Schuster.

Frank, M. (1986). *How to Get Your Point Across in 30 Seconds or Less*. New York: Pocket Books.

Hermann, N. (1988). *The Creative Brain*. Lake Lure, NC: Brain Books/Applied Creative Services.

Knapp, M. (1978). *Nonverbal Communication in Human Interaction*. New York: Holt, Rinehart and Winston.

LaFrance, M., Mayo, C. (1978). *Moving Bodies: Nonverbal communication in social relationships*. Monterey, CA: Brooks/Cole.

Leary, M.R. (1983*). Understanding Social Anxiety: Social, personality, and clinical perspectives*. Beverly Hills: Sage.

Leary, M.R., Knight, P.D., Johns. K.A. (1987). Social anxiety and dyadic conversation: A verbal response analysis. *Journal of Social and Clinical Psychology, 5*, 34-50.

Leary, M.R., Kowalski, R.M., Campbell, C. (1988). Self-presentational concerns and social anxiety: The role of generalized impression expectancies. *Journal of Research in Personality, 22*, 308-321.

Turner, S.M., Beidel, D.C., Cooley-Quille, M. (1997*). Social Effectiveness Therapy: A therapist's guide*. No. Tonowanda, NY: Multi-Health Systems.

Wlazlo, Z. Schroeder-Hartwig, K., Hand, I., Kaiser, G., Munchau, N. (1990). Exposure in vivo vs. social skills training for social phobia: Long-term outcome and differential effects. *Behavior Research and Therapy, 28*, 181-193.

Chapter 9

Alberti, R., Emmons, M. (1976). *Stand Up, Speak Out, Talk Back*. New York: Pocket Books.

Bandura, A. (1997). *Self-Efficacy: The exercise of control*. New York: W.H. Freeman.

Bootzin, R.R. (1975). *Behavior Modification and Therapy: An introduction*. Cambridge, MA: Winthrop Publishers.

Brandt, D. (1984). *Is That All There Is?: Overcoming disappointment in an age of diminished expectations*. New York: Poseidon Press.

Dayhoff, S.A. (1989). Managing your time is key to opening the door to success. *Wellesley Townsman*, September 21.

Duke University. (1998). *Stress has greater effect on hostile people*. April 22. Durham. NC: Duke University Medical Center Press Release.

Ellis, A., Knaus, W. (1977). *Overcoming Procrastination: How to think and act rationally in spite of life's inevitable hassles.* New York: New American Library.

Gordon, T. (1975). *P.E.T.: Parent-Effectiveness Training.* New York: New American Library.

Gore, M. (1959). *How To Organize Your Time.* New York: Doubleday.

Lange, A.J., Jakubowski, P. *Responsible Assertive Behavior: Cognitive/behavioral procedures for trainers.* Champaign, IL: Research Press.

Messer, M., Dillon, L.(1993). *If You're So Smart, Why Aren't You Happy?* Chicago, IL: The Anger Clinic Book Service.

Mueller, C.M., Dweck, C.S. (1998). Praise for intelligence can undermine children's motivation and performance. *Journal of Personality and Social Psychology, 75* (1), 33-52.

Paul, S. (1999). Be firm, stand firm. *Personal Effectiveness News* (May 14), shale@shalecoach.com/.

Smith, M. (1975). *When I Say No, I Feel Guilty.* New York: The Dial Press.

Williams, S.L., Turner, S.M., Peer, D.F. (1985). Guided mastery and performance desensitization treatment for severe acrophobia. *Journal of Consulting and Clinical Psychology, 52,* 502-518.

Chapter 10

Antonuccio, D.O. (1997). A cost-effectiveness analysis of cognitive-behavioral therapy and fluoxetine (Prozac) in the treatment of depression. *Behavior Therapy, 28,* 187-210.

Baker, B. (1999). Depression plus anxiety: A double whammy. *Clinical Psychiatry News, 27* (1), 22.

Beidel, D.C., Turner, S.M. (1998). *Shy Children, Phobic Adults: Nature and treatment of social phobia.* Washington, DC: American Psychological Association Press.

Beutler, L.E. (1997). Fact and fiction about prescription privileges. *Psychotherapy Bulletin, 32* (2), 4-6.

Birmaher, B., Waterman, S.G., Ryan, N., Cully, M., Balach, L. Ingram, J., Brodsky, M. (1994). Fluoxetine for childhood anxiety disorders. *Journal of the American Academy of Child and Adolescent Psychiatry, 33,* 993-999.

Borne, R.F. (1994) Serotonin: The neurotransmitter for the "90s." *Drug Topics,* October 10, 108.

Bougerol, T., Scotto, J., Patris, M. et al. (1993). Citalopram and fluoxetine in major depression: Comparison of two clinical trials in a psychiatric setting and in general practice. *Clinical Drug Investigation, 14* (2), 77-79.

Clark, D.B., Agras, W.S. (1991). The assessment and treatment of performance anxiety in musicians. *American Journal of Psychiatry, 148,* 59-65.

Davidson, J.R.T., Ford, S.M., Smith, R.D., Potts, N.W. (1991). Long-term treatment of social phobia with clonazepam. *Journal of Clinical Psychiatry, 52* (11 Supplement), 16-20.

den Boer, J.A., van Vliet, I.M., Westerberg, H.G.M. (1994). Recent advances in the psychopharmacology of social phobia. *Progress in Neuropsychopharmacology and Biological Psychiatry, 18,* 634-636.

DeNelsky, G. (1996). The case against prescription privileges for psychologists. *American Psychologist, 51* (3), 207-212.

De Vane, C.L., Ware, M.R., Emmanuel, N.P. (1995, December). *Evaluation of the safety, efficacy, and physiological effects of fluvoxamine in social phobia.* Paper presented at the Annual Meeting of the American College of Neuropsychopharmacology, San Juan, Puerto Rico.

Falloon, I.R.H., Lloyd, G.G., Harpin, R.E. (1981). The treatment of social phobia: Real life rehearsal with nonprofessional therapist. *Journal of Nervous and Mental Disease, 196,* 180-184.

Fawcett, J., Barkin, R.L. (1998). A meta-analysis of eight randomized, double-blind, controlled clinical trials of mirtazapine for the treatment of patients with major depression and symptoms of anxiety. *Journal of Clinical Psychiatry, 59* (3), 123-127.

Fisher, R., Fisher, S. (1997). Are we justified in treating children with psychotropic drugs? In S. Fisher and R. Greenberg (Eds.), *From Placebo to Panacea: Putting psychotropic drugs to the test.* New York: John Wiley and Sons.

Gardner, D.M., Shulman, K.I., Walker, S.E., Tailor, S.A.N. (1996). The Making of a user-friendly MAOI diet. *Journal of Clinical Psychiatry, 57,* 99-104.

Gerlernter, C.S., Uhde, T.W., Cimbolic, P., Arnkoff, D.B., Vittone, B.J. et al. (1991). Cognitive-behavioral and pharmacological treatments of social phobia: A controlled study. *Archives of General Psychiatry, 38,* 938-945.

Gorman, J. *Essential Guide to Psychotropic Drugs.* (1990). New York: St. Martin's Press.

Harvard College. (1996). Antidepressant interactions. *Harvard Women's Health Watch,* October.

Heimberg, R.G., Juster, H.R. (1995). Cognitive-behavioral treatment: Literature review. In R.G. Heimberg, M.R. Liebowitz, D.A. Hope, F.R. Schneier (Eds.), *Social Phobia: Diagnosis, assessment, and treatment.* New York: Guilford Press.

Heimberg, R.G., Juster, H.R., Brown, E.J., Holle, C., Makris, G.S., Leung, A.W. et al. (1994, November). *Cognitive-behavioral versus pharmacological treatment of social phobia: Posttreatment and follow-up effects.* Paper presented at the annual meeting of the Association for the Advancement of Behavior Therapy, San Diego, CA.

Liebowitz, M.R., Marshall, R.D. (1995). Pharmacological treatment: Clinical applications. In R.G. Heimberg, M.R. Liebowitz, D.A. Hope, F.R. Schneier

(Eds.), *Social phobia: Diagnosis, assessment, and treatment*. New York: Guilford Press.

Liebowitz, M.R., Schneier, F.R., Campeas, R., Hollander, E., Hatterer, J., Fyer, A. et al. (1992). Phenelzine vs. atenolol in social phobia: A placebo-controlled comparison. *Archives of General Psychiatry, 49*, 290-300.

Medical Economics Co., Inc. (1996). *Physician's Desk Reference*. 51st ed. Oradell, NJ: Author.

Munjack, D.T., Bruns, J., Baltazar, P.L., Brown, R.,Leonard, M., Nagy, R. et al. (1991). A pilot study of buspirone in the treatment of social phobia. *Journal of Anxiety Disorders, 5*, 87-88.

Potts, N.L.S., Davidson, J.R.T. (1995). Pharmacological treatment: Literature review. In R.G. Heimberg, M.R. Liebowitz, D.A. Hope, F.R. Schneier (Eds.), *Social Phobia: Diagnosis, assessment, and treatment*. New York: Guilford Press.

Roan, S. (1997). A prescription for growing concern: Medications Prozac and paxil and other antidepressants are increasingly prescribed for ailments besides depression. *Los Angeles Times*, January 8.

Reuters. (1998). *Antidepressant patch being tested*. October 22.

Schneier, F.R., Chin, S.J., Hollander, E., Liebowitz, M.R. (1992). Fluoxetine in social phobia. *Journal of Clinical Psychopharmacology, 12*, 62-63.

Schneier, F.R., Saoud, J., Campeas, R., Fallon, B., Hollander, E., Coplan, J. et al. (1993). Buspirone in social phobia. *Journal of Clinical Psychopharmacology, 13*, 251-256.

Stein, M.B., Liebowitz, M.R., Lydiard, R.B., Pitts, C.D., Bushnell, W., Gergel, I. (1998). Paroxetine treatment of generalized social phobia (social anxiety disorder). *Journal of the American Medical Association, 28*, August 26, 708-713.

Sutherland, S.M. (1999). *Personal communication* (May 3).

Turner, S.M., Beidel, D.C., Jacob, R.G. (1994). Social phobia: A comparison of behavior therapy and atenolol. *Journal of Consulting and Clinical Psychology, 62*, 350-358.

Turner, S.M., Cooley-Quille, M., Beidel, D.C. (1995). Behavioral and pharmacological treatment of social phobia: Long-term outcome. In M. Manissakalian and R. Prien (Eds.), *Anxiety Disorders: Psychological and pharmacological treatment* (pp. 343-371). Washington, DC: American Psychiatric Association Press.

U.S. Medication Access Programs. (1995). *Drug Manufacturers' Programs to Help Americans Obtain Their Medications: An information paper*. Washington, DC: Staff of Special Committee on Aging, U.S. Senate.

van Vliet, I.M., den Boer, J.A., Westenberg, H.G. (1992). The pharmacotherapy of social phobia: Chemical and biochemical effects of brofaromine, a reversible MAO-A inhibitor. *European Neuropsychopharmacology, 2*, 21-29.

Versiani, M., Mundim, F.D., Nardi, A.E., Liebowitz, M.R. (1988). Tranylcypromine in social phobia. *Journal of Clinical Psychiatry, 8*, 279-282.

Versiani, M., Nardi, A.E., Mundim, F.D., Alves, A., Liebowitz, M.R., Amrein, R. (1992). Pharmacotherapy of social phobia: A controlled study of moclobemide and phenelzine. *British Journal of Psychiatry, 161*, 353-360.

Zitrin, C.M., Klein, D.F., Woerner, M.G., Ross, D. (1983). Treatment of phobias: A comparison of imipramine and placebo. *Archives of General Psychiatry, 40*, 125-138.

Chapter 11

Bersheid, E., Walster, E. (1978). *Interpersonal Attraction*. Reading, MA: Addison-Wesley.

Blackmon, K.L. (1998). *Personal communication* (July 5-December 22).

Boergers, J., Spirito, A., Donaldson, D. (1998). Reasons for adolescent suicide attempts: Associations with psychological functioning. *Journal of the American Academy of Child and Adolescent Psychiatry, 37*, 1287-1293.

Brehm, S. (1985). *Intimate Relationships*. New York: Random House.

Burns, D. (1984). *Intimate Connections*. New York: William Morrow.

Buskirk, A.M., Duke, M.P. (1991). The relationship between coping style and loneliness in adolescents: Can "sad passivity" be adaptive? *Journal of Genetic Psychology, 152* (2), 145-157.

Freudenberger, H.J. (1982). *Situational Anxiety*. New York: Carroll & Graf Publishers.

Gliatio, M.F., Rai, A.K. (1999). Evaluation of treatment of patients with suicidal ideation. *American Family Physician, 59* (6), 1500-1513.

Green, V.A., Waldermuth, N.L. (1993). Self-focus, other-focus, and interpersonal needs as correlates of loneliness. *Psychological Reports, 73* (3 part 1), 843-850.

Hall, E.T. (1966). The *Hidden Dimension*. New York: Doubleday.

Horowitz, L.M. (1983). The toll of loneliness: Manifestations, mechanisms, and means of prevention. *Technical Advisory Report*. Washington, DC: NIMH.

Johnson, S. (1977). *First-Person Singular: Living the good life alone*. Hagerstown, MD: J.B. Lippincott.

Joiner, T.E. Jr. (1997). Shyness and low social support as interactive diastheses, with loneliness as mediator: Testing an interpersonal-personality view of vulnerability to depressive symptoms. *Journal of Abnormal Psychology, 106* (3), 386-394.

Jones, W.H. (1982). Loneliness and social behavior. In L.A. Peplau and D. Perlman (Eds.), *Loneliness: A sourcebook of current theory, research and therapy* (pp. 238-252). New York: Wiley-Interscience.

Jones, W.H., Hobbes, S.A., Hockenbury, D. (1982). Loneliness and social skills deficits. *Journal of Personality and Social Psychology, 42*, 682-689.

Novaco, R. (1975). *Anger Control: The development and evaluation of an experimental treatment.* Lexington, MA: Heath and Company.

Parmelee, P., Werner, C. (1978). Lonely losers: Stereotypes of single dwellers. *Personality and Social Psychology Bulletin, 4*, 292-295.

Peplau, L.A., Caldwell, M.A. (1978). Loneliness: A cognitive analysis. *Essence, 2*, 207-220.

Peplau. L.A., Miceli, M., Morasch, B. (1982). Loneliness and self-evaluation.. In L.A. Peplau and D. Perlman (Eds.), *Loneliness: A sourcebook of current theory, research and therapy* (pp. 135-151). New York: Wiley-Interscience.

Perlman, D. (1991). *Age differences in loneliness: A meta analysis.* Vancouver, Canada: University of British Columbia (ERIC Doc. Reproduction Service No. ED 326767).

Perlman, D., Landolt, M.A. (1999). Examination of loneliness in children/adolescents and in adults: Two solitudes or unified enterprise? In K.J. Rotenberg and S. Hymel (Eds.), *Loneliness in Childhood and Adolescence.* New York: Cambridge University Press (in press).

Perlman, D., Peplau, L.A. (1998). Loneliness. In H. Friedman (Ed.), *Encyclopedia of Mental Health* (Vol. 2, pp. 571-581). San Diego, CA: Academic Press.

Rook, K.S. (1984). Promoting social bonding: Strategies for helping the lonely and socially isolated. *American Psychologist, 39* (12), 1389-1407.

Rubenstein, C.M., Shaver, P. (1982). Loneliness in two Northeastern cities. In J. Hartog, J.R. Audy, Y.A. Cohen (Eds.), *The Anatomy of Loneliness* (pp. 319-337). New York: International Universities Press.

Schneier, F.R., Johnson, J., Hornig, C.D., Liebowitz, M.R., Weissman, M.M. (1992). Social phobia: Co-morbidity and morbidity in a epidemiologic sample. *Archives of General Psychiatry, 49*, 282-288.

Sides, R., McChristie, P. (1998). What do men/women really want on a date? *Solo Lifestyles For Singles* online, http://www.solosingles.com/wantdate.htm.

Sommer, R. (1969). *Personal Space.* Englewood Cliffs, NJ: Prentice-Hall.

Tessina, T. (1989). *Gay Relationships for Men and Women: How to find them, how to improve them, and make them last.* New York: Tarcher/Putnam.

Young,, J.E. (1982). Loneliness, depression and cognitive therapy: Theory and application. In L.A. Peplau and D. Perlman (Eds.), *Loneliness: A sourcebook of current theory, research and therapy* (pp. 379-405). New York: Wiley-Interscience.

Chapter 12

Boll, C.R. (1979). *Executive Jobs Unlimited.* New York: Macmillan.

Dayhoff, S.A. (1987) *Create Your Own Career Opportunities.* Andover, MA: Brick House Publishing.

Dayhoff, S.A. (1982). *Effects of organizational mentoring on perceptions of achievement and upward mobility.* Boston University: Unpublished manuscript.

Dayhoff, S.A. (1989). Getting that new job can be made easier by using your network. *Wellesley Townsman,* November 2.

Dayhoff, S.A. (1981).*Perceptions of mentees by third-party peer observers.* Boston University: Unpublished manuscript.

Dayhoff, S.A. (1984). *Single and Multiple Mentors: Perceived effects on managerial success.* Ann Arbor, MI: University Microfilms International.

Granovetter, M. (1973). The strength of weak ties. *American Journal of Sociology, 78* (6), 1360-1380.

Griffin, J., Mayo, C. (1979). The hired mentor. *Association for Women in Psychology Newsletter,* October/November.

Iacocca, L. (1984). *Iacocca: An autobiography.* New York: Bantam Books.

Lin, N., Ensel, W., Vaughn, J. (1981). Social resources and strength of ties: Structural factors in occupational status attainment. *American Sociological Review, 46,* 393-405.

Milgram, S. (1977). *The Individual in a Social World.* Reading, MA: Addison-Wesley.

Misserian, A. (1982). *The Corporate Connection: Why executive women need a mentor to reach the top.* Englewood Cliffs, NJ: Prentice-Hall.

Shapiro, E., Haseltine, F., Rowe, M. (1978). Moving Up: Role models, mentors, and the patron system. *Sloan Management Review, 19,* 51-58.

Turner, R. (1960). Sponsored and contest mobility and the school system. *American Sociological Review, 25,* 855-867.

Chapter 13

Bodner, J. (1987). Your brilliant career. *Changing Times,* November, 26-39.

Boll, C.R. (1979). *Executive Jobs Unlimited.* New York: Macmillan.

Dayhoff, S.A. (1990). *Get the Job You Want: Successful strategies for selling yourself in the job market.* Acton, MA: Brick House Publishing.

Goleman, D. (1998). *Working with Emotional Intelligence.* New York: Bantam.

Hopkins, T. (1982). *Master of the Art of Selling.* New York: Warner Books.

Jackson, T. (1978). *Guerrilla Tactics in the Job Market.* New York: Bantam Books.

Lant, J.A. (1987). *Money Making Marketing.* Cambridge, MA: JLA Publishing.

Lant, J.A. (1986). *Tricks of the Trade.* Cambridge, MA: JLA Publishing.

Lareau, W. (1985). *Inside Track: A successful job search method.* New York: New Century Publications.

Yate, M. (1985) *How to Knock 'Em Dead.* Holbrook, MA: Bob Adams, Inc.

Chapter 14

Beck, A., Katcher, A.H., Thomas, E.M. (1996). *Between Pets and People.* West Lafayette, IN: Purdue University Press.

Brody, J.E. (1997). Prozac alternative - a common weed. Long-term clinical trials needed to prove herb's worth. *Minneapolis Star Tribune,* September 14.

Carrigan, M.H., Levis, D.J. (1999). The contributions of eye movement to the efficacy of brief exposure treatment for reducing fear of public speaking. *Journal of Anxiety Disorders, 13* (1-2), 101-118.

Cusak, K., Spates, C.R. (1999). The cognitive dismantling of eye movement desensitization and reprocessing (EMDR) treatment of posttraumatic stress disorder (PTSD). *Journal of Anxiety Disorders, 13* (1-2), 87-99.

Center for Medical Consumers. (1996). Mixing St. John's wort with drugs. *Healthfacts, 21,* November 1, 1-2.

Denny, N.R. (1995). An orienting reflex/external inhibition model of EMDR and thought field theory. *Traumatology: International Electronic Journal of Innovations in the Study of the Traumatization Process and methods For Reducing or Eliminating Related Human Suffering,* August.

Drummond, P.D. (1989). Mechanism for social blushing. In N.W. Bond and D.A.T. Siddle (Eds.). *Psychobiology: Issues and Applications* (pp. 363-370). Amsterdam: Elsevier Science.

Feske, U., Goldstein, A.J. (1997). Eye movement desensitization and reprocessing treatment for panic disorder: A controlled outcome and partial dismantling study. *Journal of Consulting and Clinical Psychology, 65* (6), 1026-1035.

Garza, J.S. (1998). *Personal communication* (August 24-September 26).

Garza, J.S. (1998). *Thoracic sympathectomy: Minimally invasive surgical procedure.* Houston, TX: Videoscopic Surgery Center. http://www.endoscopic-surgery.com/thoracos.htm.

Heiligenstein, E., Guenther, G. (1998). Over-the-counter psychotropics: A review of melatonin, St. John's wort, and kava-kava. *Journal of American College Health, 46,* May 1, 271-277.

Heimberg, R.G. (1999). *Personal communication* (May 4).

Jacob, R.G. (1988). Panic disorder and the vestibular system. *Psychiatric Clinics of North America, 11* (2), June, 361-374.

Jacob, R.G. Furman, J.M., Turber, S.M. (1997). Surface dependence: A balance control strategy in panic disorder with agoraphobia. *Psychosomatic Medicine, 59 (3),* May, 323-330.

Jaspers, J.P. (1998). Cognitive-behavioral therapy for paruresis: A case study. *Psychological Reports, 83,* (1) August, 187-196.

Jorgenson, J. (1997). Therapeutic use of companion animals in health care. *Image. Journal of Nursing School, 29* (3), 249-254.

Levinson, H.N., Carter, S. (Ed). (1986). *Phobia Free.* New York: M. Evans and Company.

Levinson, H.N. (1989). Abnormal optokinetic and perceptual span parameters in cerebellar-vestibular dysfunction and related anxiety disorders. *Perceptual and Motor Skills, 68,* 471-484.

Levinson, H.N. (1989). The cerebellar-vestibular predisposition to anxiety disorders. *Perceptual and Motor Skills, 68,* 323-338.

Levinson, H.N. (1989). A cerebellar-vestibular explanation for fears/phobias: Hypothesis and study. *Perceptual and Motor Skills,* 68, 67-84.

Linde, K., Ramirez, G., Mulwer, C.D., Pauls, A., Weidenhammer, W., Melchart, D. (1996). *British Medical Journal, 313,* August 3 (7052), 253-258.

Miller, R.S. (1996). *Embarrassment: Poise and peril in everyday life.* New York: Guilford Press.

National Institutes of Medicine. (1997). *St. John's wort study launched,* October 3. Washington, DC: NIH Press Release.

O'Donnell, J. (1997). Neither food nor drug: Lack of science leaves safety up to consumers. *USA Today,* June 19.

Organon. (1998). *Remeron more effective, faster working than Cipramil or Paxil, study shows.* November 3. Paris, France: Organon Pharmaceutical Press Release.

Pavlov, I.P. (1927). *Conditioned Reflexes.* New York: Dover Books.

Reisfeld, R. (1997). Overview, symptoms, causes, and treatment of hyperhidrosis. Online: Center for Hyperhidrosis. http://handsweat.com/overview.html.

Shapiro, F. (1989). Efficacy of the eye movement desensitization procedure in the treatment of traumatic memories. *Journal of Traumatic Stress, 2* (2), 199-223.

Simmons, C., Simmons, M. (1998). Drugs and dietary supplements: ramifications of the Food, Drug and Cosmetic Act and Dietary Supplement Health and Education Act. *West Virginia Journal of Law and Technology, 3,* February 14.

Telaranta, T. (1998). *Stellate block patient information. Privatix Method.* Tampere, Finland: Privatix Clinic.

Telaranta, T. (1998). Treatment of social phobia by endoscopic thoracic sympathicotomy. *European Journal of Surgery, 580* (Supplement), 27-32.

Yilmaz, E.N., Dur, A.H., Cuesta, M.A., Rauwerda, J.A. (1996). Endoscopic versus transaxillary thoracic sympathectomy for primary axillary and palmar hyperhidrosis and/or facial blushing: 5-year-experience. *European Journal of Cardiothoracic Surgery, 10,* 168-172.

Zacherl, J., Imhof, M., Plas, E.G., Herbst, F., Fugger, R. (1997). Hyperhidrosis of upper extremity: Long-term outcome of endoscopic thoracic sympaticotomy. *Langenbecks Arch. Chir. Suppl. Kongressbd., 14*, 1287-1289.

Zgourides, G.D. (1987). Paruresis: Overview and implications for treatment. *Psychological Reports, 60* (Part 2), 1171-1176.

Chapter **15**

American Psychological Association. (1992). *Ethical principles of psychologists and code of ethics.* Washington, DC: Author.

Eisenberg, S. Delaney, D.J. (1977). *The Counseling Process.* New York: Rand McNally College Publishing.

Greist, J.H., Kobak, K.A., Jefferson, J.W., Katzelnick, D.J., Chene, R.L. (1995). The clinical interview. In R.G. Heimberg. M.R. Liebowitz, D.A. Hope, F.R. Schneier (Eds.), *Social Phobia: Diagnosis, assessment, and treatment.* New York: Guilford Press.

King, S.A., Moreggi, D. (1998). Internet therapy, self-help groups, and the pros and cons. In Jayne Gackenbach (Ed.) *Psychology and the Internet: Intrapersonal, interpersonal, and transpersonal implications.* New York: Academic Press (in press).

King, S.A., Poulos, S.T. (1998). Using the Internet to treat generalized social phobia and avoidant personality disorder. *CyberPsychology and Behavior, 1* (1), 29-36.

Kraut, R., Patterson, M., Lundmark, V., Kiesler, S., Muhopadlhyay, T., Sherlis, W. (1998). Internet paradox: A social technology that reduces social involvement and psychological well-being. *American Psychologist, 53* (9), 1017-1031.

Lucas, R.A., Telch, M.J. (1993, November). *Group versus individual treatment of social phobia.* Paper presented at the annual Association of Advancement of Behavior Therapy, Atlanta, GA.

National Alliance for the Mentally Ill (1996, Sept.-Oct.). SSI/SSDI. *Helpline Fact Sheet.* Arlington, VA: Author.

Newman, F.D. (1998). *PM News.* White Plains, NY: The Anxiety and Phobia Clinic of White Plains Hospital Center online, http://www.phobia-anxiety/fromthenewsletter.html.

Schneier, F.R., Welkowitz, L. (1996). *The Hidden Face of Shyness: Understanding and overcoming social anxiety.* New York: Avon Books.

Zaro, J.S., Barach, R., Nedelman, D.J., Dreiblatt, I.S. (1977). *A Guide for Beginning Psychotherapists.* New York: Cambridge University Press.

INDEX

Q

R

S

EFFECTIVENESS-PLUS PUBLICATIONS

Quick Order Form

- **Fax orders:** (914) 835-0398. Send this form.

- **Telephone orders:** Call (800) 431-1579 **toll free**. Have your credit card ready.

- **Web site orders:** http://www.book-clearing-house.com/. Click "Order"

- **Postal orders (check or money order only):** Payable to/Mail to Effectiveness-Plus Publications, P.O. Box 340, Placitas, NM 87043 USA. Postal order status: (505) 867-0094, Dr. Signe A. Dayhoff

Send me

—— **Diagonally-Parked in a Parallel Universe: Working Through Social Anxiety** by Signe A. Dayhoff, Ph.D. (ISBN 0-9671265-0-9) @ $19.95 US_____

NM sales tax_____

Shipping _____

Total_____

I understand that I may return this book to the Publisher for a full refund, excluding shipping, for any reason, no questions asked.

Name: _____

Address: _____

(If it's to be shipped to a P.O. box, include street address for check orders)

City: _____ **State:** _____ **Zip:** _____ - _____

Telephone: _____

E-mail address: _____

Sales tax: Please add 5.75% for products shipped to New Mexico addresses.

Shipping (to each address):
US: $4.00 for first book via priority mail and **$2** for each additional book.
International: $9 for first book and $5 each additional book (estimate)

Payment: ☐ Check ☐ Money Order ☐ Credit Card:

☐ Visa ☐ MasterCard ☐ AMEX ☐ Discover

Card number: _____

Name on card: _____ **Exp. Date:** ___/___

EFFECTIVENESS-PLUS PUBLICATIONS

Quick Order Form

- **Fax orders:** (914) 835-0398. Send this form.

- **Telephone orders:** Call (800) 431-1579 **toll free.** Have your credit card ready.

- **Web site orders:** http://www.book-clearing-house.com/. Click "Order"

- **Postal orders (check or money order only):** Payable to/Mail to Effectiveness-Plus Publications, P.O. Box 340, Placitas, NM 87043 USA. Postal order status: (505) 867-0094, Dr. Signe A. Dayhoff

Send me

—— **Diagonally-Parked in a Parallel Universe: Working Through Social Anxiety** by Signe A. Dayhoff, Ph.D. (ISBN 0-9671265-0-9) @ $19.95 US_____

NM sales tax_____

Shipping _____

Total_____

I understand that I may return this book to the Publisher for a full refund, excluding shipping, for any reason, no questions asked.

Name: _____

Address: _____

(If it's to be shipped to a P.O. box, include street address for check orders)

City: _____ **State:** _____ **Zip:** _____ - _____

Telephone: _____

E-mail address: _____

Sales tax: Please add 5.75% for products shipped to New Mexico addresses.

Shipping (to each address):

US: **$4.00** for first book via priority mail and **$2** for each additional book. **International:** **$9** for first book and **$5** each additional book (estimate)

Payment: ☐ Check   ☐ Money Order   ☐ Credit Card:

☐ Visa   ☐ MasterCard   ☐ AMEX   ☐ Discover

Card number: _____

Name on card: _____ **Exp. Date:** ___ / ___